Change over Time in the Iberian World

Max Planck Studies in Global Legal History of the Iberian Worlds

Editor

Thomas Duve

The book volumes in the *Max Planck Studies in Global Legal History of the Iberian Worlds* publish research on legal history of areas which have been in contact with the Iberian empires during the early Modern and Modern period, in Europe, the Americas, Asia and Africa. Its focus is global in the sense that it is not limited to the imperial spaces as such but rather looks at the globalization of normativities within the space related to these imperial formations. It is global also in another sense: The volumes in the series pay special attention to the coexistence of a variety of normativities and their cultural translations in different places and moments, decentring classical research perspectives and opening up for different modes of normativity.

The monographs, edited volumes and text editions in the series are peer reviewed, and published in print and online.

Brill's Open Access books are discoverable through DOAB and distributed free of charge in Brill's E-Book Collections, and through OAPEN and jstor.

VOLUME 8

The titles published in this series are listed at *brill.com/mpiw*

Change over Time in the Iberian World

Stabilization and Transformation of Law (16th–19th Centuries)

Edited by

Luisa Stella de Oliveira Coutinho Silva

BRILL | NIJHOFF

This book is available as an open access publication via https://www.degruyterbrill.com.

ISSN 2590-3292
ISBN 978-90-04-76441-5
ISBN 978-90-04-76442-2 (PDF)
DOI https://doi.org/10.1163/9789004764422

Library of Congress Control Number: 2026939927

Brill and Koninklijke Brill bv is part of De Gruyter Brill.
www.degruyterbrill.com

Questions about General Product Safety Regulation: productsafety@degruyterbrill.com

Cover illustration: Quadrangular dial forming a panel-type composition in the Mannerist style, with Roman numerals and figurative decoration of the winds (Aeoli or blue cherubs) at the four corners of the composition. The panel also features a border with geometrical and symmetrical decoration in blue, yellow, green, and manganese, including half-oval motifs. The inner space is filled with a representation of the sun and its rays, dividing the circle into twenty-four equal parts, circa 1585. Collection of the Municipal Museum of Santarém, Casa-Museu Anselmo Braamcamp Freire, Nuno Moreira, © Municipality of Santarém.

Contents

Preface

Legal change is a concept that has been interpreted in multiple ways and assigned a wide range of connotations. It has shaped and been shaped by diverse analytical frameworks, often taking on highly interdisciplinary dimensions. Within legal disciplines and subfields of law, various approaches have offered different interpretations of what constitutes change in law. Some suggest that law changes when individuals comply with imposed norms; others emphasise imitation of prestigious models, the dynamics of reform and development or the influence of economic performance. Change may occur through legal transplants, through adherence to foundational principles or as a result of motivation to obey the law. Some approaches argue that legal change depends on broader social transformations, everyday practices and public acceptance; others frame change in terms of legal evolution or progress, systemic transformation or differing modes of reception. Additionally, legal change has been explained through transcendental motivations, including religious, moral and philosophical influences; through the legitimacy of legal authority and the rule of law; through the criteria of legal validity and democratic reinforcement; and through political processes, such as justification and decision-making.

Therefore, different fields, such as legal theory, sociology of law, comparative law, international law and legal anthropology, have all contributed with both overlapping and divergent reflections on legal change and its causes. This is no less true for historical analysis: legal historians have long been inspired by the question of change when attempting to understand the past. Collectively, these fields engage with foundational questions in law studies, such as: what is (or was) law? How can law in the past be characterised? How does law change from one place to another, from one period to the next – even from one moment to another? How is law created and complied with in different contexts?

The chapters in this volume engage with the broader debate on legal change but from a distinct approach. Rather than offering only abstract theorisation, this book also adds a new layer of complexity by examining legal change through concrete case studies drawn from the legal histories of the Iberian empires and their colonial contexts.

The following nine chapters explore how law changed across a variety of colonial settings within the Iberian empires, investigating how legal transformations both responded to and followed social demands. The volume begins with a conceptual framework (Coutinho Silva), which proposes four analytical axes for approaching legal change: types of change, actors of change, mechanisms of change and spatial and temporal dimensions of change. Each axis is linked to a specific guiding question. First, what types of change occur when different actors shape normative transformations in Iberian continental and overseas territories in the early modern period? Second, who initiates legal change, and who is influenced by it? Third, through which normative instruments, mechanisms or channels does legal change take place? Fourth, how can global-local dynamics and non-linear or progressive perspectives be understood in colonial contexts from a legal historical standpoint?

The subsequent chapters delve into specific case studies. These include: changes in internal institutional norms (Meneses Muñoz); shifts in religious norms and arguments in missionary-Christian interactions (Ehalt); transformations in legal statuses through laws, litigation and petitions, particularly by subaltern actors, such as enslaved individuals and widows (Oliveira and Lopes); changes in institutional developments and functions in the administration of colonial spaces (Massuchetto); changes in the introduction of administrative procedures by royal agents to govern local populace (Cabral); changes in the creation of meaning for already existing normative types (Curvelo); and reforms issued by the Crown, framed as police regulations, aiming to improve efficiency and control, specifically for colonial contexts (Mancilla-Órdenes). Together, these chapters reflect on how global frameworks assumed local forms through legal change, often producing "new" law deeply embedded in practices from different actors from different statuses and positions.

Questioning Eurocentric narratives and nation-state-based legal historiography, this volume demonstrates that law did not solely change through the formal alteration of written state-driven norms. Legal change also emerged from the localised production of knowledge by a wide range of actors – missionaries, priests, inquisitors, widows, adulterous women, viceroys, governors, *ouvidores*, *superintendentes*, captain-majors and enslaved people. Each chapter addresses changes through practices and experiences from the ground up, beginning with a specific case study to explore how legal change was experienced, negotiated and understood in context. These perspectives illuminate broader lawmaking processes in the early modern Iberian empires across Asia, Europe and the Americas. Unfortunately, we were not able to include African contexts, but I wish to highlight the importance of expanding in that direction in future studies.

The origins of this volume trace back to 2022, as the world reopened after the COVID-19 pandemic. First ideas were shared at a preparatory meeting for the First Annual Conference of the *Glocalising Normativities* project, held virtually on 19–21 May 2022. From September 2022 to February 2023, the project's *Global Legal History Colloquium* was organised around the theme of legal change. The decision to structure the colloquium around this theme emerged from our first virtual encounter, which revealed a pressing need to exchange ideas and build a shared conceptual foundation. The colloquium thus became a theoretical springboard for both the conference and this volume. The conference itself was held in person in Frankfurt am Main on 20–24 March 2023, at the Max Planck Institute for Legal History and Legal Theory, where all contributing authors met in person to collectively refine their chapters.

Throughout these activities, we were guided by a core set of questions: how can we characterise legal stability (including the role of sources, archives, materiality, textuality, media and norms)? How do people perceive change and motion? Who participates in legal change, especially acknowledging gender-sensitive, subaltern and bottom-up perspectives? Is it possible to measure legal change? When and how can we determine that law has changed? How long does it take for law to change again? What role does periodisation play in legal history? What drives legal change – colonialism, transfers, adaptations, appropriations, translations of norms? Why does a particular legal change occur at a specific moment? How can legal change be connected to social change and conditions? How do we assess the speed, frequency or absence of legal transformations? The following chapters were inspired by these and other questions and offer answers from their own standpoint in the context of global empires.

Many people made this project possible. I am deeply grateful to all members of the *Glocalising Normativities* project, who contributed through discussion, writing, session moderation, organisation and feedback on the introductory chapter. Many additional scholars joined our community by submitting conference proposals that evolved into remarkable chapters. Thank you to all participants of the colloquium on legal change. I am also indebted to the thoughtful reports and analyses from our anonymous peer reviewers. The theoretical grounding on legal change owes much to the generous insights of Luca von Bogdandy, Christian Boulanger, Massimo Meccarelli, Burak Aydin, Thomas Duve, Manuel Bastias Saavedra and João Paulo Bachur, presented at our colloquium. Special thanks go to Nicole Pasakarnis and Janina Zimmerman for their editorial support, and to Genevieve Beech for her exceptional work in refining the language of this text. Finally, I thank Eduardo Charters Morais for the countless hours of discussion over the years, which led to the insights and systematisation of the analytical framework of this book.

Luisa Stella de Oliveira Coutinho Silva
Frankfurt am Main, June 2025

Figures, Charts and Tables

Figures

Charts

Tables

Notes on Contributors

Gustavo César Machado Cabral
is Professor of Legal History and Theory of the State and Dean of the Law School at the Federal University of Ceará (Brazil). He is also a Researcher at the National Council for Scientific and Technological Development (CNPq). His work specializes in early modern Iberian legal history, with a particular focus on colonial Brazil. His publications include *Legal Literature in the Early Modern Age: The Decisiones in the Kingdom of Portugal (16th–17th Centuries)* (Rio de Janeiro, 2017); *Ius Commune: An Introduction to the History of the Ius Commune between the Middle Ages and the Early Modern Period* (Rio de Janeiro, 2019); and *Law in Portuguese America: Foundations, Jurisdictions, Norms, and Practices* (16th–18th Centuries) (forthcoming, 2026).

Luisa Stella de Oliveira Coutinho Silva
is a legal historian specializing in women's history. She is currently a researcher at the Max Planck Institute for Legal History and Legal Theory and is a trained lawyer in both Portugal and Brazil. Her research focuses on women's legal history in imperial contexts and her current project examines the conversion of Japanese women to Christianity between the 1540s and 1630s. Her most recent book *Nem teúdas, nem manteúdas: História das Mulheres e Direito na capitania da Paraíba (Brasil, 1661–1822)* explores the legal lives of women in colonial Paraíba, a captaincy in northeastern Brazil.

Arthur Curvelo
is Assistant Professor in the College of History at the Federal University of Vale do São Francisco (UNIVASF). He holds a PhD in History from the *Programa Interuniversitário de Doutoramento em História*, associated with the Institute of Social Sciences – University of Lisbon (2019). His research specializes in the social history of power, institutions, and political communications in Portuguese America, with particular emphasis on local government institutions, royal governors, and governorships. He also works on entailment practices through the foundation of *morgadios* and *capelas*. His recent publications include *VINCULUM. Entailment societies. Entails in the Portuguese Atlantic (14th-17th centuries)* (Coimbra, 2025) in collaboration with other authors.

Rômulo Ehalt
is a historian of early modern global history and a researcher at the Max Planck Institute for Legal History and Legal Theory. He specializes in the legal and

intellectual history of the Society of Jesus, as well as slavery and other forms of bondage in early modern Asia. His publications include several articles on legal translation, casuistry, and the history of slavery in the Portuguese Empire.

Ana Mafalda Lopes
is a Max Weber Fellow at the European University Institute in Florence. She specializes in socio-economic history, gender, and family history, focusing on eighteenth-century Portugal and the transition into the Liberal period. Her article, *The invisibility of Portuguese stepfamilies: the relationships between step-parents, stepchildren and half-siblings in eighteenth- and nineteenth-century Porto* (2022) received the 2024 Best Early Career Article in Iberian History from the Association for Spanish and Portuguese Historical Studies. She also co-authored, with Paulo Teodoro de Matos, the book chapter *Property ownership by widows: A study of nineteenth-century inheritance practices on the island of São Jorge (Azores, Portugal)*.

Nathaly Mancilla-Órdenes
holds a PhD in Law from the University of Brasília (2023). Since 2022, she has been a postdoctoral researcher at the Faculty of Law, University of Helsinki. Her research lies at the intersection of legal history, global history, legal theory, and social theory, with a particular focus on the Portuguese Empire. Her current project examines the classification of subjects and the problem of early modern citizenship in the Iberian Empires in Asia—specifically Goa, Macao, and the Philippines—during the seventeenth and eighteenth centuries.

Vanessa Massuchetto
is a Marie Skłodowska-Curie Postdoctoral Researcher at the Max Planck Institute for Legal History and Legal Theory, Frankfurt am Main. She specializes in women's legal history, criminal justice, and sexualities in the Iberian-American worlds in the XVII and XVIII centuries. Her recent publications include *Mulheres, conflitos e normatividades: a justiça criminal e o feminino na América Meridional* (forthcoming) and *El «amor de madre» y usos de normatividades de género: maternidad y esclavitud a través del caso de Narcisa en América Meridional (XVIII)*.

Mariana Meneses Muñoz
is a PhD candidate in early modern history at *Universidade Nova de Lisboa* (FCT scholarship holder) and researcher at *CHAM – Centro de Humanidades*. Her work focuses on everyday moral and juridical discourse, inquisitorial studies, and representations of non-elite people in the 16th- and 17th-century in the

Iberian Peninsula and colonies, through a gender lens. Her thesis argues that women possessed legal knowledge and shared experiences shaped by social pressures. Using ecclesiastical court records from Lisbon (c. 1535–1640), she reconstructs how women negotiated their societal position, examining legal subjectivities, gender relations in judicial narratives, and the networks forged through female sociability.

Felipe Garcia de Oliveira
is a PhD candidate in History at at *CHAM – Centro de Humanidades*, within the School of Social Sciences and Humanities at NOVA University Lisbon (NOVA FCSH). He specializes in the study of how Africans, Indigenous peoples, and their descendants interacted with different levels of courts in Portuguese America during the seventeenth and eighteenth centuries. His recent publications include articles and book chapters on Indigenous labor regimes and the role of enslaved peoples in shaping notions of freedom, slavery, and justice.

CHAPTER 1

Change over Time in the Iberian Empires

Legal History and Experiences of Change between the Global and the Local

Luisa Stella de Oliveira Coutinho Silva

1 Change Over Time: Legal Change and Legal History in the Iberian Empires

Legal history and (post)colonial studies are deeply intertwined as the study of legal change reveals how law transformed across different colonial contexts. Traditional historiography often portrayed colonial legal systems as rigid and externally imposed, with laws applied variably based on racial or social classifications. However, recent scholarship challenges this perspective, emphasising social diversity and the agency of local actors in shaping legal transformations. Scholars now explore law as a dynamic process influenced by cultural translation, political shifts and social interactions – including asymmetrical power relations – rather than as a purely state-driven phenomenon. Legal history has been reshaped and influenced by various disciplines and subfields, as well as tendencies and paradigm changes offered by the pragmatic and archival turns. These new perspectives highlight the role of power asymmetries as well as resistance in situations involving legal change. By moving beyond Eurocentric narratives, these approaches offer a more nuanced understanding of how law was constructed, contested and transformed in colonial and postcolonial settings.

The colonial experiences in the Iberian empires, as explored in this book, also provide an alternative lens through which to understand legal change. By revisiting the relationship between the global and the local through case studies, the chapters in this book do more than just characterise change in legal history or theory – they offer crucial insights into human social practices in early modern societies and question the role of law at the local level within colonial and imperial contexts.

The cases analysed in this book demonstrate that, between the global and the local, law was never transported intact from one place to another within the Portuguese and Spanish empires. Quite the opposite; legal "systems" were not frozen, taken from one place and reproduced in another without contest,

© 2026 THE AUTHOR(S) | HTTPS://DOI.ORG/10.1163/9789004764422-002

but, on the contrary, they represented legal changes in colonial contexts that led to the creation of new knowledge related to law, even as they built upon structures assumed to be applied across imperial territories. The changes discussed here – ranging from internal normative regulations that shaped power relations, to evolving interpretations of jurisdiction over religious communities and evangelisation, shifts in normative diplomas (including legislation, but not only) affecting specific social and subaltern groups, modifications in the application of normative sources and practical legal issues and transformations in criminal law and punishments – collectively question traditional notions of power dynamics and the relationship between law and authority.

The chapters in this book explore the complexities of legal change in colonial societies by analysing experiences of change. They do so by using case studies set in the Iberian empires. The expansion of the Iberian empires – Portugal and Spain – has been widely studied across various historiographical traditions. In legal history, the colonisation of localities situated in places, such as Brazil, Angola, Japan, New Spain, Azores and Madeira, to mention a few explored in this book, and the interaction, imposition, contradictions and reactions of different legal systems have been explained in different terms, such as adaptation, transnational legal transfers, transitions, legal pluralism and many other critical explorations between postcolonialism and law.

However, this book aims to offer an alternative historiographical perspective on colonial societies in the early modern period, expanding the definition of law beyond nation-state frameworks and Eurocentric interpretations. Looking at experiences of change that prioritise local sources, the chapters in this volume examine lawmaking processes and legal change from eight case studies, focusing on practices from everyday life. The analysis goes beyond the practices alone; it also engages with what historiography has traditionally categorised as law in theory – closer to what is written in legal texts – without rigidly separating this facet from what happens on the ground. Instead, the book demonstrates the necessity of analysing practice and theory in tandem.

In general, the case studies examine the interplay between local and global influences, seeking alternative frameworks for understanding law in the early modern world, which span Iberian overseas and continental territories. Based on the case studies in this book and the experiences they describe, I propose four key dimensions for analysing legal change in the early modern world, which focus on four groups of questions.

1. Types of change: which type of change occurs when different actors shape normative transformations in Iberian continental and overseas territories in the early modern period? Which kinds of law emerge from these local contexts? How can we characterise law in the early modern period by examining these changes? Looking at the cases, I identify four types

of legal change: (a) Hermeneutical change, or shifts in legal interpretation and meanings; (b) Punitive change, or changes in legal enforcement and punishment; (c) Status change, or alterations in the legal categories of identity, belonging or hierarchy; (d) Governance change, or adjustments in governance structures, regulations and political and economic policies.

2. Actors of change: who initiates legal change, and who is influenced by it? In these terms, change may occur as top-down and bottom-up or horizontal and transversal processes that reveal upward or downward communications.
3. Mechanisms of change: through which normative instruments, mechanisms or channels does legal change take place? This section broadens the range of sources considered in legal history, moving beyond codified laws to embrace a more flexible, non-legalistic approach that challenges Eurocentric narratives. The sources used by the authors reveal three types of change: institutional, argumentative and statutory.
4. Spatial and temporal dimensions of change: how can global-local dynamics and non-linear or progressive perspectives be understood in colonial contexts from a legal historical perspective? How do global processes influence local normative environments? The consequences of these questions reflect on the value of analysing law through localised, non-linear perspectives on time. Regarding this aspect, change can be characterised as abrupt or gradual; diffused or condensed.

The four axes of analysis serve as analytical tools for exploring how legal change was addressed in relation to people of different statuses and positions in the early modern times in issues of their daily life – their social and power dynamics, inequalities and differences – and how law functioned in motion. These axes are not necessarily isolated from one another but rather complement a holistic understanding of legal change in colonial contexts.

2 Understanding Iberian Continental and Overseas Territories Through Legal Change

2.1 Types of Change

What kind of legal change occurs when multiple actors – across different social, political and geographical contexts – shape normative transformations in the Iberian empires during the early modern period? And how can these changes help us characterise law as it emerged from local, colonial and transimperial interactions? All these fundamental questions have long traditions behind them. Scholars in legal studies and legal history fields and subfields have analysed change, often referring to it as legal change. The evolution of law, how it develops, adapts, stabilises and transforms, is deeply tied to fundamental questions in legal studies: what is law? How can we characterise law in a specific historical period and place? How can change serve as a critical tool for understanding law in the past? And, finally, how does law change across different contexts, such as colonial territories?

The chapters in this book demonstrate that change is multifaceted and can take different forms that can be analysed in certain situations. These transformations include internal normative regulations to assert authority over solicitors, reinterpretations of jurisdictional principles for religious communities and evangelisation, modifications in legislation affecting the social perception of certain social groups and their prerogatives as petitioners to the King, alterations in the application and content of normative sources to address practical concerns, shifts in practices related to criminal offences surrounding women's punishments, and legal argumentation and meanings.

Based on the case studies, we can identify four types of change, depending on what is being transformed. From this starting point, in terms of characterising the change itself, by looking at the cases, I have identified four types of legal change: (a) hermeneutical change; (b) punitive change; (c) status change; and (d) governance change.

If we look to the state of the art related to these topics, we can observe that, indeed, some of these ideas were explored very differently by other scholars, and not necessarily as theories of legal change. The question of hermeneutics and legal change is mentioned in legal theory as well as in certain approaches in legal history, such as originalism.[1] Also the question of how to understand legal change in the transition of political regimes has already been addressed by legal historians.[2] Scholars focusing on this approach use legal change to

1 Yowell, "Dworkin, Interpretation and Legal Change". See also further interpretations explored by originalism, on how to interpret legal texts according (or not) to the time of their inception. Sachs, "Originalism as a Theory of Legal Change".

2 Meccarelli, "Time of Innovation", 23. Massimo Meccarelli sees in the analysis of legal change a "possibility for multiplying the levels of analysis of legal issues, by bringing its relationship with its social, political, economic and cultural dimensions to the forefront." As a historical process, he considers that the social, political, economic, technological and cultural fields influence the study of innovation in legal change and he pushes forward an understanding of legal change beyond oppositional conceptual pairs, such as continuity and discontinuity, tradition and modernisation. To study such a concept, he focuses on examples of change in political regimes in the 20th century in Italy. For other interpretations of transitions and legal change in the Common law world, see Sarat (ed.), *Transitions*.

explain changes in political systems and forms of governance and to answer questions, such as: how are democratic systems built or conquered? Why are different political systems and forms of governance possible and how do they change? The administration of colonial overseas territories and how they were governed or how they governed themselves has also been a disputed matter in different historiographical traditions.[3]

But the way the authors in this volume answer these questions is different. Drawing on the new insights explored in Ehalt's and Oliveira's chapters of this book, (a) hermeneutical change can be understood as a change that refers to shifts in the interpretation of legal principles and arguments. Examples include the reinterpretation of the principle of ignorance by different religious orders and the principle of the just price in lawsuits.

Ehalt's chapter explores how the Jesuits adapted their legal reasoning in response to external pressures. He demonstrates how the hermeneutical shift of ignorance influenced the development of religious normativity, and how these legal transformations contributed to the stabilisation of Christian doctrine in early modern Japan. The Council of Trent's decrees, whose implementation in Japan was fraught with challenges, further complicated these legal changes, particularly as Jesuits sought to maintain their authority while preventing Franciscans from altering the status quo. Ultimately, the Jesuits' reliance on dissimulation to preserve religious stability was disrupted by the mendicant friars' arrival, leading to a reconfiguration of legal strategies and the gradual imposition of Catholic positive law under episcopal oversight. In the middle of such political conflict between religious orders, the Jesuits defended their methods by invoking the doctrine of invincible ignorance, which exempted individuals from sin and religious infractions due to their lack of knowledge. This change reshaped legal discourse, as the former condemned invincible ignorance as a dangerous loophole that excused all manner of sins, whereas the latter used it to justify their gradual approach to imposing Christian norms. The clash between these approaches led to a change in the application of legal doctrines, ultimately devising a structured programme for introducing positive law selectively among Japanese Christian communities.

3 For the early modern period, debates on governance were taken as the administration of Empires, not necessarily as theories of legal change. For historiographical debates on governance and administration of the Iberian Empires or models of colonial administration, see *Center-Periphery Model* (Wallerstein, *The Modern World-System*); *Antigo Sistema Colonial* (Novais, *Estrutura e dinâmica do antigo sistema colonial*); *Corporate Model* (Hespanha, *As vésperas do Leviathan*); *Casuísmo y Sistema* (Anzoátegui, *Casuismo y sistema*); *Antigo Regime nos Trópicos* (Fragoso, Bicalho and Gouvêa (orgs.), *Antigo Regime nos trópicos*); and *Polycentric Monarchies* (Herzog et al. (eds.), *Polycentric Monarchies*).

Another hermeneutical change can be observed in Oliveira's chapter where he demonstrates how enslaved litigants employed diverse judicial strategies to substantiate their claims, drawing on the legal frameworks of the *ius commune*, ordinances and customary law. The ways in which the "opened price" argument was proven varied widely, demonstrating the complexity and adaptability of legal reasoning in these cases. This argument was not a fixed legal principle but rather a construct developed through litigation, incorporating various forms of evidence that demonstrated a master's willingness to sell. The normativities that emerged from these cases were the result of an interactive legal process in which enslaved individuals, their attorneys and their masters strategically engaged with the *ius commune* to assert their interpretations. Ultimately, this chapter highlights the active role of enslaved people in shaping legal change, even when their legal victories remained limited to individual cases of freedom.

The second classification of change encompasses cases of (b) punitive change, meaning the changes in punishment practices and law enforcement. Two cases are notable: transformations in the punishment of adulterous women, including their confinement in *recolhimentos* in Massuchetto's chapter, and the evolving legal responses to confessors accused of solicitation in Meneses Muñoz's chapter.

Meneses Muñoz's case study examines the dynamic relationship between the centre and the periphery within the Spanish Inquisition, focusing on the changing attitudes of authorities toward inquisitorial norms in the context of confessionalisation and the reinforcement of the sacrament of penance. By analysing the interactions between the *Consejo de la Suprema y General Inquisición* and district tribunals in Spanish America (in Mexico, Lima and Cartagena *de* Indias), she highlights the disciplinary transgressions of male clergy, particularly in cases of *sollicitatio ad turpia*, where the sacrament of penance was abused for sexual misconduct. This study explores how discussions on canonical and inquisitorial law led to jurisdictional conflicts and shaped the everyday religious experiences of both clergy and laity across the empire. By examining trial procedures, the circulation of pragmatic literature and the strategic use of treatises and edicts of faith (*edictos particulares*), her research reveals how priests manipulated definitions of solicitation to mitigate their offences and, consequently, their punishments.

Massuchetto's paper explores how sending deviant women to *recolhimentos*, a gathering house for women in colonial Brazil, represented a legal change that gradually solidified as a gendered punitive practice, particularly in the latter part of the 18th century. This form of punishment and penalisation was linked to perceptions about which penalties were effective in eliciting the desired social responses from historical actors. In this chapter, she analyses the social practices surrounding the punishment of sending women who deviated from moral expectations to *recolhimentos*, particularly those performed by family authorities, namely husbands, who prioritised their own honour and concerns over the needs of the women. She looks at how these norms evolved over time, the legal transformations the punishment underwent and the perspectives of the women subjected to it.

The third change, (c) status change, involves alterations to the legal and social status of individuals. In the Early Modern world, people could possess various statuses and occupy roles and positions in the world from which duties and rights derived. These statuses could vary depending on a person's freedom or, for example, their position within the family. Men and women could be fathers, mothers, sons or daughters; and, as children, they could be born to married parents, in concubinage, to unknown parents (registered as "*incógnitos*"), to enslaved parents or even be children of a priest father or a nun mother. All these statuses mattered and determined, in a complex and intertwined way, people's social roles in society and their specific legal consequences – for example, being free or enslaved (in the case of children of enslaved women) or being able to inherit from their parents, use the family name and enjoy the nobility of their ascendants.[4] Two key examples are shifts in the status of liberty (freedom) and status in the family, particularly in the cases of enslaved individuals seeking manumission and widows navigating their legal and social positions.

Oliveira's chapter analyses how lawsuits were used by enslaved people to change their legal statuses from enslaved to free. By changing normativities through arguments in lawsuits, he demonstrates how the demands of enslaved persons resulted in normativities capable of judicially defining and changing legal status, giving them the possibility to pay for their freedom. To do so, in the city of São Paulo, Brazil, in the second half of the 18th century, enslaved persons reappropriated and selected norms and legal concepts to force owners to sell their freedom. Oliveira's chapter examines how enslaved individuals and their lawyers juridically constructed the argument that a master had "opened the price", thereby allowing an enslaved person to self-purchase their freedom. By analysing legal disputes in which enslaved individuals sought recognition of a set price for manumission, the chapter explores how their demands led to legal transformations that shaped normativities capable of modifying their legal status.

---

4 Hespanha, *Como os juristas viam o mundo*.

Lopes' chapter analyses legal changes in the status of widows and the impact of these changes in women's lives through the analysis of petitions in the city of Porto, continental Portugal, in the 18th and 19th centuries. She demonstrates that the legal status of widows was shaped not only by legislative changes, but also by the ways in which women characterised widowhood in their petitions and litigations concerning inheritance, property, debts and royal favours, to assess how widows navigated legal constraints. While the transition from the *Ordenações Filipinas* to the Pombaline's legislation – which introduced legal restrictions on widows' control over their children's assets and remarriage – represented a change in a widow's status, cultural shifts also redefined widows' roles within the family and society. She demonstrates that despite legal limitations, widows actively leveraged institutional frameworks, invoking discourses of fragility and honour to secure royal mercy, defend their interests and protect their families from exploitative male relatives and authorities. Therefore, the status of widows varied according to economic, social and legal contexts, as well as their marital property regime, associating their status to the result of a cultural process and several legal changes.

Finally, some of the chapters in this volume focus on changes that belong to the governance of localities, implementing (d) governance change, or adjustments in governance structures, internal and external regulations and/or political-economic modifications. Using a variety of perspectives, the authors of this book present different cases that analyse changes in daily issues across the governance of the Iberian empires. They encompass transformations in commercial regulations (Cabral, Curvelo and Mancilla-Órdenes) and policies regarding the extraction of wealth, particularly diamonds (Mancilla-Órdenes). These shifts reflect broader changes in governance, police regulation and political-economic strategies, and not necessarily an extreme change in a political system, which is more adequately applied to more modern periods in history.

To dig into the details of specific chapters, Curvelo's contribution to this debate explores the evolving social meanings and political uses of *bandos*, broadening the analysis to encompass continental Portugal and the Portuguese Atlantic World. Originally martial in nature and issued under wartime circumstances, *bandos* gradually became one of the most significant instruments of imperial governance, regulating a wide range of legal, economic, commercial and societal aspects of colonial communities. Despite their military origins, these proclamations allowed governors and viceroys to improvise, adapt and administer policies. Over time, different types of *bandos* emerged: those that disseminated royal decrees, those that communicated decisions made by the Crown and those issued at the discretion of local governors to regulate daily life. Their content reflected the broad and complex responsibilities of colonial administrators, covering different themes, such as justice, trade, economic production, migration, morality and public health. They changed beyond their original military function to become highly adaptive governance tools that reflected and facilitated legal changes in the Portuguese Atlantic World. More than mere proclamations, they served as one of the most interventionist expressions of imperial norm, shaping the social and political landscapes of colonial territories through a martial approach to civil administration.

Cabral analyses the role of royal *ouvidores* as agents of change in the towns of Curitiba, in the Captaincy of São Paulo, and Aquiraz, in the Captaincy of Ceará, both in colonial Brazil, during the first half of the 18th century. Cabral's analysis examines how correctional decrees issued by *ouvidores* – officials responsible for ensuring that local legal order conformed to royal legislation – addressed changes in legal authority in Portuguese America. He delves into how these two *correições*, inspections that aimed to reinforce the Crown's power over localities, changed normative order locally, as these *ouvidores*, as agents of the Crown, had the jurisdictional power (and responsibility) to make changes to accommodate the needs of the Empire to Portuguese America. In his chapter, royal *ouvidores* served as agents of change, ensuring the continuity of ties to the Portuguese Crown in structural matters (such as food supply, mining, slavery and relations with Indigenous peoples) as well as the very minutiae of community life, such as town organisation. Through their enforcement of norms and the creation of a local law, *ouvidores* sought to reshape reality and secure the integration of these communities into the Portuguese legal framework and the common tradition of the early modern Portuguese Empire.

The third example of this change can be found in Mancilla-Órdenes' chapter, which explains how colonial institutions drove legal changes in a specific situation: the implementation of the Royal Extraction policy in the Diamond District in the captaincy of Minas Gerais. This chapter examines the transformation of colonial law in the Diamond District between 1771 and 1808, focusing on the administrative and legal changes initiated by the Portuguese Crown to regulate diamond extraction. Mancilla-Órdenes demonstrates how the new norms produced by the Crown to improve efficiency and control should be described as police regulations. As such, although colonial agents focused on enforcing centralisation, the royal institutions were permeable to local peculiarities. Therefore, the new struggle between the central Crown's demands and local needs paved the way to legal changes that provided new concepts of law. The shift she refers to aimed to enhance efficiency and control over production but encountered significant challenges, including jurisdictional conflicts with local authorities, necessitating the use of flexible regulatory tools. The legal change process was not characterised by sudden legal ruptures but rather by the gradual and dynamic interplay of norms shaped through communication between colonial authorities, local officials and economic actors. This chapter highlights how colonial institutions contributed to legal change, demonstrating that colonial law functioned as a flexible regulatory tool designed to navigate the complexities of the building of an empire.

2.2 Actors of Change

Who initiates legal change, who is addressed and who is influenced by it? If we observe who the actors are in the lawmaking processes that drive change, we can observe that changes occur as top-down and bottom-up processes, depending on whether the communications happen upwards or downwards. While change is rarely one-sided, identifying its primary direction helps clarify its dynamics. This means that case studies from this book focus on actors who play a crucial role in initiating and experiencing legal change. In most cases, both the initiators and those affected undergo transformations. Although changes cannot be only one-sided, because both sides change in the process, attempts to name their direction can help to reveal who the actors involved in the processes of legal change are and the kinds of social relations they are involved in.

The understanding of social connections among actors involved in lawmaking processes and legal change is not unanimous and univocal in modern social sciences. Since the inception of social disciplines in its modern format, questions of how social relations are constituted and how they influence legal change have been present. The positivist movement, as one example – asserting that (what was considered at the time) scientific methods are the only valid means of acquiring true knowledge through logic and reason – played a key role in the discussion about legal transformation and broader societal dynamics, as well as how law could reflect and shape social structures through social facts.

This raises key questions that intersect law and social thought, reflecting the intricacies of who drives legal change: does law merely reflect social, economic and political change or does it actively drive it? Can law promote social change, or is it inherently conservative, reinforcing the status quo? Can marginalised groups use law to transform society, or does legal change only follow broader social shifts?

Early sociologists, like Max Weber, Émile Durkheim and Karl Marx, engaged with these questions.[5] Sociologists and social historians have understood the

---

5 Cornelius and Liu, "Law in Classical Sociological Theory", 368.

relationships among actors in social relations and their hierarchies in different ways. They have mused on how law is a reflection of social structures and an active force in shaping them and effecting legal change, whether directly or indirectly. Legal change has, undoubtedly, played a fundamental role in the history of sociology and the humanities, raising questions about historical processes,[6] systemic interactions with the environment and transformations in communication.[7]

If we push forward the connections and understandings of social theory, social relations and how to analyse actors within historical processes and their social dynamics in colonial contexts, we can also identify shifts in how to incorporate different actors into the analysis of social dynamics according to historical narratives. In the historical tradition, the question of which individuals and groups are relevant for understanding the past has been a contentious issue in the history of the Iberian empires, often reflecting strong political agendas. To analyse this, it is also necessary to go back to the late 19th century, when legal scholars explored the legal history of empires and colonial settings initially focusing on traditional actors, usually colonisers considered white and within a colonialist approach. Of course, the history of the Iberian empires involved the relations of not only Europeans, but peoples from different parts of the world, most of them in contact for the first time. As "Others", they were added to historical narratives as belonging to certain fixed categories, such as the "Indians", "Whites", "Mulattos" and "Blacks".[8] Traditional historiography viewed colonial legal systems as separate, such as the distinction between the Spanish and Indigenous Republics or how law was often seen as an external force imposed on colonies.[9]

In Portugal, as one example, the reforms of the Marquis of Pombal shaped colonial law through state-controlled institutions which were the ones responsible for publishing and selecting the sources of overseas colonial territories. During Salazar's regime, scholars were pushed to emphasise how Portuguese colonisation was a mild and cordial process. Topics like slavery were never to be touched. The fall of Portugal's Estado Novo in 1974 allowed scholars to, very slowly, reassess colonial legal history, examining political structures, economic systems and marginalised groups differently, but keeping the myth that the

6 On the current discussion on what a historical process is from a sociological perspective, see Knöbl, *Die Soziologie vor der Geschichte*.

7 See Luhmann, *Law as a Social System*; and Luhmann, *Social Systems*.

8 See Coutinho Silva, *Nem teúdas, nem manteúdas*.

9 Herzog, "Latin American Legal Pluralism". For example, the Spanish *Derecho Indiano* initially reflected this separation of a legal order made abroad but applied in the *Indias Occidentales*. For further development of *Derecho Indiano*, see Petit, "How Was and Is Latin American Legal History Written?".

Portuguese were friendly colonisers able to adapt to different places and peoples (such as defended by the Lusotropicalism movement, for example). It took a while until,

> They gave center stage to the agency of ordinary people, as well as to Amerindians, Africans, and Asians. In addition, and in contrast to most Portuguese historians' practices, they connected their studies on Portuguese imperial rule with debates about Western European colonial rule in Asia, America, and Africa (the New Philology; Asian, African, and Amerindian sources; and social history of colonial societies). Another striking feature of these studies is their use of comparison as an interpretive tool.[10]

It was only in the second half of the 20th century that these paradigms were structurally questioned. A wave of critical theories and disciplines challenged traditional legal history, shifting its focus towards colonial critique adding intersectional interpretations and including various other actors that had been silenced in history, such as women or enslaved individuals, giving protagonism to individuals who were marginalised before. This recent scholarship challenges this view by adding more diverse actors as relevant for the historical colonial past.

Moreover, the late 20th-century "critical turns" in legal history emphasised practices over formal laws. The pragmatic turn, for example, shifted the focus to how legal meaning is shaped by context and social interactions. Rather than viewing language as a closed system of context-independent signs, the pragmatic turn emphasises how meanings are influenced by context, speakers' intentions and social practices.[11] Other "turns" were equally important for the study of legal change and colonialism, such as the cultural turn in history and the archival turn that made possible the access and use of a broader scope of sources.[12] Legal history was further transformed by Critical Legal Studies, which drew from American pragmatism, social movements, feminist jurisprudence, Black studies and postcolonial theories, highlighting how local actors shaped legal transformations.[13] Additionally, new perspectives in international and comparative law challenged the state-centred approach, allowing scholars to rethink how law operates beyond national borders.[14]

---

10 Cardim, "Reassessing the Portuguese Imperial Past", 182.
11 Giltrow and Stein (eds.), *The Pragmatic Turn in Law.*
12 Stoler, *Along the Archival Grain.*
13 Unger, *The Critical Legal Studies Movement.*
14 Osterhammel, *Colonialism*; Loomba, *Colonialism/Postcolonialism*. Spivak, *A Critique of Postcolonial Reason* and Mignolo, *The Darker Side of the Renaissance*. Chakrabarty, *Provincializing Europe.*

Finally, translation and cultural studies have also highlighted the importance of legal change for their explanations of colonial contexts. They ask: what is the role of translation (and those who translate) in processes of change? How can change be explained by analysing language and meaning? This is crucial for understanding the role of different actors in colonial societies. Translation studies and legal history are important concerning the emphasis they place on the actors who drive the translations.[15]

This subfield also has a tradition. Translation processes and the explanation of historical facts have long crossed paths. Peter Burke and Po-chia Hsia have already defended that "all major cultural exchanges in history involved translation".[16] However, the translation they mention in their work must be inserted into the cultural history of translation.

Influenced by the term cultural translation, Thomas Duve explains law as a process of constant cultural translation and knowledge of normativity.[17] But in his terms, law is not exclusively produced by learned jurists or the nation state, for example, but it is constructed by other actors as well, both individual or collective, jurists and non-jurists. Law is a cultural product, continually in the making, shaped by social processes that can happen through the state, but also by different social communities, beyond transnational borders and through practices.

Law is thus also produced in very practical contexts. The knowledge produced in such circumstances is a continuous process of cultural translation of discourses, practices, rules, norms and principles. It gives law stability but also allows for changes in concrete situations, such as the cultural translation of information into knowledge of normativity.

Many factors influence this translation process: the economy, power relations, social relations, culture, norms related to households as a domestic unit, relations between people and things, dependency ties, different forms of government, religious beliefs and practices and long- standing traditions. These conditions affect the translation of the normative information that are to become normative knowledge. Any changes to these conditions constitute the driving force that enables the creation of new knowledge of normativity.

Therefore, change within time and space has its own dynamics of transformation. As time does not stop, one should avoid using linear schemata that risk reducing the ongoing possibility of change – the only permanent

15 For more on the development of translation theories, see Pym, *Exploring Translation Theories*.

16 Burke and Hsia (eds.), *Cultural Translation in Early Modern Europe*.

17 Duve, "Legal History as a History of the Translation of Knowledge of Normativity".

possibility. Knowledge of normativity, then, is also considered to be permanently in motion regarding its content. In this understanding, change does not only happen top-down in written legal documents or in books; nor does it happen only on the ground, in action. It cannot be separated in theory or practice. Change works together with these and relies on a broad understanding of knowledge. The transformation of law happens in all these spheres: between internal and external factors, between the rules of operation already established by the system and the norms behind the norms. That is why change is deeply connected to the idea of law as a knowledge of normativity, because legal history is understood as a process of creation through the acceptance, recreation and transformation of this knowledge. The process of cultural translation is never essentialist but is always in motion as new knowledge of normativity is being created. To closely observe this translation process, one needs to look at localised situations, at ordinary people and the actions they perform in everyday life. "This is why legal change is possible: it is a consequence of the continuous process of translation of knowledge of normativity, in which the actors process, respond and react to changing conditions and circumstances and thus produce new knowledge of normativity".[18]

In this sense, change would always be the possible explanation for how law worked in the early modern period, particularly in colonial contexts. Using the explanation of law as a process of cultural translation means that it could never be moved, transplanted or coexist. Law always changed, created something new by drawing on the people's local knowledge, but also using immemorial customs and centuries-old laws, discourses and, not least, practices.

The concept of translation is one also used by Yanna Yannakakis to explain legal change. She views law as a product of knowledge production and translation. Law is described as: invention, deployment and synthesis, and translation, as this last one involves both the adjustment of meaning and the production of knowledge. According to her, translation is never purely linguistic; it involves cultural adaptation and the reinterpretation of legal concepts. The dynamic interplay between Spanish and Indigenous normative categories varied in vocabulary and jurisdiction. Therefore, her idea on translation was not merely about finding word correspondences; synthesis and invention played key roles. Rather than a two-sided interaction with their own isolated vocabularies, there was a process of negotiation, invention and interpenetration – sometimes collaborative, sometimes violent – producing new vocabularies across different jurisdictions.

---

18 Duve, "Legal History as a History of the Translation of Knowledge of Normativity", 5.

In her book, *Since Time Immemorial*, she explores the evolving significance of native custom within the legal and social fabric of colonial New Spain. She demonstrates how Indigenous communities adapted and redefined custom, integrating it into their communal life and leveraging it as a legal argument in Spanish courts. Over time, the scope of custom narrowed, reflecting broader shifts in colonial governance. By examining how native custom functioned as a reference point for legal continuity and change in the 16th century, Yannakakis contributes to the global history of law. Her analysis highlights the cross-cultural production of legal meaning, emphasising Indigenous engagement with multiple imperial institutions, from the viceroyalty's core to its peripheries. By moving beyond essentialist views of Indigenous norms, her work challenges romanticised notions of a precolonial past, instead revealing the fluid and negotiated nature of legal traditions under colonial rule.[19]

As one can see, the question of how have different actors influenced legal change beyond the fictional separation between metropolis and colonies, has been addressed by all these positions and modifications in historiographies. But, most importantly, the question of who promoted the change and who is addressed by it, or who drives legal change, shifts the focus of analysis from abstract processes to actors from various statuses and positions in their intersectional connections, considering a variety of factors, such as status regarding liberty, family position, governance hierarchy, religion, sex, gender and age, among others.

In this perspective, the case studies in this book emphasise that law does not move in isolation but requires the agency of people from different social strata, focusing on actors from different social statuses and positions within colonial and continental societies. Knowledge is not simply transferred from one place to another; rather, it is continuously produced and reshaped by individuals.

The case studies presented here illustrate how legal change was driven by diverse actors, including priests, solicitors and inquisitorial agents (Meneses Muñoz); missionaries from different religious orders (Ehalt); widows in different positions (honest; joyful; older than 50 years old; childless or with children; former wives of craft workers, merchants, businessmen, soldiers and noblemen) (Lopes); viceroys, governors and captain-majors (Curvelo); *ouvidores* (Cabral); enslaved women and men (Oliveira); women accused of adultery and their husbands (Massuchetto); and *intendentes*, royal officials and *ouvidores gerais* (Mancilla-Órdenes).

Although these actors can be identified as agents of change, their influence must be understood in the context of their social interactions within colonial

19 Yannakakis, *Since Time Immemorial*.

society. For instance, priests influenced the lives of the women they confessed (Meneses Muñoz); missionaries in Asia shaped the experiences of converted Japanese individuals and their communities (Ehalt); widows navigated legal and social challenges, impacting their families and broader communities (Lopes); viceroys, governors and captain-majors attempted to regulate merchants and enslavers (Curvelo); *ouvidores* sought to control food supply, mining, slavery and town organisation (Cabral); adulterous women risked confinement in gathering houses (Massuchetto); enslaved individuals strategically used legal arguments to contest their status and claim freedom (Oliveira); and workers, Crown officials and enslaved people in the diamond industry engaged in complex social and legal dynamics (Mancilla-Órdenes). These actors did not exist in isolation but in constant interaction with figures of power – kings, viceroys, spouses and others – demonstrating how power was both distributed and redistributed from the top down or bottom up.

Going deeper into the details of the relations among actors, Meneses Muñoz examines the *Conselho* of an Inquisitorial Court, where legal change was negotiated internally and shaped the configuration of a crime in a court, communicating their premisses upwards while priests tried to use allegations to navigate these changes in order to find a less harsh penalty. Ehalt explores a top-down process in which missionaries shaped interpretations of the lives of converted Japanese people. Lopes analyses legislation and policies, demonstrating a top-down approach, while widows' petitions illustrate a bottom-up dynamic to negotiate these new policies in their favour and in favour of those they protect. Curvelo focuses on *bandos* and their regulatory impact on society, demonstrating a top-down transformation where new normative types were used to establish order in colonial territories. Cabral examines adaptations in the *correições* as another instance of top-down legal change – similar to Ordinances, the correctional decree translated the regulation of daily issues related to the social individuals. Massuchetto investigates gendered punishments, reinforcing a top-down framework as a social and moral punishment of women. Oliveira highlights enslaved individuals striving to alter their legal status, representing a bottom-up movement. Lastly, Mancilla-Órdenes explores administrative changes in the governance of the Diamond District, illustrating a top-down shift in practices in an attempt to regulate diamond extraction according to the Crown's best interests.

Despite their differences in status and position, these agents of change acted as cultural translators, changing their legal and social environments to meet their own needs rather than simply responding to imperial demands. Legal change was often driven by the need to stabilise local social urgencies rather than by the Crown's overarching objectives. Therefore, what we take from the cases which observe the actors is that the central demands of the Crown and the local needs often did not converge, and this led to legal changes that produced new legal concepts which were shaped by new practices and institutions. These changes, in turn, acquired new meanings and political power within local communities. In this sense, subaltern positions must be examined on a case-by-case basis within colonial contexts. Categories, such as widows, merchants and enslaved individuals, are not absolute but must be analysed in relation to other axes of intersectionality. These actors contributed to the governance of territories across different regions, challenging and reshaping the status quo from which they emerged.

Furthermore, the transformations reveal the dynamic and changing features of law in the Iberian colonial world. Rather than being imposed in a rigid, top-down manner, legal norms were continually reinterpreted, contested and reconfigured through interactions between imperial authorities and local actors. Legal change can be understood not in absolute terms but as a process of upward and downward communication, where law evolved through continuous negotiation between imperial authorities and local actors. Therefore, far from a mere reproduction of metropolitan laws, the cases presented in this volume illustrate that "legal development" was never a linear process of imposition or adoption. Legal change was shaped by the participation of actors at all levels of society – whether in dominant positions of power or in socially, economically or legally subaltern positions.

Actors pursued legal change as a means of stabilising society (within a certain framework of pre-existing values and practices), responding to local needs within a decentralised law-making process. Though embedded in vast imperial structures, lawmaking was ultimately shaped by problem-oriented, decision-making processes that integrated micro-historical perspectives, broader socio-political contexts and complex legal comparisons. At its core, lawmaking in colonial contexts was always a negotiation between stability and reform.

2.3 Mechanisms of Change

Through what instruments or channels does legal change take place? Where should we look to find legal change? Which sources should one use, and what is the specific relation between legal change and media?

In this book, legal change can be observed through a wide range of sources and media. All the cases analysed in the eight chapters rely on local sources within their specific contexts. Although many of these sources were shaped by imperial bureaucratic frameworks – such as ordinances and lawsuits – they took on distinct local characteristics depending on the actors and places where they were applied and reinterpreted. This section broadens the range of sources considered in legal history, moving beyond codified laws to embrace a more flexible, non-legalistic approach that challenges Eurocentric narratives.

The specific question of which source should be incorporated into legal historical research (and into the understanding of legal change) has also been extremely polemical in various historiographical traditions. Materially speaking, where should we look to find legal change? Since the inception of legal history and legal theory disciplines and subfields, this question has intertwined with the question of what law itself is. Again, under the influences of the context of inception of modern disciplines, for instance, legal positivists, such as Hans Kelsen, have explored how legal change operates within a system that regulates its own creation and validity.[20] In Kelsen's own words, the validity of a legal norm – especially its temporal domain of validity – can be limited: its beginning and end can be determined either by itself or by another norm. The norms of a legal order remain valid as long as their validity is not terminated according to the precepts of that legal order. Since a legal system regulates its own creation and application, it dictates the beginning and end of the validity of its norms. Law can only change according to its own rules of lawmaking.[21] It is in those norms that we can find legal change. Later, Adolphus Hart expanded this discussion, introducing the "rule of change" as the only source essential for modifying legal norms.[22] These two positions are not theorisation on legal change, but reflect on the rules of how law can change and through which media.

In contrast, the German Historical School of Jurisprudence emphasised historical analysis, viewing law as a product of human interactions rather than transcendental principles. Adherents argued that legal evolution unfolds over centuries, shaped by the *Volksgeist* – the national spirit.[23] According to this perspective, legal change results from the evolution of the *Volksgeist*.

However, the source of the *Volksgeist* was a matter of debate. Romanists attributed it to the reception of Roman law, while Germanists (such as Friedrich Eichhorn, Jakob Grimm and Georg Beseler) traced it to medieval German law. Thus, different sources are presented in order to look for legal change. A key representative of the Romanist school, Karl Friedrich von

20 Kelsen, *Teoria pura do direito*, 146, translated by the author.

21 Kelsen, *Teoria pura do direito*, 146, translated by the author.

22 Hart, *The Concept of Law*. This relation between the secondary and primary rules was interpreted as similar to the separation and discussion about law in books and law in action, or black-letter law and rules in action, by legal historian Jean-Luis Hálperin, who also addressed the discussion of legal change. See Halpérin, "Law in Books and Law in Action".

23 Savigny, Of *the Vocation of our Age for Legislation and Jurisprudence*.

Savigny, argued that legal institutions are not fixed but rather products of evolutionary processes that are often unplanned.

In contrast, the jurisprudence of interests emphasised societal needs as drivers of legal development. Rudolf von Ihering, in turn, saw legal transformation as a struggle, arguing that law continuously reshapes itself through conflict.[24] There were different positions defended regarding where to look to find law and legal change.

Moving specifically onto history as a discipline, the question of where we should look materially to find change over time and through law has been disputed for centuries, as far back in time as the formation of the historical schools and all the important criticism (critical theories) that followed the School of Annales in the 1970s. This also includes questioning the archives, modifying its understanding not as a place for the depository of sources but as an institution that influenced and shaped knowledge production, revealing the archival bias, political agenda and classifications made with certain intended purposes.[25]

Legal history followed these advances. If we go back to translations and legal history, for example, Lena Foljanty worked with the connection between legal history and cultural translation to expand the uses of sources in understanding transitions.[26] Influenced by the translational turn, she explores a deeper understanding of what translation is beyond the mere correspondence of terms. On the contrary, translation is a complex process of meaning production, one that she analyses particularly in the processes of legal change in the 19th- and early 20th-century Ottoman Empire, Japan and China.[27] In all three countries, European law "was studied through translations, impacting heavily on the intellectual, normative and institutional framework of law. Translation was a key element of the legal reform projects." Her work proves that the 19th century was determinant for the development of what are considered modern features of law in those places, and translation became an "urgent matter" in the modernisation process. To make this point, she, together with other legal historians, needed to go beyond the uses and translations of codes, for instance, and to use literary works as well.

The states from the three countries used translations of European and "Western" knowledge on which to base the fundamental reforms in law and in the organisation of the society, centralising the efforts of translation activities. Reform engagement, therefore, relied on the knowledge produced by these

24 Ihering, *A luta pelo Direito*.
25 Derrida, *Archive Fever*.
26 Foljanty, "Legal Transfers".
27 Foljanty et al., *Translations and Transitions*. Co-authoring comparative monograph.

translations, performed by the states. The translations of military and technical works, as well as legislative material and legal literature, were used as materials for the legislators, courts and private practitioners, but also used in the education of the elite (beyond the key element of the state reform agenda).[28] Using translations, Foljanty et al. explored more sources in the analysis of 19th-century legal changes.

All these and other approaches to sources that came before us justify the broader and rich uses of sources (particularly local sources) in the analysis of cases of legal change in this book. Its case studies draw from a variety of legal and administrative documents, including inquisitorial correspondence and reports, petitions, regulations, trials, compilations or alphabets (*abecedarios*) and edicts (Meneses Muñoz); missionary reports, correspondence, consultations, summaries, apologies, manuals and histories of Japan (Ehalt); petitions submitted by widows, Ordinances, legal doctrine, roman law principles, *alvarás*, decrees and extravagant laws (Lopes); lawsuits initiated by enslaved individuals in the *Juízo ordinário* and the *Ouvidoria* of São Paulo (Oliveira); General Information of the Captaincy, Book of Registration of Bands, Regiment of the Governors of the Arms of the Provinces, Book of Orders, *Bandos* and Ordinances issued by the governors and captains-general of the State of Brazil and of the Governors and Captains-General, Registry of Ordinances and Orders, letters from the Governors, dictionaries and vocabularies (Curvelo); correctional decrees of the 1721 correction in Curitiba and the unpublished manuscripts of the 1729 correction in Aquiraz, regulations of the Ombudsman General, ordinances, common law and chamber books (Cabral); correspondence, requests and petitions and pragmatic normative literature (Massuchetto); and official notifications, *portaria, cartas de data, carta régia, alvará* and regiments (Mancilla-Órdenes).

The authors have gathered sources from various archives across the world, including Portugal, Spain, Japan, Italy, Mexico, Philippines and Brazil. They include the *Archivo Histórico Nacional* in Madrid; the *Archivo General de la Nación* in Mexico; the *Biblioteca Nacional de España* in Madrid; the *Archivo de la Província del Santo Rosário* in Ávila; the *Archivo General de Indias* in Seville; *Archivum Historicum Societatis Iesu* in Rome; *Biblioteca de la Real Academia de la História* in Madrid; *Biblioteca do Palácio Nacional da Ajuda* in Lisbon; Ōmura City Library in Ōmura; *Arquivo Histórico Municipal do Porto* in Porto; *Arquivo Histórico Parlamentar* in Lisbon; *Arquivo Nacional da Torre do Tombo* in Lisbon; the *Biblioteca Nacional do Rio de Janeiro* in Rio de Janeiro;

28 On the questioning of the uses of the terms reform and legal change, see Luna-Fabritius et al. (eds.), *Political Reason and the Language of Change.*

Arquivo Histórico Ultramarino in Lisbon; *Arquivo da Universidade de Coimbra* in Coimbra; *Arquivo Público do Estado do Ceará* in Fortaleza; *Arquivo Público do Estado de São Paulo* in São Paulo; *Arquivo Público Mineiro* in Belo Horizonte; and *Arquivo Histórico do Tribunal de Contas de Portugal* in Lisbon.

These sources, originating from different jurisdictions and lawmaking processes, challenge the notion of a monolithic state as the sole producer of law. Instead, they reveal a legal landscape in which multiple institutions and actors actively shaped legal practices and governance in colonial societies.

Far from being static, law was constantly subjected to negotiation, serving as a space for the exercise of political power, governance strategies and social manoeuvring. There were no laws in a modern sense that could simply be transplanted intact to different territories; rather, law was culturally translated to address concrete local issues. In practice, law assumed various forms and functions, often deviating from its original intent. It is, therefore, best understood through its application on the ground.

Through the sources above, the case studies in this book illustrate several types of normative transformation depending on the media used for the change. I group them into three distinct processes: institutional change, argumentative change and statutory change.

Institutional change is characterised by the creation and modification of institutions – such as the *Intendência dos Diamantes* (Mancilla-Órdenes) and the *recolhimentos* (Masssuchetto) – that can take on entirely new meanings in colonial contexts, promoting changes. These institutions functioned in ways distinct from their European counterparts, adapting to the realities of colonial territories.[29] The latter one was made to administrate the extraction of diamonds in a specific part of the Empire, a new institution, originally in colonial Brazil, that tried to change practices in order to reinforce specific policies to control governance. The former, although present in different parts of the Portuguese Empire, was used in colonial Brazil in a specific moment to change punitive practices against women.

Argumentative change is based on legal reasoning, which was reshaped according to local circumstances. For example, the argument of ignorance, rooted in canon law and Catholic legal traditions, was employed by missionaries in Japan (Ehalt). Similarly, enslaved individuals used the concept of the „just price" in lawsuits as a strategy to argue for their freedom in colonial Brazil, demonstrating how legal arguments changed according to one's need and struggle to change their *status libertatis* (Oliveira).

---

29 Thelen and Conran, "Institutional Change".

Finally, statutory change draws on normative instruments that took a well-known bureaucratic format, but with a different meaning, to address further issues. *Bandos*, for example, originally inspired by military regulations, were repurposed for entirely different social and administrative functions depending on local needs (Curvelo). Additionally, subaltern actors actively engaged with legal norms to claim privileges. Likewise, legal codes, such as the *Ordenações Filipinas*, were applied in novel ways in Brazilian regions: *correições* (judicial inspections) took on distinct forms in Brazil to regulate issues of daily life that occurred in colonial societies (Cabral). Legislation regarding widow status during the Pombaline laws proved a change necessary for a new political agenda (Lopes). Inquisitorial norms, such as reports and compilations, changed the application of regulation of crimes, such as solicitation (Meneses Muñoz).

2.4 Spatial and Temporal Dimensions of Change

The cases presented in this book focus on lawmaking processes and take such processes away from the central administration of empires, a perspective that has already been questioned by the historiography of the Iberian Colonial World. Instead, such cases provide evidence of how lawmaking processes unfolded from local standpoints. But this polarity is not exclusive to the local. On the contrary, the chapters stress how global processes also influenced local legal environments, offering insights into the interaction between the local and the global. By taking the focus away from a big process of global proportions, they question the uses of periodisations and linear timeframes to understand history as a progressive series of events. In such terms, legal change can occur abruptly or gradually; can be diffused or condensed.

Rather than following a linear analysis of change, these cases reject the idea of a progressive, causal chain of legal transformations, as if one change could lead directly to another. Instead, they propose studying specific problems within particular periods, taking a localised snapshot to reflect on issues that did not necessarily lead to fixed or permanent solutions. These problems were shaped by circumstances rather than metaphysical structures and solutions were often temporary, context-dependent and variable rather than absolute or eternal.

These conclusions contribute to a new historiography that has increasingly rejected the outdated idea that colonial territories are merely receivers of "European" law. Instead, they emphasise how legal change involved negotiation, adaptation and local agency. They overcome the understanding that territories beyond Europe were merely recipients of legal diffusion and legal classifications, where legal systems that had already attained maturity in Europe still seemed to be in their infancy overseas.

This outdated approach has been fed for decades when scholars analysed the interface of legal history and colonialism. One of the key questions has been to understand how law changes from one place to another, or if is it possible to speak about a law that is a specific colonial law, or even how to separate a law that is specific to the colony and other from the continent.[30] These connections or questions can be studied from a comparative perspective, looking at the interactions of different legal systems. However, the impact of colonialism on legal systems and how cultural, political and economic factors can influence legal change have also been highlighted. Scholars have argued that legal change can occur through the adoption of new legal models and the borrowing of legal concepts from other legal systems. Others have emphasised how the colonial legal system evolved (if it is possible to speak about one colonial legal system), how Indigenous legal systems were impacted and their relation to "customary law", and even how legal change was influenced by certain factors, such as religion, race, sexuality and gender.[31]

More nuanced questions explore how law responded to colonial "encounters" using concepts, such as introduction, reception, translation, imposition, diffusion, borrowing, adaptation, cultural translation of law, legal transfers, legal transplants, globalisation of law and transnationalisation of law. Each of these approaches deals differently with the question of nation-state-centred understanding of law and the position of Europe in relation to a more global perspective.

Legal pluralism is one of these concepts that also highlights understandings of colonial legal change.[32] This concept examines how multiple legal orders interacted, coexisted and evolved, and how social processes influenced the emergence, maintenance and transformation of different legal systems.[33] Lauren Benton, for instance, applied this concept in her study of colonial legal history, analysing how law functioned as a tool for legitimising and

30 Hespanha, "Porque é que existe e em que é que consiste um direito colonial brasileiro".

31 In the context of postcolonial theory and law, see the work of Comaroff, "Colonialism, Culture, and the Law" and Kapur, *Erotic Justice*. See also Krishnadas, "The Sexual Subaltern in Conversations"; Ferreira da Silva and Harris, *Postcolonialism and the Law*; Haldar, *Law, Orientalism and Postcolonialism*; Stoler, *Carnal Knowledge and Imperial Power*.

32 For a complete overview of its different meanings, see Seinecke, "What Is Legal Pluralism and What Is It Good For?".

33 See Menski, *Comparative Law in a Global Context*; Hooker, *Legal Pluralism*; Griffiths, "What Is Legal Pluralism?".

institutionalising the colonial order, even when multiple legal structures coexisted. She emphasised "the importance of legal pluralism to empires, which invariably relied on layered legal arrangements within composite polities. Empires were legally plural in their core regions as well as in their overseas or distant possessions."[34]

Another use of legal pluralism was given by the Project Group Legal Pluralism, developed at the Max Planck Institute for Social Anthropology. In a collection of papers on the dynamics of plural legal orders, scholars examine how external influences reshape local economies, power relationships and local constellations of legal ordering. Their work explores how one legal order adapts under the influence of another and how new legal forms emerge or coexist within plural legal frameworks. These transformations, they argue, are the result of dynamic and ongoing processes.

> Given the close relation between law and power, changes in relations of social, political and economic power and authority, sometimes expressed in legal form but also occurring relatively independently of legal changes, usually trigger changes in plural legal constellations. This change is in part imposed on local populations. However, [...] the ways these changes occur depend on the actions of local people who often design creative responses unintended by those initiating legal change.[35]

Another key concept in the study of legal change and legal history is legal transplant. This concept, which has greatly influenced contemporary legal history and comparative law, refers to the movement of legal norms from one system to another. While historians have long debated the adaptation of foreign legal traditions – such as the reception of Roman law in medieval Europe (as happens in Savigny's approach, for example) – the term legal transplant was first explicitly introduced by Alan Watson in the 1970s. Watson wanted to emphasise the importance of the influence of one system of law from one country into another by means of borrowing. He argued that understanding legal change requires a comparative approach that investigates why certain legal transformations occur while others do not, and why some societies resist change even when legal reforms take place. For him, the transplant was primarily about the transfer of legal rules. Legal history could be the key to understanding legal change. "Any theory of the relationship between law and society must rest, I believe, on detailed knowledge of the history of individual legal

34 Benton, *Law and Colonial Cultures*.

35 Benda-Beckmann and Benda-Beckmann (eds.), *Dynamics of Plural Legal Orders*, 31.

systems. Indeed, an investigation into several systems is necessary if one is to discover general causes of legal change."[36]

However, later scholars developed more critical perspectives on the interaction between legal systems. Pierre Legrand, for instance, challenged Watson's notion of legal transplants, arguing that legal rules cannot simply "travel" intact across borders. According to Legrand, legal systems are deeply embedded in the social, political and cultural contexts in which they operate, and when a legal rule crosses borders it inevitably transforms.[37]

Building on these debates, other scholars have explored the transnational dimensions of legal change, showing changes that appeal to the transnational dimensions of the law to explain the "making of local law" in a "postcolonial landscape".[38] While much of the literature on legal transplants treats change as a structural force, some scholars have shifted focus to the role of individual agency in shaping legal transformations. By examining legal change beyond the macro level of "the law" they highlight the micro-level interactions that contribute to legal transplant.[39]

Additionally, some scholars have emphasised the spatial and temporal dimensions of legal transplants. They argue that transplants are not merely about moving legal rules across geographical boundaries but also about reshaping the future. As one scholar put it, "besides a spatial dimension, a transplant also implies a specific conception of time that encompasses both the space of experiences and the horizon of expectations. Legal transplants not only transpose legal rules and arguments from one place to another; they fundamentally try to change the future."[40]

These discussions raise big interdisciplinary questions regarding the relation between the global and local, the macro and the micro, and how law functions between those scales, particularly in colonial and imperial contexts. [41] Scholars of micro, macro and global history point out that "both microhis-

36 Watson, "Legal Change"; and Watson, *Legal Transplants*.

37 Legrand, "The Impossibility of 'Legal Transplants'".

38 Graziadei, "Legal Transplants", 724.

39 Graziadei, "Legal Transplants".

40 Galindo, "Legal Transplants between Time and Space".

41 Microhistorians (at least some of them), which started with the Italian *Microstoria*, posed the large question of how to relate specific situations and the general conclusions they imply, turning the micro into a broader connotation. Other historiographical traditions also questioned the connection between local focuses and broader scenarios, such as the local historians in England, the *histoire de la vie privée* in France, and the German *Alltagsgeschichtes*. On the other side of this relation between the micro and the global, global historians have remarked on certain pitfalls that could take away the richness of the global approach while pursuing big questions, such as the impulse to include everyone

tory and global history need to be connected to the study of change over time", contributing largely to the understanding of law in colonial societies in the early modern Iberian empires.[42]

By emphasizing how "(…) less effective at explaining how change over time takes place in specific contexts and, more importantly, why this change happens differently in sites that are connected to one another", global historians' interest in microhistory and vice versa brought to light the importance of connecting and putting together questions that are at the core of these approaches – the necessity of "connecting local spaces and networks with global dynamics."[43] Debates vary about "combining microhistory with a field of historical analysis such as global history"[44] or the investigation of "the global frameworks of local spaces and histories".[45]

Bartolomé Casalilla suggests that global history has a lot to do with local history, and urges for the need for local knowledge of non-European societies. Localities are socially-constructed, dynamic spaces where globalisation emerges through the actions of individuals, leading to globalising structures that shape localisation processes. Practices and actions exist in a mutually dependent relationship, as actions shape practices while simultaneously being conditioned by them, creating constant change. These practices, varying in scale and impact, can extend beyond specific groups to become hegemonic and serve as drivers of multiple, divergent globalisations.[46]

Others focus on the concept of globalisation to inquire about the "relation between the micro level of individual actions and the macro level of global structures." Angelika Epple, for example, proposes an analysis of *globalisations* while integrating the micro level and global changes.[47] Another option has been the usage of glocalisation as a single word that could reflect the divergence,

---

and everything in the interpretations, the imprecise possibilities of analysing power relations and social structures and the extensive connectedness in pursuit of the importance of overcoming national historiographies and Eurocentric approaches.

42 Ghobrial (ed.), "Global History and Microhistory", 32.

43 Ghobrial (ed.), "Global History and Microhistory"; Bertrand and Calafat (eds.), "Microanalyse et histoire globale"; *Journal of Early Modern History*; Ginzburg, *Ecstasies*.

44 Ghobrial (ed.), "Global History and Microhistory".

45 Trivellato, "What Differences Make a Difference?".

46 Casalilla, "'Localism'", 668: "It is increasingly clear to historians – primarily but not only the early modernists – that historical knowledge, like law and anthropology, is a form of local knowledge; in other words, ways of observing general principles in local events […]." See also Casalilla, *Os impérios ibéricos e a globalização da Europa*.

47 Epple, "Calling for a Practice Turn in Global History".

although the term has not been widely adopted by historians or scholars working with the Iberian empires.[48]

Thomas Duve also refers to this term while defending a global legal history. According to him, it would be useful to use the tradition of global history in legal historical studies. The cultural translation of law can allow us to speak about a global legal history drawing on a wide range of sources, on a transnational scale, with special attention to the dialectics of glocalisation.[49]

This concept of *glocal* has received some attention in recent years, not only in economic studies, by also humanities. It emphasises the social construction aspect of the global and the local by arguing that both concepts are not absolute, but social constructions that vary within the writing of various social scientists.[50]

However, *glocal* is a term disputed in terms of definition and methodology. The utility of the term has unquestionably been as one worth trying to use to grasp the complexity of the local and the global as a middle-range explanation to engage theoretical conclusions from empirical research, more specifically, the case studies that were used in local circumstances that were somehow linked to the Iberian empires.

The chapters in this book are inspired by these tensions between the global and the local, or the *glocal*, so often discussed by the literature, to reconsider the social construction of the global and local scales. They do not offer a fixed, one-size-fits-all solution, but highlight the importance of the local and the global and defend that an alternative perspective on legal change from a local standpoint requires us to rethink traditional notions and overall narratives. That is why the volume as a whole focuses on analysing case studies concerning how legal changes can be seen from different local experiences in the Global Iberian World.

---

48 See Roudometof, *Glocalization*; Beyer, *Globalization/Glocalization*; Robertson, "Glocalization"; Roudometof, "Theorizing Glocalization: Three Interpretations"; Ritzer, The *Globalization of Nothing 2*.

49 Duve, "What Is Global Legal History".

50 There is a vast literature on the relation between the global and local. See Andrade, "A Chinese Farmer, Two African Boys, and a Warlord"; Davis, *Trickster Travels*; Colley, *The Ordeal of Elizabeth Marsh*; Sachsenmaier, *Global Entanglements of a Man Who Never Travelled*. Different approaches have studied this connection, calling it "connected histories" or pointing to different scales of analysis or even how local stories fit into a global world to decentre history. See Subrahmanyam, *Empires Between Islam and Christianity*; and Davis, "Decentering History". Immanuel Wallerstein's world-systems approach reflects on globalisation and the Iberian Expansion, an approach that traced the origin of the modern world-system in 16th-century Western Europe and the Americas. Wallerstein, *The Modern World-System*.

Experiences of change and case studies may offer a pathway to understand these complexities by avoiding simplistic ideas of justice as a linear progression from bad to good, unjust to just or unequal to equal, as well as linear schemata of historical periodisations. Moreover, in tackling *glocal* legal history with a focus on local contexts, the chapters aim to initiate a less Eurocentric movement, showing that law was not only made according to what Europeans thought was law, but alternatively adding more local sources and perspectives. They are not radical in the sense of completely turning to an authentic or non-European history, but they do question and reframe the position Europe had in the history-telling of our world and lawmaking processes, as well as how they invisibilised subjects who were marginalised for centuries.

Throughout the practices analysed in the case studies, conceptions could be reaffirmed, adapted and reshaped within local contexts. In many of the cases, it is recognised that the expansion of the Iberian seaborne Empires somehow facilitated the dissemination of its (always changing) legal traditions throughout the Empire's agents and institutions. Law was neither static or frozen in the early modern period, nor was it free of conflicts or cooperations … or change.

The cases examined span locations from Madrid to New Spain, Lima and Cartagena de Indias, as well as Japan, Madeira, Azores, Pernambuco, Maranhão, Pará, Goiás, Minas, Bahia and Angola; the towns of Curitiba and Aquiraz; Captaincies of Bahia, Pernambuco, Grão Pará, Rio de Janeiro and São Paulo; São Paulo city; and even specific places, such as the Diamond District, in the captaincy of Minas Gerais. Porto city and Alentejo region are the only cases in the Portuguese mainland.

The chapters are organised chronologically, and the studies focus on specific and often short periods. The earliest case dates from the 16th century, while the latest reaches the 19th. Some focus on particular years, such as 1721 and 1729 in Cabral's study, while others analyse cases spanning a century or more (Massuchetto, Oliveira, Meneses Muñoz, Ehalt, Lopes). Some chapters examine more defined intervals, such as 1771–1808 (Mancilla-Órdenes).

Put together, these studies raise the question of the speed of change – whether transformations occurred abruptly or gradually. The key issue is not simply whether a change was fast or slow but rather the conceptual challenges of identifying when a change began, when it ended and how something new emerged. How do we define the interval of change? When does one legal or social order give way to another?

Using such classification, the chapters by Curvelo, Cabral and Mancilla-Órdenes demonstrate that changes were driven by one factor in time, such as a new law, decree and/or the establishment of a new institution. They are abrupt in the sense that the reaction to change is fast, not isolated from social long-term events. The chapters by Meneses Muñoz, Ehalt, Lopes, Massuchetto and Oliveira demonstrate another type of change in terms of speed, because the changes are diffused over time, requiring the tracking of many situations throughout the years to be characterised.

As for how they specifically approach the relation between the local and the global, they propose different perspectives but always mention the importance of the local. Meneses Muñoz focuses on the process of construction of knowledge from local to global and vice versa by questioning the centre and periphery relation. She links the general regulations and their local impacts when decision-making processes in the Inquisition became decentralised between local tribunals and local trials.

Ehalt takes us through the complex interplay of global legal change, represented in his chapter by the Tridentine reformational decrees, Catholic liturgical and theological understandings and local political dynamics, such as celebrations, labour calendars and conflicts between religious orders.

Lopes analyses general rules, such as those belonging to Ordinances, and their local uses by and in local courts, such as *Relação do Porto*, but also through the application of the rules belonging to a certain status (widows) in their own uses of privileges.

Curvelo focuses on the tension between European law and local and regional legal solutions managed by local elites, local powers, local communities, local intermediaries and local/regional administrative bodies. The complex relation reflects on the lives of local settlers, local trade relations and local populace practices.

Cabral, referring to *glocalisations*, reflects on the tension between the needs of royal officials to fulfil the interests of the Crown and the needs of local communities that could not be generalised in local spaces and within their local legal order. The result is the emergence of a local law by the hands of local agents, such as the local *ouvidores*. The conflict that justified the *glocal* tension relied on the disagreement between local and general interests that had to be resolved by the action of local elites when facing local dynamics. Assuming that "every global legal issue exists in a local reality", he gives attention to how local institutions and local norms produce normativities from a local perspective, taking into consideration local communities and local experiences.

Massuchetto interweaves the local and global normativities by looking to local social order and the local normative production by local institutions and actors, explaining it by using the concept of cultural translation. In her chapter, the "dynamics of transformation are discerned through the exploration of local normative production encompassing practices, rules, discourses, norms and principles derived from archival sources spanning different regions of Portuguese America."

Oliveira stresses the tensions between local agents, local authorities and local government. By taking the general conceptions of the *ius commune*, he detaches from it the immutability of law by demonstrating that conceptions could be reiterated, reappropriated and recreated locally. The global processes generated by the "expansion of the seaborne Portuguese Empire" were never "a peaceful or even one-way movement", proving that the spread of legal traditions depended on the agents of the Empire, and relied on the agency of those considered less powerful.

Finally, in Mancilla-Órdenes' chapter, we find the conflict between the expectations of local authorities and new local circumstances, provided by "local actors" and the "local practices". Even though solutions could come from the top (the Portuguese Crown) to the bottom (the local level), on the ground, "the Crown observed local complexities and attempted to address them using the best solutions available." This meant that some "normative orders" (for example, the *ius commune*) were localised by "local problems", even allowing the interpretation of royal norms, such as the Regiment of 1771, against the grain, thereby localising the law.

3 Legal Change and the Understanding of Law in the Early Modern Period

One major conclusion, based on the classification of changes so far, allows us to also rethink the concept of law in the early modern world. To understand the types of changes mentioned in this book, I will conclude by systematising the various inferences about what law is as referred to in the next pages. First, it is worth saying that all authors share the understanding that law must be understood in the early modern period from a local point of view and, due to this local perspective, deeply embedded in practices from different actors from different statuses and positions.

All the authors explore the intricacies of jurisdiction in the early modern period. But they also comfortably navigate between jurisdictions and the tools used to apply justice, such as Inquisitorial law, Canon law, local law, *ius commune*, customary law, positive law, divine law, Church law, natural law, royal law, temporal law, ecclesiastical law, spiritual laws, Roman law, common law and criminal law. I highlight three features that stand out from the analysis contained in this book: law as local practice; law as cultural translation; and law as social practice.

Local law existed in tandem with more broader structures, meaning not the existence of two separate bodies, like the historiographical illusion of national laws (such as "Portuguese Law" or "Spanish law"), but one interconnected relation that allowed law to happen on the ground, not coming out of nowhere, and, at the same time, not being completely new or independent, frozen or static, as if created in a laboratory for a fictional society. Law was problem-oriented and served not as a pre-existing force that dictated rules with pre-stablished assumptions. As such, it can be seen as policy regulation (Mancilla-Órdenes); as social response to cultural and political realities of the Atlantic territories in relation to imperial and economic projects (Curvelo and Cabral); and as correspondence between the same institutions in different places of the Empire (Meneses Muñoz). But law was not only like that in colonial territories, as Lopes provides enough demonstration that it could also work with such malleability in the European continent too.

Therefore, law is also identified in translation processes by different actors, giving protagonism to all social strata, including enslaved people, adulterous women, religious men and widows. In the process of making law happen and solving practical issues of daily life, conceptions could be reiterated, reappropriated and recreated locally and, consequently, constantly questioned. In their uses and explanations for lawmaking processes, we can see that concepts, such as normative and knowledge of normativity, are frequently used in this book, as well as local translation of terms related to law in the early modern period, such as in Ehalt's paper (divine law [*jihiina rekisu* or *divina lex*], human law [*umaana rekisu* or *humana lex*], natural [*natsuraru*] law and positive [*pojichiiwa*] law, "old law" [*furuki go-okite*] and "new law" [*shinshiki go-okite*], *hatto*, *okite*, *hō*, *rekisu*, *rei* and *mandamentosu*). Malleable in "interpretations and disputes", Oliveira explains, law could be used by the less favourable as an instrument to change power relations and maintain orders from above, allowing for the identification of the decision-making centres and their locations. Therefore, and foremost, law was a circular process that favoured and deeply shaped social and institutional changes (Massuchetto and Lopes).

Through these diverse forms of legal change and possibilities of understanding law, this volume illustrates that legal transformations were not unilateral but emerged from the dynamic interplay between legal norms, social practices and the actors involved. The evidence suggests that legal transformations primarily aimed to regulate social life and create stability, even though they often led to instability for certain groups. The four key questions explored in this volume – concerning the actors, directionality, objects and mechanisms of legal change – shed light on the new techniques used to govern territories and daily life. Whether driven by top-down or bottom-up processes, these changes paradoxically served as a powerful force for the attempt at stabilisation that was never reached in the social life of the past.

Bibliography

Literature

Andrade, Tonio, "A Chinese Farmer, Two African Boys, and a Warlord: Toward a Global Microhistory", in *Journal of World History* 21, no. 4 (2010), 573–591.

Anzoátegui, Víctor Tau, *Casuismo y sistema: Indagación histórica sobre el espíritu del Derecho Indiano*, Seville 2021.

Benda-Beckmann, Franz von and Keebet von Benda-Beckmann (eds.), *Dynamics of Plural Legal Orders*, Münster 2006.

Benton, Laura, *Law and Colonial Cultures. Legal Regimes in World History, 1400–1900*, Cambridge 2002.

Bertrand, Romain and Guillaume Calafat (eds.), "Micro-analyse et histoire globale", in *Annales: Histoire, Sciences Sociales* 73, no. 1 (2019).

Beyer, Peter, *Globalization/Glocalization: Developments in Theory and Application*, Leiden 2022.

Burke, Peter and R. Po-chia Hsia (eds.), *Cultural Translation in Early Modern Europe*, Cambridge 2007.

Cardim, Pedro, "Reassessing the Portuguese Imperial Past: Scholarly Perspectives and Civic Engagement", in *Journal of Lusophone Studies* 8:1 (2023), 176–205.

Casalilla, Bartolomé Yun, "'Localism', Global History and Transnational History. A Reflection from the Historian of Early Modern Europe", in *Historisk Tidskrift* 127:4 (2007), 659–678.

Casalilla, Bartolomé Yun, *Os impérios ibéricos e a globalização da Europa (séculos XV a XVII)*, Lisboa 2021.

Chakrabarty, Dipesh, *Provincializing Europe: Postcolonial Thought and Historical Difference*, Princeton, NJ 2000.

Colley, Linda, *The Ordeal of Elizabeth Marsh: A Woman in World History*, London 2007.

Comaroff, John L., "Colonialism, Culture, and the Law: A Foreword", in *Law & Social Inquiry* 26:2 (2001), 305–314.

Cornelius, Eduardo and Sida Liu, "Law in Classical Sociological Theory: Coercion, Ideology, and Change", in Abrutyn, Seth and Omar Lizardo (eds.), *Handbook of Classical Sociological Theory*, Cham 2021, 367–380.

Coutinho Silva, Luisa Stella de Oliveira, *Nem teúdas, nem manteúdas: História das Mulheres e Direito na capitania da Paraíba (Brasil, 1661–1822)*, Frankfurt am Main 2020.
Davis, Natalie Zemon, *Trickster Travels: A Sixteenth-Century Muslim Between Worlds*, New York, NY 2006.
Davis, Natalie Zemon, "Decentering History: Local Stories and Cultural Crossings in A Global World", in *History and Theory* 50, no. 2 (2011), 188–202.
Derrida, Jacques, *Archive Fever: A Freudian Impression*, trans. Eric Prenowitz, Chicago, IL 1997.
Duve, Thomas, "What Is Global Legal History?", in *Comparative Legal History* 8:2 (2020), 73–115 (https://doi.org/10.1080/2049677X.2020.1830488).
Duve, Thomas, "Legal History as a History of the Translation of Knowledge of Normativity", in *Max Planck Institute for Legal History and Legal Theory Research Paper Series*, no. 2022–16 (2022), 1–12 (https://ssrn.com/abstract=4229323).
Epple, Angelika, "Calling for a Practice Turn in Global History: Practices as Drivers of Globalization/s", in *History and Theory* 57, no. 3 (2018), 390–407.
Ferreira da Silva, Denise and Mark Harris (eds.), *Postcolonialism and the Law*, London 2017.
Foljanty, Lena, "Legal Transfers as Processes of Cultural Translation: On the Consequences of a Metaphor", in *Max Planck Institute for European Legal History Research Paper Series*, no. 2015–09 (2015), 1–18 (https://ssrn.com/abstract=2682465).
Foljanty, Lena, Murat Burak Aydin, Egas Bender de Moniz Bandeira, Zheng Li, Zülâl Mulsu, Yu Wang and Zeynep Yazici Çağlar, *Translations and Transitions: Legal Practice in 19th and Early 20th Century Japan, China, and the Ottoman Empire*, forthcoming.
Fragoso, João, Maria Fernanda Bicalho and Maria de Fátima Gouvêa (orgs.), *Antigo Regime nos trópicos: a dinâmica imperial portuguesa (séculos XVI–XVIII)*, Rio de Janeiro 2001.
Galindo, George Rodrigo Bandeira, "Legal Transplants between Time and Space, Global Perspectives on Legal History", in Duve, Thomas (ed.), *Entanglements in Legal History: Conceptual Approaches*, Frankfurt am Main 2014, 129–148.
Ghobrial, John-Paul (ed.), "Global History and Microhistory", in *Past and Present* 242, issue supplement 14 (2019).
Giltrow, Janet and Dieter Stein (eds.), *The Pragmatic Turn in Law. Inference and Interpretation in Legal Discourse*, Berlin 2017.
Ginzburg, Carlo, *Ecstasies: Deciphering the Witches' Sabbath*, trans. Raymond Rosenthal, Chicago, IL 1991.
Graziadei, Michele, "Legal Transplants and the Frontiers of Legal Knowledge", in *Theoretical Inquiries in Law* 10:2 (2009), 723–743.
Griffiths, John, "What Is Legal Pluralism?", in *Journal of Legal Pluralism and Unofficial Law* 18, no. 24 (1986), 1–55.

Haldar, Piyel, *Law, Orientalism and Postcolonialism. The Jurisdiction of the Lotus Eaters*, London 2007.

Halpérin, Jean-Louis, "Law in Books and Law in Action: The Problem of Legal Change", in *Maine Law Review* 64:1 (2011), 45–76.

Hart, H. L. A., *The Concept of Law*, Oxford 2012.

Herzog, Tamar, "Latin American Legal Pluralism: The Old and the New", in *Quaderni Fiorentini per la storia del pensiero giuridico moderno* 50:2 (2021), 705–736.

Herzog, Tamar, José Javier Ruiz Ibáñez, Gaetano Sabatini and Pedro Cardim (eds.), *Polycentric Monarchies: How Did Early Modern Spain and Portugal Achieve and Maintain a Global Hegemony?*, Eastbourne 2013.

Hespanha, António Manuel, *As vésperas do Leviathan. Instituições e poder político: Portugal – séc. XVII*, Lisboa 1994.

Hespanha, António Manuel, "Porque é que existe e em que é que consiste um direito colonial brasileiro", in *Quaderni Fiorentini per la storia del pensiero giuridico moderno* 35:1 (2006), 59–81.

Hespanha, António Manuel, *Como os juristas viam o mundo. 1550–1750: Direitos, estados, pessoas, coisas, contratos, ações e crimes*, Lisboa 2015.

Hooker, M. B., *Legal Pluralism: An Introduction to Colonial and Neo-Colonial Laws*, Oxford 1975.

Ihering, Rudolf von, *A luta pelo Direito*, trans. Edson Bini, São Paulo 2019.

Journal of Early Modern History 27:1–2, special issue "Global Microhistories" (2023).

Kapur, Ratna, *Erotic Justice: Law and the New Politics of Postcolonialism*, London 2005.

Kelsen, Hans, *Teoria pura do direito*, trans. João Baptista Machado, São Paulo 1998.

Knöbl, Wolfgang, *Die Soziologie vor der Geschichte. Zur Kritik der Sozialtheorie*, Berlin 2022.

Krishnadas, Jane, "The Sexual Subaltern in Conversations 'Somewhere in Between': Law and the Old Politics of Colonialism", in *Feminist Legal Studies* 14 (2006), 53–77.

Legrand, Pierre, "The Impossibility of 'Legal Transplants'", in *Maastricht Journal of European and Comparative Law* 4:2 (1997), 111–124.

Loomba, Ania, *Colonialism/Postcolonialism*, London 1998.

Luhmann, Niklas, *Social Systems*, trans. John Bednarz, Jr. and Dirk Baecker, Stanford, CA 1995.

Luhmann, Niklas, *Law as a Social System*, trans. Klaus A. Ziegert, Oxford 2004.

Luna-Fabritius, Adriana, Ere Nokkala, Marten Seppel and Keith Tribe (eds.), *Political Reason and the Language of Change. Reform and Improvement in Early Modern Europe*, London 2022.

Meccarelli, Massimo, "Time of Innovation and Time of Transition Shaping the Legal Dimension: A Methodological Approach from Legal History", in Meccarelli, Massimo, Cristiano Paixão and Claudia Roesler (eds.), *Innovation and Transition in Law: Experiences and Theoretical Settings*, Madrid 2020.

Menski, Werner, *Comparative Law in a Global Context: The Legal Systems of Asia and Africa*, Cambridge 2006.

Mignolo, Walter, *The Darker Side of the Renaissance. Literacy, Territoriality and Colonization*, Ann Arbor, MI 1995.

Novais, Fernando, *Estrutura e dinâmica do antigo sistema colonial (séculos XVI–XVIII)*, Hucitec 2018.

Osterhammel, Jürgen, *Colonialism: A Theoretical Overview*, trans. Shelley L. Frisch, Princeton, NJ 2000.

Petit, Carlos, "How Was and Is Latin American Legal History Written?", in Duve, Thomas and Tamar Herzog (eds.), *The Cambridge History of Latin American Law in Global Perspective*, Cambridge 2024, 18–39.

Pym, Anthony, *Exploring Translation Theories*, London 2023.

Ritzer, George, *The Globalization of Nothing* 2, Thousand Oaks, CA 2007.

Robertson, Roland, "Glocalization: Time–Space and Homogeneity–Heterogeneity", in Featherstone, Mike, Scott Lash, and Roland Robertson (eds.), *Global Modernities*, London 1995, 25–44.

Roudometof, Victor, *Glocalization. A Critical Introduction*, London 2016.

Roudometof, Victor, "Theorizing Glocalization: Three Interpretations", in *European Journal of Social Theory* 19:3 (2016), 391–408.

Sachs, Stephen E., "Originalism as a Theory of Legal Change", in H*arvard Journal of Law & Public Policy* 38, no. 3 (2015), 817–888.

Sachsenmaier, Dominic, *Global Entanglements of a Man Who Never Travelled: A Seventeenth-Century Chinese Christian and His Conflicted Worlds*, New York, NY 2018.

Sarat, Austin (ed.), *Transitions: Legal Change, Legal Meanings*, Tuscaloosa, AL 2012.

Savigny, Friedrich Carl von, *Of the Vocation of our Age for Legislation and Jurisprudence*, trans. Abraham Hayward, Clark, NJ 2002.

Seinecke, Ralf, "What Is Legal Pluralism and What Is It Good For?", in Luts-Sootak, Marju, Irene Kull, Karin Sein and Hesi Siimets-Gross (eds.), *Legal Pluralism – cui bono?*, Tartu 2018, 13–28.

Spivak, Gayatri, *A Critique of Postcolonial Reason. Toward a History of the Vanishing _Present*, Cambridge, MA 1999.

Stoler, Ann Laura, *Along the Archival Grain. Epistemic Anxieties and Colonial Common Sense*, Princeton, NJ 2009.

Stoler, Ann Laura, *Carnal Knowledge and Imperial Power. Race and the Intimate in Colonial Rule*, Berkeley, CA 2010.

Subrahmanyam, Sanjay, *Empires Between Islam and Christianity, 1500–1800*, Albany, NY 2019.

Thelen, Kathleen and James Conran, "Institutional Change", in Fioretos, Orfeo, Tulia G. Falleti and Adam Sheingate (eds.), *The Oxford Handbook of Historical Institutionalism*, Oxford 2016.

Trivellato, Francesca "What Differences Make a Difference? Global History and Microanalysis Revisited", in *Journal of Early Modern History* 27 (2023), 7–31.

Unger, Roberto Mangabeira, *The Critical Legal Studies Movement: Another Times, A Greater Task*, New York, NY 2015.

Wallerstein, Immanuel, *The Modern World-System I: Capitalist Agriculture and the Origins of the European World-Economy in the Sixteenth Century*, Berkeley, CA 2011.

Watson, Alan, "Legal Change: Sources of Law and Legal Culture", in *University of Pennsylvania Law Review* 131:5 (1983), 1121–1157.

Watson, Alan, *Legal Transplants. An Approach to Comparative Law*, Athens, GA 1993.

Yannakakis, Yanna, *Since Time Immemorial. Native Custom & Law in Colonial Mexico*, Durham, NC 2023.

Yowell, Paul, "Dworkin, Interpretation and Legal Change", in Glanert, Simone and Fabien Girard (eds.), *Law's Hermeneutics: Other Investigations*, London 2017, 100–117.

CHAPTER 2

The Dynamics of Normative Change

Sollicitatio ad Turpia in the Inquisitorial Courts of Spanish America (16th and 17th Centuries)

Mariana Meneses Muñoz

1 Introduction

During the Council of Trent (1545–63), the imperative to fortify the discipline of both regular and secular clerics was deemed essential. This measure was considered crucial in drawing parishioners nearer to the Christian faith through the accurate administration of sacraments, thereby reinforcing confidence in religious individuals as representatives of both God and the ecclesiastical institution. Consequently, the deliberations of the Church, along with the conduct of its agents, were contemplated considering the diversity of topics discussed and reinforced by the Tridentine decrees. This scrutiny is particularly evident in the proceedings of Session XXII, addressing the Eucharistic ritual; Session XIV, addressing the sacrament of Marriage; and, notably, Session XIV, delving into the sacrament of Confession.

The canons encompassed elements that personalised the Christian experience, guiding individuals toward integration into collective expressions of faith, signifying participation in a religious community. However, despite the efforts by the Council of Trent pertaining to society and local communities, there was a simultaneous tightening of mechanisms for controlling clerical discipline. Among the male clergy's disciplinary transgressions, regarded as bordering on heretical conduct, was the *Sollicitatio ad turpia*. This crime was a manifestation of excessive authority unbecoming of the confessor's dignified status and an abuse of the sacrament of penance involving behaviours of a sexual nature. This means that confessors could use the intimacy of the space of the sacrament of confession and the repentant attitude of the penitent to demand sexual favours or to perform sexual abuse. These behaviours were explicitly addressed in Pope Pius IV's *bulla*,[1] *Cum Sicut Nuper* (1561):

1 In spite of the existence of other terms (like papal constitutions), I decided to use the Latin terminology, *bulla*, for this kind of documentation because of the popularisation of the term after the 13th century to refer to almost all the letters issued by the Pope and based on the

HTTPS://DOI.ORG/10.1163/9789004764422-003

"Specifically, they entice and provoke penitent women to indecent acts while hearing their confessions, tempting and enticing them, and endeavouring to seduce and provoke them, and instead of acting in place of these women through the sacrament of reconciliation to our Creator […]".[2]

Due to Pius' *bulla*, theological dialogues proliferated, leading to a heightened production of texts, including treatises, manuals and instructions, aimed at sustaining the doctrinal and disciplinary education of clergy. As the crime also represented an abuse of a sacrament, considered a heresy, the authority to discuss and judge it passed from the bishop's jurisdiction to the Holy Office's. This integration of discussions into the realms of canonical and inquisitorial law precipitated a clash between the varied 'realities' within the Catholic world. This clash involved navigating the everyday aspects of being part of the Christian community to reveal a diverse range of religious experiences among both ecclesiastical figures and the laity, also reaching different parts of the Spanish Empire on a local level.

For Spanish America, those who implemented Canon law in the 16th and 17th centuries generated a spectrum of learning, adaptations and perspectives. In this era, three inquisitorial tribunals were established: Mexico (1569), Lima (1570) and Cartagena de Indias (1610). The geographical distance from central authority, or the long-distance relationship between the district tribunals in America (Mexico, Cartagena and Lima) with the *Consejo de la Suprema y General Inquisición*,[3] the diverse subjects reflected in the demographical varieties of colonial territories and a spectrum of religious beliefs, including varied understandings of dogmas and permissible forms of sociability within the Christian community, prompted local interpretations of guidelines originating from the "Old World". Consequently, social and jurisdictional conflicts arose, presenting new challenges for district tribunals and the *Consejo de la Suprema* in Madrid.

classification used in the recompilation books of Canon Law from the Vatican Archive of *Bullarum*, produced during the second half of the 18th century and during the 19th century.

2 Gasparri, *Codicis Iuris Canonici Fontes*, vol. 1, 181: "[…] iniuriam facere vereantur: mulieres videlicet poenitentes ad actus inhonestos, dum earum audiunt confessiones alliciendo, et provocando, seu allicere, et provocare tentando, et procurando, ac loco earum per Sacramentum huiusmodi Creatori nostro reconciliationis" (all translations from Spanish and Latin are mine).

3 Hereafter, *Consejo de la Suprema*. The *Consejo de la Suprema* was the central governing body of the Spanish Inquisition. Commonly known as the "Supreme", this council was established in 1483 by King Ferdinand II of Aragon and Queen Isabella I of Castile as part of efforts to unify and strengthen religious and political control in Spain.

Therefore, drawing on the importance of this crime to the whole Empire, this chapter studies the forms of changes in internal norms regarding solicitation in the sacrament of confession and how the dissemination and internal production of regulations about the concept and practice of solicitation consolidated the procedure to judge the confessors suspected of this crime in the *Consejo de la Suprema* and the district tribunals in Spanish America. To do so, it relies on a wide range of documents produced by the Spanish Inquisition, such as correspondence, trials and trial summaries (*Relaciones de causa*) found in the National Historical Archive in Madrid (AHN), the collection of edicts from the Mexico tribunal in the General Archive of the Nation of Mexico (AGNM) and some compilations or alphabets (*abecedarios*) that are held in the National Library of Spain (BNE), from the end of the 16th century and the 17th century. The timeframe chosen to be examined is substantiated by the production of documentation from the Holy Office and the Papal authorities concerning solicitation. Emphasis will be placed on the impact of Pope Gregory XV's *breve, Universi Dominici Gregis* (1622). Interestingly, due to the completeness of this document, there was no new Canon Law produced on solicitation in the Early Modern Period. The only subsequent confirmation occurred through Pope Benedict XIV's decree, *Sacramentum Penitentiae*, in 1741.

Furthermore, this chapter will analyse the application of this documentation in the trials against the solicitant clergy and the impact it may have had on the procedural dimension. In doing so, it will be possible to identify the consolidation of and changes in the attitudes of the authorities involved in inquisitorial trials, within a context of confessionalisation and reinforcement of the sacrament of penance regarding solicitation in sacramental confession.

Finally, this chapter aims to contribute to the field of the legal history of the Inquisition by linking it to the history of knowledge. I align with Thomas Duve's overview about the translation of knowledge of normativity as a product of a communicative activity.[4] I argue that a decentralisation of the production of knowledge occurred in specific decision-making processes between the district tribunals in America and the *Consejo de la Suprema*. The geographical distance and the imperative to address local trials and conflicts gave rise to diverse decision-making centres within the local territories.

In this sense, one of the objectives of producing, circulating and preserving documents from governing bodies in the early modern period was to obtain empirical information. Arndt Brendecke describes this method as consisting of three stages: "*Informatio* could refer both to the beginning of the process

4 See Duve, "Legal History as a History of the Translation of Knowledge of Normativity"; and Duve, "Pragmatic Normative Literature", 1–36.

(the survey) as well as its intermediate result (the report) and, finally, the stated goal of the process (to be informed)".[5] This practice allowed for a differentiation in the documents between what was considered information and what was seen as knowledge production, legitimising the institutions that produced the information.

As will be demonstrated, the sections of this chapter correspond to the process that shapes normative orders: production, storage, processing and legitimation.[6] The first part sheds light on the nature of the production of the main Holy Office regulations and, more importantly, the dynamics of the circulation of documents, such as instructions and *cartas acordadas*, a form of circulars or official bulletins that conveyed the norms of the Holy Office to the district courts, as well as the rhythms and logics of communication between the district courts and the *Consejo de la Suprema*. By providing examples taken from the correspondence between the "centre and the periphery", this section shows the problem that arose around the idea of autonomy that the inquisitors in America could have, and the responses received from Spain.

The last section of this chapter presents a chronology of the arrival of cultural translation of internal norms used to prosecute solicitants. This analysis is based on a sample of chosen trials from three tribunals, particularly from the second half of the 17th century, and aims to apply the concept of knowledge of normativity, defined by Duve and applied by different authors.[7] By analysing the comments, attitudes and actions of the Holy Office and the subjects involved in the trials (in this case, clerics suspected of solicitation), it is possible to identify the individual attitudes of the subjects involved in the inquisitorial trials.

Following these steps, this chapter dialogues with the historiography on the creation, circulation and reception of internal regulations of the Holy Office. Recently, this tradition saw a surge in production towards the end of the 1970s with Gustav Henningsen's publication on the Moldenhawer Collection in Copenhague,[8] and the book *Perfiles jurídicos de la inquisición Española,*

5 Brendecke, *Imperio e información*, 111.

6 See Schuppert, *The World of Rules. A Somewhat Different Measurement of the World*, 59–136.

7 Danwerth, "The Circulation of Pragmatic Normative Literature in Spanish America", 89–130; Rex Galindo, "Shaping Colonial Behaviours", 296–327; Duve, "Pragmatic Normative Literature". This concept results from the continuous process of knowledge production, through the transformation (translation) of normative information, and over time defines specific normative orders, which, as Duve states, are important for understanding, for example, the 16th- and 17th-century Ibero-American regime of production of knowledge of normativity.

8 Henningsen, "La colección de Moldenhawer en Copenhague", 209–270.

coordinated by José Antonio Escudero López in 1986. These texts inspired a series of studies that analysed the documentation of the Holy Office, characterising it and exploring its relationship with the inquisitorial process. From the 2000s onwards, the focus shifted towards an institutional perspective, typifying the different legal instruments such as inquisitors' manuals and *cartas acordadas*. For instructions,[9] the texts concentrated on biographies of inquisitors or those who formed the *Consejo de la Suprema* and impacted the tribunal's organisation and functioning.[10]

The works published have provided a foundation for understanding the functioning of the Inquisition through its documents and archives. However, these approaches have almost exclusively dealt with the relationship between the district courts on the peninsula (Castile and Aragon), with less mention of the Inquisitorial courts in Sicily.[11] They have practically excluded the American courts and their relationship with the *Consejo de la Suprema* and the Inquisitor General from this production and documentary analysis universe, always focusing on a more general approach.[12] Despite this, there are some studies on the existing documentary types for local courts between the end of the 16th and the 17th centuries for the American case.[13]

---

9 Martín Barba, "Documentación del Consejo de Inquisición en tiempos de Torquemada", 187–221; Berdera Bravo, "La Legislación interna del Santo Oficio. Las cartas acordadas", 39–62; Pérez Fernández-Turégano, "Cartas acordadas de la Inquisición española", 13–34; Cabezas Fontanilla, "Nuevas aportaciones al estudio del archivo del Consejo de la Suprema Inquisición", 31–49; Cabezas Fontanillas, "La carta acordada", 713–726; Galende Díaz, "La recorrección de registros diplomática inquisitorial", 21–34; Bolaños Mejías, "La literatura jurídica como fuente del derecho inquisitorial", 191–220; among others.

10 Barrios Pintado, "Las competencias privativas del inquisidor general en la normativa regia de los siglos XVI y XVII", 121–140; Domínguez Nafría, "La «copilación» de las instrucciones inquisitoriales de Gaspar Isidro de Argüello", 137–276; Juanto Jiménez, "El comisario del Santo Oficio en las instrucciones inquisitoriales", 95–109; Pérez Fernández-Turégano, "El archivo de la Secretaría de Aragón del Consejo de la Inquisición", 41–73.

11 Ciaramitaro, *Santo Oficio imperial. Dinámicas globales y el caso siciliano.*

12 In terms of production regarding solicitation in the Iberian Peninsula, see Sarrión Mora, *Sexualidad y confesión*; Alejandre García, *El veneno de Dios.*

13 Millar Carvacho, "El archivo del Santo Oficio de Lima y la documentación inquisitorial existente en Chile", 101–116; Sánchez Rubio and Testón Núñez, "Por mares de olvidos. Correspondencia privada e inquisición en Nueva España. Siglos XVI–XVIII", 46–80; Levaggi (coord.), *La Inquisición en Hispanoamérica. Estudios*; Maqueda Abreu, *Estado, Iglesia e Inquisición en Indias.* On solicitation in Hispanic America see Aspell, "El sacramento de la confesión. Los manuales y las sumas de confesión", 431–447; Delgado, "Foregrounding Marginal Voices", 155–168; González Marmolejo, *Sexo y confesión*; Tortorici, *Sins against Nature.*

I decided to focus on the study of a specific practice: solicitation in confession. Despite the literature about this crime,[14] I argue that there is still some research to be done about this topic. Although this inquisitorial crime is briefly mentioned by the historiography, studies focusing on its specificities regarding normativities that also include practices are still rare.[15] On the other hand, solicitation has a specificity that makes it interesting to analyse. Being a crime specifically of the confessing clergy, its judgement should have been private. However, for it to be reported and denounced, the awareness of the act had to be made public.

Methodologically speaking, the analysis of the creation of a normative framework over two hundred years will help to understand the configuration of the dynamics of functioning, the relationship of their inquisitorial agents in the district tribunals, with the *Tribunal de la Suprema*, and the process of construction of knowledge from local to "global" and vice versa. I also argue that there has been little analysis of the correspondence books, a rich documentary series of which a large quantity is preserved in the AHN and which would complete the lack of information about solicitation trials, lost in the American archives. This concern was addressed in a 1670 response from the *Consejo de la Suprema* to the Inquisition of *Cartagena de Indias*: "By letter from that Tribunal dated April 6th of last year (1669), the Council was informed that papers cannot be preserved in that Holy Office as, within a short time, termites consume them to such an extent that those that are not normally handled cannot be read after six years".[16] Hence, this is one of the crucial reasons for sending copies of the most significant documents to Spain.

As evident throughout this chapter, there is a pronounced emphasis on the documentary dimension. In cases of solicitation, particular attention should be given to the statements of inquisitors and ecclesiastical authorities. This practice, both disciplinary and heretical, directly affected the clergy's discipline

14 I have previously written two texts about solicitation in the American courts and wanted to complete my research about solicitation during the 17th century with a more institutional and internal framework of the Holy Office, linking and decentralising the discussions. See Meneses Muñoz, "Solicitación y praxis inquisitorial en los tribunales de México, Cartagena y Lima, siglo XVII", 110–135; and Meneses Muñoz, "Male Violence and Female Resistance in the Sacrament of Penance: Accounts Before the Inquisitorial Tribunals in Colonial America (Seventeenth Century)", 177–194.

15 Mejía, "Escritura de la historiografía sobre los tribunales inquisitoriales americanos", 161–179.

16 AHN, Inquisición, lib. 345, fol. 7r: "por carta de ese Tribunal de 6 de abril del año pasado de 1669, se da cuenta al Consejo que no se pueden conservar en ese Sto. Of. los papeles, sin que dentro de breve término el comején no los consuma de tal suerte, que no se pueden ler pasados seis años los que de ordinario no se manejan [...]".

and its perception among parishioners and religious communities. This emphasis arises from the recognition that the Inquisition collection within the AHN stands as the foremost repository of documents pertaining to the Spanish Inquisition. It meticulously preserves the original order of document acquisition and organisation, offering insights into the operational dynamics of district courts and their connections with the *Consejo de la Suprema*.

The archive's reinterpretation reveals a gradual establishment of remote communication and regulation mechanisms for inquisitorial processes. This amassed knowledge, methodically organised over time by various inquisitors, served as consultation tools for their counterparts. Notably, in the case of alphabets, it facilitated the accumulation and publication of laws on specific subjects, serving as legal precedents.

2 Dissemination of Internal Regulations, Communication and Local Decisions: Questioning the Centre and Periphery Relation

The Inquisition developed a certain degree of autonomy in producing internal regulations regarding its relationship with the Crown of Castile and the Pontificial State.[17] The continuous production of norms by the Holy Office was essential for its proper functioning. These elements ensured that inquisitorial trials were conducted according to the guidelines and style of the Holy Office, guaranteeing the effectiveness of inquisitorial justice. At the same time, a series of documents were sent to local or district courts to guide their functioning. Instructions, manuals and internal regulations of this institution aimed to keep inquisitorial actions homogeneous. This goal was directed from afar by general inquisitors and the Council of the Supreme.

These regulations complemented the four constitutive elements of inquisitorial law (secular legislation, general Canon Law regulations, judicial doctrine and customs/customary law).[18] Initially, this autonomy was reflected in

---

17 Although the hierarchy of powers is reflected in the importance of the documents produced by these three entities – first Rome, then the King and finally the Council – these levels or legal ranks can be identified. They were more evident during the foundational period of the Holy Office and persisted until the first half of the 16th century. It is important to remember that the *Secretaría de Aragón* handled all matters relating to the Courts of the Crown of Aragon, Logroño, Italy and America.

18 See Gacto Fernández, "La costumbre en el derecho de la Inquisición", 215–262; and Pérez Martín, "La doctrina jurídica", 279–322.

the publication of instructions.[19] Later, towards the second half of the 16th century, *cartas acordadas*, a type of document that earned its name because it resulted from deliberations between the *Consejo de la Suprema* and the General Inquisitor, emerged as the second most important judicial document for the functioning of the Tribunal of the Holy Office.[20] *Cartas acordadas* gradually displaced the instructions as they allowed for quicker rulings on procedural aspects and concrete problems.[21]

The norms regarding the crime of solicitation were no different. One example is a letter dated 2 March 1576, in which a request was made to publish an edict against solicitants, "To be published in the edicts so that they may manifest it in the Holy Office, and so that it may be understood that his punishment is due."[22] This letter modified the instruction from 22 March 1571, where district inquisitors were asked: "not to publish this offence in the edicts". In this case the problem was not jurisdictional (that was partially resolved in 1559 by the constitution of Pope Paul IV) but related to the scandalous and possibly bad reputation of confessors. It is noteworthy that the General Inquisitor and the *Consejo de la Suprema* legislated on all aspects of the internal functioning of the Inquisition and the trials, except for dogma.[23] Therefore, sending *cartas acordadas* reflected changes in institutional attitudes toward crimes. In this case, it emphasised the necessity of making the crime of solicitation publicly known so that the Holy Office could investigate complaints. This information also circulated in the district courts in America, where particular edicts (*edictos*

19 The first significant attempt to structure the functioning of the court are the instructions of Fray Tomás de Torquemada from 1484. During the 16th century, they continued to perfect and configure the procedures, with the judicial reorganisation of the General Inquisitor Don Diego de Deza, Archbishop of Seville in 1500 and, more importantly, with the *Instrucciones* of the General Inquisitor Fernando Valdés, published in Toledo in 1536. These instructions complemented the instructions of Torquemada and defined the procedural elements of the Spanish Holy Office up until its extinction, as they were the last published ones.

20 As Gustav Henningsen and Susana Cabezas Fontanillas noted in their work, the oldest found *carta acordada* dates to 1513, but the production of this type of document became more frequent from the second half of the 16th century. See Cabezas Fontanillas, "La carta acordada", 716.

21 In addition to the instructions emanating from Spain, some local instructions were produced for the American courts by the district inquisitors, such as that of Inquisitor Cerezuela in Lima in 1569. See AHN, Inquisición, lib. 352, among others.

22 Índice abecedario, fol. 59v: "Se publique en los edictos pra que lo manifiesten en el Santo Oficio, y se entienda le toca su castigo".

23 On the competences of these two bodies, see Barros Pintado, "Las competencias privativas del Inquisidor General en la normativa regia de los siglos XVI y XVII", 129.

particulares) were pronounced on solicitation, as argued by John Chuchiak and Luis René Guerrero in the case of Nueva España.[24]

Just like the documents referring to the secular government of the American territories, the correspondence from the Holy Office was also considered official and transported in the dispatch vessels within the main postal system between America and Europe. As a result, the courts in Mexico and Lima were the biggest users of the quicksilver ships (*barcos de azogue*), as the main ports from which the postal vessel system directly operated were in these territories (Lima and Veracruz). According to Nelson Martínez, this postal system could transport correspondence of an ecclesiastical nature, as well as private letters, which made the communication between the centre and periphery more fluid.[25] A sample of the rhythms of communication can be identified in the letters and reports of Juan de Saracho, receiver (*receptor*) of the Lima Inquisition Tribunal, to the *Consejo de la Suprema* between 1584 and 1588. For this period, 14 letters are preserved, including information, reports and petitions, with de Saracho's comments on the presence or absence of ships to send information from the port of Lima.[26]

Although the correspondence and books related to case relations arrived in Madrid, in the Americas, *cartas acordadas* were used as a quicker means of communication with simpler language than the instructions. Provisions, decrees and dispatches were categorised as more regulatory and specific. The instructions were of a generic and normative nature, but they were a fundamental part of the American courts, especially during the foundational periods. The use of this legislative compendium was evident and helped *the Consejo de la Suprema* to govern local courts in a relatively homogenous manner and to impose different aspects "from the judging method to the details of keeping accounts for the inquisitorial treasury. Current knowledge of the instructions has been relatively simple due to their small number and the fact that editions from the 16th century are available".[27]

In a letter from the Supreme Council to the prosecutor of Venezuela in the Tribunal of Cartagena, it was clarified that sending all copies of the letters was unnecessary for their contents to be carried out. In another letter sent from the Tribunal of Cartagena on 24 July 1636, regarding a series of *cartas acordadas* where the sending of pecuniary condemnations along with annual cause

24 See Chuchiak IV and Guerrero Galván, *Los edictos de fe del Santo Oficio de la Inquisición de la Nueva España*.
25 See Martínez González, "Communicating an Empire and Its Many Worlds".
26 See AHN, Inquisición, lib. 4800, exp. 3.
27 Bedera Bravo, "La legislación interna del Santo Oficio. Las cartas acordadas", 43.

summaries was ordered, the inquisitors of Cartagena reinforced this consultation referring to all the *cartas acordadas* received on this subject (6 February 1631, 9 April 1633, 28 April 1633 and 30 July 1635). In the margin, there is a note from the *Consejo de la Suprema* stating: "it should be noted that not all *cartas acordadas* need to be sent to the Indies".[28]

During the period under study, there were several conflicts between *the Consejo de la Suprema* and the district courts, particularly those in the Americas, which presented an additional challenge for the Holy Office due to the distance involved. According to José María Vallejo García, the commissioners of the Holy Office required greater autonomy in the American courts compared to the commissioners and officials of the Spanish courts, as the distance between some of the territories of the district courts and the headquarters of the Holy Office made it necessary to develop this increased power.[29]

To illustrate this issue, let us discuss a case of internal conflict in the Tribunal of Cartagena. In 1670, the inquisitors Fray Pedro de Achurri and D. Matías Guerra were fined 300 pieces of gold and 20 pieces of silver for exceeding their authority. They had provided a text for the commissioner in Caracas, with copies sent to Puerto Rico, Santo Domingo, Espanola Island, Habana and Panama. The text stated that the *Consejo de la Suprema* should not be consulted in cases of faith, excluding *duplici matrimonio*. Instead, learned men in these matters, such as the provincials of the orders or "people of letters", should examine whether these issues fell under the jurisdiction of the Holy Office. They could then issue a prison order as appropriate. In response, the Council stated that:

> and having seen in the general Council //14v.// it seems that it was very surprising that the said Inquisitor D. Matías Guerra and Fray Pedro de Achurri took such an attribution so contrary to all style, instructions and causes of the Holy Office, without having consulted the council on such a serious matter, that you acted unjustly and improperly.[30]

This document highlights the potential issue of Guerra and Achurri's exercising of excessive autonomy by disregarding not only the style of the Holy Office

---

28 AHN, Inquisición, lib. 1041, fol. 12v: "Que se advierta que no todas las cartas acordadas se han de remitir a Indias".

29 See Vallejo García-Hevia, *Estudios de instituciones hispano-indianas*, tomo 2, 119.

30 AHN, lib. 345, fol. 14v: "y habiéndose visto en el Consejo //14v.// general ha parecido de ser de que se ha extrañado mucho que ve el dicho Inquisidor D. Matías Guerra y Fray Pedro de Achurri tomasen semejante atribución tan contraria a todo estilo, instrucciones y causas abordadas del Santo Oficio, sin haber para ello, siendo materia tan grave consultado al concejo, que obrasteis injusta y indebidamente (...)".

but also the principles of authority, promptness and experience on the part of the *Consejo de la Suprema*, compounded by their failure to send complaints and trials in severe cases as required. This requirement was established in the first Instructions of Torquemada in 1484 and was reiterated in subsequent instructions. However, as Henningsen has demonstrated, whether a specific order was sent to all the courts is unclear. All district courts did not uniformly observe the mandatory nature of the instructions, and conflicts arose from individual interpretations of the more general regulations of the Holy Office, often clashing with each court's customs.

During judicial arbitration in each district court, it is important not to ignore internal laws, which specify who should handle the most severe cases or whether a copy of the complaints should be sent to Madrid in case of doubt. As a result, the *Consejo de la Suprema* ordered the cancellation and erasure of the court's governance records of the American courts and all the acts related to the text sent by Achurri and Guerra on bigamy. These orders also included instructions to maintain the style and adhere to the *cartas acordadas* and instructions of the Holy Office, which were to be read in each tribunal every year, as evident from *abecedarios*[31] and general correspondence. Finally, the *Consejo de la Suprema* reminded them that in case of any doubt:

> before contravening, they should consult the Chief Inquisitor General, who, representing them, sent an opinion, and waiting for the resolution that will be given to you, without ignoring that you will be informed to comply in this way and for this purpose this order will be copied //15r.// into the Government book and kept with *the Cartas acordadas* of that Inquisition.[32]

The obligation to record all dispatches held by each district court and the *Consejo de la Suprema* has resulted in this documentary compilation, which provides insight into the administration and interactions between the different offices of the Inquisition and the rhythms of documentary production. The aim was to limit the autonomy that the district courts could hold, as argued by Berdera Bravo: "The centralising and unifying trend of the Council will

31 This was a pretty useful instrument that compiled the principal norms produced by the Holy Office about a practice or fault. It was organised, as the name indicates, in alphabetical order, including *cartas acordadas*.

32 AHN, Inquisición, lib. 345, fols. 14v–15r: "antes de contravenir, consultaren al C. Inqui. Glr. al que representándoles envío parecer, y esperando la resolución, que se os diere, sin [ignorar] de que estaréis advertidos para cumplirlo así, y para ello se copiará //15r.// esta orden en el libro de Gobierno y se guardasen y pondrá con las cartas acordadas de esa Inquisición". Translated by the author.

grow particularly during the 17th century, and with it will come an exponential increase in the number of *Cartas acordadas* produced which will make its knowledge impossible".[33] The centralising trend led to the publication of provisions during this period that reminded people of the obligation to keep these dispatch correspondence books. Additionally, an instruction was sent to the commissioners of the bishoprics to write monthly reports with the latest news and main events to reinforce the authority and comply with the aforementioned style of the Holy Office.

3 Solicitation, General Regulations and Local Impacts

Through the production of internal norms by the Holy Office, it is possible to identify how the knowledge of normativity and the manners of how to proceed in solicitation trials from the Inquisition were cumulative. There was a need for change on the part of the inquisitors in order to apply the inquisitorial process and thus justice. This can be observed in new moral discussions and Canon Law, as well as the determinations arising from the extraordinary jurisdiction of the general inquisitor and the procedural needs that arose, depending on the persons and practices judged.

This was also the case for the cases of solicitation, or *Sollicitatio ad turpia,* judged by the Inquisition. This practice generated a disciplinary issue among male clergy and had related offences, but it worried the Inquisition because of its proximity to heresy as it went against the sacrament of penance. The first precedent of the privative jurisdiction on this offence for the Spanish Inquisition is the brief or *breve* from Pope Paulo IV in 1559 for the tribunal of Granada.[34]

If we consider the chronological development of inquisitorial documentation, it reflects an institutional effort to standardise the prosecution and penalisation of solicitation. Different types of texts related to this practice were circulated and should be considered by the district inquisitors, such as inquisitorial manuals, instructions and, their improved version, *cartas acordadas,* and the Holy Office developed a set of internal regulations as part of its internal knowledge that were to be communicated to the district tribunals and that were to be in constant circulation. At the same time, it had to be an external way of communicating the inquisitorial knowledge about solicitation practices to lay people, such as inquisitorial edicts of faith (*edictos de fe*), with

33 Bedera Bravo, "La legislación interna del Santo Oficio. Las cartas acordadas", 54.

34 For more on this matter, see Teixeira Gouveia, "A jurisdição privativa da Inquisição portuguesa", 512–513.

the finality of denouncing their confessors and others involved in the profanation of the sacrament to later determine if the denounced behaviours were heretical or not. As we shall see, information was transmitted through different formats and judicial instruments, including printed materials and correspondence in the 17th century. These elements impacted the procedure and communication in a more technical way.

In addition to the texts mentioned above, specific instructions for the district courts were also published. Cardinal Diego de Espinosa, who served as General Inquisitor from 1565 to 1572, was responsible for overseeing the proper implementation of the Tribunal of the Holy Office in New Spain. To this end, he ordered the publication of special instructions that were printed in Madrid in 1570. Information about these local instructions was included in the First Book of Letters of the Inquisitorial Tribunal of Mexico to the Council of the Inquisition and the General Inquisitor, written between 1570 and 1578.[35] Based on Espinosa's *Instrucciones Especiales*, a pamphlet was printed containing the rules, procedures and essential elements that the commissaries of the Holy Office had to know. It had a more practical format and circulated more rapidly. Fray Diego de Bobadilla, commissioner of the Mexican Holy Office, mentioned that the mandatory requirement for the commissioners was to observe what was established in these regulations and to follow the terms of the booklet that were mentioned in the instructions: "to whom you shall give your commission *according to the copy* that you carry with this instruction".[36]

In this short text entitled "Instruction that must be observed by the commissioners and notaries of the Tribunal of the Holy Inquisition in Mexico in the office of business of faith and others related to its knowledge",[37] the characteristics, functions and ways for the two agents of the Inquisition to proceed are defined. In different sections, cases of solicitation are referenced:

> VII. Appointment and election of the Notary […] it is emphasised to the commissioner that the Notary for the cases of Confessor Solicitants ad turpia must always be a priest […] IX. Cases of Sollicitatio ad turpia.

35 A copy of this text is present in the Riva Palacio Collection of the AGN: AGN, Riva Palacio, tomo 44, no. 2. In the same collection, there is also a publication of a booklet with instructions for the commissioners and notaries of the Inquisition in Mexico.

36 García Icazbalceta, *Bibliografía mexicana del siglo XVI*, mentioned by Piña y Palacios, "Cartilla de comisarios del Santo Oficio de la Inquisición de México", 644.

37 *Instrucción que deben observar los comisarios y notarios del Tribunal de la Santa Inquisición en México en el despacho de los negocios de fe y demás tocantes a su conocimiento*, in Piña y Palacios, "Cartilla de comisarios del Santo Oficio de la Inquisición de México", 644–667.

> Write down everything as it happened. XI. If they have been warned about the obligation to denounce, XII. Examination of solicited individuals through general questions.[38]

While the text deals with 20 questions, four focus on how to deal with trials of solicitation, one deals with bigamy and the rest address the elements of a trial and the attitudes the notary should hold. These instructions served as a model for centuries until the end of the Holy Office. They were useful as complements that helped judges adapt judicial concepts from the Holy Office to specific criminal cases and define the circumstances, people and aggravating and attenuating places in each case.

The legislative organisation of the Holy Office around solicitation gradually became more complex as it adopted the structure and function of the *Consejo de la Suprema*. This organisation produced a constant flow of information from Pope Gregory XV's *bulla Universi dominici gregis* of 30 August 1622 – in this ordination Gregory XV confirmed the jurisdiction of the Holy Office to prosecute the crime of *Sollicitatio ad turpia* - resulting in a more consolidated judicial corpus and common knowledge for the district courts through the precedents set in previous cases. This is why the need to send information to Madrid became more frequent in the documents sent to the district courts from the 1570s onwards. As the cases involved religious people, it was indispensable that the *Consejo de la Suprema* gave an opinion on these cases. In a manuscript, the *Abecedario* index of the Council of the *Consejo de la Suprema* in 1662, there is a letter requesting the consignment of "the names, titles and offices of the solicitants against whom no procedure had been initiated or against whom the cases are suspended, along with the number of witnesses, and this information is sent to other Inquisitions. After the C. A. [Carta Acordada] from 10 Nov. 1601".[39] The names ended up appearing in the testimonial books and other documents of the registry of the Holy Office.

Shortly after, in 1576, *Instrucciones para procesar a Solicitantes en el tribunal de la inquisición de México* were issued in response to Pope Pius IV's *bulla Cum sicut nuper* (1561), which granted to the Spanish Holy Office privative jurisdiction over the crime of solicitation.[40] These instructions were sent by

38 See Piña y Palacios, "Cartilla de comisarios del Santo Oficio de la Inquisición de México", 644–650. Translated by the author.

39 BNE, Índice abecedario, mss. 854, fol. 96r. Carlos Pérez Fernández Turégano attributes the authorship of this compilation to the secretary of the Council, José de Ribera: "los nombres, títulos, y oficios de los solicitantes, contra quien no se [h]a procedido, o están suspensas sus causas con el número de testigos y se envía a las demás inquisiciones. Is de C. A [Carta Acordada] 10 de nov. de 1601".

40 See Gasparri, *Codicis Iuris Canonici Fontes*, vol. 1, 181.

the *Consejo de la Suprema* to the court in New Spain and then to the court in Lima. At that time, the Inquisition's internal laws on this practice were in the early stages of development, as demonstrated by the analysis of the *Promptuario alfabético* by Miguel Antonio de Cortaverria y Echave.[41] During the last decades of the 16th century and until the Gregorian *bulla*, the positions of the Spanish Holy Office on the prosecution of solicitants were changing towards practices that better suited the needs of protection and, at the same time, discipline of the Catholic Church. There was a dispute over whether this offence should be kept secret and what its penalty should be.

Before the *bulla* of Gregory XV, there was a series of document remissions in the format of instructions sent by the *Consejo de la Suprema* to the American courts regarding solicitation. Three of these instructions date back to 1577, two of which were sent on 16 April to the court in Mexico, and a third sent on 8 May to the court in Lima. They contained "dispositions on how to proceed against Solicitant priests"[42] as well as "instructions on how to proceed in the cases of Solicitant priests".[43] In March 1581, a "Relation of letters sent to the Inquisition of Mexico regarding the agreed dispositions on how to proceed in the cases of Solicitant priests"[44] was sent. However, these documents have not been found beyond their reference in correspondence.

Local conflicts over whether special secrecy should be kept on solicitation continued in the American district courts, as demonstrated by a letter received by the *Consejo de la Suprema* on 16 December 1636. In this letter, dated 15 May of the same year, the inquisitors of the court in Lima – solicitors Juan de Mañozca, Andrés Juan Gaitán and Don Antonio de Castro del Castillo – wrote that they had received a letter from the *Consejo de la Suprema* in 1634, in which they were asked to mask the language in the edicts of faith related to the penance of solicitants. The reason given was the multiple complaints received in Madrid about the disclosure of the cases of the solicitants. The letter stated:

> I have given less that it is not clearly expressed, in the edicts of the faith be nothing in them, than by seizure of the Brief of the Holiness of Gregory XV issued on the 30th of August of the last year of 1622.[45]

---

41 BNE, Promptuario alfabético y compendioso, mss. 12891.

42 "disposiciones de cómo proceder contra los curas solicitantes", AHN, Inquisición, lib. 352, fols. 109r–110r.

43 "instrucciones sobre cómo proceder en los casos de curas solicitantes", AHN, Inquisición, lib. 352, fols. 140r–141v.

44 AHN, Inquisición, lib. 352.

45 AHN, Inquisición, lib. 1041, fol. 10r: "(…) he dando menos que no se exprese con claridad, en los edictos de la fee – sea nada en ellos, que por embargo del Breve de la Santidad de Gregorio XV expedido en 30 de Agosto del año pasado de 1622". Translated by the author.

Despite this, Mañozca, Gaitán and de Castro argued in their letter about the obligation of including solicitation in the edicts of faith, referring to Gregory XV, and emphasising the need to comply with this pontifical document:[46]

> Due to the foreclosure of the Brief from the Holy See of Gregory XV, issued on August 30th of last year, 1622, declaring the said act a stronghold, to the Holy Office, so that it may be known by all that this harm that has been done should be addressed, it will be complied with what is ordered and commanded, although many acts in this Holy Office may express this clause and knowledge of this offence in the edicts of faith that are published in these kingdoms.[47]

In the specific cases and correspondence, not only is the application of the pontifical laws evident, but also the impact that normative literature had on the trials of solicitation and its dissemination at the time of judging the confessors. This is reflected in the book of trial summaries covering the period from 21 April 1663 to 15 May 1665, sent by the court of Cartagena de Indias to the *Consejo La Suprema* in April 1665. In this book, a letter from Madrid is answered, dated 11 September 1664, asking the district inquisitors about the sentencing given to the priest Andrés Mendez de Valdivieso for being a solicitant who "with merit was warned and reprehended". His sentence was dealt with through collective punishments applied to the solicitant religious men, such as temporary imprisonment and suspension of giving the sacrament of confession, in this case, permanently. An element to highlight in this sentence is that Mendez de Valdivieso was not asked to abjure *de levi*,[48] a common way to reconcile solicitants. The explanation of the inquisitors was:

> We respond (sir) that, considering the trial, it appeared to everyone that, given the qualities of the witnesses, their discrepancies and some enmity resulting from the defences, the accused was not convicted of solicitation, but rather

46 This information can also be found in the *Carta Acordada* from 2 March 1576 in the Abecedario from 1662 and in the Promptuario.

47 AHN, Inquisición, lib. 1041., fols. 10r–10v: "que por embargo del Breve de la Santidad de Gregorio XV expedido en 30 de Agosto del año pasado de 1622, por declarar suya loca para baluarte, al Santo Oficio para que a todos sea Notorio se acuda al reparo de este daño q se ha diciendo= se cumplirá lo que ordena y manda= aunque muchos autos que esta cláusula y conocimiento de este delito // fol.10v.// en este Sancto Oficio esta puede [ser] espresado en los edictos de la fe que se publiquen en estos reinos [...]".

48 This was the lesser of the formal ways of renouncing a heresy in front of the Holy Office after a trial. This was applied for the person who was sentenced as lightly suspected of heresy.

> there was strong suspicion against him. In this case, we follow the doctrine of Mr. Escobar de Confesariis Solicitantibus, q 4a.sv. n.3 te.245, who says he has seen it practiced in the Council.[49]

This section refers to the work of Juan Escobar del Corro, *Confesariis Solicitantibus*, which was published in Córdoba in 1642. Escobar del Corro had a career as a prosecutor in the courts of Zaragoza and Granada, and later became an inquisitor in Llerena and Córdoba. Finally, he served as a prosecutor and then a councillor for the *Consejo de la Suprema*. This is why the inquisitors Diego del Corro Carrascal and Dr, Pedro de Salas y Pedrosa alluded to his experience and trusted the criteria outlined in Escobar del Corro's text. It appears that the inquisitors of Cartagena acted and judged Mendez de Valdivieso without first consulting the *Consejo de la Suprema*, as the customary usage by the inquisitors of Cartagena provided enough guidance for this case. In this sense, the district inquisitors went against what was established in the *Instrucciones Nuevas*, which mandated that it was 'mandatory' to consult the Council if a case dealt directly with people of high social standing, especially religious people.

This example highlights how the use of the treatises on solicitation, in conjunction with internal regulations, indirectly contributed to the development of the normative framework of the Inquisition. One of the guiding principles of the Inquisition was to apply the norm and respect the procedure, depending on the circumstances of the accused. The dissemination of normative knowledge, particularly those related to the clergy, was facilitated by the presence of ecclesiastical agents and contributed to the formation of local inquisitorial practices.

The circulation and possession of texts by the clergy were essential to understanding the acquisition of pragmatic literature. As noted by Otto Danwerth, "Even in places where the reach of law was limited, the practice of regulations and notions of 'proper' behaviour were mediated through ecclesiastical institutions and actors, but also through religious symbols and practice".[50] These regulatory literary texts can be found in the inventories of confiscated property that list the books owned by religious men. Fray Bernardo Gaitán, a Franciscan friar accused of soliciting seven women in the province of Guatemala in 1665,

---

49 AHN, Inquisición, lib. 1022, fols. 297r–298v: "a que respondemos (señor) que visto el proceso, pareció a todos, que atentas las calidades de los testigos, su variación y alguna enemiga que resultaba de las defensas no estaba convencido el reo de la solicitación, sino que resultaba vehemente sospecha //fol. 297v.// contra él, y en este caso seguimos la doctrina del señor Escobar de Confesariis Solicitantibus. q 4a.sv. n.3 te.245 que dice haberlo visto practicar así en el Consejo=". Translated by the author.

50 Danwerth, "The Circulation of Pragmatic Normative Literature", 90.

had a book, titled *Questiones prácticas de casos morales*, confiscated. The book was written by the Augustinian Iván Henriques and was published in Córdoba in 1646.

These readings provided religious men with erudition that was used in the confessional and as a means of defence. Some solicitants used their knowledge of the definition of solicitation to defend themselves and to pass off their transgressions as simple fornication or minor offences resulting in only admonishments from the Holy Office and disciplinary failures on behalf of their confessors. In 1648, Rafael Vanegas, from the college of the Jesuits in Santiago de Chile, was accused by nine women of solicitation during his trial before the court in Lima. For his defence, he argued that he used the confessional as a space to approach women due to the closeness provided by this space and because of the local prohibition in the Society of Jesus to speak to women in churches:

> But he never had the intention or made the first move to confess the women he called, nor did he simulate confession, implying that he confessed them or discussing anything related to confession in conversation, but only with the purpose mentioned, to have an excuse with the prelates. He completely ignored the Breve of His Holiness Gregory XV.[51]

Vanegas manipulated the definition of solicitation to his advantage. He used his knowledge about the sacrament of penance from his disciplinary offence and, with his arguments, transformed potential heresy into a sin of lust.

Finally, beyond the uses of pragmatic literature to build and acquire knowledge about solicitation, there was also the content and circulation of particular edicts of faith (*edictos particulares*). As demonstrated by the *cartas acordadas*, when an edict of faith arrived in the jurisdiction of a district court, it had to be affixed to the wall of the church, and the document had to be read after the reading of the gospels during the great mass. In 1570, the Council of the Inquisition asked Inquisitor of México Pedro de Contreras to monitor that the edicts of faith were published in the parishes every year during Lent. To achieve this, he had to implement the mechanism of visitation.[52] Similarly, the

51 AHN, Inquisición, lib. 1648, exp. 1. fol. 68r: "pero nunca tuvo intención ni primero movimiento de confesar a las mujeres que llamaba, ni de simular confesión, dando a entender que las confesaba ni tratando en ella conversación cosa concerniente a la confesión, sino solo con el fin que tiene referido de tener escusa con los prelados y que ignoró totalmente el breve de su Santidad de Gregorio décimo quinto". Translated by the author.

52 AGN, Ramo de Inquisición, vol. 223, exp. 7, fol. 1r.

edict was made known in local monasteries and convents so that the whole community, whether learned or not, could come before the court to confess or denounce: "A decree from La Suprema ordered, at the beginning of 1575, that it was mandatory for the edicts of faith to be proclaimed and published on the doors of all monasteries and churches".[53]

The limited number of edicts on solicitation that still exist in archives, along with correspondence about the dissemination of these documents, suggest that these edicts were published more frequently during the 17th century, particularly after the *bulla* of Gregory XV. In the course of researching this chapter, I found references to five such edicts: one for the court in Lima from February 1617 and four for Mexico (one in 1620, one in 1621 and two in 1624). In terms of content, it is possible to identify a genealogy in the construction of the offences that constituted solicitation, as well as the strategies used by confessors to conceal their intentions. One example of such strategies is the submission of a "Copy of the particular edict of faith on the decrees of Popes Pius IV and Gregory XV against Confessors who solicit their spiritual daughters, by deed or by word, for indecent and dishonest acts in confession".[54] This edict was dated May 1624 and was found in the AGNM.

4 Conclusions

As evidenced by this chapter, the establishment of a trial to deal with solicitants was gradual, cumulative and long-term. Over the course of more than a hundred years (c. 1570–1670), internal laws were developed to address this practice. Various edicts and *cartas acordadas* circulated during the period under study, particularly in the 17th century, and the positions of the *Consejo de la Suprema* and the General Inquisitor changed in response to the evolving definition of solicitation, culminating in the publication of the *bulla* of Gregory XV (1622).

Regarding the correspondence, it is evident that this communication mechanism was used to disseminate the various legal bodies that would guide the district courts after their establishment. Additionally, it provided a platform to

53 Chuchiak IV and Guerrero Galván, *Los edictos de fe del Santo Oficio de la Inquisición de la Nueva España*, 12: "Una *carta acordada* de la Suprema ordenó, a principios de 1575, que era obligatorio que los *edictos de fe* se proclamaran y publicaran en las puertas de todos los monasterios y las iglesias". Translated by the author.

54 "Copia del edicto particular de fe sobre los decretos de los Papas Pio IV y Gregorio XV en contra de los Confesores que solicitan a sus hijas espirituales, por obra o de palabra, para actos torpes y deshonestos en la confesión", in Chuchiak IV and Guerrero Galván, *Los edictos de fe del Santo Oficio de la Inquisición de la Nueva España*, 206. Translated by the author.

witness the numerous difficulties faced by inquisitors when adapting to local contexts, and the persistent conflicts with civil authorities and members of the clergy, who regarded the presence of the Holy Office as a threat to their power. Despite the effectiveness of internal regulations and the implementation of mechanisms, such as the *cartas acordadas* in the American Courts, local resistance to publicly addressing practices like solicitation was still apparent.

The letters recommended the *Consejo de la Suprema's* directives to seek consultation on trials involving religious individuals and in serious cases, such as those involving confessors and doubts held by the inquisitors. However, they also revealed instances of non-compliance with the centralisation of power in the Inquisition, as stipulated in Madrid, through decision-making and knowledge accumulation on cases and the local administration of courts. The 1670 offence of the inquisitors in Cartagena serves as an example of attempts at autonomy that some district inquisitors developed as judicial practices evolved. As mentioned previously, distance was a contributing factor that led local inquisitors to consider themselves independent in making their own decisions.

As evident, while the *Consejo de la Suprema* consolidated information from district courts, it did not singularly serve as the exclusive "centre" for knowledge production, but primarily as a hub for internal norm production, reliant on information supplied by the district courts. The inquisitorial practice, coupled with the autonomy asserted by some local inquisitors, facilitated a diverse system of justice administration in Spanish America during the late 16th century and throughout the 17th century. This can be seen as a change, one that challenges the relation between centre and periphery.

Finally, the trials of Guerra and Achurri, as documented in inquisitorial books of correspondence, reflect the construction of knowledge of normativity on a specific practice and demonstrate the legitimacy that came from the lengthy process of applying inquisitorial justice to solicitants. The role of pragmatic literature and moral codes of conduct in these documents helped inquisitors and the accused concerning what to do and how to lead themselves in legal processes. I would like to highlight the importance of the public edicts, which were also a means of disseminating knowledge of what solicitation was, through their publication. The edicts and their language were tools that combined *bullas* and Briefs, the language and inquisitorial jurisdiction and the moralising discourse that led people to come closer to this court where priests who were condemned had the potential to turn "into deadly poison the healthy medicine that Christ himself left".[55] By public or internal means,

55 "Edicto particular de fe sobre los decretos de los Papas Pio IV y Gregorio XV en contra de los confesores que solicitan a sus hijas espirituales, por obra o de palabra, para actos torpes

the Holy Office attempted to shape the ways in which people denounced and testified against priests, petitioners, making clear what solicitation was and how it was configured in the *sacremento* of confession.

Acknowledgments

This paper had the support of CHAM (NOVA FCSH/UAc), through the strategic project sponsored by FCT (UIDB/04666/2020). I would like to thank MEMIC (Medieval and Early Modern Iberian Cultures) colleagues for their generous comments on the construction of this text.

Bibliography

Manuscripts

Archivo General de la Nación, Ciudad de México (AGN), Ramo de Inquisición, vol. 223, exp. 7.

Archivo General de la Nación, Ciudad de México (AGN), Riva Palacio Collection, tomo 44, no. 2.

Archivo Histórico Nacional, Madrid (AHN), Inquisición, lib. 345.

Archivo Histórico Nacional, Madrid (AHN), Inquisición, lib. 352.

Archivo Histórico Nacional, Madrid (AHN), Inquisición, lib. 1022.

Archivo Histórico Nacional, Madrid (AHN), Inquisición, lib. 1041.

Archivo Histórico Nacional, Madrid (AHN), Inquisición, lib. 1648, exp. 1.

Archivo Histórico Nacional, Madrid (AHN), Inquisición, lib. 4800, exp. 3.

Biblioteca Nacional de España, Madrid (BNE), Índice abecedario de instrucciones y cartas acordadas del Sancto Officio, antiguas y modernas, dispuesto por materias generales conforme a las instrucciones impresas y dos tomos de cartas acordadas que están en el Consejo Supremo de Inquisición, mss. 854.

Biblioteca Nacional de España, Madrid (BNE), Papeles referentes a la Inquisición, mss. 848.

Biblioteca Nacional de España, Madrid (BNE), Promptuario alfabético y compendioso de todas las instrucciones, cartas acordadas, bullas pontificias y Cédulas Reales, pertenecientes al Santo Officio de la Inquisición, mss. 12891.

---

y deshonestos en el confesión", 13 de mayo de 1624, in Chuchiak IV and Guerrero Gaitán, *Los edictos de fe del Santo Oficio de la Inquisición de la Nueva España*, 215: Translated by the author. "convirtiendo en veneno mortífero la saludable medicina que el mismo Cristo dejó [...]".

Printed Sources

[Anon.,] "Instrucciones para procesar a solicitantes en el Tribunal de la Inquisición de México", trans. Antonio M. García-Molina Riquelme, in *Revista de la Inquisición* 8 (1999), 85–100.

Gasparri, Pietro, *Codicis Iuris Canonici Fontes*, vol. 1, Rome 1947.

Literature

Alejandre García, Juan Antonio, *El veneno de Dios. La Inquisición de Sevilla ante el delito de solicitación en confesión*, Madrid 1994.

Alonso, María Luz, "Vías de revisión de la sentencia en el proceso inquisitorial", in *Cuadernos de historia del Derecho* 2 (1995), 151–188.

Aspell, Marcela, "El sacramento de la confesión. Los manuales y las sumas de confesión", in *Anuario del CIJS*, no. 11 (2008), 431–447.

Barros Pintado, Feliciano, "Las competencias privativas del Inquisidor General en la normativa regia de los siglos XVI y XVII. Una aproximación al tema", in *Revista de la Inquisición* 1 (1991), 121–140.

Berdera Bravo, Mario, "La Legislación interna del Santo Oficio. Las cartas acordadas", in *Revista de la Inquisición. Intolerncia y Derechos Humanos* 22 (2018), 39–62.

Bolaños Mejías, Carmen, "La literatura jurídica como fuente del derecho inquisitorial", in *Revista de la Inquisición* 9 (2000), 191–220.

Brendecke, Arndt, *Imperio e información: funciones del saber en el dominio colonial español*, Madrid 2016.

Cabezas Fontanilla, Susana, "La carta acordada: nacimiento y consolidación de un documento inquisitorial", in *Hidalguía. La revista de la genealogía, nobleza y armas* 294 (2002), 713–726.

Cabezas Fontanilla, Susana, "Nuevas aportaciones al estudio del archivo del Consejo de la Suprema Inquisición", in *Documenta & instrumenta* 5 (2007), 31–49.

Chuchiak IV, John and Luis René Guerrero Galván, *Los edictos de fe del Santo Oficio de la Inquisición de la Nueva España,* México D.F. 2018.

Ciaramitaro, Fernando, *Santo Oficio imperial. Dinámicas globales y el caso siciliano*, Ciudad de México, 2022.

Danwerth, Otto, "The Circulation of Pragmatic Normative Literature in Spanish America (16th–17th Centuries)", in Duve, Thomas and Otto Danwerth (eds.), *Knowledge of the Pragmatici. Legal and Moral Theological Literature and the Formation of Early Modern Ibero-America*, Leiden 2020, 89–130.

Delgado, Jessica, "Foregrounding Marginal Voices: Writing Women's Stories Using Solicitation Trials", in Melvin, Karen and Sylvia Sellers-García (eds.), *Imagining*

Histories of Colonial Latin America. Synoptic Methods and Practices, Albuquerque, NM 2017, 155–168.

Domínguez Nafría, Juan Carlos, "La «copilación» de las instrucciones inquisitoriales de Gaspar Isidro de Argüello", in *Revista de la Inquisición*, no. 12 (2006), 137–276.

Duve, Thomas, "Pragmatic Normative Literature and the Production of Normative Knowledge in the Early Modern Iberian Empires (16th–17th Centuries)", in Duve, Thomas and Otto Danwerth (eds.), *Knowledge of the Pragmatici. Legal and Moral Theological Literature and the Formation of Early Modern Ibero-America*, Leiden 2020, 1–36.

Duve, Thomas, "Legal History as a History of the Translation of Knowledge of Normativity", in *Max Planck Institute for Legal History and Legal Theory Research Paper Series*, no. 16 (2022), 1–12.

Gacto Fernández, Enrique, "La costumbre en el derecho de la Inquisición", in Iglesia Ferreiros, Aquilino (ed.), *El dret comú i Catalunya, Actes del IV Simposi Internacional Homenatge al professor Josep M. Gay Escoda*, Barcelona 1995, 215–262.

Galende Díaz, Juan Carlos, "Documentación Inquisitorial", in Ávila, Nicolás and Juan Carlos Galende (eds.), *La diplomática y sus fuentes documentales*, Madrid 2020, 263–282.

Galende Díaz, Juan Carlos, "La recorrección de registros: diplomática inquisitorial", in *Documenta & instrumenta* 1 (2004), 21–34.

Galende Díaz, Juan Carlos and Susana Cabezas Fontanillas, "Historia y documentación del Santo Oficio Español: el período fundacional", in Franco, José María de and Javier de Santiago Fernández (eds.), *III Jornadas Científicas sobre documentación en Época de los Reyes Católicos*, Madrid 2004, 119–146.

García Icazbalceta, Joaquín, *Bibliografía mexicana del siglo XVI*, México D.F. 1954.

García-Molina Riquelme, Antonio M., "Instrucciones para procesar a solicitantes en el Tribunal de la Inquisición de México", in *Revista de la Inquisición* 8 (1999), 85–100.

Gilliland, Anne, "Afterword: in and out of the archives", in *Archival Science* 10 (2010), 333–343.

González Marmolejo, Jorge René, *Sexo y confesión. La iglesia y la penitencia en los siglos XVIII y XIX en la Nueva España*, Plaza y Valdés 2002.

Henningsen, Gustav, "La colección de Moldenhawer en Copenhague: una aportación a la archivología de la Inquisición española", in *Revista de archivos, bibliotecas y museos* LXXX, no. 2 (1977), 209–270.

Juanto Jiménez, Consuelo, "El comisario del Santo Oficio en las instrucciones inquisitoriales", in *Revista de la Inquisición* (*Intolerancia y Derechos Humanos*) 18 (2014), 95–109.

Levaggi, Abelardo (ed.), *La inquisición en Hispanoamérica. Estudios*, Buenos Aires 1997.

Maqueda Abreu, Consuelo, *Estado, Iglesia e Inquisición en Indias. Un permanente conflicto*, Madrid 2000.

Martín Barba, José Julio, "Documentación del Consejo de Inquisición en tiempos de Torquemada", in *Documenta & Instrumenta* 18 (2020), 187–221.

Martínez González, Nelson Fernando, "Communicating an Empire and Its Many Worlds. Spanish American Mail, Logistics and Postal Agents: 1492–1620", in *Hispanic American Historical Review* 101:4 (2021), 567–596.

Mejía, Pilar, "Escritura de la historiografía sobre los tribunales inquisitoriales americanos", in Duve, Thomas (ed.), *Actas del XIX congreso del Instituto Internacional de Historia de Derecho Indiano: Berlín 2016*, vol. 1, Madrid 2017, 161–179.

Meneses Muñoz, Mariana, "Male Violence and Female Resistance in the Sacrament of Penance: Accounts Before the Inquisitorial Tribunals in Colonial America (Seventeenth Century)", in Sánchez León, Pablo and Benita Herreros Cleret de Langavant (eds.), *Resistance in the Iberian Worlds from the Fifteenth to the Eighteenth Century. Dissent and Disobedience from Within*, Cham 2024, 177–194.

Meneses Muñoz, Mariana, "Solicitación y praxis inquisitorial en los tribunales de México, Cartagena y Lima, siglo XVII", in *Fronteras de la Historia* 24:2 (2019), 110–135.

Millar Carvacho, René, "El archivo del Santo Oficio de Lima y la documentación inquisitorial existente en Chile", in *Revista de la Inquisición* 6 (1997), 101–116.

Pérez Fernández-Turégano, Carlos, "Cartas acordadas de la Inquisición española", in *Revista de la Inquisición. Intolerancia y Derechos Humanos* 21 (2017), 13–34.

Pérez Fernández-Turégano, Carlos, "El archivo de la Secretaría de Aragón del Consejo de la Inquisición: Domingo de la Cantolla Miera y su labor recopiladora en el tránsito del XVII al XVIII", in *Revista de la Inquisición. Intolerancia y Derechos Humanos* 19 (2015), 41–73.

Pérez Martín, Antonio, "La doctrina jurídica y el proceso inquisitorial", in Escudero Pérez, José Antonio (coord.), *Perfiles jurídicos de la Inquisición española*, Madrid 1986, 279–322.

Piña y Palacios, Javier, "Cartilla de comisarios del Santo Oficio de la Inquisición de México. Estudio introductorio", in *Anuario Jurídico* VII (1980), 637–667.

Rex Galindo, David, "Shaping Colonial Behaviours: Franciscan Missionary Literature and the Implementation of Religious Normative Knowledge in Colonial Mexico (1530s– 1640s)", in Duve, Thomas and Otto Danwerth (eds.), *Knowledge of the Pragmatici. Legal and Moral Theological Literature and the Formation of Early Modern Ibero-America*, Leiden 2020, 296–327.

Sánchez Rubio, Rocío and Isabel Testón Núñez, "Por mares de olvidos. Correspondencia privada e inquisición en Nueva España. Siglos XVI–XVIII", in Vieira, Alberto, António Castillo, Henrique Rodrigues, Verónica Sierra Blas (coords.), *Escritas das mobilidades*, Funchal 2011, 46–80.

Sarrión Mora, Adelina, *Sexualidad y confesión. La solicitación ante el Tribunal del Santo Oficio (siglos XVI–XIX)*, Madrid, 1994.

Schuppert, Gunnar Folke, *The World of Rules. A Somewhat Different Measurement of the World*, trans. Rhodes Barrett, Frankfurt am Main 2017.

Teixeira Gouveia, Jaime Ricardo, "A jurisdição privativa da Inquisição portuguesa sobre o delito de solicitação: De facto ou de iure?", in *Investigaciones históricas. Época moderna y contemporánea* 42 (2022), 507–548.

Tellkamp, Jörg (ed.), *A Companion to Early Modern Spanish Imperial Political and Social Thought*, Leiden 2020.

Tortorici, Zeb, *Sins against Nature. Sex and Archives in Colonial New Spain*, Durham, NC 2018.

Vallejo García-Hevia, José María, *Estudios de instituciones hispano-indianas*, tomo 2, Madrid 2015.

Wright, Anthony D., *The Counter-Reformation Catholic Europe and the Non-Christian World*, Oxfordshire 2005.

CHAPTER 3

Ignorance Lost

The Arrival of Franciscan Missionaries and the Jesuit Normative Discourse in Japan (16–17th Centuries)

Rômulo Ehalt

> Thought would destroy their Paradise.
>
> Thomas Gray, *Ode on a Distant Prospect of Eton College* (1742)

> Now I seem to recall you telling me that you were a christian, And I recall answering, more or less, sir, more or less, What does that mean, though, are you or are you not a christian, Well, I was baptised in India when I was a child, And then, Then, nothing (…).[1]
>
> José Saramago, *The Elephant's Journey* (2010)

1 Introduction

On 31 May 1557, Giovanni Morone (1509–1580) was imprisoned in the Castel Sant'Angelo. One of the most important cardinals of the Roman Curia at the time, the prelate and a number of other members of the cardinalate were accused by Pope Paul IV (b. 1536, r. 1555–1559) on suspicion of heresy concerning statements that allegedly contradicted matters discussed by the ongoing Council of Trent. Morone claimed he could not have committed any heresy since his statements dated back to years before the council.[2] The prelate was using one of the most powerful arguments of the period: ignorance. To posit one's lack of knowledge regarding a norm was a strategy widely adopted to excuse individuals not only from criminal accusations but also from sin and other religious infractions.

1 Saramago, *The Elephant's Journey*, 47. Saramago, *A viagem do elefante*, 71: "Creio recordar-me que disseste que és cristão, E eu recordo-me de ter respondido, mais ou menos, meu comandante, mais ou menos, Que quer isso dizer na realidade, és ou não és cristão, Batizaram-me na índia quando eu era pequeno, E depois, Depois, nada (…)."

2 Prosperi, *Tribunali della coscienza*, 200–202, 208–209. On Morone's clashes with the Inquisition, see Firpo, *Inquisizione Romana e Controriforma*; and the two homonymous collections by Firpo and Marcatto (eds.), *Il Processo Inquisitoriale del Cardinal Giovanni Morone*.

Indeed, the legal doctrine of ignorance had a long tradition in both law and theology. This tradition led many confessors in areas remote from Rome to apply the doctrine when hearing confessions from non-Europeans. Consequently, on the other side of the globe, a particular set of circumstances made ignorance a powerful tool in saving a whole Christian community.

Until the mid-1580s, missionaries of the Society of Jesus enjoyed a period of steady political, economic, and social stability in Japan, despite their limited influence. They had established close relationships with several powerful individuals, obtained local sources of revenue, actively participated in trade, governed the port city of Nagasaki and established schools to train a new generation of preachers in the country. Soon, the success of the enterprise drew the attention of members of other religious orders.

The impending problems brought by the arrival of non-Jesuit missionaries were noticed by the visitor Alessandro Valignano (1539–1606), an Italian priest nominated by the Jesuit Curia to inspect the Province of India, the administrative unit of the Society of Jesus encompassing all missions of the order from East Africa to Japan.[3] His assessment of the situation in the archipelago was shaped by his training and previous experience. Indeed, the Italian-born lawyer was in Rome during the troubles of Cardinal Morone, when the legal value of ignorance set the stage for the prelate's defence, and he may have come across a rumour or two about the prelate's legal strategy.

After failing to obtain an office at the Curia, Valignano reemerged in the historical record upon his entrance into the Society of Jesus in 1566.[4] His career as a strategist and political figure in Asia started with his arrival in Goa in 1575, the centre of the Jesuit Province of India. It was during his first stint in Japan, between 1579 and 1582, that Valignano realised the legal and religious circumstances of the islands and their missionaries. Since the arrival of the first Jesuits in 1549, the mission was entirely in the hands of the Society of Jesus: no other religious order would set foot in Japan until the 1580s. This prompted a situation of double monopoly over, first, the knowledge that Japanese Christians had about the religion and, second, the publication of positive law.[5]

3 On Valignano and hierarchical disputes among Jesuits and with other orders in this context, see Alberts, *Conflict and Conversion*, 17–46.

4 Schütte, *Valignanos Missionsgrundsätze für Japan*, 37–39.

5 The idea of positive law appears in Japan Jesuit sources interchangeably as *derecho positivo* or *precepto positivo*, always with the same meaning and covering different topics, such as matrimony, liturgical calendar and fasting periods. Learning from the Second Scholastics, they generally followed Thomas Aquinas' notion that positive law was a norm "which [has] given to natural law some specific determination for a given community." Finnis, *Aquinas*, 135. Antoni Ucerler summarises the issue by defining a positive precept as "an externally

This chapter delves into the uses of the doctrine of invincible ignorance as a common thread through the troubling times that the Jesuits in Japan faced in the late 16th and early 17th centuries. I begin with an overview of the status of the doctrine and its main thinkers in the early modern period, followed by the identification of the special circumstances of Japan and how they influenced decisions regarding the use of positive law in the country. The focus shifts to the criticism raised by the Franciscans about the Jesuit methods, which brought the doctrine of invincible ignorance to the forefront of the debate. Following that, I analyse the uses of the doctrine by Jesuits as a fundamental part of their project, when after the arrival of the mendicants, the declaration of positive law in Japan became unavoidable. Finally, the chapter concludes with reflections on changes in normative discourse as a result of political disputes between missionary orders in Japan. The objective here is to underline the case of Japan as an example of legal change of religious normativities as prompted by political disputes concerning missionary territories and the interests of different political actors.[6]

In this chapter, we can identify two actors who play a pivotal role in the analysis presented here: Valignano and Cerqueira. While the former defended the maintenance of the relative stability obtained in previous decades by the Society of Jesus in Japan, the second used his episcopal authority to advance an agenda of reform that appealed to external pressures while defending internal interests of the order in the country.

From his early days in the archipelago, Valignano recognised the complex situation of Japan. In a 1583 letter addressed to the Superior General Claudio Acquaviva (1543–1615), Valignano pointed out two major events as threatening to the mission. First, the visitor drew attention to the consequences of the death of the last King of the Portuguese Aviz dynasty, Henrique (1512–1580),

promulgated law in contrast with an individual's dictate (or lack thereof) of conscience. Thus a 'positive law' could either prescribe a course of action or forbid it." Ucerler, *The Samurai and the Cross*, 77.

6 The idea of normativity expressed in this text follows the concept of *multinormativity*, i.e., norms originated in various orders of actions and in human interactions. The concept has been further developed in recent years by taking on the multiple meanings that interactions may carry in the normative process, including actions that go beyond classical ideas of legal utterance. This turn to the normative meaning of action has allowed an approximation between legal and social historians. See Duve, "Was ist Multinormativität?"; Duve, "Legal History as a History of the Translation of Knowledge of Normativity"; Duve, "Legal History as an Observation of Historical Regimes of Normativity". One can see in Thomas Duve's more recent perspectives parallels with the Weberian *Verstehen* and anthropological ideas concerning the various meanings carried by social action. D'Avray, *Rationalities in History*, 25; Geertz, *The Interpretation of Cultures*.

which led to the handover of the crown to Filipe II of Spain (1527–1598), now Filipe I of Portugal. Valignano feared that, with the Iberian Union, mendicant friars from Manila would swiftly attempt to enter Japan. He also warned against the waves caused by the death of Melchior Carneiro, S.J. (1516–1583) in August of 1583. At that time, Carneiro had acted as Bishop of China in Macau for decades. According to the visitor, the Bishop had blocked the passage of the friars to the islands. With his death, mendicants would try to use the Chinese port as a springboard into Japan. Valignano's fears were soon confirmed.[7]

His calls for Roman support in maintaining the state of Japanese Christianity and the primacy of the Society of Jesus were based on the information he collected from his colleagues regarding the state of Buddhism in Japan. In a report written after his first visitation, Valignano explained that dogmatic differences among different Japanese sects and the unity of opinion among Christians were among the chief reasons behind the Japanese decision to leave Buddhism and adopt Christianity. If other orders with differing ways of proceeding and opinions (*modos de proceder y diversas opiniones*) were to enter Japan, the priests would also be targeted with similar suspicions regarding the uniformity of their dogma. For the visitor, these circumstances demanded prudence, experience, and attention in the teaching of the doctrine and in the propagation of the positive law of the Church.[8] His plan was to regulate the application of Catholic positive law to the community in order to avoid jeopardising their salvation. By controlling their ignorance regarding the rules they were breaking, their access to Christian paradise would not be lost. In his view, the entry of other orders would bring about ruin to the Japanese church.

Valignano's defence was based on two doctrines: invincible ignorance and *bona fides*.[9] In this chapter, I focus on the uses of the doctrine of invincible ignorance in Japan in the context of the disputes between Jesuits and Franciscans and with the arrival of the Tridentine rules in the background. The main question is how the arrival of missionaries from other orders to the country, starting in 1585, affected the legal discourse employed by Jesuits in the process

7 Wicki, *Documenta Indica*, vol. 12, 832. Apparently, Carneiro supported the creation of a Franciscan custody covering the area between Malacca and the Philippines, but it is unclear if the project included Japan. Alberts, *Conflict and Conversion*, 28.

8 Valignano, *Sumario*, 143–144. The same warning against the diversity of opinion as detrimental to the missionary project was repeated in 1598. Valignano, *Apologia*, 45.

9 I have previously analysed the use of these two doctrines in Jesuit dealings with slavery in Japan. See Ehalt, *Jesuits and the Problem of Slavery*. For a general overview of ignorance in the context of confession, see Lea, *History of Auricular Confession*, vol. 2, 248ff. Takase Kōichirō has also drawn attention to the importance of invincible ignorance for the overlooking of actions contrary to Catholic morals: Takase, *Kirishitan jidai*, 589–590.

of the creation of religious norms for Japanese Christianity and in their communications with Rome. Sources indicate that it was only after the Franciscans arrived in the country that the Jesuits' normative discourse began to use the doctrine of invincible ignorance.[10] Eventually, from 1598 onwards, the new Bishop of Japan, Cerqueira, adopted a different stance, using the doctrine as an argument in favour of the controlled publication of positive law in specific areas of Japanese Christianity.

The background to the argumentation regarding the privileged position of the Society of Jesus in Japan as the sole source for Christian knowledge and, more importantly, the positive law of the Church was based on the recognition that Japanese Christians were living in a state of controlled invincible ignorance. In fact, the conditions for legal change were given with the transformation of the assumed ignorance of the Japanese into a political strategy. Needless to say, the legal change of which I speak is not that of reactive legislation or as a means to reach a given agenda, or even the search for the historical causality of alterations in the normative codes of a given society.[11] As German sociologist Niklas Luhmann reminds us, this type of change becomes easily normalised.[12] This study focuses on a more consistent and deeper type of change, i.e., the transformations in the legal discourses that serve as the basis for the creation of knowledge of normativity and its stabilisation. In the case discussed here, this transformation concerns the regulation of the missionary–Christian relationship in Japan. The plan is to understand how this reasoning was forcefully brought to light after the arrival of the mendicant orders in the 1580s. If previous scholarship on the Jesuit and Franciscan clashes in Japan has focused on the political disputes between the two camps, this chapter presents a distinct perspective by focusing on their stances regarding law. Indeed, the shift of the Jesuit attitude towards the implementation of certain aspects of positive law that were deemed problematic in Japan came in response to the threat of mendicant criticism against the balance between ignorance and knowledge among Japanese Christians. The friars were, insofar as positive law is concerned, new sources of knowledge of normativity. In response to the criticism levelled at them, Japan Jesuits adopted a strategy in which they viewed ignorance as instrumental to the consolidation of the Catholic Church in the country, using

---

10 There is an extensive bibliography on the Franciscan–Jesuit dispute in Japan: Uyttenbroeck, *Early Franciscans*; Alvarez-Taladriz, "Notas para la historia de la entrada en Japón de los franciscanos"; Willeke, "Biographical data on early Franciscans"; Sola, *Historia de un Desencuentro*; Tronu, "The Rivalry between the Society of Jesus and Mendicant Orders"; Bernabé, *Fé e prática entre os Kirishitan*.

11 As summarised in Watson, "Legal Change".

12 Luhmann, *Law as a Social System*, 261.

it as a tool for the implementation of positive law. In this chapter, legal change is understood as the result of transformations in the circumstances surrounding the production of knowledge of normativity.[13]

2 Invincible and Probable

The basis for all early modern readings of the doctrine of ignorance is Thomas Aquinas' *Ia-IIae*, q. 76.[14] In the growing tension rising from the finding of new peoples and new lands, as well as the ever-challenging issue of harmonising often conflicting legal texts,[15] theologians found solid ground in Aquinas' works. The *Doctor Angelicus* discussed the nature of ignorance and its relationship with sin, putting forward a two-pronged classification: vincible and invincible ignorance (*Ia-IIae*, q. 76, art. 2). This was one among many different categorisations of the term, which inherited a long tradition of debates concerning its use as an argument for the exemption of culpability. For the period here in question, invincible ignorance came to be defined as the condition of the individual who, despite their efforts, could not overcome their ignorance regarding a specific aspect of Church law.[16]

In Aquinas' thought, invincible ignorance indicated a mistake of our conscience, meaning one could in fact avoid being accused of sinning. That was not true for vincible ignorance, which denoted the voluntary act of ignoring the dictates of one's conscience by willingly acting against it and, thus, against divine law, since the human conscience was one's source of knowledge of divine morality.[17] Despite its relative lack of emphasis among medieval philosophers, ignorance became central for early modern thinkers. Yet, the

13 Legal change "is a consequence of the continuous process of translation of knowledge of normativity, in which the actors process, respond and react to changing conditions and circumstances and thus produce new knowledge of normativity": Duve, "Legal History as a History of the Translation of Knowledge of Normativity", 5. See also Duve, "Legal History as an Observation of Historical Regimes of Normativity".

14 For a survey on the doctrine up to Aquinas, see Lottin, *Psychologie et Morale*, 11–96. Beyond that, see Laemers, *Invincible Ignorance and the Discovery of the Americas*; Walser, *Die Rechtshandlung im Kanonischen Recht*, 201–210. For a general summary, see Walser, "Ignorantia II. Kirchenrechtlich", 413; Meier-Oeser, "Unwissenheit", 341–348. For more on the argument of *ignorantia* (and *error*) in the *ius commune* tradition, see Zimmermann, *The Law of Obligations*, 606–620, 869–871.

15 Tierney, "Vitoria and Suarez", 103.

16 Toste, "Invincible Ignorance and the Americas", 284–285.

17 Although, Aquinas himself admits the possibility of a failing conscience and erring reason (*Ia-IIae*, q. 19, art. 5 and 6). Tutino, *Uncertainty in Post-Reformation Catholicism*, 7–9.

expansion of the horizons of the world posited the difficult challenge of interpreting the possibility of salvation of peoples that were clearly ignorant of the Gospel. So, while medieval thinkers considered the doctrine of invincible ignorance a weakness and a sign of blameworthiness, the School of Salamanca completely redefined the idea based on the experiences of the New World.

The first to offer a theological solution for this conundrum was Matías de Paz (c. 1470–1517), professor at the universities of Valladolid and Salamanca in the 1510s. Following Aquinas' classification of invincible and vincible ignorance, De Paz admitted the exculpatory force of ignorance with regards to the Indigenous peoples of the American continent. For him, the resistance shown by the Indigenous peoples against the wars waged by the Spanish was due solely to their ignorance regarding the true nature of the *conquistadores* and the friars that accompanied them as servants of God. Theological ignorance was not "restricted to a purely religious sphere", but with De Paz it was also understood "as a part of a civilizing gap with many political and juridical implications."[18]

After De Paz, Francisco de Vitoria (c. 1492–1546) dissociated the doctrine of invincible ignorance from any moral connotation, thus understanding the ignorance of God displayed by Indigenous peoples in America as indicative of the need for persuasion in their conversion rather than pure brute force. These arguments were later repeated and refined by Domingo de Soto (1494–1560), who went on to argue that even the idolatry shown by the Indigenous peoples did not go against faith but only against natural reason. For that reason, idolatry could not be taken as an argument in favour of invasion and domination.[19] Undoubtedly, the need for persuasion as prescribed by De Vitoria was one of the chief driving forces of the Jesuit mission in Japan.

The foundation provided by the *salmanticenses* were quickly spread to the missions through De Soto's *De iustitia et iure* (1553) and Martin de Azpilcueta's confession manual.[20] Available in the Americas, Africa and Asia, the latter instructed confessors throughout the world on how to deal with the numerous problems faced in new missionary frontiers and colonial societies, playing a crucial role in reconciling frequently contradictory theological, legal and canonical sources of authority. Due to its widespread acceptance, the manual

18 Egío Garcia, "Matías De Paz and the Introduction of Thomism in the *Asuntos De Indias*". See also Egío Garcia, "Pragmatic or Heretic?", 258.

19 Toste, "Invincible Ignorance and the Americas", 284–297.

20 On Azpilcueta and his manual, see Bragagnolo, "Managing Legal Knowledge in Early Modern Times"; Bragagnolo (ed.), *The Production of Knowledge of Normativity in the Age of the Printing Press*.

participated in the popularisation of the idea of invincible ignorance as a valid spiritual remedy for the moral issues of the period. Numerous passages of the book use ignorance as a valid argument in exempting Christians from sin due to certain issues, such as restitution, heresy and sacraments administered to excommunicated individuals.[21]

However, the crux of the problem here was how to prove ignorance. Effectively, in his definitions of different types of ignorance, Azpilcueta, albeit a canonist, drew not only from Aquinas but also from summists, such as Antonino di Firenze, Angelo di Chivasso and Silvestro Mazzolini.[22] Taking a step back from theology, he employed legal definitions, preferring *probable ignorance* to *invincible ignorance*, a choice that underlines his view of the necessity of proof.[23] The same is true for his treatment of the issue of conscience and guilt. Azpilcueta's "selective certainty", which guaranteed freedom of agency of the penitent while still maintaining the moral authority of the confessor, placed most of the responsibility in the hands of the latter in judging the internal certainty of the former's conscience when performing dubious actions.[24] As Azpilcueta's project was to collate the juristic view of uncertainty with theology and canon law, it is unsurprising that his treatment of ignorance resembles that of mid-16th-century jurists.[25]

Given his legal training, Valignano was particularly fond of Azpilcueta's approach.[26] It was the "Doctor Navarrus's" proceduralist spirit that had a

21 Azpilcueta, *Manual de Confessores*, cap. IX, no. 2; cap. 11, no. 17, 18, 21 and 32; cap. 12, no. 6; cap. 14, no. 31; cap. 17, no. 82 and 83; cap. 24, no. 44 and 45. Nevertheless, there are a number of cases in which Azpilcueta does not accept the argument, such as luxury (cap. 16, no. 1) and for those who knowingly purchased stolen items (cap. 17, no. 84).

22 On the summists, see Dietterle, "Die Summae confessorum"; Michaud-Quantin, "Sommes de casuistique et manuels de confession"; Tentler, "The Summa for Confessors as an Instrument of Social Control".

23 Azpilcueta, *Manual de Confessores*, cap. 23, no. 44, "Ignorancia, que los theologos llaman, inuencible, y los nuestros prouable, es la del que haze lo que vn hombre diligente y cuerdo deue, para saber, y no lo sabe, segun S. Tho. quel es la del que pide parecer a hombres reputados por de sciencia, y consciencia bastante para ello por hombres cuerdos, y ellos se lo dan falso". All references to Azpilcueta's Manual use the 1556 digitised version available at https://www.salamanca.school/en/index.html. See also Tutino, *Uncertainty in Post-Reformation Catholicism*, 27–29.

24 Tutino, *Uncertainty in Post-Reformation Catholicism*, 31–35.

25 Hespanha, *Como os Juristas Viam o Mundo*, 6.4.1 § 1607.

26 The visitor commented on the uses of Azpilcueta's work on a number of occasions, including in his reports from Japan to the general of the Society of Jesus in 1583 and 1592. Furthermore, the manual was included in the list of books set by Valignano that were to be purchased and sent periodically to Japan. Valignano, *Sumario*, 220–221; Valignano, *Adiciones*, 497; Biblioteca do Palácio Nacional da Ajuda, 49-IV-66, fol. 19r.

formative impact on the Jesuit missionaries in Japan. Consequently, their rich descriptions of Japanese society, including their assessment of local norms and punishments, can be understood as a reflection of their deep concern with the legal and religious consequences of actions taken by Christians in Japan – both foreigners and locals – rather than a kind of *avant-la-lettre* ethnographic interest. These concerns are evident in the reports written by the visitor during his first two tours in the country (1579–1582 and 1590–1592).

3 Gradual Revelation

The first to notice Japan's legal situation was Francis Xavier. In November 1549, less than three months after disembarking in Kagoshima, he wrote that the Japanese lived in error (*vivem em muitos erros*) due to their ignorance.[27] In the first decades of the mission, Jesuits also spoke of moral blindness, blamed on the influence of Buddhism in the country.[28] Yet, it would not be until the 1580s that the position of the Society of Jesus as the sole source of knowledge regarding Catholicism or the *ius commune* would enter the Jesuit discourse.

This recognition came in the context of Valignano's first visit to Japan. It was then that he noticed the political meanings behind Japanese courtesy and social ceremonies. In order to improve the chances of missionaries in dealing with powerful locals, the visitor compiled a manual of Japanese etiquette (the *Advertimentos e avisos acerca dos costumes e catangues de Jappão*, or "Warnings and Notices regarding the Customs of the Japanese", 1581). In its second chapter, where he discusses how to curry favour with the locals, Valignano understood that Japanese Christianity was too immature to receive the positive precepts of the Church. For him, it was necessary to slowly make them capable of receiving and understanding the sacraments, given that the Japanese had lived for so long under such depraved customs (*costumes tão depravados*) and were so ignorant and lacking in the divine doctrine (*tanta ignorancia e falta de doutrina acerca das cousas de Deus*) that the Jesuits needed to first bind them through love with the Church. Only then would they comprehend the religion and derive the benefits of the sacraments (*com proveito usar dos sacramentos*).[29] Valignano identified the Japanese ignorance of natural law as an impediment to the declaration of the positive law of the Church.[30]

27 Ruiz-de-Medina, *Documentos del Japón*, vol. 1, 182.

28 Ruiz-de-Medina, *Documentos del Japón*, vol. 2, 358 and 453.

29 Valignano, *Il Ceremoniali per i Missionari del Giappone*, 168–170.

30 Ignorance of natural law was a delicate subject. Even though most authors did not admit this possibility, given that "admitting the ignorance of natural law would mean to deny

Designed for inexperienced churchmen in Japan, the manual displayed Valignano's first planned reformation of the Japan mission. At that moment, for the visitor, it did not matter whether Christians in Japan received the sacraments properly or not, despite their importance. For him, it was much more relevant to convince new converts to fully accept their teachings before running the risk of administering the sacraments for those who had not yet earned the moniker of Christian.

The convincing came through gradual revelation and through educating the new converts, a process that largely followed methods first instituted by Xavier in the early years of the mission. The idea was to deny a number of Japanese beliefs – polytheism, the belief in an eternal world absent from eschatology, Shinto cosmogony and the divinity of Japanese gods. Based on the rational deconstruction of these beliefs by proving them to be falsehoods, one of the methods was a series of ten sermons which, following the chronological order of the Bible, told the story from Creation to the Passion.[31] Other plans involved the use of catechisms for two, eight, ten, 15, 20 days or more.[32] At this point, the main issue was not whether the Japanese were ignorant about the doctrine or not – rather, the concern was with regulating the methods and the rate with which the doctrine was transmitted. As shown by later Japanese sources, the process of translating the Christian dogma into Japanese, a necessary step for the teaching of the religion, employed local terms charged with social expectations and values that skilfully supported the mission.[33]

Alongside the basic knowledge necessary for one's recognition as a member of a Christian community, the obligation of following the positive law of the Church was not a concern in the first decades of the mission. The Jesuits in Japan first heard of the news of the end of the Council of Trent in 1566, a couple of years before the publication of the Constitutions of the Archbishopric of Goa (1568).[34] But despite the synodal constitutions theoretically paving the way for the introduction of Trent in Japan – since the country was under the auspices of the Archbishop of Goa – their influence was small in the 1560s.

[...] human nature": Toste, "Invincible Ignorance and the Americas", 285. Some, such as De Soto, accepted violations of secondary precepts of natural law due to invincible ignorance, as in the case of the Indigenous peoples of the Americas. Laemers, *Invincible Ignorance and the Discovery of the Americas*, 292–293.

31 Ehalt, "A Difficult Enterprise".

32 Lopez-Gay, *El Catecumenado en la Misión del Japón*, 36–57.

33 Ehalt, "In Their Likeness".

34 In September 1566, Luís Fróis wrote that he had received news of the conclusion of the Council of Trent in August. ARSI, Japonica Sinica (henceforth JapSin) 6, fol. 116r. On Trent in Portuguese India, see Xavier, "Gaspar de Leão e a Recepção do Concílio de Trento no Estado da Índia", 133.

Instead, Christian liturgy and festivities often mixed local and Catholic elements. Marriages, for instance, were celebrated as natural matrimonies in Japan – some were followed by pompous baptisms in order to create exemplar Christians for local communities.[35] Christian festivities, such as Lent, were, according to the missionaries, simulated, although it is not certain what they meant by that.[36] Meanwhile, Cosme de Torres (1510–1570), the second superior of the mission in the country, requested guidance from the Superior General of the Society of Jesus, Diego Laínez (1512–1565), regarding Japanese matrimonies and those who wanted Christian marriages.[37] In this context, Francisco Rodrigues, professor of casuistry in the College of São Paulo in Goa, responded to a consultation from Japan allowing the priests to refrain from declaring and enforcing canon law that could be detrimental to conversions.[38] Religious normative stability in the 1560s among Japanese Christians was characterised by intense syncretism of local and imported religious practices, made possible by the country's distance from Rome and other centres of hierarchical power in the Society of Jesus. The news of the conclusion of the Council of Trent was just the start of a process of legal change that would be intensified after the arrival of mendicant friars in the country.

As in missions all around the globe, the impact of Trent was first felt in warnings and requests for special exemptions for Japan. Jesuit calls asking for the authority to enact dispensations for the Japanese regarding positive law began in 1571, in the wake of consultations with Goa in the 1560s.[39] By the 1580s, Valignano was exhorting his confreres to exercise caution when considering the exposition of the Church's precepts.[40] Eventually, in the 1592 rules

35 ARSI, JapSin 6, fol. 142v.

36 ARSI, JapSin 6, fol. 124v. Yet, since the first years of the mission, Lent was a particularly significant time for Japanese Christians as it was the preferred time for yearly confession. López-Gay, *La Liturgia en la Misión*, 56–61, 113–130.

37 ARSI, JapSin 6, fols. 4r–5v.

38 Ucerler, *The Samurai and the Cross*, 78. On Rodrigues, see references listed in Ehalt, "Casuística nos Trópicos".

39 In 1571, Gaspar Vilela asked for papal concession so the priests could dispense on issues of matrimonies between cousins and other close relatives in Japan that were prohibited by canon law due to consanguinity. ARSI, JapSin 7-III, fol. 79v. Francisco Cabral, writing in that same year to the Superior General Diego Laínez, asked for general dispensations regarding positive law in Japan, a jurisdiction that he believed should be delegated to the Bishop of China. ARSI, JapSin 8-I, fol. 13r. On the Japan consultations in this period, see Fernandes Pinto and Remédio Pires, "The 'resposta que alguns padres do Japão mandaram perguntar'".

40 Of course, by 'precept' Valignano is referring to the general obligations derived from the legal dispositions of the Church, such as canon law and the Decalogue, and not just to the five Catholic precepts as understood today (obligation to attend mass, communion,

delineated by the visitor for Japan, he expressly condemned the publication of positive law without the authorisation of the Vice-Provincial, due to the risks represented to local Christians.[41] The initial waves created by Trent were, at best, minimal.

In the following decade, though, things looked different. At that time, Valignano was fighting for the right to reserve for the Jesuits the primacy in publishing positive precepts in Japan. Based on De Soto and his *De iustitia et iure* (1553), the visitor defended that the Church should not burden Christians with norms that could bring harm to them.[42] Jesuit letters exhibit concern with the arrival of the mendicants as early as 1580 – more than a decade after the news of the end of Trent. During the three meetings of the 1580–1581 consultation, the priests agreed that, despite the apparent advantages of having more missionaries to tend to the growing community of Christians, the arrival of clergy other than members of the Society of Jesus would be problematic not only from an economic point of view, since there were not enough Christians to maintain a large number of missionaries, but also due to the possible "inconvenience and scandal" resulting from the diversity of opinion and judgement, reflected in controversies and contradictions among the different orders.[43]

The result would be detrimental to the prestige already acquired by the religion at that point and led the Japanese to view Christianity as just another human invention. One of the main points made by the consultation was that a diversity of opinion would be unmanageable for the Japanese, since they were still not properly habilitated to discern between right and wrong in matters of faith, even though Valignano believed that, with time, the Japanese would become capable of such discernment. A comparison between the success enjoyed by the Jesuits in Japan with the little progress in missions observed in other regions, namely India and Europe, was put forward as evidence of his assessment. Furthermore, numerous references were made to the exotic and strange ways of the Japanese as arguments in favour of keeping the special circumstances under which the

confession, etc.). A clear delimitation of precept in the canonical and theological context has been difficult to carry out, and the term is generally accepted as a reflection of God's will summarised in a commandment or law. Joest, "Gebot II. Systematisch-Theologisch", 130; Korff and Winger, "Gebot III. Theologisch-ethisch", 327.

41 Lopez Gay, *El Catecumenado en la Misión del Japón*, 70–71; ARSI, JapSin 2, fol. 94r; Vu Thanh, "Introducing Tridentine Marriage", 148.

42 Ucerler, *The Samurai and the Cross*, 76–77. Valignano was referring to De Soto's discussion on the publication of law and exemption based on ignorance, *De iustitia et iure*, lib. 1, q. 1, art. 4.

43 On the theological notion of scandal and its particular meanings, see Schwartz, *The Political Morality of the Late Scholastics*, 101–103.

Jesuit mission found itself in the archipelago.[44] In order to successfully conduct the mission in the country, Valignano believed that missionaries needed patience and, eventually, to denaturalise (*desnaturalizarse*) themselves due to the unexpected ways of the Japanese.[45] The idea that Japan was so different that it demanded unorthodox solutions was constant in Jesuit documents of the early modern period, although not all were convinced by it.[46] Eventually, a successful campaign promoted by Jesuit procurators in the Iberian courts and in Rome managed to obtain a papal brief – the 1585 *Ex pastorali officio* – from Pope Gregorius XIII, and a royal letter from 1586 preventing the entrance of missionaries from any order but the Society of Jesus in Japan.[47] The text of King Filipe II's prohibition explained that, due to the Japanese not being used to the divine and human precepts – here, divine and positive law – there was the need for extreme caution (*mucha prudencia*) in transmitting the Christian faith (*nuestra sagrada doctrina*) and in enforcing them to abide by the positive law of the Church (*obligarlos a los preçeptos positivos de la Santa Iglesia*). The solution was to maintain the uniformity of opinion, i.e., the Japan Jesuits acting as the sole missionaries in the country.[48] Despite the success, Valignano's list of reasons against the entrance of missionaries from other orders in Japan was still

44 ARSI, JapSin 2, fols. 5r–5v, 43v–45v, 70r–70v; ARSI, JapSin 9-I, fol. 116r. This idea of Japan as being impossible to be understood by those who had not visited it is constant in Valignano's epistles. See, for example, Wicki, *Documenta Indica*, vol. 12, 831, as well as chapters 7 and 22 of Valignano, *Sumario*.

45 Colin, *Labor Evangelica*, 298.

46 Acquaviva, for instance, rejected the idea, claiming that Transylvania and Poland were much more exotic than Japan. ARSI, JapSin 3, fol. 76r. As for the effects of this notion on the administration of the Jesuit provinces in Asia, see Friedrich, "Government in India and Japan".

47 Magnino, *Pontificia Nipponica*, 24–27. The papal bull was published by the Viceroy of Goa on 12 April 1586. Alvarez-Taladriz, "Pro y Contra de la Linea", 7; ARSI, JapSin 27, fols. 8r–8v. The royal decision was supported by a decision of the Council of the Portuguese Indies in favour of the prohibition. ARSI, JapSin 9-I, fol. 16r; Magnino, *Pontificia Nipponica*, 25. However, Sixtus V's *Dum ad uberes* brief guaranteeing to the Franciscans the right to establish missions in Asia triggered a long dispute between Jesuits and mendicants for Japan. Schütte, "Die Wirksamkeit der Päpste für Japan", 187. Gregorius XIII's brief was finally revoked by Pope Clement VIII's constitution *Onerosa* in 1600. Jann, *Die katholischen Missionen in Indien, China und Japan*, 182. The need to consult Rome on local issues began in the 1580s as a result of the threat posed by the mendicants to Jesuit primacy in Japan, which was then intensified by the end of the decade due to local political instability (mainly the loss of Nagasaki and the planned invasion of Korea), not because of the incapacity of Goa to solve their problems in the 1590s or just because "Valignano felt a definite settlement was needed", as has been argued before. Vu Thanh, "Introducing Tridentine Marriage", 144–146.

48 ARSI, JapSin 27, fol. 8r.

making the rounds in Rome even after Gregorius XIII's bull, where it reached the new Pontifex, Pope Sixtus V, in May 1585.[49]

In 1580, the Japanese Christian warlords Bartolomeu Ōmura Sumitada and his son, Sancho Ōmura Sumiaki, donated the ports of Nagasaki and Mogi to the Jesuits in Japan. Nagasaki, the most important of the two, was progressively turned into a Christian enclave by the missionaries.[50] But despite the secular authority included in the donation, the administration of the city posited a legal challenge for the missionaries: could they execute criminals? The solution was to delegate criminal jurisdiction to Jesuit-appointed justices, while the missionaries oversaw other aspects of the city's administration.[51] Effectively, the argument of ignorance in Japan – more specifically, the ignorance of positive law – was key in the negotiations between the Jesuit Curia and the Pope when they applied for papal approval on the Japan Jesuit plan for Nagasaki.[52]

But despite their secular administrative powers in the port city, Valignano's 1583 report on Japan highlighted the limited and fragile authority that the Jesuits had over Christians in most of the archipelago. Among the chief reasons listed against the entrance of missionaries from other orders, the visitor explained that the need for uniform opinion and judgement among the members of the mission, impossible if other orders were allowed in, was fundamental to the decision-making on numerous topics, such as doubtful cases of conscience, ecclesiastical dispensations and penances given or denied to the Japanese, the administration of the sacraments and preventing the non-Christian Japanese from entering churches or burying their dead in Christian cemeteries. After all, these were the only coercive powers Jesuits had over their flock in the country.[53] The presence of mendicant friars in the country would only serve to cause great inconveniences, scandals and damage to the government of Japanese Christianity.[54] Similar arguments regarding limited Jesuit coercive powers in Japan and the dwindling state of their presence were repeated throughout the period, such as in the apologetic defence of the mission written by Valignano in 1598.[55]

In August of 1584, the first group of mendicant missionaries arrived in Japan. The four churchmen – Franciscan Brothers Juan "Pobre" Díaz Pardo

49 ARSI, JapSin 27, fol. 3r–6v.

50 Hesselink, *The Dream of a Christian Nagasaki*; Ehalt, "From Tenants to Landlords".

51 Other aspects of the administration were also divided with the newly-founded *Misericórdia* of the city. Ehalt, "In Their Likeness".

52 Ucerler, *The Samurai and the Cross*, 185.

53 Valignano, *Sumario*, 144.

54 ARSI, JapSin 9-I, fol. 116r.

55 Valignano, *Apologia*, 497.

(1514–1616)[56] and Diego Bernal (d. 1584), and Augustinians Francisco Manrique (d. 1588) and Mateo de Mendoza (d. 1605)[57] – arrived in Hirado and soon passed to Nagasaki, where they were received by the Jesuit Vice-Provincial Gaspar Coelho (c. 1529–1590). The band left the country a couple of months later, but their short passage through Japan prompted other mendicants in Manila to start planning their crossing of the Philippine Sea.[58] Díaz Pardo and the others were possibly the carriers of Coelho's requests to Spanish authorities in the Philippines for mendicant assistance for the Jesuit mission, in spite of Valignano's resolve and the ongoing campaign for papal and royal prohibitions.[59]

In 1587, Toyotomi Hideyoshi ordered the expulsion of all missionaries from Japan.[60] Although they managed to go into hiding and avoid the deportation process, pressure was mounting. Since 1586, the missionaries were aware that the Japanese leader was planning to invade the Korean Peninsula.[61] Jesuits in Japan feared the numerous problems the massive military campaign would bring to them and Japanese Christianity, including the justice of the war in Korea, the ownership of people imprisoned during the conflict, homicide and the conscience of Japanese Christians who had to follow heathen generals and orders with doubtful morals.[62]

The crisis prompted by Hideyoshi's 1587 decree and the impending war brought Valignano back to Japan in 1590. In November of that year, after consulting the elder members of the Vice-Province on whether missionaries should advise Japanese Christians on matters of war, the visitor set out his opinion on the matter in a list of decisions taken after the second consultation

---

56 Not to be confused with Friar Juan Pobre de Zamora, OFM (1550–1615), Diaz Pardo was procurator of the Franciscans in Manila and *encomendero* in Otón. He became a Franciscan brother between 1579 and 1584. AGI, Filipinas 84, n. 14; Iaccarino, "Early Spanish Intruders in China", 245–262; Zamora, *Historia de la Pérdida*, 18–19; Uyttenbroeck, *Early Franciscans in Japan*, 2–3; Valignano, *Apologia*, 26–28.

57 On Manrique and Mendoza, see Hartmann, *The Augustinians in Seventeenth Century Japan*, 12.

58 Valignano, *Apologia*, 26–30; Zamora, *Historia de la Pérdida*, 137–139.

59 Aduarte and González, *Historia de la Provincia del Santo Rosario*, 249–250. There were many other Jesuits, especially Spaniards, in favour of the participation of mendicant orders in the mission, such as Pero de la Cruz and Pero Gómez. Taladriz, "Opinión de un teólogo de la Compañia de Jesús."

60 Scholarship on this event is vast, although mostly in Japanese. Fujiki, *Toyotomi heiwarei to sengoku shakai*; Anno, *Bateren tsuihōrei*; Shimizu, *Shokuhō seiken to kirishitan*; Shimizu, "Hideyoshi ha naze kiristukyō wo kinshi shita no ka?"; Shimizu, "Kirishitan kinseishi no kenkyū jōkyō to kadai".

61 Boxer, *The Christian Century in Japan*, 140–143.

62 These were among the most sensitive topics of the consultation sent to Europe in 1592 by the Japan Jesuits. See López Gay, "Un Documento Inédito".

of Japan, held in August of that year. Upon showing great concern with the effects of the conflict on the consciences of faithful warlords and soldiers, Valignano underlined that, since Jesuits were the only missionary order in Japan (*estamos hasta ahora solos y como pastores de esta cristiandad de Japón*) the issue could be solved through careful analysis of each aspect of the cases (*casos*).[63] Furthermore, internal prohibitions would be enough to prevent the priests from personally meddling with issues of war by threatening penitents with admonitions, providing support with weapons or other materials or holding hostages for one of the sides in a given conflict.[64] The distance from Rome and their isolation as the only missionary order in the country would be an advantage to the solution of these and other matters pertaining to the doctrine and the positive law of the Church. Valignano planned to keep the stability of the norms regulating the lives of Japanese Christians through the controlled use of ignorance.

In 1592, the visitor gathered thirteen of the highest-ranking Japan Jesuits for the first congregation of the Vice-Province.[65] Although they repeated the arguments given during the first consultation of 1580–1581 against the entrance of missionaries from other orders by referring to its proceedings, due to the imminent arrival of the mendicants they requested special powers for the future Bishop of Japan.[66] Envisioning a prelate that would be able to regulate missionaries from other orders beyond the Society of Jesus according to the specificities of Japan and the vicissitudes of the mission, Jesuits wished for a bishop able to selectively promulgate or concede dispensations regarding the *ius positivum*, as well as enjoying sufficient independence from the See of Goa and its constitutions.[67] This was not surprising given the ample authority and jurisdiction of the prelate.[68] If the entrance of Franciscans, Dominicans and Augustinians was unavoidable, Jesuits in Japan would have to change their strategy.

---

63 Valignano, *Adiciones*, 649.

64 Valignano, *Adiciones*, 648–653.

65 The congregation was, however, limited in its powers and capacities, since Japan was a Jesuit Vice-Province. ARSI, JapSin 51, fol. 276v; Wicki, *Documenta Indica*, XIII, 372–373 and 581; Wicki, *Documenta Indica*, XIV, 816–817 and 887.

66 The first bishop chosen to head the Diocese of Funai (erected in 1588) was Sebastião de Morais, who died on his way to India. The second was Pedro Martins and the third Cerqueira. Costa, *O Cristianismo no Japão*, 240–247; Magnino, *Pontificia Nipponica*, 39–58.

67 Valignano, *Adiciones*, 715; ARSI, Congregatio 46, fol. 329v. The need for such powers was a constant concern regarding the administration of provinces, dioceses and missions in Asia. See Friedrich, "Government in India and Japan", 13–14.

68 On the episcopal authority, see Traslosheros, "Audiencia Episcopal" and Assimakópulos, "Oficios Eclesiásticos", 22–34.

4 A cloak for Sinners

In the early 1590s, Japan Jesuits explicitly adopted the doctrine of invincible ignorance as the legal foundation for their decisions regarding the imposition of positive law in Japan. The forthcoming arrival of mendicants meant that Jesuits could no longer hold exclusive control over the methods, order, or rate at which the dogma was taught to Christians, nor prevent other missionaries from publishing positive precepts in the country. It was time to justify their *modus procedendi* and request arrangements that would keep the normative status quo as long as possible. One key point was to argue in favour of the slow pace at which the doctrine was transmitted, based not only to the capacities of the individuals but also to the regional characteristics of each community. Publishing the Church's positive precepts for the Christians of Nagasaki was much different from declaring positive law for new converts in the countryside.[69]

The doctrine of invincible ignorance is brought up in two documents of the early 1590s in regard to a key element of the *ius positivum*: marriage.[70] In a report on Valignano's second visit to the country, the 1592 *Adiciones del Sumário de Japón* points to invincible ignorance as a remedy for the problem of repudiation in Japan. As he explains, the common doctrine of the Church followed Pope Innocent III's *Gaudemus de divortiis* by considering marriages among non-Christians to be true and indissoluble.[71] However, the visitor explores possible exceptions to the chapter in order to defend the invalidity of Japanese marriages. After all, Japanese marriages were non-permanent contracts, believed in good faith (*bona fides*) to be dissoluble. Since that belief

---

69 On how the geography of the mission in Japan influenced Jesuit administration, see Vu Thanh, "Principles of Missionary Geography".

70 Japanese matrimony was a concern for the missionaries as early as 1557. Ruiz-de-Medina, *Documentos del Japón*, vol. 1, 692. By the mid-1560s, even before the news of the end of the Council of Trent reached Japan, there were calls from Japanese Christians who wanted to marry *in face ecclesiae*. See, for example, ARSI, JapSin 6, fols. 71v, 190v–191r. Other relevant works on this topic for other regions of the early modern period include Broggio, Castelnau-L'Estoile and Pizzorusso (eds.), "Administrer les sacrements en Europe et au Nouveau Monde"; Albani, *Sposarsi nel Nuovo Mondo*; Albani, Aranha and Catto (eds.), "Tridentine Marriage in a Global Perspective".

71 After Innocent III's *Gaudemus de divortiis*. *Gregorius IX, Decretales*, lib. IV, tit. XIX, cap. 8. For a general overview of matrimony in canon law, see Zaballa Beascoechea, "Matrimonio" and Reynold, *How Marriage Became One of the Sacraments*. For a legal historical and comparative analysis of Christian and Japanese understandings of marriage in early modernity, see Coutinho Silva, "The Janus Face". In Japanese, a thorough analysis is made in Ahn, *Kirishitan jidai no kon'in mondai*. More recently, see Asami, *Kirishitan jidai no ryōshin mondai*, 91–118.

meant repudiation provoked no injury to any of the involved parties, the visitor asked the Roman Jesuit Curia to rule *in favorem fidei* and consider Japanese marriages invalid. This would allow priests to ignore marriages with non-Christian spouses as well as all legal, political and religious complications derived from them. Valignano also envisioned the missionaries as middlemen between the determinations of Rome and Japan, responsible for keeping Christians safe from laws of the Church that could bring unnecessary punishment and damage (*peñas y daños*) by preventing their publication and thus keeping them protected by the principle of invincible ignorance.[72] This was all in accordance with their repeated requests for the power to dispense on matters of canon law.

Around the same time, Japan Jesuits circulated a list of questions and propositions in universities in Évora, Coimbra, Alcalá de Henares and Salamanca. Invincible ignorance was presented as an argument in the debates concerning ritual suicide and idolatry. The former referred to the norms surrounding dishonourable death at the hands of enemies – when death was imminent, Japanese warriors would ask a relative or friend to kill them instead of letting themselves be killed by a foe. But if invincible ignorance was posited as a legitimate defence for the practice, the same was not true for idolatry. Rituals and general practices related to heathenism were understood as signs of a depraved mind – a reference to Romans 1:28. For that reason, the ignorance of the Japanese of religious practices was not invincible, but rather *ignorantia crassa* or *supina*, which meant their blame could be mitigated but they could not be completely exempt from it.[73]

In parallel with the ongoing debate concerning Jesuit claims of exclusivity over Japan, there were concerns among mendicants that managed to enter the country regarding the methods established by the Society of Jesus. The uses of invincible ignorance, for instance, seem to have gone beyond what Jesuits reported to Rome, as suggested in the numerous papers written against them. Due to the difficulties met by the Society of Jesus in moving around Japan in the years following the 1587 decree by Hideyoshi, a growing number of individuals, both Japanese Christians and warlords interested in having priests nearby either for liturgical or trading reasons, started requesting missionaries from Manila. Franciscans swiftly responded to the petitions by preparing their

72 Valignano, *Adiciones*, 474–478. Ahn, *Kirishitan jidai no kon'in mondai*, 70–83.

73 López Gay, "Un Documento Inédito", 135, 139–140, 149, 154–155; Takase, *Kirishitan jidai no bunka to shosō*, 590–608. Although debates were held in a number of universities, the only extant response to the questionnaire seems to be the one given by Gabriel Vázquez (1549–1604) in 1594.

entrance to the country.[74] Yet, due to the heavy punishments prescribed by the 1585 papal brief for all non-Jesuit missionaries entering Japan, their plans required careful consideration. After debating the issue, the Spanish secular and ecclesiastical authorities agreed that Franciscans should be sent to the archipelago as ambassadors of the governor. Despite their mission being diplomatic, the 1586 brief of Sixtus V guaranteeing the mendicants freedom to erect new houses and convents in any country in Asia, including Japan, was used as an argument in support of the expedition.[75]

The Franciscan mission had its supporters among the Jesuit ranks, including the Vice-Provincial Pero Gómez (1533–1600).[76] After their arrival in the early 1590s, the Franciscans were sent written instructions by Gómez regarding what they termed the "soft means" (*suaves medios*) of conversion. These focused on sermons delivered by Japanese catechists over six or seven days – an adaptation of the Jesuit method established by Xavier. If any doubts were raised during the conversion process, the Japanese brothers were told to answer as best as they could or explain that the priests were not proficient enough in the language to reply to the questions. Many Christians were confused about the friars, and disputes began concerning allegiance to one or another order – even though Franciscans declared that the faithful were to be loyal to Jesus Christ, not to the Jesuits or the mendicants.[77]

Once they started talking to the Japanese Christians, the friars realised the community's lack of knowledge regarding the dogma and the positive laws of the Church. According to the mendicants, Jesuits had taught only the Ten Commandments since they believed other teachings would become obstacles to the maintenance of the faith. As the mendicants began transmitting other positive precepts, the Japanese started interpreting this as further evidence of Franciscans and Jesuits not preaching the same faith.[78]

Concerned with the non-observance of the Church's laws, Pedro Bautista (1542–1597), superior of the Franciscans in Japan, decided to instruct the

74 Uyttenbroeck, *Early Franciscans in Japan*, 4–6. A perspective that is often overlooked in the study of the Jesuit–mendicant disputes is that, due to the Franciscans losing space in the Spanish Americas for at least three decades prior to their entrance in Japan, the archipelago represented an important new enterprise for the global mendicant effort. Crewe, *The Mexican Mission*, 204–205.

75 Uyttenbroeck, *Early Franciscans in Japan*, 6–7; Lage Reis, "Alessandro Valignano's attitude", 81–85; Magnino, *Pontificia Nipponica*, 35–39.

76 Also, Sebastião Gonçalves (1533–1597) and Francisco Calderón (1548–1618), both Jesuit veterans. Pérez, *Cartas y Relaciones*, vol. II, 84–85.

77 Pérez, *Cartas y Relaciones*, vol. II, 78–80.

78 Pérez, *Cartas y Relaciones*, vol. II, 81.

Christian community regarding the annual feasts, fasts and other precepts mandatory for the faithful. According to him, the authority to do so was guaranteed by the 1522 brief *Exponi nobis fecisti* (the *Omnimoda*), issued by Pope Adrian VI (b. 1459, r. 1522–1523), which gave the Franciscans the right to establish missions without episcopal oversight.[79] But even though they had started publishing positive law, the Franciscans would still give dispensations whenever they felt the need to do so in order to safeguard the communities, at least until the Bishop of Japan arrived and solved the issue once and for all.[80]

Meanwhile, other friars critical of Jesuit methods in Japan, such as Martín Ignacio de Loyola (c. 1550–1606), Martin de la Ascensión (1566–1597) and Marcelo de Ribadeneira (dates unknown), addressed their complaints to Rome. As their writings reached Europe, the Franciscan and the Jesuit camps waged a paper war, fueled periodically by the arrival of critical and apologetic reports sent from Asia.[81] While Bautista corrected things ad hoc, De Loyola, De la Ascensión and De Ribadeneira aimed at disputing missionary rights at European courts. Their criticism, however, targeted the extensive use of ignorance as an exculpatory argument regarding positive law.

The earliest Franciscan to raise his voice against Jesuit primacy in Japan was De Loyola.[82] His involvement with the issue began in 1587, when he was trying to reinstall the friars in Macau. Upon being notified by Portuguese authorities of the papal bull and the royal letter expelling the order from Japan,[83] De Loyola, with five other Franciscans, signed a rebuttal of both decisions. According to them, the decrees were invalid since the pontiff and the king had been misinformed by the Jesuits in Japan – in his view, if the Pope and the Crown

79 Matritensi, *Bullarium Fratrum Ordinis Minorum*, 112–114; Crewe, *The Mexican Mission*, 204.

80 Pérez, *Cartas y Relaciones*, vol. II, 81.

81 On the Roman side of the dispute, see Tronu, "The rivalry between the Jesuits and the Mendicant orders", 29–33. From the addressees of the documents, it is possible to envision the dimension of the conflict. Besides the King and the Pope, numerous powerful and influential figures in Rome, Madrid and Lisbon were involved, such as Francisco de Toledo, Antonio Carafa, Fabio de Fabi, Gaspar de Quiroga y Vela, Juan Azor, Roberto Belarmino, Miguel Vázquez de Padilla and Muzio de Angelis. ARSI, JapSin 27, fols. 16r–17v; JapSin 33, fols. 48r–49v; JapSin 11, fols. 210r–211v;; JapSin 10, fols. 147r–148v; JapSin 11, fols. 200r–201v; López Gay, *El Matrimonio de los Japoneses*, 60, 67.

82 Before venturing into Japan, De Loyola was actively enmeshed in the jurisdictional disputes concerning the missions between Manila, Macau and Malacca. Alberts, *Conflict and Conversion*, 28–29. His globetrotting peregrinations were also perused in Gruzinski, *Les quatre parties du monde*, 278–285.

83 Portuguese efforts to expel Spanish mendicants from the Eastern ports of the Estado da Índia had been going on since the early 1580s. Tang, *Setting Off from Macau*, 17–18.

had been properly informed, no friar would have been stopped from entering Japan. He classified as presumptuous and reckless the argument used by the Jesuits to exclude the Franciscans from the country, as the Society of Jesus had underlined the need for prudence, discretion, doctrinal uniformity and experience in preaching (*prudencia y discreción, unidad de doctrina, experiencia en la predicación*) the many precepts of the Church and maturity in declaring positive law and in using dispensations in Japan.[84]

Effectively, De Loyola emphasised that there had been no need to exclude specific religious orders from missions led by mendicant orders in other parts of the world. The friar painted a rosy picture of the collective memory of Franciscan missions, where there had been no separation between missionaries, or diversity in the precepts declared, or the involvement of clergymen with trading. He also drew attention to the incapacity of the Society of Jesus in tending to the whole of Japanese Christianity, and the commissary even mentioned the fact that the lord of Hirado, Matsura Takanobu (1529–1599), had previously asked the authorities in Manila for mendicant priests rather than Jesuits to preach in his city. The friar took a dramatic turn when criticising the Jesuit notion that diversity would be detrimental to the missionary enterprise: who could say a garden with different types of flowers is ugly? (*¿Quién dirá que un jardín de diversas flores es cosa fea?*) or that an army of soldiers wielding different weapons and with many specialisations is a bad thing? (*¿Parece mal un ejército de soldados de diversas armas y oficios?*) The Jesuit monopoly on Japanese Christianity was, according to him, contrary to positive law, since it prevented locals from obtaining the necessary doctrine and the sacraments due to the small number of priests available in the archipelago.[85] For De Loyola, the Pope and the King had been duped. Because of that, their unjust prohibitions could be disregarded.

The second friar to express to Rome his dissatisfaction with the Jesuits in Japan was De la Ascensión. After spending a couple of years in Manila studying the state of Japanese Christianity, De la Ascensión sailed to Japan in 1596. Between June and September, he penned two *Relaciones* wherein he denounced abuses among the Jesuit methods.[86] In conversations with an unnamed high-ranking Jesuit,[87] the Franciscan became aware of a common

84 Alvarez-Taladriz, "Pro y Contra de la Linea", 8.
85 Alvarez-Taladriz, "Pro y Contra de la Linea", 7–11.
86 Alvarez-Taladriz, *Documentos Franciscanos*, 12–14.
87 José Luiz Alvarez-Taladriz believes this was Pedro Ramón, an *opositor* to Valignano in the Jesuit Vice-Province who worked as interpreter for the Franciscans. Alvarez-Taladriz, *Documentos Franciscanos*, 80.

practice in the mission: Jesuits performed no in-depth examinations of candidates during conversion in regard to matrimonies, usury and restitutions, something unheard of in Manila. The reason was, in the words of De la Ascensión's interlocutor, that "twisting the nose produces blood" (Proverbs 30:33), i.e., to put too much pressure on the neophytes would be detrimental to the mission itself: "no preguntan nada de esto al bautismo porque nadie se haría Cristiano" ("they ask nothing about these issues at the Baptism; otherwise, no one would become Christian"). The fundamental proposition involved, according to the informant, leaving the Japanese in a state of invincible ignorance until they learned the doctrine, little by little, during confession. The report gives as an example the case of Arima Harunobu (1567–1612), whose complicated marital situation was allegedly overlooked by Valignano at the occasion of his conversion.[88] The Jesuit conclusion was that penitents could be forgiven by resorting to invincible ignorance whenever there was any sinful action that they were not instructed about before. Invincible ignorance was, De la Ascensión pointed out, a cloak for sinners (*capa de pecadores*), excusing the Japanese from all sorts of murder, robbery, usury, deceit and rape, since uninformed Christians did not understand any of these as sinful actions.[89]

A similar strategy was described by the Franciscan De Ribadeneira. Author of a *Historia* of the missions in Japan where he stayed between 1594 and 1597, the friar wrote two reports after leaving the country: the *Quejas y respuestas* and the *Memoria de las Cosas de Japón*.[90] De Ribadeneira repeated the accusations about the lack of indoctrination and proper examination before the baptism, although he added a significant detail: Jesuit priests used the occasion of the first confession of the newly baptised Japanese to examine whether the individual – particularly powerful individuals – resorted to any kind of abusive

88 The complicated marital situation of Harunobu has been a contentious point, adding to the numerous variances in the records of his life in Japanese and Western sources. See Shimizu, "Fujiwara Arima seifu", 62–102; Fróis, *História de Japam*, vol. II, 498–499; Fróis, *História de Japam*, vol. III, 138–141; Schütte, *Valignanos Missionsgrundsätze für Japan*, 401–407; Nawata Ward, *Women Religious Leaders*, 73, 324–325; *Nihon Kirisuto-kyō Rekishi Daijiten*, 68; Ōmura City Library, Ōmura Keki, vol. 1, 30–31; Ōmura-ke Oboegaki, vol. 3, 8–9; Ōmura Kafu, vol. 2, 36; Ōmura-shi Hankanfu, unnumbered page; and Hotta, *Kansei Chōshū Shokafu*, vol. 4, 1015–1016.

89 As pointed out by Alvarez-Taladriz, *capa de pecadores* was a reference to the Spanish adage *capa de pecadores, el verano con sus flores* (cloak for sinners, the summer with its flowers), that is to say, the many temptations of a given circumstance become an occasion for sin. Alvarez-Taladriz, *Documentos Franciscanos*, 80–82, 86.

90 Here I use the abbreviated titles suggested in Alvarez-Taladriz, *Documentos Franciscanos*, 151, 154, 156. On De Ribadeneira's *Historia*, see Busquets Alemany, "Huellas de Japón en las crónicas misioneras del siglo xvii"; Padrón, *The Indies of the Setting Sun*, 205–231.

usury, tyrannical actions, excessive taxation or the practice of polygamy.[91] The observation confirms much of what the Jesuits had previously declared in regard to this point: that due to their lack of secular authority, the only tool they had to correct the path followed by Japanese Christians was admonition through confession.[92]

That does not mean, however, that Franciscans did not resort to the doctrine themselves. In a sense, ignorance and simplicity walked hand in hand as fundamental values for the friars, who understood them as indispensable virtues in avoiding integration into a sinful society.[93] Both De la Ascensión and De Ribadeneira described the mendicants' use of invincible ignorance to exempt and protect Japanese Christians from sin. Yet, the difference between the Franciscans and the Jesuits, both argued, was that the friars were purportedly more careful when applying the doctrine.[94] For the Japan Franciscans, invincible ignorance could be used exclusively to forgive sins regarding positive law, hence it was not applied in cases of natural or divine law.[95]

Valignano's rebuttal came in 1598, in the form of his *Apologia de la Compañia de Jesús de Japón y China*. His text reproduced passages from numerous Franciscan reports – inflammatory libels (*libelos inflamatorios*, as he put it)[96] – on Jesuit activities in Japan, although Valignano's citations often left out sections that could be more compromising for his defence. After consultation in Macau with the Bishop of Japan, Pedro Martins, and his substitute, Cerqueira,[97] the visitor explained that the apparently mistaken decision to maintain the Japanese in a state of ignorance had actually been the result of numerous internal discussions, as well as consultations with the Jesuit Curia, which had cleared

91 Alvarez-Taladriz, *Documentos Franciscanos*, 223–224, 240.

92 Since the earliest days of the mission, confession was a major medium of indoctrination. Uncoincidentally, the picture painted by Xavier of the protoconverts Paulo de Santa Fé and his companions in Malacca, a couple of years after their conversion, displays the Japanese as recognising confession and communion as "the best thing we have in our law". Ruiz-de-Medina, *Documentos del Japón*, vol. I, 120. See also Ehalt, *Jesuits and the Problem*, 241–242, 289–290; López Gay, "Un Documento Inédito", 137, 150.

93 Lage Reis, "Alessandro Valignano's attitude", 91.

94 Seemingly, this was the opposite of what took place in China, where Jesuits were the ones accusing Franciscans of carelessness in, for example, their assessment of Confucianism. Also, this change of Franciscan attitudes can be seen as caused by the absence of secular authorities enforcing their will upon candidates for conversion. Brockey, *Journey to the East*, 106–107.

95 Alvarez-Taladriz, *Documentos Franciscanos*, 83, 224.

96 Alvarez-Taladriz, "Documentos de 1597", 55.

97 The consultation took place between July and November 1597. Alvarez-Taladriz, "Documentos de 1597", 49 and 58.

the strategy with both the Roman College and the Pope.[98] Valignano argued that his position was in accordance with the doctrine of the Church, which declared that new Christian communities – such as those in Japan – could not be under the same rules as the Christians in Europe.[99]

Regarding the complicated marital status of Arima Harunobu, which the Franciscans said had been ignored by Valignano, the visitor explained that the priests had been informed that the warlord had a concubine, whom he was unwilling to dismiss, despite knowing that it would be an obstacle to receiving baptism. Valignano even expressed regret over his knowledge of the concubine, given that had they been unaware of her existence, they could have baptised Harunobu in good conscience. Valignano explained that, eventually, Harunobu chose Christianity over his lover, and that there had been no mistake in that case.[100]

On the issue of ignorance, the *Apologia* did not deny the friars' accusations, but rather reiterated that the application of the doctrine of invincible ignorance was approved by their superiors in Rome and by the Pontifex. The intention was to use dissimulation when interacting with the local Christians, refraining from either condemning or endorsing their conduct.[101] In Valignano's view, the Franciscans had disingenuously misunderstood the strategy. For the Jesuits, the plan was to keep Japanese Christians safe according to their circumstances while gradually but decisively promulgating positive law in Japan.[102] Valignano's general tone is explanatory, as he wished to prove that their plan was not only in accordance with canonical jurisprudence and theological casuistry but that it had also been approved by all higher authorities in Rome.

The visitor's apology employs uncertain and controversial points to justify the Jesuit methods in Japan. When Franciscans accused Jesuits of leaving aside instructions regarding natural law, thus allowing Japanese Christian soldiers to murder and ransack under the command of heathen warlords, Valignano pointed out the various grey areas of theology and canon law concerning these issues. The visitor also edited out a key phrase from the mendicant accusation, where De la Ascensión admits the possibility of exemption as expressed by numerous doctors of the Church. Rather than addressing the excessive use of invincible ignorance in cases of natural law, Valignano instead cunningly

98 Ucerler, *The Samurai and the Cross*, 82.
99 Valignano, *Apologia*, 248.
100 Valignano, *Apologia*, 250–251.
101 Bernabé, "Los jesuitas contra el método de los franciscanos", 92–93. On dissimulation as an institution of canon law, see Roca, "Disimulación". On Jesuit dissimulation, see Tutino, "Jesuit Accommodation, Dissimulation, Mental Reservation", 216–240.
102 Valignano, *Apologia*, 252–253.

reiterated the indecisiveness of the issue as enough to justify their ways.[103] This was an unsurprising strategy, given the way the visitor's writings often employed ambiguity and uncertainty as legal arguments in his negotiations with Rome and other authorities.[104]

In addition to the apologetic text of the visitor, the new policy directions established by Cerqueira, the new Bishop of Japan, exerted a decisive influence on the uses of the doctrine of invincible ignorance and the implementation of positive law in the country.[105] Arriving in August 1598, Cerqueira had had a distinguished academic career in Portugal, where he was a close colleague of Luis de Molina (1535–1600).[106] After disembarking in Nagasaki, he immediately called a series of consultations to discuss the most pressing matters of the mission.[107] On one of these occasions, the prelate realised that the problem lay not in whether positive law was declared to Japanese Christians, but rather the way in which these precepts were introduced.[108] From this point on, the *ius positivum* could no longer be avoided. After half a century of the mission, Japanese Christianity community contained pockets of believers ready to receive the positive law of the Church.

Of course, the role played by the Council of Trent's decrees in Japan cannot be overlooked. Recent studies have ascribed to Cerqueira the role of adapter of the Tridentine decrees in Japan, in an attempt to avoid their publication.[109] Sources, however, point to a rather complex story, as many indicate the publication of the decrees in parts of Japan. In 1595, Gil de la Mata (1547–1599), a representative of the Japan Jesuits, informed the Superior General Claudio

---

103 Homicide was an issue of natural law, as it was the opposite of the conservation of human life. Olaza Pallero, "Homicidas". The description is analogous to the practice of *ranbō rōzeki*, a form of pillaging and slaughter that was allowed by warlords in exchange for monetary payments for their soldiers. Fujiki, *Zōhyōtachi no senjō*. Valignano, *Apologia*, 252; Alvarez-Taladriz, *Documentos Franciscanos*, 81.

104 See, for instance, Valignano's racial taxonomy. Ehalt, "Os Japoneses no Pensamento Racial", 665–677.

105 Cerqueira's episcopal career in Japan has been the focus of numerous studies. The most representative are Costa, *O Cristianismo no Japão*; and Kataoka, *A Vida e a Acção Pastoral*.

106 Cerqueira's thought as a theologian is still far from being properly discussed and understood in the context of the mission in Japan. For an analysis of the theological works written before his departure to Asia, see Díez-Alegría, *El desarrollo de la doctrina*, 138–140, 257–273.

107 Costa, *O Cristianismo no Japão*, 309–10; Lopez-Gay, *El Catecumenado*, 181–182; Schütte, *Valignanos Missionsgrundsätze für Japan*, L-LI; Kataoka, *A Vida e a Acção Pastoral*, 87–8.

108 Lopez Gay, *El Catecumenado*, 71. See also Lopez Gay, "La Consulta 'Ad Modum Synodi'", 251–266.

109 Vu Thanh, "Un évêque tridentin au Japon?", 209–231; Vu Thanh, "Introducing Tridentine Marriage", 143–150.

Acquaviva in Rome that the Tridentine *De matrimoniis* had already been published for some of the older Christian communities in Japan.[110] The same was repeated in Gabriel Vázquez's answers to the 1592 questionnaire brought to him by De la Mata, in which he declares that the council had already been published in a few Japanese parishes.[111] Later accounts of Cerqueira's career in Japan celebrated him as the one responsible for promoting Tridentine regulations within the country regarding marriages.[112]

Despite the difficulty in pinpointing the areas and the timing of the publication of Trent in Japan, this is a key point for understanding the Jesuits' change of position regarding the introduction of *ius positivum* in the country. Writing in the 1620s, Afonso de Lucena (1551–1623), confessor of the Ōmura clan and the main Jesuit in their lands between 1578 and 1614, claimed that some areas of the fief were already under the new rules of Trent during his time. Furthermore, he reiterated that the enforcement of these rules depended on the students of the local novitiate, who, through preaching, admonitions and example, persuaded the locals to comply.[113] Similarly, Luís Fróis (1532–1597) had already affirmed in November 1584 that in some areas surrounding Nagasaki the missionaries had started to declare the necessity of the sacrament of matrimony, as determined by the Tridentine council, in order to suppress the widespread practice of repudiation. The architect of the initiative had been the Vice-Provincial of Japan, Coelho.[114] Indeed, the obvious next choice to publish the positive precepts of the Church was Nagasaki, although the chronology of this process remains unclear. Yet, from the introduction of the Tridentine parish system in the city, first instituted in 1601 and finally consolidated in 1606 with the ordaining of the first local diocesan priest under Cerqueira's prelacy, the adoption of positive law did not begin until the end of the sixteenth century in the country.[115]

Clear recommendations regarding Trent in Japan came from authorities intermediating in the Nagasaki–Rome dialogue. In the early 1590s, Jesuit theologians in Goa gathered to discuss the issues presented by the 1592 questionnaire sent to Europe.[116] Upon receiving De la Mata in the College of São Paulo, the Jesuit teachers reiterated Valignano's warnings against the publication of

110 ARSI, JapSin 3, fol. 62r.
111 Lopez Gay, "Un Documento Inédito", 133–134, 146–147.
112 BRAH, 9/7236, fol. 322r; Cardim, *Batalhas da Companhia de Jesus*, 6.
113 Lucena, *Erinnerungen aus der Christenheit von Ōmura*, 176–177.
114 ARSI, JapSin 9-II, fol. 312v. Alvarez-Taladriz misunderstands that the rules of Trent had been declared for the Christians of Ōmura. Valignano, *Apologia*, 249.
115 Tronu, "The post-Tridentine parish system", 85–87.
116 On the role of the Goa Jesuit theologians in the debate, see Ehalt, "Goa no iezusukai shingakusha to nihon no doreika".

the decrees as well as any positive law in Japan, recognising that any positive law in Japan would be a clear obstacle to their conversion (*manifiesto estorvo para su conversión*).[117] The alert was, of course, a reference to areas not as strongly Christianised as Ōmura or Nagasaki. The assembled theologians advised Japan Jesuits that the rules should be adopted only in places where "all were Christians" (*donde son todos Xpianos*), namely: in the islands of Amakusa,[118] in the port of Takase, in the lands of Ōmura and in Nagasaki.[119] Of course, these were the areas where a relatively established presence of the Church could enforce the rules, although the role played by the Bishop in judging Japanese adherence to Trent is still unclear. For those heavily Christianised areas, Jesuits in Goa devised actions that could help in supporting compliance to the decree of the reformed matrimony (*el decreto de reformatione Matrimonij del Concilio tridentino*). These included constant exhortations through sermons in favour of the Catholic form of the marriage, celebrated by a diocesan priest in the presence of two witnesses; formalization of existing marriages now *in face ecclesiae*; and the careful consideration of dispensations of certain elements pertaining to the decrees according to the specific situation of each parish.[120] Their assessment highlighted which areas of Japan were then under consideration for the introduction of positive law in the 1590s. Meanwhile in Rome, Pope Clement VIII (b. 1536, r. 1592–1605) recognised in 1595 the impossibility of observing the Tridentine rules in all of Japan, bestowed on the Bishop of Japan (and, in his absence, the Jesuit Vice-Provincial) the right to dispense on issues of matrimonies in the country.[121]

That does not mean, however, that the Jesuit education plan in Japan lacked instructions on law. In 1593, Vice-Provincial Gómez wrote a manual of Catholic teachings to be used at the local Jesuit college, the *Compendium catholicae veritatis*, which was translated into Japanese a couple of years later.[122] In the translation, Gómez delineates a traditional taxonomy between divine law (*jihiina rekisu*, or *divina lex*), human law (*umaana rekisu*, or *humana lex*),

117 APSR, Consultas 2, fol. 321r.
118 By 1601, more than 100,000 Christians lived on the islands and the lands of Higo, under the protection of Agostinho Konishi Yukinaga. ARSI, JapSin 14-I, fol. 56v.
119 Cerqueira followed suit. In 1599, he confirmed the need to implement calendar reforms, impose fasting and administer the sacraments differently in each area of Japan according to their specific circumstances. ARSI, JapSin 20, fol. 54r.
120 APSR, Consultas 2, fol. 330r.
121 Magnino, *Pontificia Nipponica*, 58; Ucerler, *The Samurai and the Cross*, 82.
122 Both edited in facsimile. Gómez, *Compedium catholicae Veritatis*, 3 vols.

natural (*natsuraru*) law and positive (*pojichiiwa*) law.[123] By correlating Western and Japanese concepts, he offered a rather sophisticated understanding of the *ius commune* for Japanese novices. Divine positive law, for instance, is divided into "old law" (*furuki go-okite*) and "new law" (*shinshiki go-okite*), while human law is classified as either ecclesiastical law (*rei*, from the Portuguese *lei*) or secular law (*secularis*). In general, the manual uses six different normative categories to classify the Church's precepts and other norms: *hatto*, *okite*, *hō*, *rekisu*, *rei* and *mandamentosu*, three borrowed from Japanese legal tradition and three adapted from European languages.[124] As with other instances of Jesuit translation in Japan, the choice of words denoted the seizing of specific meanings and understandings concerning normativities to the benefit of the missionary enterprise.[125] Moreover, this taxonomical impulse is also present in the *Compendium*'s exposition on ignorance. After a brief introduction to Aquinas' definitions of ignorance, Gómez discusses who could employ the argument, with a mention of Juan de Ginés Sepulveda's doctrine of idolatry. He also explores the possibility of ignorance of divine law (now *juro jibiino*, in the Japanese version), which he confirms by evoking the authorities of Aquinas, Alfonso de Castro and De Soto. Although his answers do not comment on the specifics of the Japanese situation, his short exposition of the basics of the doctrine underlines the specific role of invincible ignorance (the only type actually discussed) for the mission.[126] Nevertheless, the extent to which Gómez's textbook reflected Trent still remains to be better understood.

Sometime before the 1620s, however, Trent was invalidated in Japan. In February 1614, the Bishop Cerqueira died in Nagasaki; months later, the Tokugawa Bakufu decided to expel all missionaries from the country – only 48 missionaries decided to remain and go into hiding.[127] This dramatic turn of events certainly had an effect on the maintenance of the Tridentine rules. By the end of the decade, the decrees were considered invalid for all parts of Japan. In the early 1620s, the Manila-based Dominican rector of the College of Santo Thomás, Domingo González, discussed the case of Spaniards wishing to marry in Japan by the rules of the council in spite of their suspension. However, there was still doubt among the mendicants about whether the obligations derived

123 For a similar example of legal taxonomy in the period, see Decock, "From Law to Paradise", 17.

124 Ucerler, *The Samurai and the Cross*, 12, 78–80.

125 As with the translations of social obligations in the rules of lay brotherhoods. Ehalt, "In Their Likeness".

126 Gómez, *Compendium catholicae veritatis*, vol. I, fols. 380v–381v; Gómez, *Compendium catholicae veritatis*, vol. II, fols. 330v–332v.

127 Shimizu et al. (eds.), *Kinsei Nagasaki*, 100–101; Schütte, *Introductio*, 182–183, 200.

from publishing Trent had been suspended for all Christians in Japan, including Europeans residing in the country, or just for the Japanese.[128] If at first Trent reforms were tentatively adopted during the first half of the 1580s, it was the entrance of the mendicant missionaries in the 1590s that accelerated the changes in the religious normative scenario. With the introduction of positive precepts by Franciscans, Jesuits were forced to shift their position and adopt a programmatic framework for the introduction of Tridentine marriage and other precepts of the Church's *ius positivum*.

5 Reformed Ways

Once the systematic introduction of positive law began, Jesuit leadership and the Bishop of Japan became increasingly concerned with how Japanese Christians implemented the precepts in their daily lives. The issue of matrimony was certainly of grave concern, as shown by the extensive research that has been dedicated to the introduction of Tridentine marriage in Japan in recent years.[129] However, Trent was but one of the many challenges posed by the adoption of positive law in Japan.

As a teaching and a correctional device, confession was among the chief weapons in checking the virtuousness of local believers as well as for (slowly) instructing new converts. For the Japanese, penance reiterated their allegiance to the community, although the various forms it took (donation of alms, mortification and fasting) were heavily syncretic forms during the first decades of the mission.[130] Just like in the Spanish Americas, confession in Japan followed a medieval interrogatory style, in spite of the innovations introduced in Trent.[131] As explained by Jaime Valenzuela Márquez, instead of the Triden-

128 APSR, Consultas 2, fols. 317r–317v. In Europe, however, the general assumption was that Trent was still valid for Japan even by the mid-1620s. Pizzorusso, *Propaganda Fide*, vol. I, 221.

129 Lopez Gay, *El Matrimonio de los Japoneses*; Vu Thanh, "Un évêque tridentin au Japon?"; Vu Thanh, "Introducing Tridentine Marriage"; Ahn, *Kirishitan jidai no kon'in mondai*; Tutino, *Uncertainty in Post-Reformation Catholicism*, 295–312; Wirbser, "A Law Too Strict?"; Coutinho Silva, "The Janus Face".

130 Fujitani, "Penance in the Jesuit Mission to Japan"; Kawamura, "Konchirisan no Riyaku no seiritsu haikei to igi". For other aspects of allegiance to the faith and social organisations related to Christianity in Japan, see Ehalt, "In Their Likeness". Also, one must not forget that the Decalogue itself was a rather new framing of moral expectations imposed by the Church in the 16th century. See Bossy, "Moral arithmetic".

131 This is of course a reference to the tradition established by Raymond of Peñaforte's confession. Tentler, "The Summa for Confessors", 113–117.

tine "free" examination of one's conscience, American confession followed a pre-determined questionnaire, given that this Christianity was not seen "with the same level of maturity and 'adult' responsibility" held by their European counterparts. This opinion was asserted by the invincible ignorance of native people, which made them "unable to declare their sins unless they were questioned in a detailed manner." Furthermore, confession manuals closely followed the example set by Azpilcueta, which followed the order of the Decalogue in exploring the issues of confession. The result was that confession became an exhaustive assessment of the individual's sins, with questions detailing "the number of places in which the penitent committed them, and of their details and circumstances."[132]

In Japan, Franciscans noticed that the questionnaires adopted locally by the Society of Jesus were designed in a specific way to avoid prompting sinful behaviours. According to their informants, the idea was to protect the penitents through their invincible ignorance.[133] Yet, Jesuits began to expand the repertoire of knowledge offered to the Japanese regarding sinful actions at roughly the same time that the mendicants arrived. Frequent confessions by Japanese Christians led the priests to produce a number of instructional prints in Japanese as soon as the printing machine arrived in the country, introduced by Valignano in 1590. These included the *Moromoro no Christan xirubeqi giô giô no coto* (1592), the various *Dochiriina Kirishitan* (1591, 1592, and two editions in 1600) and the *Salvator Mundi* (1598), all published in the first decade of the Japan Jesuit printing press.[134] Yet, these materials often omitted certain elements that could be controversial in the Japanese context.[135] Some, like the aforementioned *Salvator Mundi*, had questionnaires on the Ten Commandments and the seven mortal sins designed for use by Japanese assistants in hearing confession from local Christians.[136] Nevertheless, these were products of a new normative order, altered by the entrance of the mendicants in Japan, where varying levels of demand for normative instruction could be found

132 Valenzuela Márquez, "Guilt Discourse and Acculturation", 173–174; Decock, "Azpilcueta", 124–125. See also, Rex Galindo, "Shaping Colonial Behaviours".

133 Alvarez-Taladriz, *Documentos Franciscanos*, 80.

134 Humbertclaude, "Doctrina en dix Articles et Doctrina en onze Articles"; Toyoshima, *Kirishitan to shuppan*, 2–4 (appendix); Orii, "The Dispersion of Jesuit Books". The *Dochiriina Kirishitan* was a translation of Marcos Jorge's *Doctrina Christam*, which was met with wide acceptance (as evidenced by its numerous translations) since its first publication in Latin in 1566. See Cristóvão, "Catequese e Catecismos", 308.

135 Orii, "The Dispersion of Jesuit Books", 199.

136 Collado, *Koryaado Zangeroku*, 627–671; Urushizaki, "Honkoku".

among the members of the Japanese Christian community, from the new convert in the countryside to the novice of the Jesuit school in Nagasaki.

This last group would also be targeted by the production of various pedagogical and pragmatic works, such as the *Dialogue Concerning the Mission of the Japanese Ambassadors to the Roman Curia* (1590),[137] the aforementioned *Compendium* by Gómez and, in the early 17th century, Cerqueira's manuals of sacraments (the *Manuale ad sacramenta administranda* [1605]) and of cases of conscience. While a number of extant copies of his manuals of sacraments exist, the fact that no copies of the manuals of cases of conscience have been located makes it difficult to discern certain specifics, such as the date of its printing and whether it had a questionnaire for confession. Yet, contemporary sources indicate that the book – often referred to in Jesuit catalogues as *Manuale casuum conscientiae* – was printed and translated into Japanese so that it could be used by parish priests in Japan.[138] Years later, Diego Collado (1589–1641), the Dominican who represented the Holy Congregation of the *Propaganda Fide* in its fervent fight against the Jesuit monopoly over Japan, published in Rome the *Niffon no cotōbani yō confesion* or *Modus confitendi et examinandi poenitentem iaponensem* (1632). Despite its quasi-bogus Japanese title, the book contains a long questionnaire for examining the penitent's conscience. It touches on a series of issues, such as the Decalogue, works of mercy and a number of cases specific to Japanese Christianity.[139] Given his extensive efforts in collecting materials from Japan related to the Jesuit mission, it would not be surprising if Collado's book had in fact drawn upon Cerqueira's confession manual.

Yet, while confession served to suppress infractions to the positive precepts of the Church, another representative aspect of the declaration of positive law for Japanese Christianity was the publication of the Christian calendar. Despite earlier efforts, the first critical attempts were made in the 1590s. In his second visitation to Japan, Valignano instructed missionaries to inform Christians of the obligation to observe major holy days of the liturgical year, such as Christmas, Easter, Ascension and Corpus Christi. However, there was still some leeway for the priests to dispense the Japanese from observance of positive

137 Massarella (ed.), *Japanese Travellers in Sixteenth-Century Europe*.

138 Alegambe, *Bibliotheca Scriptorum Societatis Iesu*, 309. Philippe Alegambe's review of De Ribadeneira's catalogue is the first to mention Cerqueira's manual, and seems to be the source for later references, such as Sommervogel's. See Laures, *Kirishitan bunko*, 93; Kataoka, *A Vida e a Acção Pastoral*, 99 and 122; Trigault, *De Christianis Apvd Iaponios Trivmphis*, 269.

139 Pedor, *La S.C. De Propaganda Fide*; Collado, *Koryaado Zangeroku*; Boxer and Cummins, "The Dominican Mission in Japan".

precepts whenever they regarded it as necessary.[140] Franciscans frowned upon the Jesuit stance, noting that there was no official calendar or any admonitions concerning the observance of religious fasts in the mid-1590s.[141] The friars often opted to refrain from declaring any holy days or fasts, but Bautista, superior of the mendicant mission, published in 1595 a Christian calendar for the communities under his guidance.[142]

The dispensation was necessary due to the fact that many lived under unbaptised lords or in non-Christian communities, which often resulted in Christians having to attend local celebrations or follow local labour cycles that did not usually fit well with the calendar of the priests or the friars.[143] Due to that reason, Franciscans were also forced to accept dispensing Christians from holy days whenever circumstances were unfavourable to them.[144] As with most issues of positive law, the solution was given by the agency of Cerqueira. In 1601, the prelate complained that Franciscans were following a different calendar from the one the Jesuits had been using for quite some time.[145] Four years later, Cerqueira published an official calendar in his *Manuale ad sacramenta administranda*. In the book, the Bishop established two calendars for Japanese Christianity: one for the Japanese and a different one for foreigners. While the latter followed the calendar as defined by the Archbishopric of Goa, the locals were to follow a particular table established by Cerqueira in his manual. And even in this special case, the Bishop identified three stages of Christianisation, according to which the calendar to be followed differed.[146] Indeed, calendars were different for local and foreign Christians, highlighting the close relation between positive law and the view missionaries held of the Japanese. Furthermore, the manual also established the Tridentine rules for matrimonies, including the possibility of dispensation as practiced in Angola, Ethiopia, Brazil and India, a right guaranteed by popes Pius V and Gregory XIII.[147]

Eventually, Rome responded to the criticism of the use of ignorance in Japan. In 1609, the Jesuit Curia responded to an accusatory letter sent years earlier

140 ARSI, JapSin 2, fol. 14v.

141 Alvarez-Taladriz, *Documentos Franciscanos*, 211.

142 Alvarez-Taladriz, *Documentos Franciscanos*, 83; Pérez, *Cartas y Relaciones del Japón*, vol. I, 78.

143 These included *corvée* labour for local elites and communal celebrations. López Gay, *La Liturgia en la Misión*, 34–35; Ehalt, "From Tenants to Landlords", 115–117; and Ehalt, "Theology in the Dark", 263–264; Ehalt, "In Their Likeness".

144 Pérez, *Cartas y Relaciones del Japón*, vol. I, 43.

145 ARSI, JapSin 20-I, fol. 108r.

146 López Gay, *La Liturgia en la Misión*, 45–51.

147 Cerqueira, *Manuale ad sacramenta administranda*, 151–157.

from the archipelago which asked for a thorough examination of the doctrines implemented by the Jesuits in Japan. Suspicions were raised concerning the frequent use of dissimulation in the country to prevent *scandalum* (theological scandal) among local Christians.[148] The Jesuit Curia replied that the strategy adopted in Japan had been extensively scrutinised both in the mission and in Rome, furthermore, it was absolutely necessary, particularly in areas where Christianity was still in its developmental stage, as shown in analogous cases decided by ancient papal decrees and their interpretation by theologians and casuists.[149] Effectively, the letter reads:

> To dissimulate with the ignorant in order not to scandalise them and leave them in their ignorance, when they blamelessly ignore, even though what they ignore is an obligation according to any law, is to abide by what the instructions of the holy canons and the scholastic doctors teach.[150]

By then, it was an formal policy of the Jesuit leadership in Rome to leave ignorant people in their ignorance whenever the promulgation of positive law threatened to be detrimental to their situation, be it spiritual or physical. Acting in this manner was an obligation derived from the principle of *correctio raternal*, according to which one should not put another individual at risk of sinning. That approach was framed as acceptable in regard to any legal precept, be it of natural law, divine law, or positive law. Their understanding was that no law could compel an individual to perform futile or idle actions (*actos inútiles o ociosos*). Also, given there was no hope of correcting the actions of others due to their particular environment, one should not enforce any law that would deprive those Christians of the security guaranteed by their good faith (*los sacaría del buen estado y de la buena fé*) without putting them in danger of sin, a course of action supported by the principle of *correctio fraterna*.[151]

---

148 BRAH, 9/2665, fols. 301–332v. Alvarez-Taladriz reads the date of the accusatory letter as 1601, while Josef Franz Schütte reads it as 1607. Neither could be located in known collections. Valignano, *Apologia*, 253; Schütte, *Documentos sobre el Japón*, 72.

149 BRAH, 9/2665, Maço 13, no. 11, fols. 301r–301v.

150 BRAH, 9/2665, Maço 13, no. 11, fol. 301v: "Disimular con los ignorantes por no escandalizarlos y dejarlos estar en su ignorancia, cuando ignoran sin culpa suya, aunque a lo que ignoran los obligue cualquier derecho, es hacer lo que mandan los sagrados cánones y enseñan los doctores escolásticos". Translated by the author.

151 BRAH, 9/2665, Maço 13, no. 11, fols. 301r–307v. On the *correctio fraterna*, see Gründel, "Brüderliche Zurechtweisung".

6 Conclusion

In the story of the implementation of positive law in Japan, the periodisation proposed here can be separated into three different moments, characterized initially by stability through the use of dissimulation regarding certain legal questions which allowed the Jesuits to maintain a certain level of religious normative stability. Even after hearing about the conclusion of the Council of Trent, Jesuits did not seek effective ways to impose legal precepts of the Church onto Japanese Christianity. A concrete shift would be felt only in the 1580s, when the entrance of mendicant orders in Japan threatened the practices established by the Society of Jesus in the country. During this second stage, confronted by the publication of positive precepts of the Church in the country, the general strategy was to maintain the normative status quo by preventing the entrance of Franciscans and responding to growing criticisms by resorting to the doctrine of invincible ignorance. Eventually, with the arrival of the permanent episcopal authority of Luís Cerqueira in 1598, a systematic programme for the publication of positive law in the country was developed by the prelate in close collaboration with the Jesuits in Japan. In this final and third moment, invincible ignorance played a fundamental role in delimiting the areas and communities deemed capable of receiving the precepts.

The change of perspective explored here integrates two topics that have been developed in parallel yet seldom been examined in conjunction: the arrival of the rules of the Council of Trent in Japan, especially those concerning matrimonies, and the conflicts between Jesuits and Franciscans in the country. For the first theme, the starting point has usually been the arrival or reception of the new Tridentine decrees as part of a global effort of universalisation of liturgical and theological norms inside the Catholic world. However, when seen from the perspective of the mission, including its political, financial and social needs and its particular exigencies and internal disputes, the Tridentine decrees cannot be divorced from the broader corpus of ecclesiastical law, that it affected as a council and that underwent significant local scrutiny. Ultimately, this process remains inextricably linked to the political tussle between polities and religious orders, where the positive law of the Catholic Church assumed a central role. The Franciscan and Jesuit tug of war, commonly seen as a political dispute immersed in the complex Luso-Spanish relations of the late 16th century, entailed significant consequences for the normativisation of Christian life for non-European populations given their distinct attitudes towards conversion and the spiritual governing of Christian communities.

Back to the first point, it should be emphasised that the process of global legal change prompted by the Council of Trent has to be analysed in both its macro- and micro-dimensions.[152] Yet, from the perspective of the specific vicissitudes of a mission, if globally it seems that the whole body of the Church struggled to implement the reformation brought about by Trent in all corners of the world, locally it represented a single component within the broader conflict between Jesuits and mendicants in Japan. Although the immediate stakes were relatively regional, the clash took place in various areas of the globe (Nagasaki, Macau, Manila, Goa, Lisbon, Madrid, Rome). Overlooking these nuances in the larger process of legal change of religious normativity in the early modern Iberian world precludes the opportunity to appreciate the various consequences these events had on different levels. After all, the promulgation of positive precepts of the Church in Japan was determined by missionary disputes, political circumstances, regional war, financial difficulties and global processes of legal (counter)reformation.

In this complex scenario, the doctrine of invincible ignorance appears as a unifying element among these multiple historical threads. After all, while traditional periodisation of the Christian mission in Japan is typically defined by the different forms and degrees of relationship that the missionaries established with local authorities – acceptance of Jesuit activities, the persecution of 1587 and the expulsion of 1614, for instance – from a legal historical perspective the identification of the importance of the doctrine of invincible ignorance for the normative history of the Christian missions in early modern Japan offers a distinct approach that highlights the different effects of the arrival of the Franciscans in the country. In the end, the challenge for priests and friars alike lay not in deciding whether the Japanese were ignorant or not – any analogy to the situation in the Americas made the answer self-evident. The point was how Jesuit or Franciscan expectations concerning the morality and the conduct of Japanese Christians determined the ways missionaries navigated and intrumentalised ignorance to their advantage.

Acknowledgements

I would like to thank the generous reading and comments made by Liam Matthew Brockey (Michigan State University) and Ana Isabel Soler (mpilhlt). I am particularly grateful for the insightful exchanges on law and social systems with Filippo Contarini (University of Lausanne). I am also thankful for the comments received during the two conferences at the Max Planck Institute for

152 As it has been clearly demonstrated by more recent works on Trent. See, for instance, François and Soen (eds.), *The Council of Trent*.

Legal History and Legal Theory (2022 and 2023) where earlier versions of this chapter were discussed.

Bibliography

Manuscripts

Archivo de la Província del Santo Rosário, Ávila (APSR), Consultas 2.
Archivo General de Indias, Sevilla (AGI), Filipinas 84.
Archivum Historicum Societatis Iesu (ARSI), Japonica Sinica 2, 3, 6, 7-III, 8-I, 9-I, 9-II, 10, 11, 14-I, 20, 20-I, 27, 33, 51; Congregatio 46.
Biblioteca de la Real Academia de la História, Madrid (BRAH), 9/2665, 9/7236.
Biblioteca do Palácio Nacional da Ajuda, Lisbon (Ajuda), 49-IV-66.
Ōmura City Library, Ōmura, Ōmura Keki, Ōmura-ke Oboegaki, Ōmura Kafu, Ōmura-shi Hankanfu

Printed Sources

Aduarte, Diego de and Domingo González, *Tomo Primero de la Historia de la Provincia del Santo Rosario de Filipinas, Japon, y China, de la sagrada orden de Predicadores*, Zaragoza 1693: Domingo Gascon.
Alegambe, Philippo, *Bibliotheca Scriptorum Societatis Iesu*, Antwerp 1643: Ioannem Meursium.
Alvarez-Taladriz, José Luis, *Documentos Franciscanos de la Cristandad de Japón (1593–1597): San Martin de la Ascensión y Fray Marcelo de Ribadeneira, Relaciones e Informaciones*, Osaka 1973: private edition.
Azpilcueta, Martin de, *Manual de Confessores y Penitentes*, Salamanca 1556: Portonarijs (https://www.salamanca.school/en/index.html).
Cardim, António, *Batalhas da Companhia de Jesus na Provincia do Japão*, Lisbon 1894: Imprensa Nacional.
Cerqueira, Luís, *Manuale ad sacramenta administranda*, Nagasaki 1605: Collegio Japonico Societatis Iesu.
Colin, Francisco, *Labor Evangelica: Ministerios Apostolicos de los Obreros de la Compañia de Jesús*, I, ed. Pastells, Pablo, Barcelona 1900.
Collado, Diego, *Koryaado Zangeroku: Kirishitan jidai nihonjin shinto no nikusei*, ed. Hiroshi, Hino, Tokyo 2016.
Fernandes Pinto, Ana and Silvana Remédio Pires, "The 'resposta que alguns padres do Japão mandaram perguntar': a clash of strategies?", in *Bulletin of Portuguese-Japanese Studies* 10–11 (2005), 9–60.

Fróis, Luís, *Historia de Japam*, 5 vols., ed. Wicki, Josef, Lisbon 1976–1984.

Gómez, Pedro, *Compedium catholicae Veritatis*, 3 vols., Tokyo 1997: Ōzorasha.

Gregorius IX, *Decretales D. Gregorii Papae IX*, Paris 1612.

Hotta, Masaatsu, *Kansei Chōshū Shokafu*, vol. 4, Tokyo 1923: Kokumin Tosho.

Kinsei Nagasaki hōsei shiryōshū 1: Tenshō 8 nen – Kyōhō gannen, ed. Shimizu, Hirokazu, Kisaki Hiromi, Yanagida Mitsuhiro and Ujie Takeshi, Tokyo 2014.

Lucena, Afonso de, *Erinnerungen aus der Christenheit von Ōmura, De Algumas Cousas que Ainda se Alembra o P. Afonso de Lucena que Pertencem à Christandade de Ōmura [1578–1614]*, ed. Schütte, Josef Franz, Rome 1972.

Magnino, Leo, *Pontificia Nipponica: La relazione tra la Santa Sede e il Giappone attraverso i documenti pontifici, Parte Prima (secc. XVI–XVIII)*, Rome 1947: Officium Libri Catholici.

Massarella, Derek (ed.), *Japanese Travellers in Sixteenth-Century Europe: A Dialogue Concerning the Mission of the Japanese Ambassadors to the Roman Curia (1590)*, trans. J.F. Moran, Surrey, UK 2013: Ashgate Publishing.

Matritensi, Francisco, *Bullarium Fratrum Ordinis Minorum Sancti Francisci Strictioris Observantiae Discalceatorum, simulque Sacrarum Congregationum Decissiones spectantes ad Discalceatos*, vol. 1, Madrid 1744: Emmanuelis Fernandez.

Nihon Kirisutokyō rekishi daijiten, Tokyo 1988: Kyōbunkan.

Pérez, Lorenzo, *Cartas y Relaciones del Japón, vol. I: Cartas de San Pedro Bautista*, Madrid 1916: López del Horno.

Pérez, Lorenzo, *Cartas y Relaciones del Japón, vol. II: Informes sobre el modo de proceder de los Franciscanos antes de la persecución de 1596*, Madrid 1920: López del Horno.

Ruiz-de-Medina, Juan, *Documentos del Japón*, 2 vols., Rome 1990–1995: Institutum Historicum Societatis Iesu.

Schütte, Jose Franz, *Documentos sobre el Japón conservados en la Collección "Cortes" de la Real Academia de la Historia*, Madrid 1961: Maestre.

Soto, Domingo de, *De iustitia et iure*, Salamanca 1553: Portonarijs.

Trigault, Nicolas, *De Christianis Apvd Iaponios Trivmphis*, München 1623: R. Sadeler.

Valignano, Alessandro, *Apologia de la Compañia de Jesús em Japón y China*, ed. Alvarez-Taladriz, José Luis, Osaka 1998.

Valignano, Alessandro, *Il Ceremoniali per i Missionari del Giappone*, ed. Schütte, Josef Franz, Rome 1946.

Valignano, Alessandro, *Sumario de las Cosas de Japón (1583), Adiciones del Sumario de Japón (1592)*, ed. Alvarez-Taladriz, José Luis, Tokyo 1954.

Wicki, Josef, *Documenta Indica*, 18 vols., Rome 1948–1988: Institutum Historicum Societatis Iesu.

Zamora, Juan Pobre, *Historia de la Pérdida y Descubrimiento del Galeón "San Felipe"*, ed. Pérez, Jesús Martínez, Ávila 1997.

Literature

Ahn Jung Won, *Kirishitan jidai no kon'in mondai*, Tokyo 2012.

Albani, Benedetta, *Sposarsi nel Nuovo Mondo: Politica, dottrina e pratiche della concessione di dispense matrimoniali tra la Nuova Spagna e la Santa Sede (1585–1670)* (Ph.D. Thesis), Rome 2008–2009.

Albani, Benedetta, Paolo Aranha and Michela Catto (eds.), "Tridentine Marriage in a Global Perspective: Tensions and Adaptations" (special issue), *Rechtsgeschichte – Legal History* 27 (2019).

Alberts, Tara, *Conflict and Conversion: Catholicism in Southeast Asia, 1500–1700*, Oxford 2013.

Alvarez-Taladriz, José Luis, "Opinión de un teólogo de la Compañia de Jesús sobre la pluralidad de Ordenes religiosas em Japón (1593)", in *Tenri Daigaku Gakuhō* 22 (1971), 119–136.

Alvarez-Taladriz, José Luis, "Documentos de 1597 del P. Alejandro Valignano para el Estudio de su Apologia (1598)", in *Sapientia* 10 (1976), 49–67.

Alvarez-Taladriz, José Luis, "Pro y Contra de la Linea de Demarcación Misional en Oriente", in *Ōsaka Gaikokugo Daigaku Gakuhō* 38 (1977), 7–11.

Alvarez-Taladriz, José Luiz, "Notas para la historia de la entrada en Japón de los franciscanos", in Sanchez Gil, Víctor (ed.), *España en Extremo Oriente. Filipinas, China, Japón, presencia franciscana, 1578–1978*, Madrid 1979, 3–32.

Anno Masaki, *Bateren tsuihōrei: 16 seiki no Nichiō taiketsu*, Tokyo 1989.

Asami Masakazu, *Kirishitan jidai no ryōshin mondai: Indo, Nihon, Chūgoku no rinri no ashiato*, Toyko 2022.

Assimakópulos, Anastasía, "Oficios Eclesiásticos (DCH)", *Max Planck Institute for European Legal History Research Paper Series*, no. 2019–23 (https://ssrn.com/abstract=3468252).

Bernabé, Renata Cabral, *Fé e prática entre os Kirishitan: jesuítas, franciscanos e as reações japonesas ao cristianismo* (Ph.D. Thesis), São Paulo 2018.

Bernabé, Renata Cabral, "Los jesuitas contra el método de los franciscanos: el caso de la misión japonesa", in Orii Yoshimi and María Jesús Zamora Calvo (eds.), *Cruces y áncoras: la influencia de Japón y España en un siglo de oro global*, Madrid 2020, 81–103.

Bossy, John, "Moral arithmetic: Seven Sins into Ten Comandments", in Leites, Edmund (ed.), *Conscience and Casuistry in Early Modern Europe*, Cambridge, MA 1998, 214–234.

Boxer, Charles Ralph, *The Christian Century in Japan, 1549–1650*, Berkeley, CA 1951.

Boxer, Charles Ralph and James S. Cummins, "The Dominican Mission in Japan (1602–1622) and Lope de Vega", in *Archivum Fratrum Praedicatorum* 33 (1963), 5–88.

Bragagnolo, Manuela, "Managing Legal Knowledge in Early Modern Times. Martín de Azpilcueta's Manual for Confessors and the Phenomenom of 'Epitomisation'", in Duve, Thomas and Otto Danwerth (eds.), *Knowledge of the Pragmatici. Legal and Moral Theological Literature and the Formation of Early Modern Ibero-America*, Leiden 2020, 187–242.

Bragagnolo, Manuela (ed.), *The Production of Knowledge of Normativity in the Age of the Printing Press. Martín de Azpilcueta's Manual de Confessores from a Global Perspective*, Leiden 2024.

Brockey, Liam Matthew, *Journey to the East: The Jesuit Mission to China, 1579–1724*, Cambridge, MA 2007.

Broggio, Paolo, Charlotte de Castelnau-L'Estoile and Giovanni Pizzorusso (eds.), "Administrer les sacrements en Europe et au Nouveau Monde: la curie romaine et les dubia circa sacramenta" (special issue), in *Mélanges de l'École française de Rome. Italie et Méditerranée* 121:1 (2009).

Busquets Alemany, Anna, "Huellas de Japón en las crónicas misioneras del siglo xvii: la historia de Marcelo de Ribadeneira", in *Mirai. Estudios japones* 1 (2017), 169–180.

Costa, João Paulo Oliveira e, *O Cristianismo no Japão e o Episcopado de D. Luís Cerqueira* (Ph.D. Thesis), Lisbon 1998.

Coutinho Silva, Luisa Stella de Oliveira, "The Janus Face of Normativities in a Global Mirror: Viewing 16th-Century Marriage Practices in Japan from Christian and Japanese Traditions", in Bastias Saavedra, Manuel (ed.), *Norms beyond Empires. Law-Making and Local Normativities in Iberian Asia, 1500–1800*, Leiden 2022, 171–206.

Crewe, Ryan Dominic, *The Mexican Mission: Indigenous Reconstruction and Mendicant Enterprise in New Spain, 1521–1600*, Cambridge, MA 2019.

Cristóvão, Francisco da Silva, "Catequese e Catecismos", in Azevedo, Carlos Moreira (ed.), *Dicionário de História Religiosa de Portugal*, vol. A–C, Lisbon 2000, 302–310.

D'Avray, Daniel L., *Rationalities in History: A Weberian Essay in Comparison*, Cambridge, MA 2010.

Decock, Wim, "From Law to Paradise: Confessional Catholicism and Legal Scholarship", in *Rechtsgeschichte* 18 (2011), 12–34.

Decock, Wim, "Azpilcueta", in Domingo, Rafael and Javier Martínez-Torrón (eds.), *Great Christian Jurists in Spanish History*, Cambridge, MA 2018, 116–133.

Dietterle, Johannes, "Die Summae confessorum (sive de casibus conscientiae): von ihren Anfängen an bis zu Silvester Prierias (unter besonderer Berücksichtigung ihrer Bestimmungen über den Ablaß)", in *Zeitschrift fur Kirchengeschichte* 24 (1903), 353–363.

Díez-Alegría, José Maria, *El desarrollo de la doctrina de la ley natural en Luis de Molina y en los Maestros de la Universidad de Evora de 1565 a 1591*, Barcelona 1951.

Duve, Thomas, "Was ist Multinormativität? Einführende Bemerkungen", in *Rechtsgeschichte – Legal History* 25 (2017), 88–101.

Duve, Thomas, "Legal History as a History of the Translation of Knowledge of Normativity Knowledge", *Max Planck Institute for Legal History and Legal Theory Research Paper Series*, no. 2022-16 (https://ssrn.com/abstract=4229323).

Duve, Thomas, "Legal History as an Observation of Historical Regimes of Normativity", *Max Planck Institute for Legal History and Legal Theory Research Paper Series*, no. 2022-17 (https://ssrn.com/abstract=4229345).

Egío Garcia, José Luis, "Matías De Paz and the Introduction of Thomism in the *Asuntos De Indias*: A Conceptual Revolution", in *Rechtsgeschichte – Legal History* 26 (2018), 236–262.

Egío Garcia, José Luis, "Pragmatic or Heretic? Editing Catechisms in Mexico in the Age of Discoveries and Reformation (1539–1547)", in Duve, Thomas and Otto Danwerth (eds.), *Knowledge of the Pragmatici. Legal and Moral Theological Literature and the Formation of Early Modern Ibero-America*, Leiden 2020, 243–281.

Ehalt, Rômulo da Silva, *Jesuits and the Problem of Slavery in Early Modern Japan* (Ph.D. Thesis), Tokyo 2017.

Ehalt, Rômulo da Silva, "A Difficult Enterprise: Rules for Preaching in Late Sixteenth-Century Japan", in *Bulletin of Portuguese-Japanese Studies* 2:4 (2018), 117–134.

Ehalt, Rômulo da Silva, "Os Japoneses no Pensamento Racial de Alessandro Valignano, SJ (1539–1606)", in Alveal, Carmen Margarida Oliveira et al. (eds.), *Anais VII EIHC*, Mossoró 2018, 665–677.

Ehalt, Rômulo da Silva, "Casuística nos Trópicos: a pragmática teológico-moral de Francisco Rodrigues na Ásia portuguesa (séculos XVI e XVII)", in *Revista de História da Sociedade e da Cultura* 19 (2019), 399–418.

Ehalt, Rômulo da Silva, "Goa no iezusukai shingakusha to nihon no doreika", in *Kirishitan bunka kenkyūkai kaihō* 154 (2019), 1–14.

Ehalt, Rômulo da Silva, "From Tenants to Landlords: Jesuits and Land Ownership in Japan (1552–1614)", in Županov, Ines G. and Hélène Vu Thanh (eds.), *Trade and Finance in Global Missions (16th– 18th centuries)*, Leiden 2021, 97–123.

Ehalt, Rômulo da Silva, "Theology in the Dark: The Missionary Casuistry of Japan Jesuits and Dominicans during the Tokugawa Persecution (1616–1622)", in Bastias Saavedra, Manuel (ed.), *Norms beyond Empire. Law-Making and Local Normativities in Iberian Asia, 1500–1800*, Leiden 2022, 249–284.

Ehalt, Rômulo da Silva, "In Their Likeness: Japanese Misericórdias and the Limits of the Misericórdia in Japan (1553–1633)", in Sá, Isabel dos Guimarães and Lisbeth Rodrigues (eds.), *The Confraternities of Misericórdias and the Portuguese Diasporas in the Early Modern Period*, Leiden 2023, 134–156.

Finnis, John, *Aquinas: Moral, Political, and Legal Theory*, Oxford 1999.

Firpo, Massimo, *Inquisizione Romana e Controriforma: Studi sul Cardinal Morone e il suo Processo d'Eresia*, Bologna 1992.

Firpo, Massimo and Dario Marcatto (eds.), *Il Processo Inquisitoriale del Cardinal Giovanni Morone*, 6 vols., Rome 1981–1995.

Firpo, Massimo and Dario Marcatto (eds.), *Il Processo Inquisitoriale del Cardinal Giovanni Morone*, 3 vols., Vatican 2011–2015.

François, Wim and Violet Soen (eds.), *The Council of Trent: Reform and Controversy in Europe and Beyond (1545–1700)*, 3 vols., Leuven 2018.

Friedrich, Markus, "Government in India and Japan is different from government in Europe," in *Journal of Jesuit Studies* 4:1 (2017), 1–27.

Fujiki Hisashi, *Toyotomi heiwarei to sengoku shakai*, Tokyo 1985.

Fujiki Hisashi, *Zōhyōtachi no senjō: chūsei no yōhei to doreigari*, Tokyo 1995.

Fujitani, James, "Penance in the Jesuit Mission to Japan, 1549–1562", in *Journal of Ecclesiastical History* 67:2 (2016), 306–324.

Geertz, Clifford, *The Interpretation of Cultures*, London 1973.

Gründel, Johannes, "Brüderliche Zurechtweisung II, Theologisch-ethisch", in *Lexikon für Theologie und Kirche*, vol. 2, Freiburg im Breisgau 1958, 716–717.

Gruzinski, Serge, *Les quatre parties du monde: histoire d'une mondialisation*, Paris 2006.

Hartmann, Arnulf, *The Augustinians in Seventeenth Century Japan*, Marylake, ON 1965.

Hespanha, António Manuel, *Como os Juristas Viam o Mundo, 1550–1750: Direitos, estados, coisas, contratos, ações e crimes*, Lisbon 2015.

Hesselink, Reinier H., *The Dream of Christian Nagasaki: World Trade and the Clash of Cultures, 1560–1640*, Jefferson, NC 2016.

Humbertclaude, Pierre, "Doctrina en dix Articles et Doctrina en onze Articles", in *Monumenta Nipponica* 5:1 (1942), 234–243.

Iaccarino, Ubaldo, "Early Spanish Intruders in China: The 1579 Mission of Pedro de Alfaro, O.F.M., Reconsidered", in *Journal of Jesuit Studies* 9:2 (2022), 245–262.

Jann, Adelhelm, *Die katholischen Missionen in Indien, China und Japan: Ihre Organisation und das portugiesische Patronat vom 15. bis ins 18. Jahrhundert*, Paderborn 1915.

Joest, Wilfrid, "Gebot II. Systematisch-Theologisch", *Theologische Realenzyklopädie* 12, Berlin 1984, 130.

Kataoka, Inácia Rumiko, *A Vida e a Acção Pastoral de D. Luís Cerqueira S.J., Bispo do Japão (1598–1614)*, Lisbon 1997.

Kawamura, Shinzō, "Konchirisan no Riyaku no seiritsu haikei to igi: kirishitan no seishin-teki shichū to shite no tokuisei", in *Bulletin of Cultural Research Institute, Aoyama Gakuin Women's Junior College* 9 (2001), 97–125.

Korff, Wilhelm and Wolfram Winger, "Gebot III. Theologisch-ethisch", in *Lexikon für Theologie und Kirche* 4, Freiburg im Breisgau 1960, 327.

Laemers, Jeroen Willem Joseph, *Invincible Ignorance and the Discovery of the Americas: the History of an idea from Scotus to Suárez* (Ph.D. Thesis), Iowa City, IA 2011.

Lage Reis, Pedro, "Alessandro Valignano's attitude towards Jesuit and Franciscan concepts of evangelization in Japan (1587–1597)", in *Bulletin of Portuguese-Japanese Studies* 2 (2001), 79–108.

Laures, Johannes, *Kirishitan bunko: a manual of books and documents on the early Christian missions in Japan: with special reference to the principal libraries in Japan and more particularly to the collection at Sophia University, Tōkyō*, Tokyo 1940.

Lea, Henry Charles, *History of Auricular Confession and Indulgences in the Latin Church*, vol. 2, Philadelphia, PA 1896.

Lopez Gay, Jesús, "Un Documento Inédito del P. G. Vázquez (1549–1604) sobre los Problemas Morales del Japón", in *Monumenta Nipponica* 16:1/2 (1960), 118–160.

Lopez Gay, Jesús, *El Matrimonio de los Japoneses: Problemas y soluciones según un ms. inédito de Gil de la Mata, S.J. (1547–1599)*, Rome 1964.

Lopez Gay, Jesús, *El Catecumenado en la Misión del Japón del S. XVI*, Rome 1966.

Lopez Gay, Jesús, *La Liturgia en la Misión del Japón del Siglo XVI*, Rome 1970.

Lopez Gay, Jesús, "La Consulta 'Ad Modum Synodi' di Nagasaki, 1598", in Henkel, Willi (ed.), *Ecclesiae Memoria: Miscellanea in Onore del R. P. Josef Metzler O.M.I., Prefetto dell'Archivio Segreto Vaticano*, Rome 1991, 251–266.

Lottin, Odon, *Psychologie et Morale aux XIIe et XIIIe Siècles, Tome III, Second Partie I*, Louvain 1949.

Luhmann, Niklas, *Law as a Social System*, trans. Klaus A. Ziegert, Oxford 2004.

Meier-Oeser, Stephan, "Unwissenheit", in *Historisches Wörterbuch der Philosophie*, vol. 11, Basel 2001, 341–348.

Michaud-Quantin, Pierre, "Sommes de casuistique et manuels de confession au Moyen Âge (XII–XVI siecles)", in *Analecta Mediaevalia Namurcensia* 13 (1962), 3–42, 103–106.

Nawata Ward, Haruko, *Women Religious Leaders in Japan's Christian Century, 1549–1650*, London 2009.

Olaza Pallero, Sandro, "Homicidas (DCH)", in *Max Planck Institute for Legal History and Legal Theory Research Paper Series*, no. 2022–07 (https://ssrn.com/abstract=4060941).

Orii Yoshimi, "The Dispersion of Jesuit Books Printed in Japan: Trends in Bibliographical Research and in Intellectual History", in *Journal of Jesuit Studies* 2:2 (2015), 189–207.

Padrón, Ricardo, *The Indies of the Setting Sun: How Early Modern Spain Mapped the Far East as the Transpacific West*, Chicago, IL 2020.

Pedor, Lino, *La S.C. De Propaganda Fide e le Missioni del Giappone, 1622–1838*, Vicenza 1946.

Pizzorusso, Giovanni, *Propaganda Fide I: La congregazione pontifícia e la giurisdizione sulle missioni*, Rome 2022.

Prosperi, Adriano, *Tribunali della coscienza: Inquisitori, confessori, missionari*, Rome 2009.
Rex Galindo, David, "Shaping Colonial Behaviours: Franciscan Missionary Literature and the Implementation of Religious Normative Knowledge in Colonial Mexico (1530s–1640s)", in Duve, Thomas and Otto Danwerth (eds.), *Knowledge of the Pragmatici. Legal and Moral Theological Literature and the Formation of Early Modern Ibero-America*, Leiden 2020, 296–327.
Reynold, Philip L., *How Marriage Became One of the Sacraments*, Cambridge, MA 2016.
Roca, Maria J., "Disimulación", in Otaduy, Javier, Antonio Viana and Joaquín Sedano (eds.), *Diccionario General de Derecho Canónico*, vol. 3, Pamplona 2012, 379–381.
Saramago, José, *A viagem do elefante*, Lisbon 2008.
Saramago, José, *The Elephant's Journey*, trans. Margaret Jull Costa, London 2010.
Schütte, Josef Franz, *Valignanos Missionsgrundsätze für Japan, Erster Band 1573–1582, Erster Teil 1573–1580*, Rome 1951.
Schütte, Josef Franz, "Die Wirksamkeit der Päpste für Japan im ersten Jahrhundert der japanischen Kirchengeschichte (1549–1650): Versuch einer Zusammenfassung", in *Archivum Historiae Pontificiae* 5 (1967), 175–261.
Schütte, Josef Franz, *Introductio ad historiam Societatis Iesu in Japonia 1549–1650*, Rome 1968.
Schwartz, Daniel, *The Political Morality of the Late Scholastics*, Cambridge, MA 2019.
Shimizu Hirokazu, "Fujiwara Arima seifu: Arima Harunobu kenkyū shiryō", in *Kenkyū Kirishitan Gaku* 3:3 (2000), 62–102.
Shimizu Hirokazu, *Shokuhō seiken to kirishitan: Nichiō kōshō no kigen to tenkai*, Tokyo 2001.
Shimizu Yūko, "Hideyoshi ha naze kiristukyō wo kinshi shita no ka?", in Nihonshi Shiryō Kenkyūkai (ed.), *Hideyoshi kenkyū no saizensen: koko made wakatta 'tenkabito' no jitsuroku*, Tokyo 2015, 215–233.
Shimizu Yūko, "Kirishitan kinseishi no kenkyū jōkyō to kadai", in Kawamura, Shinzō (ed.), *Kirishitan rekishi tankyū no genzai to mirai*, Tokyo 2021, 77–100.
Sola, Emilio, *Historia de un Desencuentro: España y Japón, 1580–1614*, Madrid 1999.
Takase Kōichirō, *Kirishitan jidai no bunka to shosō*, Tokyo 2001.
Tang Kaijian, *Setting Off from Macau: Essays on Jesuit History during the Ming and Qing Dynasties*, Leiden 2012.
Tentler, Thomas N., "The Summa for Confessors as an Instrument of Social Control", in Oberman, Heiko A. and Charles Edward Trinkaus (eds.), *The Pursuit of Holiness in Late Medieval and Renaissance Religion: Papers from the University of Michigan conference (20, 21 and 22 April 1972)*, Leiden 1974.
Tierney, Brian, "Vitoria and Suarez on *ius gentium*, natural law, and custom", in Perreau-Saussine, Amanda and James Bernard Murphy (eds.), *The Nature of Customary Law*, Cambridge, MA 2007.

Toste, Marco, “Invincible Ignorance and the Americas: Why and How the Salamancan Theologians Made Use of a Medieval Notion”, in *Rechtsgeschichte – Legal History* 26 (2018), 284–297.

Toyoshima, Masayuki (ed.), *Kirishitan to shuppan*, Tokyo 2013.

Traslosheros, Jorge, “Audiencia Episcopal (DCH)”, in *Max Planck Institute for Legal History and Legal Theory Research Paper Series*, no. 2021–12 (https://ssrn.com/abstract=3869661).

Tronu, Carla, “The Rivalry between the Society of Jesus and Mendicant Orders in Early Modern Nagasaki”, in *Agora: Journal of International Center for Regional Studies* 12 (2015), 25–39.

Tronu, Carla, “The post-Tridentine parish system in the port city of Nagasaki”, in Amsler, Nadine, Andrea Badea, Bernard Heyberger and Christian Windler (eds), *Catholic Missionaries in Early Modern Asia: Patterns of Localization*, London 2020.

Tutino, Stefania, “Jesuit Accommodation, Dissimulation, Mental Reservation”, in Županov, Ines G. (ed.), *The Oxford Handbook of the Jesuits*, Oxford 2017, 216–240.

Tutino, Stefania, *Uncertainty in Post-Reformation Catholicism: A History of Probabilism*, Oxford 2018.

Uçerler, M. Antoni J., *The Samurai and the Cross: The Jesuit Enterprise in Early Modern Japan*, Oxford 2022.

Urushizaki Masato, “Honkoku: Kirishitan-ban no Sarubatoru Munji”, in *Fuji Joshi Daigaku Kokubungaku Zasshi* 97 (2017), 35–52.

Uyttenbroeck, Thomas, *Early Franciscans in Japan*, Himeji 1959.

Valenzuela Márquez, Jaime, “Guilt Discourse and Acculturation in Early Spanish America”, in Muldoon, James (ed.), *The Spiritual Conversion of the Americas*, Gainsville, FL 2004.

Vu Thanh, Hélène, “Principles of Missionary Geography in Jesuit Spirituality and their Implementation in Japan (16th–17th centuries)”, in *Bulletin of Portuguese-Japanese Studies* 18–19 (2009), 175–191.

Vu Thanh, Hélène, “Un évêque tridentin au Japon? Le rôle de Luís Cerqueira dans l’application des réformes du Concile de Trente au sein de la mission japonaise (1549–1614)”, in François, Wim and Violet Soen (eds.), *The Council of Trent: Reform and Controversy in Europe and Beyond* (*1545–1700*), vol. 3: Between Artists and Adventurers, Göttingen 2018, 209–231.

Vu Thanh, Hélène, “Introducing Tridentine Marriage: The Jesuits’ Strategy in Japan (Sixteenth and Seventeenth Centuries)”, in *Rechtsgeschichte – Legal History* 27 (2019), 143–150.

Walser, Markus, “Ignorantia II. Kirchenrechtlich”, in *Lexikon für Theologie und Kirche*, vol. 5, Freiburg im Breisgau 1960, 413.

Walser, Markus, *Die Rechtshandlung im Kanonischen Recht: ihre Gültigkeit und Ungültigkeit gemäss dem Codex Iuris Canonici*, Göttingen 1994.

Watson, Alan, "Legal Change: Sources of Law and Legal Culture", in *University of Pennsylvania Law Review* 131:5 (1983), 1121–1157.

Willeke, Bernward, "Biographical data on early Franciscans in Japan (1582–1640)", in *Archivum Franciscanum Historicum* 83:1–2 (1990), 169–180.

Wirbser, Rouven, "A Law Too Strict? The Cultural Translation of Catholic Marriage in the Jesuit Mission to Japan", in Flüchter, Antje and Rouven Wirbser (eds.), *Translating Catechisms, Translating Cultures: The Expansion of Catholicism in the Early Modern World*, Leiden 2017, 252–284.

Xavier, Ângela Barreto, "Gaspar de Leão e a Recepção do Concílio de Trento no Estado da Índia", in Gouveia, António Camões, David Sampaio Barbosa and José Pedro Paiva (eds.), *O Concílio de Trento em Portugal e nas suas conquistas: olhares novos*, Lisbon 2014, 133–156.

Zaballa Beascoechea, Ana de, "Matrimonio (DCH)", in *Max Planck Institute for European Legal History Research Paper Series*, no. 2018–15 (https://ssrn.com/abstract=3299914).

Zimmermann, Reinhard, *The Law of Obligations: Roman Foundations of the Civilian Tradition*, Oxford 1990.

CHAPTER 4

Negotiating their Lives

Normativity in Widows' Petitions over Inheritance, Properties and Debts in 18th- and 19th-Century Porto, Portugal

Ana Mafalda Pereira Lopes

1 Introduction

In 1793, Dona Josefa Cândida Carvalhais, widow of João de Sequeira Almeida Carvalhais, requested a *Juíz Privativo* for the probate inventory of her father-in-law's estate but her brothers-in-law contested her petition. The widow defended herself at the high court, stating that she "brought a large dowry to this couple, which had saved the house of her deceased husband from total decay and ruin, and this same dowry had also saved her brothers-in-law from indigence and penury".[1] She also affirmed that "during the life of their late brother and after his death, they had found in the house the wealth and support they needed, and it would never be possible if her marriage and her dowry had not entered this house".[2] The widow was aware of the importance of her dowry in saving her husband's family from economic difficulties and in placing its members in a subordinate position relative to her. The dowry she brought to her marriage gave her the possibility to request a private judge for her father-in-law's inventory and supervise the assets left after his death, thereby safeguarding her own children's interests. The decision of the high court was "that the supplicant, both for her good behaviour, as well as for her sex, widowhood and the minority of her children, deserved all the favour and real consideration", not seeing any inconvenience in her request.

Widows were aware of their legal possibilities and were very active in defending their assets. The legal status of widows has been considered an exceptional one because, despite being women, they could become heads of the household

1 Translated by the author. ANTT, Desembargo do Paço, Repartição de Minho e Trás-os-Montes, mç. 1440, no. 31.
2 Translated by the author. ANTT, Desembargo do Paço, Repartição de Minho e Trás-os-Montes, mç. 1440, no. 31.

and were not under male authority.[3] Portuguese studies mainly focus on the agency of widows and acceptance of a widow's action in a patriarchal society. However, if we go further into the analysis of a widow's legal status, what we find is a very complex and ambiguous one, marked by several ideas and changes that legally framed their actions. In fact, the legal status of widows combined several ideas about women's inferiority, honesty and economical position and needs. At the same time, widows needed great autonomy to manage the family's assets or be their children's tutors in the absence of the husband.

Thus, this chapter analyses legal changes in the status of widows and the related normativities. In doing so, it evaluates the impact of these changes on women's lives through the analysis of petitions. I analyse petitions addressed by widows in order to resolve litigation processes over inheritance, property and debts, or to receive royal favours (*mercê* ou *graça*).[4] The aim is to understand how their prerogatives as heads of the household, guardians of their children or administrators of their assets were challenged or limited by the legal changes and normativities related to their status, but also by the way individuals understood their role within the family and society.[5] We will find that widows were very active in using their legal possibilities, as well as the institutions of misery and of the honourable widow, to reach the monarchs' favour, to fight for their interests and to defend their families and themselves from male kin or civil and ecclesiastical authorities who tried to take advantage of women who were seen as weaker or more vulnerable when their husbands died.

Petitions are important sources to access the voices of widows and provide insight not only into their discourses but also into the impact that widowhood had on their daily experiences, the difficulties they faced and the choices they made to circumvent them. Here, I analyse petitions drawn up by the *Desembargo do Paço*, the high Portuguese court, which concentrated on the most serious judicial proceedings; the *Juízo das Justificações Ultramarinas*, the court in charge of inheritance processes; and the *Cortes Gerais e Extraordinárias* (1821–1822), which functioned as an appeal to ordinary justice. The analyses

3 Some works have focused on the agency of Portuguese women and widows, namely Abreu-Ferreira, *Women, Crime, and Forgiveness*, 287–290; Abreu-Ferreira, "Women, law and legal intervention", 293–313; Polónia, "Women's contributions to family", 269–285; Sá, *O Regresso dos Mortos*; Coutinho Silva, *Nem teúdas, nem manteúdas*; Lopes, "Viuvez e Doação de Bens"; Lopes, *As viúvas do Porto*, 52.

4 On these two types of petitions (*queixas* and *súplicas*), see Slemian, *Entre graça e direitos*, 1–38.

5 On familial arrangements, litigations and property regimes in Italy, Germany, Austrian territories, Nordic countries, Western Pyrenees and England, see Lanzinger et al. (eds.), *Negotiations of Gender and Property*.

focus on petitions by widows from Porto, the second largest city in Portugal (circa 50,000 inhabitants in the 18th century) and a seaport connected to the empire, Brazil in particular. I analyse 21 petitions, but the petitionary world of these widows is wider, with over 200 petitions related to family issues, property acquisitions, businesses and pensions.[6] These sources are related to the intermediate and high strata of the population and the elite of the city, but who are still far from the court's aristocracy.

Widows from the city of Porto represented one-third of the people who participated in notarial acts, showing themselves as very active in the management of their properties, inheritance, debts or other issues related to their patrimony. Also, 41% of them were able to sign their deeds, which proves their experience in dealing with daily affairs. The majority of these widows with good literacy levels were widows of merchants and businessmen (29%), followed by widows of soldiers (22%) and widows of noblemen and *Cavaleiros da Ordem de Cristo* (16%). Widows of craft workers also knew how to sign (16%), revealing their importance in running the shop.[7]

This chapter is divided into five parts. First, I analyse the status of women in Portuguese law; second, I demonstrate how widows were perceived by the producers of the law and individuals and how this perception changed over time; third, I study the inheritance system in Portugal and the disputes incited against widows; fourth, I explore their role as guardians of their children; and fifth, I focus on the debts that widows tried to recover and the difficulties they faced during this process. Lastly, the conclusion confirms that widows were aware of their legal possibilities and normativities and that they used them to reach the grace of the monarch.

---

6 On these petitions, see Lopes, *As viúvas do Porto*. Miriam Halpern Pereira also noted that widows asked for pensions in their petitions, but they also managed important estates and commercial enterprises. Widows participated "regularly in petitions seeking to give form to the collective will of the business or commercial world": Pereira, *Negociantes, fabricantes e artesãos*, 12–13, 91. The petitions addressed to the *Comissão da Justiça Civil* were requests for personal interest or complaints against the justice system, as well as petitions not to pay fees, to receive compensation or higher wages, to pay debts in instalments, among other matters: Vieira, *A Justiça civil na transição*, 36. Other widows have asked for pensions or tried to recover their rents: Pinheiro, *Os Portugueses e as finanças*, 24, 79, 85, 147. The study of women's collective petitions in the constitutional period was carried out by Palacios Cerezales, who looked at the petitioning movement from a political point of view and at women's participation as a point of affirmation of their status as "citizens": Palacios Cerezales, "Assinem assinem, que a alma não tem sexo", 740–765. On the petitionary practice in Portugal and its empire in the modern period, see Cruz (ed.), *Petitioning in the Atlantic World*; Slemian, *Entre graça e direitos*, 1–38.

7 Lopes, *As viúvas do Porto*, 91–95.

2 Women in Portuguese Legal History

The *Ordenações Filipinas*, the main Portuguese legal compilation from 1603, ruling in Portugal and in the Empire, stipulated that Portuguese women were under paternal power until they reached the age of 25. Women under this age could also be emancipated through paternal authorisation or marriage, although the emancipation would not be granted by the father's death. In these situations, paternal power would pass to the women's mother or grandparent, guardian or curator through a request to the *Desembargo do Paço*, the high Portuguese court which was responsible for dispatching petitions of grace addressed to the monarch. Women could ask for emancipation if they were at least 18 years old (20 years old for a man).[8]

Also, at the age of 25, women could acquire and hold property, alienate, donate, inherit and manage assets and businesses, make a will, lend money, sue others in court or mortgage their assets. However, Portuguese women were forbidden from performing some public acts, such as being witnesses in wills, but the law did not prohibit them from giving other testimonies.[9] The woman could not yet be a proxy or be present in court without a proxy. Women were also forbidden from holding public offices, such as being judges or performing any magistracy.[10] Finally, the idea of female fragility led to more benevolent laws regarding women's punishment for crimes.[11]

The law granted to women the *Benefício de Veleiano*, a tradition inherited from Roman law, in which they were forbidden to give bail in favour of others, preventing them from debtors' abuse. However, in the modern period, this law was rarely mentioned in the notary records since it became incongruous with the ordinances, which granted women the ability to be guardians or be responsible for legal contracts, thus revealing several women acting as guarantors in the notarial records.[12] The decree of 2 December 1791 stipulated that the merchant's

8 The request should be addressed to the king through the *Desembargo do Paço*, *Ordenações Filipinas*, lib. III, tit. 42, 625–627. They could also request emancipation in specific situations, such as severe aggression from the father; if the father accepted a legacy with the condition of emancipating them; if he forced them to sin; or refused to feed them, that is, when the father did not fulfill his duties as head of the family. Lobão, *Notas de uso prático*, lib. II, 604–610; Teles, *Digesto português*, lib. II, 99.

9 *Ordenações Filipinas*, lib. IV, tit. 81, 908–911. Women could only be witnesses in spoken wills but in 1835, the jurist José Correia Teles also allowed the participation of women in other wills, as long as they could read and write: Teles, *Digesto português*, lib. III, 291.

10 *Ordenações Filipinas*, lib. III, tit. 47, 631–633; lib. V, tit. 124, 1288–1294.

11 *Ordenações Filipinas*, lib. V, tit. 140, § 2, 1318–1319.

12 Abreu-Ferreira, "Women, law and legal intervention", 296–297.

wife could not enjoy the *Benefício de Veleiano* and was obligated to give bail.[13] Also, if they were under the age of 25, women could enjoy the *Benefício de Restituição*, a legal protection that annulled injurious acts or business deals. With the law of 29 March 1814, women of legal age, including widows, were excluded from this benefit, becoming responsible for the patrimonial damages.

Portuguese women could succeed in entailed property and were not totally excluded from succession in the crown estate, even though the 15th-century *Lei Mental* excluded them due to military and judging functions.[14] The *morgado* or *morgadio* was a legal institution that aimed to avoid the division of inheritance, ensuring the transmission and preservation of the family estate to a single successor, usually the eldest son. The *morgado* was also associated with pious obligations to remember their deceased ancestors until eternity.[15] Although male succession was preferred, in practice, preference was given to daughters or granddaughters of the first-born sons over second-born uncles and the second lines of succession, contrary to what happened in England.[16] The nobility and the family name could also be transmitted by paternal and maternal lines, and they could use the coat of arms of both father and mother.[17]

Furthermore, certain advantages were granted to married women. Marriage could be contracted in three ways: communion of goods called *carta de ametade* and two types of dowry contracts (*dote* and *dote e arras*), which functioned as regimes for property and goods division in marriage. These last two contracts were signed before the marriage. This privilege of having their own goods came from Roman law and consisted of an advancement of the *legítima* from the parents to the bride, and the *parafernal* or *extradotal* goods, that is, goods that were left out of the dowry but entered the marriage, which the woman could administer.[18]

Even though the husband was the head of the household, during the marriage they were equal holders of the assets and any patrimonial transaction

---

13 Tomás, *Repertório geral ou índice alfabético das leis extravagantes*, Tomo II, L–Z.

14 On this law, see *Ordenações Filipinas*, lib. II, tit. 35, § 4, 455.

15 The *morgado* was a form of entailment, as were the chapels (*capelas*), associated with pious charges. On the foundation of *morgados and capelas* in Portugal, see Monteiro, *O crepúsculo dos grandes*; Rosa, *Almas Herdeiras*; Rodrigues, "Valorização e exploração", 123–134; Aguiar, *Imagining and organizing kinship*; Nóvoa, *Entailment identity*; Rocha, *Power: Entailment, status, and social mobility*; Rosa, *Privilege, Memory and Perpetuity*. On the role of widows in entailed property, see Coolidge, "'Neither Dumb, Deaf, nor Destitute of Understanding'", 673–693; Backer, *Widowhood in Early Modern Spain*, 153–156.

16 Monteiro, O *crepúsculo dos grandes*, 85. On England, see Erickson, *Property and widowhood*, 145–163; Stretton, *Widows at law*, 193–195.

17 Oliveira, *Privilégios da Nobreza de Fidalguia de Portugal*.

18 Gilissen, *Introdução histórica ao direito*, 601.

required the approval of both spouses. Husbands could not dispose of common property without the consent of their wives, who were required to sign contracts on immovable goods. The husband was not allowed to sell, rent, lease or give away any property without a power of attorney or without the express consent of his wife, whether they were married in a communion of goods or a separate property. In turn, married women could not form contracts or debts, alienate movable or immovable property, sell, mortgage or give away goods without the consent of their husbands, under penalty of the contracts and alienations being considered null. The consent had to be proven by public deed, which gave the woman the opportunity to participate in the management of the couple's common property and to represent herself in notary and judicial institutions. This legal prerogative may have contributed to preparing future widows to face the new responsibilities as heads of the households.

Women could bring actions against their husbands in cases of mismanagement of the assets or dispose of property without the husband's consent in cases of dissipation, absence or mental illness of the husbands. If the husband disposed of property without the consent of his wife, whether for sale, pledge or bail, the contracts would be made null, and the wife would be allowed to revoke these acts. Donations made by the husband of movable property or money without the wife's consent were to be made only with his share of the property.[19] The husband could also not be given bail without the wife's consent, nor could he bind himself to bail on half of the wife's property if they were married by community of property, or on the wife's endowment property if they were married by dowry contract. Husbands could give bail without the wife's consent on movable goods and on immovable goods only on their half of the goods, in the case of Crown rents.[20]

The dowry gave the woman a special status within marriage and constituted an economic security, ensuring some protection to the married woman if she had a dissipating husband or in case of widowhood. As the dowry and other goods passed to the husband's guardianship during the marriage, and it could be mismanaged, there were several laws to protect the married woman's dowry. The dowry helped to protect the family from bad businesses as it separated the survival of the woman from the economic activities of the husband and prevented women from falling into poverty.[21]

The dowry was inalienable and incommunicable with the husband. He could not use the dowry to pay debts incurred before or after the marriage

19 *Ordenações Filipinas*, lib. IV, tit. 64, 867–868, tit. 65, 868–870, tit. 66, 870–871.

20 *Ordenações Filipinas*, lib. IV, tit. 60, 836–837.

21 Sá and Fernandes, "A mulher e a estruturação do património familiar", 101.

unless they were already liable for debts. The wife could also take legal action against her husband or his creditors to secure or recover her dowry. If husband and wife unduly alienated the dowry they could revoke the alienation, but they had to repair the losses of those they had deceived. After the woman's death, the dowry would be inherited by her children, and if she died without children the dowry would pass to her family and not to that of her husband.[22]

Even though these laws tried to protect women's patrimony, sometimes husbands still destroyed their wealth, causing their families to fall into poverty and ruin. There could be several circumstances that led to this situation, from dissipation of goods, incurring debts, bail bonds or even gambling, alcohol or having mistresses. These people who squandered property were considered profligates, and a curator had to be appointed for them. The *Ordenações Filipinas* allowed a married woman to be the curator of her husband's property in case of his incapacity to administer the property for health reasons. She was allowed to become the guardian and administrator of her mentally ill husband or to deal with matters related to their houses, such as leases or sub-letting of bonded property.[23]

The obligation of a woman's consent on immovable goods and the possibility of administering the family assets gave the married woman the opportunity to manage the property in common with her husband and to be represented in notary and judicial institutions, which gave her the capacity for action that she could take advantage of when widowed. As Helena Osswald reminds us, "women enjoyed power and a certain degree of authority if their status was that of wives and widows. This was in part due to the right to inherit and to hold property and manage it, and in part to the place they had in the reproduction and production process".[24] In this way, there is a certain idea of continuity between the status of the married woman and the widow regarding the movement of property, as I will demonstrate. Therefore, the communion of goods was one part of the matrimonial regime that gave a special status to Portuguese women, revealing the importance they had in the economy and government of the households.[25]

---

22 Lobão, *Notas de uso prático*, lib. II, 493; Teles, *Digesto Português*, lib. II, 26–32.

23 *Ordenações Filipinas*, lib. IV, tit. 103, § 6, 1004–1008.

24 Osswald, "Dowry, norms, and household formation", 223.

25 In England, on the contrary, a woman was totally subordinated to her husband during their marriage due to the *coverture law*, since the man and the woman became one legal person. Married women were considered *femes covert*, living under the legal restrictions of their husband and were not able to hold property, litigate or be sued in their own name, nor make contracts or a will without the husband's consent. Unless there was a contract that specified the bride's part, everything that the woman owned could be alienated and dissipated by the husband without the need for the woman's approval. Married women

Finally, in Portugal, the husband's social status directly influenced the woman's social status, as married woman enjoyed their nobility and social privileges. These privileges were important when they became widows since they continued to enjoy their husband's *tenças* or privileges, the social and economic means to live their widowhood.[26]

The legal status of women, influenced by ideas of the inferiority and fragility of the female sex, oscillated between the impediment of exercising certain functions and the attribution of privileges in relation to men. It was economic and political necessity that led to some ideas about the inferiority of women to be set aside, due to their decisive role in matrimonial matters and in the transmission of patrimony, as well as the need to protect them from a future of poverty and dependence. However, everyday situations pushed Portuguese widowed women towards greater participation in public life and in the management of the family and property. Therefore, this chapter pushes forward a different approach to widows' participation in social and economic life in the city of Porto, beyond the rules established in the *Ordenações Filipinas* just analysed. Looking for everyday practices in the sources, I will demonstrate in the next paragraphs how widowhood can also be a status which can lead to an analysis of normativities in the Portuguese society of the 18th and 19th centuries.

3 A Fluid Status: Widowhood and the Changes in the Pombaline Period

The establishment of a widows' legal status was the result of a cultural process and several legal changes. To analyse it, we begin with Thomas Duve's idea that legal history is the result of a production of normativity that comprises the theory and practice of law, cultural assimilations and political and economic changes, as well as everyday experiences. Normative knowledge considers social, religious and legal norms, and implicit or explicit knowledge perceived from theory or from certain events. On the other hand, practice is not only a simple action or the result of these normativities but can also produce a new practice as it can influence and modify actions and transform

only regained their ability to act after the husband's death and, therefore, widowhood represented to English women a release from all restrictions imposed by coverture. Erickson, "Property and widowhood", 145–163; Stretton, "Widows at law", 193–195.

26 The *tenças* are a type of pension that was given in remuneration for royal or municipal services.

habits into traditions.[27] Thus, law was a result of the jurists' work, but, at the same time, it was deeply influenced by ideas that were spread by tradition and individuals.

The status of widows changed according to economic, social and power relations. These changes, that reflect this normativity that was culturally translated, can be observed through written forms, such as petitions. Widows were seen by the *Ordenações Filipinas* in the same way as virgins, who should be protected by law and by the family.[28] The Bible founded the ideal of the poor and miserable widow in Christianity and was concerned with the protection of widows and orphans, who were considered God's protégés.[29] The Judeo-Christian tradition gave rise to the topos of charity towards widows and orphans and defended that family and close kin should provide them with what they needed to survive.[30] Widows were considered miserable, acquiring not only economic but also legal protection.[31] Categorisation as a miserable person conferred a special status on its holder, and the ecclesiastical and civil courts had a duty to protect widows in litigation, due to their fragility and misery. The poverty of widows was not only material but was also a consequence of their gender vulnerability. Although men were also at risk of poverty with widowhood, the category of poor widower was never created.

At the same time, the Church and moralists criticised widows' second marriages and encouraged them to lead a life of chastity, charity and seclusion. The precepts of the Church and, later, of treatises and manuals of conduct, played an important role in spreading the idea that the widow should be virtuous. The honourable widow was the one who lived in seclusion and perpetual

---

27 Duve, "What is global legal history?", 110.

28 On the relationship between virginity and widowhood, see Carlson and Weisl (eds.), *Constructions of Widowhood and Virginity*, 1999; Lopes, *As viúvas do Porto*.

29 *Bíblia Sagrada*, Êxodo (Ex.) 22, 21–23, 137; Deuteronómio (Dt.) 10, 18, 275; Deuteronómio (Dt.) 24, 17–21, 291–292; Deuteronómio (Dt.) 26, 12–13. Cf. also Job (Jb.) 29, 11–13, 822–823 and Primeiro Isaías (Is.) 1, 17–23, 1167–1168.

30 The Bible also defended the practice of *levirato* as a form of support for the widow, which consisted of forcing the brother of her deceased husband to marry her if she was still of childbearing age and had no children. This practice was later banned by the Church (*Bíblia Sagrada*, Génesis (Gn.) 38 and nota 8, 77–79; Deuteronómio (Dt.) 25, nota 5–10, 292–293; Rute (Rt.), 3–4, 381–382; São Mateus (Mt.) 22, nota 24, 1606; São Lucas (Lc.) 20, nota 28, 1715). See Goody, *Família e casamento na Europa*, 58–61.

31 See Hespanha, *Imbecillitas*. In Portugal, widows' pensions appeared in the 18th century, and until then their care was specially provided by the Misericórdias, confraternities or craft guilds: Lopes, *As viúvas do Porto*, *76*. On widows' pensions, see Hellwege (ed.), *A Comparative History of Insurance*.

mourning to safeguard her honour, who used her wealth to practice charity and who helped other widows and the miserable.[32]

In this way, the *Ordenações Filipinas* reflected most of all these ideas of the honourable widow.[33] The *Ordenações Filipinas* protected widows and single women from any kind of sexual enticement, punishing the man who slept with a virgin woman or honest widow against her will. Some of these measures were applied to virgin and widowed women under 25 years old, living under the custody of their father or paternal grandfather.[34] In the 17th century, extravagant laws controlled the interaction between men and women on the street or in other public places, establishing that men could not talk to single women or widows under the age of 50 in churches and that unmarried daughters could not work in inns.[35] The virgin woman was connected to the honest widow in what concerns the need for protection.

These ideas coexisted with notions of female inferiority, emphasizing the figure of the wasteful and lustful widow, in contrast to the honest widow. The former category was associated with women who chose to enter a second marriage.[36] Even though widows were allowed to be heads of the household and administrators of the assets, the *Ordenações Filipinas* stated that a curator could be appointed for them because it was necessary "to overcome the

---

32 Some of these Church priests were Saint Paul (c. 5–67 A.D.), whose teachings were echoed in the works of Saint Ambrose (c. 340–397 A.D.), in *De Viduis*, and the work of Saint Augustine (354–430 A.D.), *De Bono Viduitatis*. Saint Jerome (c. 347–420 A.D.) also prescribed some decent behaviours that should be followed by widows. Also, we should highlight the well-known works of Erasmo (1466–1536), *La viuda cristiana*, and Juan Luis de Vives (1493–1540), *De institutione feminae christianae*. The first studies on widows in Portugal focused on this perspective of the virtuous widow and the criticism of second marriages through analysing treatises and ecclesiastical sources: Fernandes, "Viúvas ideais, viúvas reais", 117–124; Braga, "Notas para o estudo da mulher viúva", 51–86. On this topic in England, Brazil and France, see Todd, "The virtuous widow", 66–83; Beauvalet-Boutouyrie, *Être veuve sous l'Ancien Régime*; Lanza, *From Wives to Widows*; Veiga, *Vida após a morte*, 60–81.

33 Portuguese law was influenced by the *ius commune*, with its great influence of Roman law and Canon Law, but also by national law (*ius patrium*). The *Ordenações* was not always applied, and other practices circumvented these legal provisions through mercies. On the evolution of law, see Gilissen, *Introdução histórica ao direito*; Cabral, *Uma introdução à história do direito comum*. On the evolution of women's juridical status in Portugal and its empire, see Hespanha, "O estatuto jurídico da mulher", 53–64; Coutinho Silva, *Nem teúdas, nem manteúdas*.

34 *Ordenações Filipinas*, lib. V, tit. 16, 1165–1166, tit. 18, 1168–1170, tit. 23, 1172–1174.

35 Tomás, *Repertório geral ou índice alfabético das leis extravagantes*, Tomo II, L–Z.

36 In this chapter, we only look at remarriage from the perspective of its implications on the inheritance transmission. On remarriage and stepfamilies, see Lopes, "The invisibility of Portuguese stepfamilies", 521–545.

weakness of mind of widowed women, who after the death of their husbands squander what they have and become poor and needy".[37] If she was the widow of a nobleman, judge or knight, "for the honour of her husband and his lineage, they should make him known before anything else, so that we can send what is lawful without scandal to his generation".[38]

The *Ordenações Filipinas* tried to control wasteful widows (*viúvas gastadoras*), stating that if the widow maliciously or wrongfully squandered or disposed of her property, the ordinary or orphan's judge had to give the property to whoever administered it, giving the widow the necessary maintenance. The reason for the law to protect widows could either lie in wanting to curb the luxury of widows or in the performance of an obligation to protect widows and the children's inheritance.[39] This legislation proves how their actions were controlled and not dissociated from the belief that women had the inability to govern themselves.

During the so-called *Período Pombalino*, ideas related to the natural law were used to reinforce the power of the monarch, who was considered the father of his subjects. The legislation enacted during this period enriched, but did not replace, the *Ordenações Filipinas* and changed some of the practices about the transmission of inheritance, reinforcing royal intervention in these fields. Influenced by the fact that economy was the main concern of the Marquis of Pombal (1699–1782), the minister during King D. José I's reign (1750–1777), and considering the central role widows had within the family and in the management of property, legislation about widows reflected these concerns as we will see below.

The perception of widows changed from the caste and honoured widow to the merry and joyful widow. During the Pombaline period, legislation sought to alleviate some of the measures imposed on widows' mourning. The *Alvará* of 17 August 1761, referring to the abuses of some families regarding mourning practices, prohibited the isolation and seclusion of widows of upper strata for a year after the death of their husbands. It determined that they could not be locked up in dark chambers deprived of the decent use of their beds or become reclusive in their houses.[40] These measures against abuse in widows' mourning can be read in the light of the great importance that widows began to have

37 Translated by the author. *Ordenações Filipinas*, lib. IV, tit. 107, 1015–1016.

38 Translated by the author. *Ordenações Filipinas*, lib. IV, tit. 107, 1015–1016.

39 *Ordenações Filipinas*, lib. IV, tit. 107, 1015–1016; Lobão, *Notas de uso prático*, lib. II, 618–620. The word lust could refer not only to the inordinate spending of goods but also to erotic activities, but both senses of the word reflected preconceived ideas, namely that of the merry, foolish, dishonest and dissipating widow: Hespanha, *Imbecillitas*, 74–76.

40 *Ordenações Filipinas*, lib. IV, Alvará de 17 agosto de 1761, 1033.

from the political point of view due to their central role in the management of property and family affairs, but also due to a cultural transformation during this period.

In fact, in the second half of the 18th century, there was a shift towards a greater openness to socialising and women's education and a greater closeness between men and women. Widows questioned the obligation to be cloistered and they sought to alleviate the constraints imposed on them. This new attitude had repercussions in the literature, as the image of the cheerful widow began to spread throughout 18th-century comedies and novels.[41] They focused on the involvement of widows with younger gallant men (known as *cicisbeo*) and the idea of fake mourning. Literature considered widows who married as cheerful and lascivious, especially if they were old and unlikely to have children, while future husbands were seen as opportunists.[42] The fact that women were seen as evil may have contributed to the proliferation of this image of the merry widow and the pejorative ideas about her. However, the decision to remarry was mostly related to her age and period of fertility, the existence of children and her social status.[43]

Finally, the post-Pombaline jurists strengthened the widows' role as mothers of the family. Manuel Almeida de Sousa e Lobão (1745–1817) and José Correia Teles (1780–1849) defended their role as tutors.[44] They were probably influenced by the *Ordenações*, which established that since the birth of the child, the mother should breastfeed him until the age of three at least, to create a bond with the child, making the use of wet nurses inadvisable.[45] This obligation extended to all mothers, even those who lived outside the norm, whether they were public women or single mothers. Although the use of wet nurses was common in elite families, noble mothers should likewise not be prevented from breastfeeding their children until the age of three.[46]

---

41 Some of these Portuguese comedies include a theatre play entitled *Academia de casquilhos*; another called *Os peraltas mascarados em Almada* (1790); and another written by Manuel de Figueiredo, entitled *João Fernandes feito homem* (1756): Lopes, *Mulheres, Espaço e Sociabilidade*, 135–137.

42 On this topic, see Lopes, *Mulheres, Espaço e Sociabilidade*, 93–146; Foyster, "Marrying the experienced widow", 108–124.

43 In the same way, stepmothers were seen as evil as well: Lopes, "The invisibility of Portuguese stepfamilies", 521–545; Lopes, *As viúvas do Porto*, 334.

44 Lobão, *Collecção de dissertações juridicas*; Lobão, *Notas de uso prático*, lib. I–III, 1816; Teles, *Digesto português*, lib. II, 1835.

45 *Ordenações Filipinas*, lib. I, tit. 88. On the idea of maternal love, see Hespanha, "Carne de uma só carne", 951–973; Backer, *Widowhood in Early Modern Spain*; Lopes, "The invisibility of Portuguese stepfamilies"; Lopes, *As viúvas do Porto*, 65-70.

46 Oliveira, *Privilégios da Nobreza de Fidalguia de Portugal*, 140.

Lobão also admitted that the mother should exercise power over their children because she should have the same piety, honour, obeisance and reverence as the father. Finally, "while the mother is not remarried, she represents the memory and image of her husband, and continues the old consortium, still being considered one flesh and soul with her husband".[47] The mother had to therefore look after the family, exercising her power over her children, if they lived with her, until she remarried. It was also the widows' responsibility to administer the children's property, except for the children's accrued property, that is, received outside the inheritance or donated to them.[48] As we will see below, widows were very active in the management of their assets and their families and were not just able to use their experience as married women, but also their legal possibilities to circumvent the obstacles of their daily lives.

As I have demonstrated, the legal status of widows was marked by several changes, not only by the obvious one, that is, the change of matrimonial status, but also by changes that were the consequence of the existence of normativities. In the second half of the 18th century, a widow was no longer seen by the legislation as an idyllic, virtuous figure within the family, and started to be increasingly seen as an active member, whose actions could have serious implications for their families' patrimony and well-being. There was a cultural, political and social change towards the opening of women's participation in the domestic sphere, but also in society itself, that led to these juridical changes and that pushed mothers and widowed mothers to have an increasing role in their children's education and upbringing. These normativities ended up strengthening the legal position of widows within the family and annulled harmful laws towards them. We will now evaluate the impact of these

---

47 Translated by the author. The father's right over his children was justified by the fact that they were "of his seed, and a portion of his body", and he should not only feed, but also educate his children in the spiritual and moral, as well civil sense: Lobão, *Notas de uso prático,* lib. II, 71, 76. Children were the extension of their parents and the transmission of acquisitions, debts or insults was allowed, but doing business with each other or for the son to accuse his father in court or kill him was not allowed: *Ordenações Filipinas,* lib. IV, tit. 12, 791–793; Lobão, *Notas de uso prático,* lib. III, 298–339.

48 *Ordenações Filipinas,* lib. IV, tit. 98, 938–985; Teles, *Digesto português,* lib. III, 103–104. The need for parents to educate their children became increasingly evident, either through learning a trade, minor studies or pursuing higher studies, depending on the condition and quality of the family; this obligation was extended to illegitimate children: Lobão, *Collecção de dissertações juridicas,* 450–451. With the Civil Code of 1867 widowed mothers were considered the natural guardians of their children and had the power to appoint a guardian. However, the mother's capacity was seen as inferior to that of her husband and he could appoint whomever he wanted to guide the widow's guardian: Brandão, *Terra, Herança e Família,* 331–338.

changes on women's lives through the analysis of specific court cases related to inheritance, property and debts, expecting to see which strategies they used to succeed.

4 Widows and Normativities: Cases Involving Inheritance and Property Disputes in Porto City, 18th and 19th Centuries

After her husband's death, the widow became head of the household and the administrator of the family assets, acquiring legal autonomy. The widow under 25 years old was not obliged to return to her parents' home, because she had been emancipated through marriage.[49] Under the joint marital regime (*carta de ametade*), the widow was entitled to receive half of the assets of the couple (*meação*), whether they had been acquired before or after marriage.[50] The other half (*legítima*) should be shared equally between the children. The third part of the assets (*terça*) was free to be bequeathed to whomever the husband chose. When a marriage contract was settled, widows regained control over their dowry (parental inheritance) and over the *arras* (dower, the groom's gift). If there were no children, the law did not prevent the widow from being benefited by her husband with the other half of the inheritance, and if there were children, he could also leave her his third, that is, the free and available share that would be taken from the *legítima*, as a way to care for the future of the widow and her children.[51] In the absence of children, the husband could leave his wife as heiress to all the property or nominate her in property succession.

Widows could receive her dowry but also the dower (*arras*), that is, a gift that the groom gave to the bride corresponding to an annuity that she should

---

49 In Florence, the widow had to return to her parents' home along with her dowry due to lineage strategies, a practice known as *tornata* and an important ritual of mourning: Chabot, "Lineage strategies", 132.

50 They had to be married in the Church and to prove that they were living in the same house, in public voice and fame as husband and wife. This means that the consummation of the marriage was fundamental for the widow to enjoy her rights as *meeiros*: *Ordenações Filipinas*, lib. IV, tit. 46, 832–835.

51 If the widow was pregnant when her husband died, she had to wait for the birth to know if the inheritance would be granted after the opening of the will: Lobão, *Notas de uso prático*, lib. III, 368. During pregnancy, the widow could request the preservation of the couple's property and be fed by the deceased's estate, but if there was any doubt about the pregnancy, an examination was to be done by experts. The woman would incur serious punishment if she pretended to be pregnant: Teles, *Digesto português*, lib. II, 103–104.

receive when becoming a widow. This amount could not exceed one-third of the dowry, and if the husband had legitimate children or other descendants, the promise of *arras* could not exceed the value of his third (*terça*).[52] The woman would lose the *arras* if she was convicted of adultery, but not if she remarried, unless there was a contractual clause. If it consisted of property, they could not pass it to the children of the second marriage if there were children from the first marriage.[53] These contracts were fundamental pieces in the transmission of the assets and properties within a family, with direct implications for widows, being one of the first necessary guarantees to ensure economic subsistence in widowhood and one of the complements to the assets she would inherit after her husband's death.

The dowries and dowers of the aristocracy were made up of large sums of money that could bring their houses into debt or impoverish them.[54] It meant a great economic effort by the houses to comply with these obligations towards women. For that reason, in the 18th century, legislation introduced some legal changes into the dowry system. The *Alvará* of 17 August 1761 began by restricting the ostentation of the weddings of families that had at least three *contos* of annual income, prohibiting the presence of people beyond the first degree of kinship and godparents. It also sought to control the large dowries made to their daughters, only permitting an *enxoval* composed of white clothes that could not cost more than 1.6 *contos*.[55] The same law abolished the attribution of the *legítima* to the daughters of the nobility because the practice of dividing the inheritance in equal portions prevented the male heirs from having the necessary means to serve the monarch.[56] A year later, during the reign of Queen D. Maria I (1777–1816), the decree of 17 July 1778 revoked this law maintaining, however, the establishment of the value of dowries and tabulating

---

52 *Ordenações Filipinas*, lib. IV, tit. 47, 835–837.

53 Teles, *Digesto português*, lib. II, 33–35.

54 However, contrary to what some authors have argued, there is no direct relationship between the matrimonial regimes chosen and the social strata to which they belonged, since dowry contracts are found not only in the families of the elite but also in the lower strata. John Gilissen was one of those defending this idea, relating dowry and dower contracts to the elite, and communion of goods contracts to the lower strata, claiming the lower value they attributed to lineage strategies, Gilissen, *Introdução histórica ao direito*, 502. We know, though, that in Portugal this was not the case since the middle strata resorted to making dowry contracts and even contracts of *dote e arras:* Sá and Fernandes, "A mulher e a estruturação do património familiar", 92–115; Faria, "Entre o campo e a cidade", 171–192; Lopes, "The invisibility of Portuguese stepfamilies", 521–545.

55 Monteiro, *O crepúsculo dos grandes*, 103–128.

56 Silva, "A legislação pombalina", 405–410.

the value of jewellery at 8,000 *cruzados*.[57] It was still important to protect the houses of the great from ruin.

The marital status of the widow was, however, considered worthy of "all favour, and compassion".[58] In order to support and feed them during their lifetime, it was practice to give at the time of the marriage, along with the dowry and dower, the *alfinetes*, an allowance that the groom promised his wife not only for her subsistence, but also to maintain her noble condition while she remained a widow, and whose value ranged between 40,000 and 50,000 *réis* per month.[59] The law of 1761 stipulated that the dower should consist of 10% of the annual income from the houses and that the widows should remain in possession of all the couple's property.[60]

The law of 4 February 1765 confirmed and extended the obligation to grant allowances to widows, stipulating that wives whose husbands died before succeeding their parents in their houses should continue to receive their *alfinetes* until they contracted second marriages or until the death of the in-laws, since only then would it be possible to separate 10% of the annual income. It was also established that in cases of succession of two widows, as mother-in-law or daughter-in-law, or widowed sisters-in-law of two brothers, the mother-in-law and the widowed sister-in-law of the first-born son should always be given 10% of the couples' property, if they were alive; and daughters-in-law and widowed sisters-in-law of second or third sons should only be given the maintenance allowances or *alfinetes*.[61] The house could not be harmed with the two-tenths payments on the property, and the need to legislate to prevent these situations shows that some families had doubts about how to proceed when there were two widows in the same family and may have experienced precarious situations.

Petitions reveal that some family members tried to harm the widows' house administration, but I did not find petitions related to the payment of widows' dowers. Portuguese women could found or administer entailed property (*morgados*) as their successors or guardians of their children or due to widowhood, overseeing management of the land, facing lawsuits or making decisions about the property. In Porto, entailed property emerged within the local elites, linked

57 Lopes, *Mulheres, Espaço e Sociabilidade*, 192.

58 *Ordenações Filipinas*, lib. IV, Aditamentos, Alvará de 17 de agosto de 1761, 1033–1034.

59 Monteiro, *O crepúsculo dos grandes*, 110.

60 *Ordenações Filipinas*, Aditamentos, lib. IV, Alvará de 17 de agosto de 1761, 1033.

61 Silva, "A legislação pombalina", 405–414; Monteiro, *O crepúsculo dos grandes*, 103–128.

to the governance of the city, who used this institution to assert their power and social status and consolidate their patrimony.

Dona Ana Casimira de Lima e Melo, widow of Diogo Francisco Leite Pereira, a nobleman, succeeded in the entail that was founded by her parents and sought to benefit her youngest son, Diogo Leite Pereira da Costa Lima e Melo, to be her only successor. In a petition addressed to the *Desembargo do Paço* in 1772, the widow wished to confirm the appointment of her youngest son to be the successor of this entail "not only in return for the filial love and service he had rendered" to her but also because he was "the only one among all his brothers who, sensitive to the obligations of nature, had assisted her in the inseparable troubles of widowhood".[62] The widow also claimed that her youngest son had been harmed by his brothers, who had not conveniently fed him, since the successor son was obliged to provide for the needs of the dependents of the house, to ensure the marriage dowries for his sisters or some career for his brothers.

She finally stated that she had several disputes with her first-born son, who had taken her to a convent "so full of impostures that Your Majesty, being informed of the supplicant's requests, restored to her home and freedom". Thus, the first-born son was not worthy of succeeding her entailed property, even though the *Ordenações Filipinas* law appointed the contrary.[63] The high court considered "that the supplicant was worthy of compassion because [she was] in the miserable state of widowhood" and the youngest son could succeed the entail instead.[64] The argument of the helpless widow had a positive impact on her claims.

Not only did first-born sons make it difficult for their widowed mothers to manage their property, but second-born sons did too. Dona Jerónima Luísa de Magalhães, widow of the nobleman Henrique Carlos Bandeira, asked for a provision to hold the entail that she wrongly ceded to her second son Jerónimo Henrique Freire de Andrade. She succeeded in two entails of her father and, in 1782, petitioned the *Desembargo do Paço* claiming that "ignoring the laws,

---

62 Translated by the author. ANTT, Desembargo do Paço, Repartição do Minho e Trás-os-Montes, Expediente com as Secretarias de Estado e Monarca, Consultas Lavradas, mç. 1434, no. 55.

63 Translated by the author. The law of 3 August 1770 limited the freedom of administrators to appoint a successor to the entail, imposing that the *morgados regulares* should be succeeded and administered only by first-born sons.

64 Translated by the author. ANTT, Desembargo do Paço, Repartição do Minho e Trás-os--Montes, Expediente com as Secretarias de Estado e Monarca, Consultas Lavradas, mç. 1434, no. 55

persuaded by her second son", she transferred one of the entails to him. She claimed that she was insulted by him "with indecent words and actions", and asked for the cancellation of the assignment, and to recover the assets of the bond.[65] Seeing himself in a disadvantageous position in relation to the first-born son, the second son took advantage of his widowed mother to deceive her. Once again, her position as a widow, and the argument of her ignorance and vulnerability, was decisive for the widow to get her property back and for the unity of her household.

The most important change in the legal status of widows was related to remarriage, which was the target of several changes during the so-called *Período Pombalino* due to the impact on patrimonial management. As we have seen, remarriage was a topic of several moral treatises and was revised by the church, which promoted the chastity and the seclusion of widows. The legislation itself did not oppose widows marrying within a year after the death of their husband even though it was not recommended for paternity issues. According to the law, widows who married a year after the death of their husbands should not be penalised or treated as infamous persons. Widows aged over 50 with children or grandchildren could dispose of only one-third of the assets of the first marriage but could administer the maternal and paternal *legítimas*. These older widows were considered too old to marry because they no longer had a reproductive role.[66]

The royal decree of 9 September 1769 was even more restrictive for widows and compelled them to complete a probate inventory. The inventory was mandatory after the death of the husband and had to be completed within two months when minor children were involved, but also before remarriage, to make known the property that existed at the time of the husband's death and thus safeguard the inheritance of his descendants. If the heads of a couple hid assets, they were given the penalty of paying double the amount of the hidden assets on behalf of the orphans, and if any of the parents did not fulfil their obligation to make an inventory, they would be deprived of the succession of

65 Translated by the author. ANTT, Desembargo do Paço, Repartição do Minho e Trás-os-Montes, Expediente com as Secretarias de Estado e Monarca, Consultas Lavradas, mç. 1436, no. 99.

66 The earlier royal French edict of 1560 on second marriages had introduced restrictions on widowed mothers although the edict was later extended to widowers remarrying with children, limiting the amount of property that could be granted to a new spouse. To prevent the goods of a deceased parent from going astray and to protect the children of a previous marriage, the new spouse or his or her relatives could only receive the amount of property and movable goods given to the (step)child of the first marriage who received the least: Warner, "Widows, widowers", 84–107; Lanza, *From Wives to Widows*, 27–39.

their children and the usufruct of their assets. The competence of the *Juíz dos Órfãos* ended when the heirs reached the age of 25. If there were no children, the spouse was not obliged to make the inventory, and if the children were of age, they could request it.[67]

However, the Marquis of Pombal reformed the *Ordenações Filipinas* to address the situation of the widowed mother or grandmother who remarried and imperilled the inheritance of her offspring. This new law also included widowers. Some of Pombal's concerns involved preventing the ruin of economically endangered families and protecting the children from a first marriage. In this law of 9 September 1769 both widower fathers and widow mothers were considered too permissive with their new spouses. The law sought to protect the children from the first marriage from stepfathers who were seen as greedy usurpers of children's inheritance or stepmothers who instigated and generated conflict.[68]

The laws of 1769 were mainly concerned with aristocratic families, and they compelled widows to complete a probate inventory and forbade widows over 50 years old from alienating assets and transmitting them to second husbands. These remarrying widows also lost control of their paternal and maternal shares of inheritance and could dispose of only one-third for their daily living. In addition, a curator would be appointed to administer the property of the children from the first marriage. Another law of 23 November 1770 reaffirmed that even if the widow was only contracted to get married, she would lose the possibility to dispose of her paternal and maternal share.

The laws of 9 September 1769 and 23 November 1770 reveal some differences between remarrying widows and widowers, as the remarrying widows were deprived of using the maternal and paternal shares of the inheritance, while widowers were not.[69] In the *Ordenações Filipinas*, widows had the right to administer the maternal and paternal *legítimas*, but the 18th-century reforms removed this financial management and thus reinforced the protection of their children's share from the stepfathers. Both the 1769 and 1770 laws were revoked in 1778 during the reign of Queen D. Maria I, and widows regained their right to receive the paternal *legítimas* while their children were underage. One explanation for this change could be the fact that these laws were too restrictive and did not allow the mother to be able to raise her children on a

67 On Portuguese widows' inventories, see Matos and Lopes, "Property ownership by widows", 203–222.

68 *Ordenações Filipinas*, lib. IV, tit. 105, 1011–1014; lib. IV, Aditamentos, Lei 9 de setembro de 1769, § 27 and 29, 1040–1041.

69 *Ordenações Filipinas*, lib. IV, Aditamentos, Lei de 23 de novembro de 1770, 1062.

small share of the property of the marital household. The *Ordenações Filipinas* was reinstated. Portuguese laws concerning remarrying fathers and mothers changed three times, in 1769, 1770 and 1778, hardening the position toward widows and widowers until D. Maria I's intervention.[70]

In Porto, there is evidence of stepfathers' dilapidations after the 1800s. In 1804, a few months before she died, Teresa Margarida de Oliveira made a petition because she wanted to use her dowry to pay debts contracted by her second husband Francisco Alves de Sousa Guimarães. She wanted to take two urban properties out of her dowry and to convert them into allodial assets. The children of the first marriage, all minors, and their curator were heard at court, and claimed that "their stepfather was the driving force behind their mother's claim because he not only absorbed all the capital entrusted to him by their mother but was also destroying their inheritance". The stepchildren considered their stepfather's administration "disgraceful and bad", resulting in several debts that their mother wanted to relieve by using her dowry.[71] Teresa's petition was refused.

In 1816, Henrique da Silva da Fonseca, a nobleman, sued his stepfather at the *Desembargo do Paço* accusing him of managing the house as if he wanted its entire dilapidation and claiming that he was "forgetful of the duties of a good family father". He claimed that his stepfather was "a second son deprived of property" and that he "only cared about enjoying himself, forcing his wife to sign several donations, which she had done out of fear and little resolution".[72] His stepfather sold real estate, had transformed entailed assets into allodial ones and did not make the annual payment to his stepdaughters' *recolhimentos*. Henrique petitioned the court to have another administrator assigned to his household and the court's decision was favourable to him. His 48-year-old mother was not able to protect the assets of her first-born children. Despite a Portuguese wife's legal capacities or the safeguards of the *Juíz dos Órfãos*, some stepfathers could be very damaging to stepchildren and their financial interests.

Obstacles to widows' administration seem to arise if they had good wealth or a prominent social position. In 1819, Dona Quitéria de Mesquita Gouveia,

70 On Portuguese widows' remarriage, see Lopes, "The invisibility of Portuguese stepfamilies", 521–545.

71 Translated by the author. ANTT, Desembargo do Paço, Repartição de Minho e Trás-os-Montes, Expediente com as Secretarias de Estado e Monarca, Consultas Lavradas, mç. 1442, no. 47.

72 Translated by the author. ANTT, Desembargo do Paço, Repartição de Minho e Trás-os-Montes, Expediente com as Secretarias de Estado e Monarca, Consultas Lavradas, mç. 1445 [not numbered].

five years after her husband's death, found herself involved in a lawsuit initiated by her own brother. Her husband, João José de Abreu e Silva, was a judge of crime (*desembargador corregedor do crime*) in Relação do Porto. In a petition addressed to *the Desembargo do Paço*, she reported that her brother started a lawsuit against her in which he upheld that she donated assets to his wife. She complained that her brother had appealed to his own father-in-law, the new judge of crime, and other influential people, to take legal action and set up a real plot against her, which ended up with an order of arrest of the widow. Dona Quitéria thus denounced the "scandalous violence of issuing an arrest warrant" and asked, "not to be imprisoned in a public jail, but in her home, because she was a widow, who enjoyed the privileges of her deceased husband, a judge".[73]

In this way, she managed to have the arrest declared null for lack of evidence, but claimed that she was "vexed, and publicly insulted by such violence and injustice repugnant to the law and to all the rules of jurisprudence". She complained "full of pain and sorrow" that this was "the result of the arrogance and pride of her brother's father-in-law" and of "his partial friends and companions in abuse of the sacred authority entrusted to them by Your Majesty".[74] The high court believed the widow had already been released from prison and that the case would be closed. The widow tried to use her social status and the privileges acquired upon her husband's death to avoid imprisonment and protect herself in court from the plot hatched by her own brother.

Widows' administration was also harmed by neighbours, and by the ecclesiastical and civil authorities from the city of Porto. Widows were legally autonomous in managing property and were granted property rights that often had been jeopardised by men. In 1774, the widow Teresa Angélica de Jesus stated that her husband José da Conceição Pereira had bought a farm and that he made an agreement with his neighbour regarding the passage of water between their properties. When he died, realising that the widow intended to continue with the work, the defendant retracted the contract and began some proceedings to

73 Translated by the author. ANTT, Desembargo do Paço, Repartição do Minho e Trás-os-Montes, Expediente com as Secretarias de Estado e Monarca, Consultas Lavradas, mç. 1445 [not numbered]. The widows of magistrates (*desembargadores*) had certain privileges, such as being able to choose the *Juízo das Ações Novas* or the ordinary from their domicile, whether as plaintiff or defendant. *Ordenações Filipinas*, lib. III, tit., § 3, 566–567; Lobão, *Collecção de dissertações*, lib. II, 665–670.

74 Translated by the author. ANTT, Desembargo do Paço, Repartição do Minho e Trás-os-Montes, Expediente com as Secretarias de Estado e Monarca, Consultas Lavradas, mç. 1445 [not numbered].

"vex the widow petitioner, who had a clear right to the property".[75] The *Desembargo do Paço* was of the opinion that she had five minor children and that the work she wanted to lead would not damage the neighbour's building, so she won the dispute. The neighbour tried to take advantage of the fact that, after her husband's death, the widow was alone and without her husband's authority in order to retract the agreement, which would end up harming her access to water.

Widows also experienced obstacles to their intentions to increase their property or to be compensated in the event of land expropriation. In 1805, Dona Brites Maria Felizarda de Castro, widow of Luís de Almeida de Morais, intended to increase the property of her palace. However, her claim was rejected by a judge who did not allow the land to be awarded to her, performing "manifest violence, worthy of reparation". She declared that he knew that her palace was "the most beautiful, and the worthiest of contemplation" and that it was necessary to acquire this property "in order to avoid great deformity".[76] Addressing the petition to the *Desembargo do Paço*, and appealing to the fact that she was a respected widow, she ended up getting the land.

In 1782, the widow Luísa Maria felt aggrieved at the amount she was paid after an expropriation process, claiming to have been defrauded by the religious people of the convent of São Domingos, who wanted to retain a large part of the money from the sale of the houses. The local court (*Relação do Porto*) decided to give almost all the money from the properties to the priests, leaving Luísa with a small amount which was not enough to compensate her for the money invested, the taxes and the costs of the rebuilding, so she asked for the case to be reviewed by the *Desembargo do Paço*. The high court recognised that the widow was harmed ("irreparável prejuízo") and that she was "a helpless widow, who should enjoy the protection of Your Majesty's laws".[77] This statement shows how the canonical ideal of the helpless widow echoed into judicial institutions. However, the court stated that the problem was the priests' abuse and that the law and the compensation was given to the owners, and for that reason they could do nothing in this matter.

---

75 Translated by the author. ANTT, Desembargo do Paço, Repartição do Minho e Trás-os-Montes, Expediente com as Secretarias de Estado e Monarca, Consultas Lavradas, mç. 1434, no. 76.

76 Translated by the author. ANTT, Desembargo do Paço, Repartição do Minho e Trás-os-Montes, Expediente com as Secretarias de Estado e Monarca, Consultas Lavradas, mç. 1442, no. 105.

77 Translated by the author. ANTT, Desembargo do Paço, Repartição do Minho e Trás-os-Montes, Expediente com as Secretarias de Estado e Monarca, Consultas Lavradas, mç. 1438, no. 24.

Lastly, the priests had great influence over widows and could take advantage of their old age and religiosity to defraud them. In 1772, the widow Rosa Teresa de Jesus complained that she had been betrayed by the Franciscan friar Luís de Santa Ana Porto, who, taking advantage of her good faith and age, took up residence in her house to extort a large part of her fortune. Living in the company of the widow's niece, "with great honour and praiseworthy conduct", the friar "had deflowered her". This concubinage lasted for seven years, leading the niece to hand over all the money, pieces of gold and silver and public debt instruments that the widow possessed, without her realising it. The amount extorted exceeded three *contos*. These facts had "prostrated the good reputation of the supplicant in such a terrible state" and the widow asked the monarch to have the friar arrested to be punished.[78]

These daily experiences, visible through the petitions, show that some male family members, neighbours and civil or religious authorities tried to take advantage of those widows who had some economic and social power. However, they also reveal the importance attached to the identity of widows, all of them evoking in their discourses the fact that they were vulnerable and honest widows, sometimes ignorant of the laws, as a means to have their requests granted. In fact, even though there were several law changes towards a greater accountability of widows' attitudes, in practice the deep-rooted tradition of the poor, miserable and helpless widow prevailed compared to the image of the reckless widow of the *Período Pombalino*. The main difference in widows' discourses is whether they were remarried or not, as remarried widows tended to be blamed for allowing the squandering of their children's assets, although the interveners were aware that they might have felt afraid or acted out of obedience to their husbands. On the other hand, the lonely widows were seen as deserving of all compassion, whether they lived alone or with children.

The decision-makers ended up favouring them, mainly due to the existing canonical conceptions of widowhood. The fact that petitions tended to be favourable to them when they evoked their widowhood, fragility or the existence of minor children clearly shows that normativities influenced the ways that widows petitioned. Also, they used the word "violence" to emphasise the

---

78 Translated by the author. ANTT, Desembargo do Paço, Repartição do Minho e Trás-os-Montes, Expediente com as Secretarias de Estado e Monarca, Consultas Lavradas, mç. 1434, no. 56. In Mexico, "los frailes de las órdenes presentes en la Nueva España se tornaron exigentes, arrogantes y maltratadores. Sus primeras víctimas fueron, como muestran los documentos, las mujeres solas y los niños sin padres": Gonzalbo Aizpuru, "La milpa por paisaje", 295. On other petitions of women and widows, in particular, in Spain and Latin America, see García González, *Vivir en soledad*; Ghirardi and Celton, *Las viudas de Córdoba*, 347–370.

fact that it was against the norm to harm or hurt widows since, by tradition, they should always be the target of compassion. It can also be expected that other widows were aware of the great influence of these types of discourse in obtaining a favourable response, and that they had repeatedly used them in litigations related to inheritance, property and family conflicts in order to win lawsuits. These normativities, translated into the petitionary practice, relativise the power of written laws, as typical of this period. Normativities were also important in placing women as the guardians of their children, as the law did not grant them this prerogative unless it was stated in their husbands' last wills. We will next see how the active role women played within the family was crucial to circumventing this legal limitation.

5 Guardianship of the Children

Guardianship of children was not immediately granted after the father's death and depended on his will. As a rule, husbands usually chose their wives as the guardians of their minor children, considering them the most capable persons to administer their property and keep it in the family. Guardianship of children could be testamentary, conferred by the father, mother or grandfather of the orphan in a will; legitimate, determined by law, and usually given to uncles, brothers or grandfathers; or donative, that is, a suitable person with assets and quality (dative guardian) should be appointed by the *Juíz dos Orfãos*.[79] When the custody of the children was given to the widow, she assumed the responsibility that the father had previously assumed as *pater familias* and had the privilege of holding the guardianship of their children until they turned 25.

The mother could apply to the court to become the guardian of her children. In fact, if she had not been named in her husband's will, or if the previously appointed guardians had been mismanaged, the widow could petition, presenting a justification stating that she lived honestly and had the capacity to manage the property, providing security over the *legítima*. The request would then be analysed by the *Desembargo do Paço* and granted by the monarch. According to the *Ordenações Filipinas*, "women are in general excluded, except the mother and grandmothers, because the law presumes that the affection they have for the children, and the grandchildren, would make up for any lack of capacity".[80] In turn, the widow would not have any interest in inheriting what belonged to her children and thus did not represent a risk for the orphan.

79 *Ordenações Filipinas*, lib. IV, tit. 102, 994–1004. On this topic, see Lopes, *As viúvas do Porto*, 65-70.

80 Translated by the author. *Ordenações Filipinas*, lib. IV, tit. 102, 994–1004.

In 1791, Rita Joana Rosa e Silva, widow of Manuel Ferreira da Silva Guimarães, became the guardian of two daughters by the provision of the *Desembargo do Paço*, stating that she wished to be guardian and administrator "of their persons and property to raise and teach them and educate them", and it was declared that an inventory should be made and the *legítima* handed over by her under bail.[81] In 1815, Ana Margarida, widow of Manuel Coelho da Silva, stated in her request for guardianship that "she has a great love for the said girl, her daughter, and wishes to be her guardian and administrator, and lives with great honour, procedure and honesty". The guardianship was conceded to her, stating to the court that the *legítima* and property should be given to the widow under bail, "until she marries, obliging herself first to indoctrinate, and feed herself with everything necessary at her own expense".[82]

The mother also had the legal prerogative to refuse the guardianship and it could also not be given to her if she was under 21 years old or from another religion. Some widows made use of the privileges granted by law and excused themselves from the responsibility of being guardians of their children. Alternatively, uncles assumed the task, especially secular-religious uncles who, according to the *Ordenações*, were not prevented from exercising guardianship, unlike the professed religious. However, the authorities favoured non-ecclesiastical relatives, possibly because they had more time for the orphan, and whenever possible they sought to ascertain whether there was another relative capable of acting as guardian. In 1784, Custódio Barbosa Carneiro, a secular cleric and lawyer, asked to take over the guardianship of two nephews. He stated that his brother-in-law Manuel José Monteiro de Lemos had died without a will, and "because the mother of these, Dona Maria Josefa de Barbosa, did not want to be guardian, nor was there any secular relative of the said orphans in that district who could accept the guardianship, and the petitioner, their uncle, did not doubt to exercise it".[83] He stated that, although he was not well-off in terms of property, "he was an honest person, and skilful for the good of his nephews" and could provide a guarantor if necessary. The guardianship was granted to him.

In 1787, Margarida Feliciana Teixeira de Magalhães e Lacerda, the widow of Manuel Cardoso de Mendonça Figueira, a nobleman, with a daughter under the age of five, was obliged to appoint a guardian to administer her property.

---

81 Translated by the author. ANTT, Juízo das Justificações Ultramarinas, África, mç. 30, no. 5.

82 Translated by the author. ANTT, Juízo das Justificações Ultramarinas, Brasil, mç. 19, no. 3.

83 Translated by the author. ANTT, Desembargo do Paço, Repartição do Minho e Trás-os-Montes, Expediente com as Secretarias de Estado e Monarca, Consultas Lavradas, mç. 1437, no. 47.

She claimed that, of all her husband's relatives, her brother José Cardoso de Mendonça Figueira de Azevedo, abbot of Sanfins, was most capable "because he knew all the affairs of the house", but also because she believed that this would have been the will of her late husband.[84] The latter had three other brothers, two of whom were ecclesiastics, and another served as steward. The guardianship was granted since, although he had a secular brother-in-law, he was unable to take over the guardianship of the orphaned child because of his professional duties.

In 1775, another priest, José da Costa Pereira, brother of Teresa de Jesus, widow of Manuel Borges Campos, a captain, asked to become the guardian of his orphaned nephews. The minor children of his late sister were in his company and he "had always administered them" since their father's death. As he had no other relative who could be their guardian, and as he "was a priest of good life and manners and wished to educate the said nephews well with all diligence, and they were the ones who were to succeed the petitioner as heirs", the request was granted to him.[85]

Finally, if widows remarried, they would lose the guardianship and the prerogative to manage the assets of their children from their first marriage. Even if the stepfather died, a widowed mother could never recover the guardianship of her children. Stepfathers, on the other hand, were considered enemies of the orphan and were not allowed to be guardians, while stepmothers, since they were under the husband's administration, did not represent any real danger and were not, therefore, considered enemies.[86]

In 1765, Pedro da Costa Ferreira de Almeida e Bessa, a priest, brother of Dona Doroteia Angélica de Almeida, a second-time widow, asked to be the guardian of a niece from the second marriage of his sister, having already been the guardian of two other children from his sister's first marriage. He stated that, when his brother-in-law died, he left two minor children, and his sister was their guardian. However, her guardianship ended when she decided to get married again. When her second husband died, she was left with a daughter under two years of age, and as he was "the closest relative, with the most respect and comfort, to support the said orphans, both from the first and second marriages, to administer

84 Translated by the author. ANTT, Desembargo do Paço, Repartição do Minho e Trás-os-Montes, Expediente com as Secretarias de Estado e Monarca, Consultas Lavradas, mç. 1438, no. 57.

85 Translated by the author. ANTT, Desembargo do Paço, Repartição do Minho e Trás-os-Montes, Expediente com as Secretarias de Estado e Monarca, Consultas Lavradas, mç. 1434, no. 86.

86 Lopes, "The invisibility of Portuguese stepfamilies", 521–545; Lopes, *As viúvas do Porto*, 101–103, 334.

them well and govern their property and the orphans themselves", he asked for royal provision. With no other relative with his "capacity and understanding", the guardianship was accepted, and he was obliged to give bail to hand over the orphans' *legítimas* until they got married or became emancipated.[87]

As we can see, the guardianship was not granted to the mother right after the death of the husband and depended on his last will. Although he often chose his wife to be the children's guardians, sometimes the suddenness of his death did not allow him to stipulate it through the last will and the mothers were led to ask for provision. The central role women had in the management of the household and in the upbringing and education of the children was certainly important to concede the guardianship to the mothers when they asked for it. Once again, normativities were important to influence court decisions and to circumvent the general prohibition of conceding the guardianship to women. Nevertheless, the choice to remarry or, on the other hand, the influence exerted by male relatives on the house affairs, sometimes deprived them of being the children's guardians, and their ecclesiastical brothers or brothers-in-law were considered by the court as the most suitable family members to hold guardianship in the absence of the widowed mothers.

6 Debt Litigations in Widow's Petitions

A person inherits not only property, privileges or shares, but also debts. These could include the costs of illness, medicines and surgeons, and funeral expenses, which had to be paid out of the couple's estate if they were married by the communion of goods, after which the inheritance could be divided. Legislation protected both the widow's *meação* and/or dowry from the payment of debts, as they were guarantors of the woman's economic survival.[88] Thus, if one of them had debts when they were married, the other spouse would not be obliged to pay them, nor should these be paid from the goods brought into the marriage. The execution of the debts should be made only on the goods of the debtor spouse and on his/her half of the goods acquired after they were

87 Translated by the author. ANTT, Desembargo do Paço, Repartição do Minho e Trás-os-Montes, Expediente com as Secretarias de Estado e Monarca, Consultas Lavradas, mç. 1433, no. 25.

88 In Minas Gerais, at the end of the 18th century, the sale of husbands' *meação* to women to avoid the division of property or to help the widow to pay off debts to creditors was a practice that left these women in a better position to guarantee the well-being of their family and the unit of their assets: Dantas, "Succession of Property", 222–238; Dantas, "Mulheres e Mães Negras", 100–101.

married.[89] However, debts incurred during the marriage had to be paid from the couple's assets. João José de Abreu e Silva, married to Dona Quitéria de Mesquita Gouveia e Castro by dowry contract, stated that debts contracted during the marriage should come out of the couple's assets, but the debts contracted before he married should be paid by his own estate, protecting his wife from paying debts that did not belong to her.[90]

Sometimes widows might not have enough liquidity to pay the debts and were forced to sell properties or to work to make ends meet.[91] Due to the negative consequences that debts could have for the deceased heirs, the legislation provided the *Benefício do Inventário*, that is, the heirs could accept their share of the inheritance after the inventory was made in order to see if the inventoried assets were enough for the payment of the debts.[92] The heirs could also refuse the entire inheritance, preventing themselves from being burdened with debts that exceeded the value of the *meação* or the *legítima*.

In 1776, Maria Gertrudes Pereira de Faria, widow of António da Costa, a sailor, requested in her habilitation process, together with her three minor children, to be his heir using this legal benefit, protecting herself from possible debts. The fact that her husband had emigrated to Luanda may have increased the widow's mistrust in receiving this inheritance. The widow stated that she did not make an inventory in the *Juíz dos Órfãos* after her husband's death because she "had no assets, and she was poor, and had only given guardianship to her minor children".[93] Another widow, Ana Rita de Meneses e Silva, also accepted the inheritance of her brother-in-law, António de Sousa Teles de Meneses, a captain who had died in the empire, using the *Benefício do Inventário* to protect herself from possible debts.[94]

89 *Ordenações Filipinas*, lib. IV, tit. 95, 949–954; Lobão, *Collecção de dissertações*, 447 e 467–470.

90 AHMP, Registo Geral de Testamentos, lib. 2279, fols. 27–32.

91 In Portuguese America, some widows became poor not only because of their husbands' debts, but also due to bureaucratic delays in the distribution of the inheritance. In Rio de Janeiro, widows' inventories revealed that, after deducting creditors' debts and expenses that arose after the husband's death, there was a loss of accumulated wealth, with the final amount representing on average of 86% of the total (*monte-mor*), an amount that would then be divided between the heirs and the widow: Russell-Wood, "Women and society", 22–26; Freitas and Alencar, "'Dona', viúva e 'cabeça de casal'", 92–94; Dantas, "Mulheres e Mães Negras", 88–104; Veiga, *Vida após a morte*.

92 Lobão, *Notas de uso prático*, lib. III, 361–369; Teles, *Digesto português*, lib. II, 163–166. The *Benefício do Inventário* was not included in the *Ordenações Filipinas*, but it was included in Roman law and was common practice.

93 Translated by the author. ANTT, Juízo das Justificações Ultramarinas, África, mç. 25, no. 2.

94 ANTT, Juízo das Justificações Ultramarinas, Brasil, mç. 30, no. 6.

Public traders could not enjoy this benefit since, being legally responsible for the business management, they were to be held liable for the contracted debts. Even if they were bankrupt, they could not avoid their liability because otherwise the tax authorities and creditors would be harmed. The widows of artisans, merchants or businessmen were therefore responsible for settling outstanding accounts and paying the debts that remained from the business. However, as the investment was always subject to risk, the couple had to find other solutions for not losing their assets.[95] In 1822, Dona Maria Margarida Máxima de Sousa Monteiro, widow of Joaquim José de Sousa Pires, a merchant, was sued after her husband's death for allegedly having transferred the couple's assets to her dowry to protect their property from her husband's creditors. She stated that to prevent the couple "from going into decay due to the misfortunes of their trade", she was obliged to pledge the couple's property, some of which was set aside to pay creditors and others of which were awarded to the dowry. After her husband's death, she was sentenced to pay a tax over this transaction, but she alleged that there was no sale between the couple because these goods were already part of the couple's assets.

She denounced to the *Comissão da Justiça Civil* explaining that such a sentence was engineered by a financial solicitor (*solicitador da fazenda*), who had oppressed her on other occasions too. She defended herself by stating that this practice was common among other merchants and, therefore, she denounced that such "execution is machinated by the financial solicitor". However, the request was rejected on the grounds that the couple tried to circumvent the law by "providing themselves with privileges to avoid paying the creditors".[96] In 1829, she declared in her last will that, due to her husband's death, she did not make an inventory, "but for myself, as the administrator of my children, I signed a term of abstention from the inheritance, and therefore what I possess is my dowry, in which I preserved my possession".[97] When dealing with large debts, she tried to avoid paying them by signing a deed of abstention from the inheritance since she could not use the *Benefício do Inventário*. Her will also revealed the existence of several debts, which she asked her heirs to settle, transmitting to them only her dowry.

Husbands also relied on their wives to collect debts owed to him, although this could be a difficult task as debtors could try to evade payment, or because the debts were often scattered throughout the empire. In cases where widows felt aggrieved by their husband's debts, which could range from 30 to 100

95 Lobão, *Notas de uso prático*, lib. III, 361–369; Teles, *Digesto português*, lib II, 163–166.
96 Translated by the author. AHP, Comissão de Justiça Civil, Secção I/II, box 61, mç. 35, no. 31.
97 Translated by the author. AHMP, Registo Geral de Testamentos, lib. 2267, fols. 218–219.

contos, they could petition to delay payment. In 1808, Ana Raimunda da Trindade continued the process of her husband João António Pinheiro, a businessman, in which he asked for a delay in paying some debts he had contracted. Her husband had requested a moratorium from his creditors to delay the payment and declared "with sorrow, he has suffered stagnation in his wholesale trade, by extraordinary circumstances lived in this kingdom, in Brazil, and in foreign squares", seeing himself unable to make prompt payment to creditors "with the good faith, and honour with which he used to".[98] He declared that he had more than 307 *contos* in funds and interests and that after paying what he owed, 211 *contos*, he would still have 96 *contos* left, showing that he was still well-off in assets. He had also asked for a private judge to be assigned to him since he was owed more than 120 *contos* in various lands of the kingdom and the empire, and he needed to collect them to pay his creditors.

The widow continued the process as head of the couple, overseeing the "administration of the goods and business of her house, for which she has the capacity and intelligence".[99] She applied for a moratorium, which was rejected because of the creditors' resistance. The habilitation for a private judge was also rejected because it could only be exceptionally granted to people who contracted debts in the service of the crown and not for perceiving their own fortune. Therefore, there was resistance to grant a private judge to merchants. The *Juíz Privativo* was an institutional device granted as a privilege to the great noble houses; it could be assigned to a house to deal with matters relating to its administration, such as the collection of rents owed to them by the insurrection of the people, whether on manorial lands and crown property or on other property under its administration. The judge ensured that if the houses were heavily in debt, the creditors could not collect more than what was allowed for them to maintain their survival and decency, thus preserving the first nobility of the kingdom.[100]

Another merchant's widow made a request for a private judge. In 1829, Dona Josefa Joaquina de Sousa Alão Veiga, widow of Matias Vieira de Araújo Veiga, a merchant, sent a petition to the *Desembargo do Paço* in which she explained that "since the business house of her deceased husband was of great value, which she was currently managing as head of the couple", she needed to pay

98 Translated by the author. ANTT, Desembargo do Paço, Repartição do Minho e Trás-os-Montes, Expediente com as Secretarias de Estado e Monarca, Consultas Lavradas, mç. 1443, no. 68.

99 Translated by the author. ANTT, Desembargo do Paço, Repartição do Minho e Trás-os-Montes, Expediente com as Secretarias de Estado e Monarca, Consultas Lavradas, mç. 1443, no. 68.

100 Monteiro, *O crepúsculo dos grandes*, 483–486.

her debts and to receive debts owed to her since there were more than 800 debtors both in the kingdom and across the border.[101] She claimed that if she used "the ordinary actions against so many and such insane debtors, she would receive almost nothing in her lifetime, and all that she may receive would be consumed in lawsuits because the debtors were from different lands". She thus wanted to obtain a private judge so that she could sue them, but once again the petition was rejected because this grace was only "granted to some corporations, or even to private individuals for reasons of public utility, distinguished nobility and relevant services".[102]

As one can see, collecting debts could be a complex and time-consuming process, especially if there were legal obstacles, such as resistance to the granting of a private judge or moratoriums, but also if some of their husbands' partners tried to deceive them by forcing them to pay debts previously settled.[103] In addition, not all women knew about their husbands' businesses and could be easy targets for fraudulent practices. In 1821, Ana Josefa, the widow of the merchant José Caetano da Silva, submitted a request to the *Comissão da Justiça Civil* stating that her husband had contracted a debt to Angélica Maria do Nascimento and that it was almost all paid. Angélica's husband stated that the widow should pay a sum that her husband supposedly owed to him, and Ana Josefa stated that, "rustic, inert, and very ignorant of the state of the affairs of his said deceased", she almost accepted to pay the debt until she found that it was already paid by her husband.[104]

The same situation happened to Dona Ana Rosa de Abreu Guimarães. In 1822, she reported in a petition that, after the death of her first husband, João Alves de Abreu Guimarães, and after having inventoried the couple's assets and dealt with the division of their children, she was forced to flee for 14 years to Brazil due to the French Invasions. On her return to Porto, the *Solicitador da Fazenda* asked the widow to pay a debt of seven *contos*, followed by a "violent procedure of seizure of the assets" and property without going to court. She was sued "with the greatest vexation" and deprived of her administration and income, and for that reason claimed that the broker had already received all the

101 Translated by the author. ANTT, Desembargo do Paço, Repartição do Minho e Trás-os--Montes, Expediente com as Secretarias de Estado e Monarca, Consultas Lavradas, mç. 1450.

102 Translated by the author. ANTT, Desembargo do Paço, Repartição do Minho e Trás-os-Montes, Expediente com as Secretarias de Estado e Monarca, Consultas Lavradas, mç. 1450.

103 On debt litigations in the Portuguese courts, see Rodrigues, "Debt Litigation", 237–264.

104 Translated by the author. AHP, Cortes Gerais e Constituintes, Comissão de Justiça Civil, box 55, mç. 32, doc. 18.

money she owed. In view of this "damaging and violent" process, she asked the *Corte Gerais* to granted her with an extraordinary resource to defend herself, but the Congress declared that these issues were not within their competence.[105]

Widows were able to criticise the behaviour of the authorities, denouncing their partiality, gender bias and corruption. They petitioned to reclaim their money when business partners refused to give them their share in profits or claimed debts that had already been settled. Petitions allow us to learn about the mechanisms used by widows to deal with the debts: the benefit of the inventory, the adjudication of the couple's assets to the dowry, the petition to delay the payment of debts or the request for a private judge. These merchants' and businessmen's widows used a variety of strategies, compared to other widows facing inheritance and property problems, and focused their discourse on the idea of the vulnerable widow. The first ones probably accompanied their husbands' work and were aware of the mechanisms they used to circumvent such problems. They also knew that being a woman or a widow would not be enough to meet their petition wishes because they were dealing with creditors and huge amounts of money involved in the business. The law itself did not protect these women in the same way, and for that reason they were forced to reconcile their strategies. However, like all widows, they also focused on the idea of ignorance, vulnerability and violence in order to reach favourable decisions. Not always successful, these women were nevertheless able to denounce debts that were being collected unfairly as well as practices of corruption on the part of business partners and the civil authorities. It was no coincidence that their husbands entrusted them with the collection and the payment of debts.

7 Conclusion

Widows acquired a new legal status and prerogatives to reinforce their role as the heads of the household, guardians of the children and administrators of the assets, due to their responsibilities in relation to their family and due to the maintenance of the patrimony. However, everyday experiences show the difficulties they faced precisely with respect to these new prerogatives. The loss of guardianship of their children or the prohibition to manage children's assets if they remarried may have influenced this choice. On the other hand, a curator could be appointed to administer their assets if they were not considered capable of it. In this sense, the new prerogatives seem to have brought advantages

105 Translated by the author. AHP, Cortes Gerais e Constituintes, Comissão de Petições, box 22, mç. 13, doc. 176.

to the widow's family, by allowing them to keep property and inheritance to ensure its well-being, but not to the widow herself, due to the restrictions imposed on her personal decisions.

The death of husbands was seen by some men and authorities as an opportunity to harm those widows who had economic and social power. Most of the widows that addressed petitions to *Desembargo do Paço* were identified as *Donas*, which reveals the prevalence of petitioners belonging to a high social status. They were mostly widows of noblemen or connected to the city's council administration, with social influence and economic possibilities to pay for the legal costs. This status provided them with some options that other widows from lower classes would not have had, either because they lacked the financial means to pay for the proceedings or because they lacked a recognised status that would allow them to enjoy certain privileges. Petitions addressed to the *Corte Gerais e Extraordinárias* or to *Juízo das Justificações Ultramarinas* were extended to other social strata, especially related to commerce and to military service and maritime activities, who could also afford this type of proceedings. While the first group of widows was concerned with protecting their patrimony and properties from male kin and the authorities that tried to undermine their ownership, the second group of petitioners was more worried about collecting their husbands' debts and regaining some economic relief.

Widows managed their property under pressure and external coercion from family members, neighbours or civil or religious authorities, confirming their great capacity to act in a male environment. In what concerns the guardianship of the children, widows were indeed harmed because they had to appeal in court for their guardianship if this was not granted to them or they would lose it if they remarried. Judicial processes of remarrying widows also reveal that some were defrauded by the second husbands, but the legislation was strong enough to protect the children's assets. Widows appeared in court when they needed royal protection; when their interests were challenged, when they became involved in litigation to recover property; to avoid debts that were being unfairly collected; or to denounce illicit practices on the part of the authorities. Widows were exposed to situations of vulnerability, but they also demonstrated a great capacity to react to adversities.

On the one hand, petitions reveal that normativity and legal change had an impact on widows' lives. There was a clear change in the legal status of widows from the *Ordenações Filipinas* to the Pombaline period in the way that legislation began to increasingly limit the widows' administration of her children's assets and control their remarriages. On the other hand, there was a cultural change in the way widows were understood by the jurists and individuals. In the 18th century, widows were seen less from the perspective of the honoured, secluded and virtuous widow and seen more as people with an active and key role within the family and in the management of the assets. However, because the loss of the husband's income may have represented economic decay for the widow and her family, the discourse of the poor widow persisted in petitionary practice.

Finally, these widows were not only aware of all their legal possibilities but also appealed to the self-representation of the poor, miserable and helpless widow, even though, in most cases, they were not. By tradition, widows and orphans could not be harmed and were worthy of pity and compassion. For that reason, it was a common practice among widows to use these ideas to positively influence the decision makers and have their claims attended to. In this sense, they assimilated very well into their petitions the discourses of fragility, vulnerability, ignorance or violence to become worthy of the monarch's charity and win judicial litigations. However, remarried widows were treated differently, as they were blamed for allowing the squandering of their children's assets, even though the interveners knew that these women may have been afraid to go against their new husbands' wishes. Also, the law did not protect merchants' or businessmen's widows in the same way it did other women, and they were forced to reconcile these discourses with other strategies in order to try to win their litigations. Their petitions were only refused because the creditors or business partners could not be affected regarding their income, or due to conflicts on the competences between the ordinary and extraordinary courts.

In sum, the court's decisions were favourable to widows, largely due to the existing legal and canonical conceptions of widowhood. Although it is undeniable that the legal status of widows was subject to certain limitations in practice, they were successful in circumventing such barriers, revealing a great deal of resilience as they negotiated their lives.

Bibliography

Manuscripts

Arquivo Histórico Municipal do Porto, Porto (AHMP), Registo Geral de Testamentos, lib. 2267; lib. 2279.

Arquivo Histórico Parlamentar, Lisboa (AHP), Cortes Gerais e Constituintes (1821–1822), Comissão de Justiça Civil, box 55, mç. 32, doc. 18; box 61, mç. 35, doc. 31.

Arquivo Histórico Parlamentar, Lisboa (AHP), Cortes Gerais e Constituintes (1821–1822), Comissão de Petições, box 22, mç. 13, doc. 176.

Arquivo Nacional da Torre do Tombo, Lisboa (ANTT), Desembargo do Paço, Repartição do Minho e Trás-os-Montes, Expediente com as Secretarias de Estado e Monarca, Consultas Lavradas, mç. 1433, no. 25; mç. 1434, no. 55, no. 56, no. 76, no. 86; mç. 1436, no. 99; mç. 1440, no. 31.; mç. 1437, no. 47; mç. 1438, no. 24, no. 57; mç. 1443, no. 68; mç. 1442, no. 47; mç. 1442, no. 105; mç. 1445 [not numbered]; mç. 1450 [not numbered].

Arquivo Nacional da Torre do Tombo, Lisboa (ANTT), Juízo das Justificações Ultramarinas, África, mç. 25, no. 2; mç. 30, no. 5.

Arquivo Nacional da Torre do Tombo, Lisboa (ANTT), Juízo das Justificações Ultramarinas, Brasil, mç. 19, no. 3; mç. 30, no. 6.

Printed Sources

Bíblia Sagrada, Lisboa 2003: Difusora Bíblica.

Lara, Silvia Hunold (ed.). *Ordenações Filipinas*, Livro V, São Paulo 1999: Companhia das Letras, 1999.

Lobão, Manuel de Almeida de Sousa, *Collecção de dissertações juridicas, e práticas*, Lisboa 1808: Lacerdina.

Lobão, Manuel de Almeida de Sousa, *Notas de uso prático e críticas adições ilustrações e remissões sobre todos os títulos e todos os do livro primeiro das Instituições do direito civil lusitano do doutor Paschoal José de Melo Freire e Collecção de dissertações juríd-ico-práticas*, Livro I a III, Lisboa 1816: Na impressão regia.

Oliveira, Luís da Silva Pereira de, *Privilégios da Nobreza de Fidalguia de Portugal*. Lisboa 2002 [1806]: ANHP – Associação da Nobreza Histórica de Portugal.

Ordenações Filipinas, Livro I a IV, Lisboa 1603: Fundação Calouste Gulbenkian.

Teles, José Correia, *Digesto português ou tratado dos direitos e obrigações civis, acomodado às leis e costumes da Nação Portuguesa para servir de subsídio ao novo código civil*, Livro I a III, Coimbra 1835: Imprensa da Universidade.

Tomás, Fernandes, *Repertório geral ou índice alfabético das leis extravagantes do Reino de Portugal, publicadas depois das Ordenações, compreendendo também algumas anteriores, que se acham em observância*, Tomo II, L–Z, Coimbra 1825: Imprensa da Universidade.

Literature

Abreu-Ferreira, Darlene, Women, Crime, and Forgiveness in Early Modern Portugal, Farnham 2015.

Abreu-Ferreira, Darlene, "Women, law and legal intervention in early modern Portugal", in *Continuity and Change* 33:3 (2018), 293–313 (https://doi.org/10.1017/S026841601800022X).

Aguiar, Miguel, *Imagining and organising kinship. The entailment system (14th-17th centuries)*, Coimbra 2024.

Beauvalet-Boutouyrie, Scarlett, *Être veuve sous l'Ancien Régime*, Paris 2001.

Braga, Ana Maria, "Notas para o estudo da mulher viúva em Portugal nos finais do Antigo Regime", in *Revista de Ciências Históricas* 8 (1993), 117–124.

Brandão, Maria de Fátima, *Terra, Herança e Família no Noroeste de Portugal. O caso de Mosteiro no século XIX*, Lisboa 1994.

Cabral, Gustavo César Machado, *Uma introdução à história do direito comum do Medievo à Idade Moderna*, Rio de Janeiro 2019.

Carlson, Cindy L. and Angela Jane Weisl (eds.), *Constructions of Widowhood and Virginity in the Middle Ages*, London 1999.

Chabot, Isabelle, "Lineage strategies and the control of widows in Renaissance Florence", in Cavallo, Sandra and Lyndan Warner (eds.), *Widowhood in Medieval and Early Modern Europe*, London 1999, 127–144.

Coolidge, Grace, "'Neither Dumb, Deaf, nor Destitute of Understanding': Women as Guardians in Early Modern Spain", in *The Sixteenth Century Journal* 36:3 (2005), 673–693 (https://doi.org/10.2307/20477485).

Coutinho Silva, Luisa Stella de Oliveira, *Nem teúdas, nem manteúdas: História das Mulheres e Direito na capitania da Paraíba (Brasil, 1661–1822)*, Frankfurt am Main 2020.

Cruz, Miguel Dantas (ed.), *Petitioning in the Atlantic World, c. 1500–1840. Empire, Revolutions and Social Movements*, London 2022.

Dantas, Mariana, "Succession of Property, Sales of Meação, and the Economic Empowerment of Widows of African Descent in Colonial Minas Gerais, Brazil", in *Journal of Family History* 39:3 (2014), 222–238 (https://doi.org/10.1177/0363199014535024).

Dantas, Mariana, "Mulheres e Mães Negras: mobilidade social e estratégias sucessórias em Minas Gerais na segunda metade do século XVIII", in *Almanack* 12 (2016), 88–104.

Duve, Thomas, "What is global legal history?", in *Comparative Legal History* 8:2 (2020), 7–115.

Erickson, Amy, "Property and widowhood in England 1660–1840", in Cavallo, Sandra and Lyndan Warner (eds.), *Widowhood in Medieval and Early Modern Europe*, London 1999, 145–163.

Faria, Rui, "Entre o campo e a cidade: bens móveis e de raiz nos dotes de casamento em Guimarães", in Sá, Isabel dos Guimarães and Máximo García Fernández (eds.), *Portas Adentro: comer, vestir e habitar na Península Ibérica (ss. XVI–XIX)*, Coimbra 2010, 171–192.

Fernandes, Maria de Lurdes Correia, "Viúvas ideais, viúvas reais: modelos comportamentais e solidão feminina (séculos XVI–XVII)", in *Faces de Eva* 1–2 (1999), 51–86.

Fink de Backer, Stephanie, *Widowhood in Early Modern Spain Protectors, Proprietors, and Patrons*, Leiden 2010.

Foyster, Elizabeth, "Marrying the Experienced Widow in Early Modern England: The Male Perspective", in Cavallo, Sandra and Lyndan Warner (eds.), *Widowhood in Medieval and Early Modern Europe*, London 1999, 108–124.

Freitas, Antônio and Ana Alencar, "'Dona', viúva e 'cabeça de casal': mulheres administradoras de bens nos sertões de Quixeramobim, Ceará, Brasil (século XVIII)", in *Revista de Historiografia* 26 (2017), 85–106.

García González, Francisco, *Vivir en soledad. Viudedad, soltería y abandono en el mundo rural (España y América Latina, siglos XVI–XXI)*, Madrid 2020.

Ghirardi, Mónica and Dora Celton, "Las viudas de Córdoba, Argentina, en la transición del Antiguo al Nuevo Régimen ¿'Escapadas o sobrevivientes del ciclo vital de dependencia patriarcal'?", in García González, Francisco (ed.), *Vivir en soledad: viudedad, soltería y abandono en el mundo rural (España y América Latina, siglos XVI–XXI)*, Madrid 2020, 347–370.

Gilissen, John, *Introdução histórica ao direito*, Lisboa 2008.

Gonzalbo Aizpuru, Pilar, "La milpa por paisaje, los itzcuintlis por compañía. Vivir sin família en el medio rural novohispano", in García González, Francisco (ed.), *Vivir en soledad. Viudedad, soltería y abandono en el mundo rural (España y América Latina, siglos XVI–XXI)*, Madrid 2020, 271–304.

Goody, Jack, *Família e casamento na Europa*, trans. Ana Barradas, Oeiras 1995.

Hellwege, Philip (ed.), *A Comparative History of Insurance Law in Europe: A Research Agenda*, Berlin 2021.

Hespanha, António Manuel, "Carne de uma só carne. Para uma compreensão histórico-antropológica da família na época moderna", in *Análise Social* 28:123–124 (1993), 951–973.

Hespanha, António Manuel, "O estatuto jurídico da mulher na época da expansão", in Comissão para a Igualdade e para os Direitos das Mulheres (org.), *O rosto feminino da expansão portuguesa: Actas/Congresso Internacional*, Lisboa 1995, 53–64.

Hespanha, António Manuel, *Imbecillitas: as bem-aventuranças da inferioridade nas sociedades de Antigo Regime*, São Paulo 2010.

Lanza, Janine, *From Wives to Widows in Early Modern Paris: Gender, Economy, and Law*, Farnham 2007.

Lanzinger, Margareth, Janine Maegraith, Siglinde Clementi, Ellinor Foster and Christian Hagen (eds.), *Negotiations of Gender and Property through Legal Regimes (14th-19th Century). Stipulating, Litigating, Mediating*, Leiden 2021.

Lopes, Ana Mafalda, "Viuvez e Doação de Bens à Misericórdia do Porto no Século XVIII: O caso de Clara Maria do Rosário", in Santa Casa da Misericórdia do Porto (ed.), *Pessoa(s), Arte e Benemerência: IV Congresso de História da Santa Casa da Misericórdia do Porto*, Porto 2020, 203–220.

Lopes, Ana Mafalda, "The invisibility of Portuguese stepfamilies: the relationships between stepparents, stepchildren and half-siblings in the eighteenth and

nineteenth century Porto", in *The History of The Family* 27:3 (2022), 521–545 (https://doi.org/10.1080/1081602X.2022.2103166).
Lopes, Ana Mafalda, *As viúvas do Porto: património, negócios e família (1700–1832)* (Ph.D. Thesis), Lisboa 2024.
Lopes, Maria Antónia, *Mulheres, Espaço e Sociabilidade: A Transformação dos Papéis Femininos em Portugal à Luz de Fontes Literárias (Segunda Metade do Século XVIII)*, Lisboa 1989.
Matos, Paulo Teodoro and Ana Mafalda Lopes, "Property ownership by widows. A study of nineteenth-century inheritance practices in the island of São Jorge (Azores archipelago), Portugal", in Moring, Beatrice (ed.), *Women and Family Property*, New York, NY 2024.
Monteiro, Nuno Gonçalo, *O crepúsculo dos grandes: a casa e o património da aristocracia em Portugal (1750–1832)*, Lisboa 2003.
Nóvoa, Rita Sampaio da, *Entailment identity: construction, transmission, perpetuation (14th-17th centuries)*. Coimbra 2024.
Osswald, Helena, "Dowry, norms, and household formation: a case study from North Portugal", in *Journal of Family History* 15:2 (1990), 201–224 (https://doi.org/10.1177/036319909001500112).
Palácios Cerezales, Diego, "Assinem assinem, que a alma não tem sexo!: Petição coletiva e cidadania feminina no Portugal Constitucional (1820–1910)", in *Análise Social* 205 (2012), 740–765.
Pereira, Miriam Halpern, *Negociantes, fabricantes e artesãos entre velhas e novas instituições*, Lisboa 1992.
Pinheiro, Magda, *Os Portugueses e as finanças no dealbar do Liberalismo*, Lisboa 1992.
Polónia, Amélia, "Women's contributions to family, economy and social range in maritime communities in sixteenth-century Portugal", in *Portuguese Studies Review* 13:1 (2005), 269–285.
Rocha, Ana Rita, *Power: Entailment, status, and social mobility (14th-17th centuries)*, Coimbra 2024.
Rodrigues, José Damião, "Valorização e exploração do património vinculado em São Miguel (séculos XVII–XVIII)", in Serrão, José Vicente, Bárbara Direito, Eugénia Rodrigues and Susana Münch Miranda (eds.), *Property Rights, Land and Territory in the European Overseas Empires*, Lisboa 2014, 123–134.
Rodrigues, Lisbeth, "Debt Litigation and the Performance of Law Courts in Eighteenth Century Portugal", in *The Journal of Interdisciplinary History* 50:2 (2019), 237–264 (https://doi.org/10.1162/jinh_a_01411).
Rosa, Maria de Lurdes, *Almas Herdeiras: fundação de capelas fúnebres e afirmação da alma como sujeito de direito (Portugal, 1400–1521)* (Ph.D. Thesis), Lisboa 2005.
Rosa, Maria de Lurdes (ed.), *Privilege, Memory and Perpetuity: Entails and Entailment in Europe, ca. 1300–1800*, Coimbra 2024.

Russell-Wood, Anthony John R., "Women and society in colonial Brazil", in Russell-Wood, Anthony John R., *Society and Government in Colonial Brazil, 1500–1822*, London 1992, 1–34.

Sá, Isabel dos Guimarães, *O Regresso dos Mortos: Os doadores da Misericórdia do Portoe a Expansão Oceânica (séculos XVI–XVII)*, Lisboa 2018.

Sá, Isabel dos Guimarães and Maria Eugénia Matos Fernandes, "A mulher e a estruturação do património familiar: um estudo sobre dotes de casamento", in *A mulher na sociedade portuguesa: visão histórica e perspectivas actuais. Colóquio 20–22 de março de 1985*, vol. 1, Coimbra 1986.

Silva, Maria Beatriz Nizza da, "A legislação pombalina e a estrutura da família no Antigo Regime português", in Santos, Maria Helena Carvalho dos (coord.), *Pombal Revisitado*, vol. 1, Lisboa 1984.

Slemian, Andréa, "Entre graça e direitos: apontamentos sobre como entender as petições na América portuguesa, século XVIII", in *Almanack* 34 (2023), 1–38 (https://doi.org/10.1590/2236-463334ed00223).

Stretton, Tim, "Widows at law in Tudor and Stuart England", in Cavallo, Sandra and Lyndan Warner (eds.), *Widowhood in Medieval and Early Modern Europe*, London 1999, 193–208.

Todd, Barbara, "The virtuous widow in Protestant England", in Cavallo, Sandra Cavallo and Lyndan Warner (eds.), *Widowhood in Medieval and Early Modern Europe*, London 1999, 66–83.

Veiga, Cristiane, *Vida após a morte: mulheres viúvas nas malhas do Império Luso – Rio de Janeiro (c. 1763–1808)* (Ph.D. Thesis), São Paulo 2017.

Vieira, Benedicta Duque, *A Justiça civil na transição para o estado liberal*, Lisboa 1992.

Warner, Lyndan, "Widows, widowers and the problem of 'second marriages' in sixteenth-century France", in Cavallo, Sandra and Lyndan Warner (eds.), *Widowhood in Medieval and Early Modern Europe*, London 1999, 84–107.

CHAPTER 5

Conveying Normativity to the Sound of Drums

An Exploration of the Normative Production of *Bandos* by Governors of the Portuguese Atlantic World (17th–18th Centuries)

Arthur Curvelo

1 Introduction

Large scale political formations, like the Early Modern European empires, were legally and politically sustained by multiple regimes of normativity.[1] As pointed out by António Manuel Hespanha, political architecture was strongly pluralistic, so that the Crown and a vast universe of ruling bodies shared jurisdiction in matters of law.[2] As a result, those regimes of normativity held a great degree of complexity, comprising legislations promulgated in Europe, but also the local and regional layers of normative production that defined the governance of cities, regions, parishes and communities.[3] In practice, as juridical doctrine rejected the automatic application of European Law to imperial communities, local or regional legal solutions and normativities often prevailed.[4] Thus, although the contours of the imperial legal regimes were originally drawn from the European legal traditions, it can be said that normative production within imperial contexts needed to respond to material factors, such as distance and time,[5] but also, and mainly, to accommodate imperial and economic projects with the social, cultural and political realities of the Atlantic territories. It seems also reasonable to suggest that the process of empire building during the Early Modern Era not only produced legal changes but also legal differences in the ways that communities within Europe and communities under European domination experienced law and normative production.[6] In imperial contexts, such legal differences were translated into a broad repertoire of policies that regulated relations between different social, economic and racial

1 Duve, "What Is Global Legal History?", 7–115.
2 Hespanha, *Poder e instituições na Europa do Antigo Regime*, 35.
3 Herzog, "Colonial Law: Early Modern Normativity in Spanish America", 105.
4 Hespanha, "Modalidades e limites do imperialismo jurídico na colonização portuguesa", 118.
5 Sellers-García, *Distance and Documents at the Spanish Empire's Periphery*, 1.
6 Garavaglia, "La cuestión colonial", 25.

HTTPS://DOI.ORG/10.1163/9789004764422-006

groups, Europeans and non-Europeans, defining segregation and integration practices that were broadly defined by Burbank and Cooper as "politics of difference".[7]

To understand the ways in which such legal changes and legal differences were formed in the Portuguese Atlantic territories, this chapter explores the social and political importance of *bandos*, one of many normative dispositions used by viceroys, governors and captain-majors to produce and create knowledge of normativity. A *bando* can be defined as an instrument of legal communication[8] with local or regional effects, through which a general statement was addressed directly to a political community according to a ritualised form of promulgation that involved the reading aloud of a proclamation preceded by the ruffling of snare drums. Essentially, *bandos* can be regarded as communicative tools that made multiple layers of normativity become known and intelligible to societies under Portuguese rule, because they mostly comprised the proclamation of governor's orders, but also of royal dispositions, treaties and agreements. While trying to understand the political uses of this normative tool, I agree with Thomas Duve when he stresses that "a critical history of the production of normativity" should be understood and treated as "a process of distributed knowledge production", in ways that "law and other modes of normativity are simply knowledge and thus part of the 'totality of propositions that the members of a culture consider to be true'".[9]

It is not unusual to find mentions of *bandos* in academic literature, but, surprisingly, few authors have systematically reflected on them as a specific research subject. The studies currently available on *bandos* were developed in different fields of research, such as history, anthropology and linguistics. One of the first authors to explore their importance as tools for imperial governance was Ana Rita Monteiro, through the case of Mozambique in the second half of the 18th century. She argued that *bandos* allowed governors to experience more "pragmatic ways to exercise power",[10] allowing them to practice more arbitrary-based repertoires of rule, firmly grounded in casuistic political-administrative solutions that often "depended on the ruling governor's will".[11] However important her contribution may be, I consider such personalistic approaches to be problematic, since they ignore that the continuous registration of *bandos* in specific register books could lead to the establishment of

7 Cooper and Burbank, *Empires in World History*, 11–12.
8 Ross, "Legal Communications and Imperial Governance", 104.
9 Duve, "What Is Global Legal History?", 111.
10 Monteiro, "Moçambique, 1750–1800: Os 'Bandos' na administração do território", 26–31.
11 Monteiro, "Moçambique, 1750–1800: Os 'Bandos' na administração do território", 26.

legal traditions within territories, and that they could be not merely replicated through time, but also mentioned as legal sources by succeeding governors.

In the field of linguistic studies, an astonishing contribution was made by Cínthya da Silva Martins regarding *bandos* laid down in the captaincy of Ceará Grande.[12] Concerned with textual and contextual forms assumed by *bandos* as a discursive genre, she systematically analysed the lexical meanings and social definitions of the word in Iberian dictionaries and military literature, observing how those meanings changed between the 17th and the 19th centuries. She then confronted those lexical meanings with a case study of 90 *bandos* that were proclaimed in Ceará between 1670 and 1832, showing that their thematic diversity implied an enormous variety of matters that were distanced from the strictly martial definitions of *bandos* that prevailed in Portugal. But as Martins' interests are strictly related to the linguistic expression of the discourse conveyed in *bandos*, she pays little attention to the different sorts of such normative dispositions, putting together those that were issued by the captain-majors of Ceará with those that merely replicated laws and other normative dispositions issued by the Portuguese Crown. Nevertheless, taking this historical interest into account, her most important contribution is that *bandos* were used in Portuguese America to address a variety of questions that go far beyond the strictly military uses they had in Portugal. This is a strong hypothesis that needs to be tested with greater samples of documents in a wider spatial scope of analysis.

Finally, establishing a solid dialogue with ethnology and historical anthropology, Ricardo Roque has offered a groundbreaking contribution regarding the use of *bandos* in Portuguese Timor during the 19th and 20th centuries.[13] Roque is less concerned with normative definitions of *bandos* than he is with their ritual effects and reception by local communities. By stressing the importance of the ritual and sound effects involved in their promulgation, Roque considered that *bandos* were key instruments for the communication of authority between Portuguese governors and local indigenous rulers in Timor. One of the most interesting topics of Roque's study is the appropriation of such normative dispositions by the indigenous rulers, the *Liurais*, who started to use them to declare war and regulate many aspects of daily life in the communities, such as crime, justice, commerce and marriage.

Through interesting case studies, those three works have illuminated different aspects of the political, social and lexical uses of *bandos* in different regions of the Portuguese empire. However, there is still much to be done. Conclusions

---

12 Martins, *Ao rufar das caixas, leia-se o bando*.

13 Roque, "A voz dos bandos".

taken from the experience of one territory or another must be tested in other geographies and a clear legal definition of *bando* must also be reached. My contribution to this debate involves exploring changes in the social meanings and political uses that surrounded the normative production of *bandos*, taking a broader scale of analyses that comprises Portugal and the Portuguese Atlantic World. To this end, and following some clues given by the works of Martins, I analyse how the *bando*, a normative disposition originally produced under martial circumstances during times of war, acquired wider political use, becoming one of the most important tools for imperial governance within the Portuguese domains and being used for the regulation of numerous legal, economic, commercial and societal aspects of communities.

Therefore, this chapter is divided into three parts. The first part approaches the normative definitions of *Bando*, analysing some clues provided by dictionaries, legal texts and styles books (*livros de estilo*)[14] that brought patterns for their standardisation as official documents. The second part approaches the social contexts of documental production and the diffusion of *bandos*, suggesting a typification of their different kinds. In the third part, through cases collected from a diverse set of territories of the Portuguese Atlantic, I explore and examine the diversity of matters conveyed in the *bandos*, observing how governors used them to create knowledge of normativity. I argue that *bandos* were essential to regulate the governance of local communities but also to organise maritime connections in the Portuguese Atlantic. In conclusion, I present some insights on the normative effects of *bandos*, approaching the mechanisms materially available for their surveillance and the penalties imposed on them. In this sense, I argue that however martial they were at their origins, *bandos* allowed governors and viceroys to improvise, adapt and administrate political repertoires focused on a great variety of matters that we would nowadays associate with civil governance.

2 Documents and Methodological Approaches

It is indispensable to start with a reflection on the archival background of the historical sources used in this chapter to justify the kind of approach it

14 *Livros de estilos* or, literally, "styles books" compiled many official standards for the production of documents and circulated as manuscripts between secretaries and clerks. There are few works regarding *livros de estilos* in the Portuguese world. However, it is important to highlight Andrea Slemian's contribution on the subject: Slemian, "Estilos das relações".

undertakes. A basic question would be where and how were *bandos* registered? Where can we find them? *Bandos* were so politically important to Portuguese rule over colonial territories that governorships produced specific, even separate, books to record them. As I will demonstrate in the next pages, an 18th-century styles book suggests that the documental registration of *bandos* was meant to be mandatory. Some of these books were exclusively made for recording *bandos*, like the one produced by the Government of Bahia, between 1759 and 1822, which is preserved in the *Biblioteca Nacional do Rio de Janeiro* today.[15] In other territories some books served to record *bandos* and other normative dispositions issued by governors, such as two record books of *portarias* and edicts produced by the General Government of the Azores in the last quarter of the 18th century.[16]

Unfortunately, those record books were not as abundant as they may seem, since a substantial part of 17th- and 18th-century colonial archives was lost, stolen or severely displaced from their original documental landscapes. Thankfully, many *bandos* and other normative dispositions survived through copy books, which could be divided into two basic categories. First, there are personal copies made by some governors who decided to create backups of the dispositions signed during their own mandates, probably to defend themselves against eventual accusations that could be made during or after their mandates, or to present testimonies of their conduct while governing overseas territories.[17] These books, often called *livros de copiadores*, were thus part of family archives that were sold and later incorporated into public archives. As personal copies, it is not always clear whether they contain the whole of an individual's normative production or merely a selection of documents. Such books not only contain *bandos*, but also letters, edicts, orders, *portarias* and other kinds of normative dispositions. This chapter uses five books of this sort that today can be found deposited in the Portuguese National Archive *Torre do Tombo*, in the Portuguese National Library, in the National Library of the Palace of Ajuda and in *Arquivo Histórico Ultramarino*.[18]

The second sort of copy books has not a personal but rather a territorial criterion of production, spawning through the 17th and 18th centuries. One of the most systematic efforts to produce them was made under the patronage of D. Marcos de Noronha e Brito, sixth *Conde dos Arcos*, during his term in Brazil

---

15 BNRJ, Livro de Bandos, ms. 07, 03, 009.

16 BPARLSR, CGA, liv. 49, liv. 50.

17 Curvelo, *Governar Pernambuco e as "capitanias anexas"*, 48–49.

18 BNP, PBA, cod. 239 and 115; ANTT, Arquivo da Casa dos Condes de Povolide, suplemento 1, no. 3; BNPA, 51-XI-34; BNPA, 51-V-43, fol. 21v; AHU, cod. 1634.

as governor and viceroy from 1746 to 1759. This governor ordered his personal clerks to copy thousands of normative dispositions preserved in the archives of Pernambuco, Goiás and Bahia dating back to the mid-17th century. Although the motivations behind the production of those territorial copy books are still unclear, the results of his efforts constitute one of the most important collections of colonial documents of Brazil, resulting in at least 38 books that were bought from his descendants in the 1970s by the University of Coimbra and are now deposited in the *Coleção Conde dos Arcos* in the University's Archive. It is hard, however, to determine the exactitude and the completeness of such copies. In other words, do they reflect all normative dispositions ever produced during a given period by one or more governors or were they merely a selection made by the clerks in eighteenth century? Comparing those copies with some of the *livros de copiadores* made by governors of Pernambuco, it is very clear that those made by Governor Noronha e Brito were surely not extensive copies of all normative dispositions recorded in the secretaries of those three captaincies, but instead represent a robust archival fond containing hundreds of *bandos*.

While writing this chapter I faced severe difficulties in locating *bandos* produced in continental Portugal. This may cause some surprise, since the sixth chapter of the *Regimento dos Governadores de Armas* issued in 1678 established that all *bandos* laid down by such military commanders had to be recorded in one specific record book that had to be made by order and kept by the *Auditor da Gente de Guerra*.[19] It would be ideal to have access to such books, but apparently they simply disappeared from national and regional Portuguese archives.[20] Since *Governadores de Armas* had merely military jurisdiction, they organised no permanent archives in their districts and, for this reason, it is very likely that *bandos* were not as systematically stored in Portugal as in other parts of the Portuguese Empire. They were probably registered in the town councils' record books alongside royal legislation, as happened in Angra,[21] for example, but I could not confirm this information yet and further research will be necessary to prove it. However, we can indeed locate some *bandos* issued during the Wars of the Portuguese Restoration that were annexed in the letters written by the military commanders of Alentejo to the King or to the Council of War in Lisbon.[22]

19 Costa, *Insubmissão*, 40.

20 At least, there is no mention of their existence in the information repositories available.

21 BPARLSR, ALL, CMAGH, C-A, 005, 008.

22 These letters were transcribed and published in the 1940s: *Cartas dos Governadores da Província do Alentejo a El-Rei D. Afonso VI*, vol. III, publ. and pref. P. M. Laranjo Coelho, Lisboa 1940: Academia Portuguesa da História.

While writing this chapter, I selected *bandos* from either original record books, copies or published documents, from Alentejo, Madeira, Azores, Pernambuco, Maranhão, Pará, Goiás, Minas, Bahia and Angola. Ranging from the mid-17th to the late 18th century, these books served different objectives and have diverse material contexts of production, some served in the royal governorship's secretaries and others were made for the personal and household use of former governors. Some of these books were more complete than others; some cover whole centuries and others just the duration of mandates. For this reason, *bandos* collected in this research must be regarded as just a small exploratory sample that does not reflect the totality of *bandos* produced in any of the abovementioned territories. As it is not feasible to approach them quantitatively or statistically, nor make solid territorial comparisons based on the quantities of *bandos* produced here and there, I have proceeded to do a more qualitative-based analysis that is less oriented toward following legal changes over time and more toward approaching them typologically, stressing a transformation in the social and political uses of *bandos*. The main objective here is to suggest that there was a possible difference between Portugal and the overseas territories in terms of normative production. Comparisons were not made to highlight differences between territories in America, Africa and Asia, but rather to stress that *bandos* had equivalent normative patterns and addressed similar topics of imperial governance no matter how socially and culturally the territories differed from one another.

3 Towards a Normative Definition of *Bandos*

What is a *bando*? It appears that royal legislation presented no precise legal definition of *bandos*, nor establish very clearly which political authorities were allowed to make them. For this reason, a normative definition of *bandos* must be located in alternative sources of information.

3.1 Lexical Definitions

Following the Martins' footsteps, dictionaries and social vocabulary provide a starting point for our reflection.[23] *Bandos* existed and were used in similar circumstances in both Portugal and Spain, and if we search for meaning of the word in Iberian dictionaries of the Early Modern Era, we find very close, but

23 Martins, *Ao rufar das caixas, leia-se o bando*, 18–58.

not identical, definitions that can be traced back to Ancient Rome. Tau Anzoátegui traces their remote origins within the ancient Roman custom to perform public lectures of edicts and laws to ensure that the social norms were known and obeyed by the populace.[24] Martins endorses this position associating the etymological origins of the word *bando* with the Latin word *bannum*, that of a "determination or prohibitive precept" normally associated with five meanings: "order of authority, fine, penalty, seizure of assets, [and] deprivation of privileges and public rights with penalty of exile".[25] In 1611, Covarrubias defined it as a "*pregón* that is issued, calling any delinquent that has runaway".[26] The Spanish *Real Academia Española* noted, in 1726, that *bando* is a synonym of "Edict, law or solemnly published mandate of superior order".[27] In the first dictionary of the Portuguese language, published by Father Rafael Bluteau in 1721, we find that *bando* was originally derived from an ancient German word, *Bam*, from which "the Italians made their *Bandire*, which means publish through *bando*, like when a decree or law is declared public". However, he stresses that "among us [Portuguese], *Bando* is *pregão* of war, to the sound of drums, with punishment imposed on the transgressors of some military law".[28] The word "pregão" is defined in the same dictionary as "the publication of anything, which everyone should know".[29] Martins highlights a change in the definition of *bando* in the dictionary of Morais e Silva, published in 1789, where it no longer appears associated with a martial context, but rather as "public *pregão*, through which some order or decree is made public". She considers that this subtle shift in the definition may indicate a change in discursive traditions, where *bandos* had wider political uses than the strict martial contexts alluded to by Bluteau, and therefore it became closer to the definitions we find in Castilian dictionaries.[30]

In this sense, the lexical definition of *bando* appears as a promulgation of a general communication, or statement, issued by a superior authority, read in public and addressed to a specific community. The proclamation attempted to guarantee the fulfilment of an order through the imposition of some penalties on transgressors. In a certain sense, the early 18th-century Portuguese definition goes a bit further than its Castilian counterparts and stresses a specific

---

24 Anzoátegui, *Los bandos de buen gobierno*, as cited in Kluger, "Disciplinamiento familiar y social en el Rio de La Plata, Tucumán y Cuyo", 131–158.
25 Martins, *Ao rufar das caixas, leia-se o bando*, 30.
26 Covarrubias Orozco, *Tesoro de la lengua castellana o española*, v. 1, 237.
27 Real Academia Española, *Diccionario de la lengua castellana*, vol. 1, 545.
28 Bluteau, *Vocabulario portuguez e latino*, vol. 2, 32.
29 Bluteau, *Vocabulario portuguez e latino*, vol. 6, 692.
30 Martins, *Ao rufar das caixas, leia-se o bando*, 32.

martial context of production. Indeed, in the Portuguese case, *bandos* were ordinarily issued by military commanders.

3.2 Bandos as an Expression of Military Jurisdiction

But what legal grounds granted military commanders the exclusivity to launch *bandos*? The jurisdiction to produce such normative dispositions was granted by some royal instructions (*regimentos*). The first *Regimento das Fronteiras*, made in 1645, regulated the relations that the *Vedor Geral do Exército* should maintain with the *Governadores das Armas*, and reserved the jurisdiction to launch *bandos* to the latter. The *Vedor* had to ask the Governor to issue *bandos* on three occasions: to summon the troops for inspection and payment; to prevent the sale of horses; and to restrict the purchase of looted assets by soldiers and officers.[31] After the War's end, the *Regimento dos Governadores de Armas das Províncias*, issued in 1678, clearly established that the governors should promulgate *bandos* to avoid military crimes, mutiny, rebellions and desertion, granting them the jurisdiction to even threaten the death penalty in such cases.[32] This created a certain sphere of precautions for the use of *bandos* that, in theory, had to be respected.[33] The death penalty would be applied after a martial trial and would be unappealable if the crime happened during a war. Moreover, in times of peace, a special commission composed of five members had to vote in the application of the death penalty, which consisted of the Governor, the *Mestre de Campo*, the *Auditor da Gente de Guerra*, the *Corregedor* or *Juiz de Fora* and a local magistrate.[34]

Looking closely at documents and correspondence exchanged between the *Governadores de Armas* of Alentejo province and the King of Portugal during the Restoration War (1640–1668), we can find references and even some copies of military *bandos*, such as the ones prescribed by the two *regimentos*. Probably, the most common were the ones circulated in most towns and villages ordering the enlistment of local populace in the army or forbidding desertion among troops. However, this phenomenon became so frequent among Portuguese ranks that *bandos*, like the one issued in Estremoz by Martinho Afonso de Melo in May 1662, promised a royal pardon for deserters who presented

31 ANTT, Regimento das Fronteiras, art. 29.
32 BNP, Regimento dos Governadores das Armas das Províncias, cod. 105, fol. 396.
33 Costa, *Insubmissão*, 40.
34 BNP, Regimento dos Governadores das Armas das Províncias, cod. 105, fol. 396.

themselves before the commanders and continued to serve in the army.[35] Others were related to specific war circumstances, such as one launched in 1661 by D. Afonso de Portugal, Count of Vimioso regarding horses. He made a *bando* ordering that all horse owners should immediately enlist their horses before a commissioned clerk, who would make a list of the available animals. If the horses were hidden, withdrawn or not enlisted, the penalty of confiscation and 30 days in jail would be applied to the transgressors.[36] Both cases are strictly related to war circumstances and were meant to keep infantry and cavalry units regularly supplied in the army, but their social effects somewhat reached the civil population as well.

Military discipline was also one of the key matters conveyed through such normative dispositions. One of the most interesting cases regarding this appears in a letter sent by Governor D. Rodrigo de Castro to King Afonso VI in 1662, mentioning that he issued a *bando* with a "life penalty" against some freshly arrived English soldiers to reprehend insubordination and insolences committed by them, such as stealing food from the local population, duelling and refusing to accept orders from their Portuguese commanders. One of the greatest difficulties faced by Governor Castro when implementing his dispositions was the translation of this *bando* for the soldiers, since they had no interpreter on their regiment and henceforth alleged that they remained ignorant of its contents.[37] This case very clearly shows that intelligibility was paramount in the publication of *bandos*. Despite the expectations posed on their normative effectiveness in the martial context, their full comprehension was essentially restricted to the Portuguese-speaking community or depended on the role of interpreters.

Cases such as these are probably episodical in Portugal, but in overseas territories, where Portuguese administration lived with several other linguistic communities, translation was a serious issue. In Asian territories, for example, viceroys and captain-generals responded to this problem by ordering the explicit translation of local idioms, as exemplified in a *bando* made in Goa and addressed to the inhabitants of Bicholim and Sanquelim in 1781, that was to be "published to the sound of drums in public and usual spaces of the mentioned provinces of Bicholim and Sanquelim; and in their districts and towns, and

35 Coelho, Laranjo (ed.), *Cartas dos Governadores da Província do Alentejo a El-Rei D. João IV e a El-Rei D. Afonso VI*, vol. II, 12–13.

36 Coelho, Laranjo (ed.), *Cartas dos Governadores da Província do Alentejo a El-Rei D. João IV e a El-Rei D. Afonso VI*, vol. II, 4–5.

37 Coelho, Laranjo (ed.), *Cartas dos Governadores da Província do Alentejo a El-Rei D. Afonso VI*, vol. III, 263.

translated into the language of the country".[38] I could not find similar concerns in Brazilian or African territories, but there are some nuances that are worth highlighting. In a *bando* of 1761, addressed to the villages and to the newly established Indian villages of Pernambuco, the Governor explicitly delegated its publication to the captain-majors of all districts with instructions to not only publish this disposition to the sound of drums but also to "match it to the intelligence" of the people of such districts.[39] The intention of the Governor to communicate the order and make it intelligible is thus very clear and, we can imagine that in doing so he was targeting not only Portuguese-speaking communities but also the Amerindians that were recently established in the villages, since in some cases they could not speak Portuguese. Although the methods to create this intelligibility were not made clear, some sort of translation could be expected.

Further, some documental evidence shows that there was an apparent tacit understanding that only governors and viceroys had the jurisdiction to produce *bandos*, even though such exclusivity was never fully expressed in legal texts beyond sparse mentions that appeared in the *Regimento das Fronteiras* of 1645 and the *Regimento dos Governadores de Armas* of 1679. Such a prerogative emerges, precisely, when other agents tried to produce their own *bandos*. The *Provedor* of Itamaracá received a harsh reprehension from the Governor of Pernambuco in 1690 when he tried to publish a *bando* in that subordinate captaincy. The Governor stressed that in the captaincies of his jurisdiction "no one has more authority to publish *bandos* than me" and if by the force of circumstance someone was urged to do so, he would need first "to require it directly from me", or otherwise publish *editais* (edicts) instead of *bandos*.[40] It is interesting to note that in the late 18th-century Azores, a provisional *junta* formed after a vacancy on the General-Government between 1795 and 1797 took some cautions and produced *editais* that were virtually identical to *bandos*, and were even published to the snare of drums, but were not promulgated with this name, probably because they understood that this was a prerogative of the General-Governors.[41] During the trials led on the rebels of the Revolution of 1817 in Pernambuco, a sentence derogated one *bando* issued by the town council of Recife, stating that "It never belonged to the town council nor to the judges to order the publication of *bandos*", nor were "the orders of the town council published through *bandos*, but only by edicts and affixation.

38 Xavier, *Collecção de Bandos e outras diferentes providências*, 26.
39 BNRJ, Livro de registos, I-12-03-035, fol. 41v.
40 AUC, CCA, cod. 31, fol. 545v.
41 BPARLSR, CGA, liv. 50, fols. 120v–121, 161v–162, 176v–177, 192.

Bando is the notification made to the people to the snare of drums from the orders that the government sends to the commanders".[42] However, such normative dispositions could also be launched by any authority in charge of the supreme military command of a given district. For this reason, some interim governors, such as bishops, *juntas* or municipal councils, occupying a post left vacant by a governor or viceroy could issue them, like the town council of São Cristóvão in Sergipe in 1657 that issued a *bando* during a rebellion that led the captain-major to escape from the captaincy.[43]

3.3 Diplomatic Features of *Bandos*

This is very interesting but, if we move on from addressing symbolic appropriations by local communities in the imperial context, it might be useful to provide a textual or diplomatic definition of a *bando*. A manuscript styles book, meant to provide models for the production of official documents in the Secretary of Government in Pernambuco in the middle of the 18th century, defines a sort of basic formulary for the writing of *bandos*. An official *bando* should follow this basic structure:

> Dom *Fuam*, from his Majesty's Council, Governor and Captain General of Pernambuco and of the other annexed captaincies etc. Inasmuch as etc. what I make public etc. And for so that the news may come to everyone, this bando will be published to the sound of drums and fixed in the public parts of this place, recording it first in the Secretary of this Government and in other competent parts. Made in place or village of such part at so-called number of such month and year. Dom *Fuam*. Signet.[44]

The underlined words, such as "Fuam", "etc.", "such" and "so-called number", should be regarded as functional equivalents of the blank spaces of our contemporary formularies. They were meant to create an official standard and indicate where new information should be filled in. On the right side of the formulary, a marginal note explicitly stated that "It should be noted that all these

---

42 BNRJ, Coleção Documentos Históricos, vol. 107, 160.

43 AHU, CU, Bahia, Luísa da Fonseca, box 14, d. 1688, fol. 1v.

44 ANTT, ms. liv., no. 2611, fol. 17. Free translation of: "Dom Fuam, do Conselho de Sua Majestade, Governador e Capitão General de Pernambuco e mais capitanias anexas &tc. Porquanto &tc. o que faço público &tc. E para a que venha a notícia de todos se lançará este Bando ao som de caixas e se fixará na parte pública desta praça, registando-se primeiro na Secretaria deste Governo e mais partes a que tocar. Dado na Praça ou Vila de tal parte aos tantos de tal mês e ano. Dom Fuam. Sinete."

bandos must be registered". This not only confirms the importance of such documents, but also suggests that not all information and normative dispositions gained register in the secretariat. As mentioned above, in Pernambuco's secretary, a separate book was meant to register all orders, *bandos*, *portarias* and edicts signed by the governors,[45] like in the General Government in Bahia.[46] Under this formulary appears another one, much smaller, containing a model for an acknowledgement record that should be written on the margins of the *bando* after the *Tenente General* had proceeded with its proclamation.

Following the guidelines of the mentioned formulary, a regular *bando* would normally have five or six indispensable elements. To facilitate the reader's understanding, I have presented all of them in Table 1, through an example also derived from Pernambuco. The left column shows the transcription of the *bando* and the right the identification of the structural element.

First, all *bandos* started with an evocative mention of the name, rank or post and also the noble titles of the authority that ordered their publication, such

TABLE 5.1 Diplomatic structure of a *Bando*[47]

Structural elements	**Original transcription**	**Translation**
Evocative mention of the author	*Fernão de Sousa Coutinho, Governador das Capitanias de Pernambuco e as mais anexas, por Sua Majestade que Deus Guarde provido etc.*	Fernão de Sousa Coutinho, Governor of the Captaincies of Pernambuco and the most annexed, appointed by His Majesty may God Protect him, etc.
Motives and justifications	*Por andar já muito esquecida a disciplina militar, e se cometerem entre soldados abusos dignos de grande castigo, com mui prejudicial exemplo, contra a observação da obediência;*	Because military discipline is now largely forgotten, and abuses worthy of great punishment are committed among soldiers, with a very harmful example, against the observance of obedience;
Order/ Prohibitions	*ordeno que todo o soldado e oficial até o posto de Sargento que puxar pela espada contra quaisquer oficiais maiores;*	I order that every soldier and officer up to the rank of Sergeant draw his sword against any higher officers;

45 Melo, *A ideia de Arquivo*, 134.
46 BNRJ, Livro de Bandos, ms. 07, 03, 009; AHU, cod. 1634, fols. 1r–22v.
47 AUC, CCA, cod. 31, fol. 252v. Translated by the author.

TABLE 5.1 Diplomatic structure of a *Bando* (*cont.*)

Structural elements	Original transcription	Translation
Penalties	sejam arcabuzeados, e do posto de Alferes para cima todos os que puxarem pela espada contra os oficiais de maiores postos que aqueles que cometerem o dito crime serão condenados à morte, que se lhe dará irremissivelmente conforme aos privilégios dos postos que ocuparem, na forma em que por todas as leis militares se observa em todo o mundo;	must be executed by shot of a harquebus, and from the rank of *Alferes* upwards all those who draw the sword against officers of higher ranks than those who committed the said crime will be condemned to death, that will be given irrevocably according to the privileges of the posts they occupy, in the manner in which all military laws are observed throughout the world;
Instructions for publication	*e para que venha à notícia de todos, e se não poder alegar a ignorância, se registrará este bando depois de publicado ao som de caixas e se fixará nos Corpos da Guarda desta vila de Olinda e do Recife.*	and so that the news may come to everyone, and none can plead ignorance, this *bando* will be recorded after its publication to the sound of drums, and it will be fixed on the Guard Corps of this town of Olinda and in Recife.
Place, date and signature	*Dado nela [vila de Olinda] ao primeiro de Abril de 1671. Fernão de Sousa Coutinho.*	Signed in [Olinda] on 1 April 1671. Fernão de Sousa Coutinho.

as governors, viceroys and captain-majors. This could be regarded as a means to affirm, externalise and legitimise the political authority of the governor or viceroy in public spaces. By pronouncing the name of the individual and all his titles in a loud voice, settlers were regularly reminded that they had a royal governor and that this man was one of the most distinguished subjects of his majesty and even of noble birth. Those elements were paramount in *Ancien-Régime* societies, where those distinctions reflected the dignity of the ruled territory and indicated the degree of closeness of the governors with the king himself.[48] One should also bear in mind that those proclamations were made in the more distant areas of a governorship's district, thus far away from the

48 Monteiro, *Elites e poder*, 136–137.

governor's residence, in places where he could not be seen in person, at least not very often, and could be regarded as a reminder for distant settlers that they were governed by a representative of the King's authority.

Continuing with the structure, the second element declares the motives or situations that justified the promulgation of the *bando*, usually a crime or a transgression that needed to be appeased. In the case presented above, the motive is the simple lack of military discipline among soldiers and officers.

The third element, which could sometimes barely be dissociated from the fourth, is the declaration of the order and/or the prohibitions issued by the *bando*. In this specific case, the governor forbids the soldiers and officers from "pulling the sword out" against their superiors, that is, threatening or calling them to duels. In the case shown, such disobedience would be punished with the death penalty, by a shot with a harquebus.

The fifth part brings specific instructions for publication, mentioning the places where the *bando* should be proclaimed, the use of snare drums during the promulgation and the latter affixation of the paper in public spaces where it would be visible to everyone. It is usual to find variations on this fifth element. Some *bandos* were meant to circulate in a single fortress or town, others could be sent as copies to a whole region; some could be published in public squares, others in markets or in the doors of churches and chapels. As suggested above, some could mention the need for translation into local languages; in rare cases, some could even not mention or suppress the instructions for the use of snare drums, which could be perhaps implicit in this sort of normative disposition. Finally, the sixth and last element was the indication of date and place in which the document was issued.

The publication to the sound of snare drums shows that the authority conveyed in such dispositions was not merely confined to the words transmitted orally or the penalties they prescribed. It was rather enhanced through a ritualised proclamation, in which the loud public reading in the most frequented places of a town, city or fortress was made in the presence of soldiers and preceded or accompanied by the ruffling of snare drums. The ritual elements associated with the *bando* would create an atmosphere both audible and visual, a soundscape,[49] which amplified the performative effectiveness and thus the reception of the discourse of authority communicated in it. In this sense, the publication of *bandos* resembles the ritualised practices of royal proclamations adopted in the Iberian kingdoms since the late Middle Ages, but, of course, with a more modest ritual apparatus and different musical instruments, since,

49 Coronado Schwindt, "La dimensión auditiva del poder", 44.

in Castille and Portugal, royal *pregões* were proclaimed to the sound of trumpets and not drums.[50] As mentioned above, Roque stresses that in 19th-century Timor *bandos* became one of the most effective ways for Portuguese colonial administrators to communicate authority to local communities precisely for the performative and ritual effects they produced.[51] In fact, even the Timorese *liurais* incorporated and adapted the fashion of Portuguese *bandos* to rule communities locally, creating their own version, later named *bandu*.[52] Those Timorese *bandus* could be very different from their Portuguese counterparts, sometimes having no spoken words but merely symbols and signs publicly displayed in some key spaces of the community. The combination of those signs – such as leaves, parts of animal's bodies, ropes, eggs, and so on – communicated prohibitions or the establishment of taxation practices.[53]

To resume, we could define the Portuguese *bando* as a normative disposition, issued by authorities invested with military powers, that addressed a statement, order or mere communication to a community under a ritual form of promulgation that united the reading of the document out loud to the sound of snare drums and in the presence of soldiers. This public or collective form of legal communication was meant to work as a sort of martial law, not only because it was issued by commanders invested with some military authority, but also due to the punitive effects they could possibly prescribe to transgressors.

Even though their martial and military uses were strictly maintained, the normative production of *bandos* by the governors of the Portuguese Empire evolved far beyond the sphere of military jurisdiction, directly impacting the regulation of local communities in several other aspects of daily life. To explain this diversification, it is necessary to point out a crucial difference between the functions and scope of action of the *Governadores de Armas* that served in continental Portugal and the governors and viceroys of the Empire. A fundamental issue is that governors in the Portuguese overseas territories accumulated the highest military command within their captaincies with the highest civil command. This was approached particularly well in a comparative study grounded in political communication, where authors demonstrated that "the *governadores de armas*, and even the Governor of Algarve, performed fundamentally military functions, while Governors of the *conquistas* and Azores

50 Nieto Soria, "El pregón real en la vida política de la castilla Trastámara", 77–102.
51 Roque, "A voz dos bandos", 235–265.
52 Roque, "A voz dos bandos", 255–260.
53 Roque, "A voz dos bandos", 258.

held several responsibilities that comprised governance".[54] Beyond military questions, such authors demonstrated that governors of the Empire communicated a wide array of fiscal, judicial, economic, commercial and even religious matters with the King through the *Conselho Ultramarino* and the *Secretarias de Estado*.[55] However, before we explore such thematic diversity in the *bandos*, we must first understand their different social uses and what exactly triggered their production in colonial contexts.

4 Patterns of Normative Production of *Bandos* in the Portuguese Empire

To understand the patterns of normative production of *bandos*, it is interesting to start with distinguishing between two of their uses as instruments of legal communication. First, we have *bandos* that were issued specifically for the diffusion and promulgation of royal decrees and laws in public spaces. This sort of *bandos* merely replicated the texts of royal normative dispositions or, sometimes, summarised them. The practice of a lecture, out loud, of the Crown's legal dispositions was paramount to making law intelligible and accessible to a predominantly illiterate population, as highlighted by Pedro Cardim and Miguel Baltazar.[56] The lecture was frequently combined with other measures, such as the affixation of the written texts in public spaces. The doors of churches were regularly used for this purpose, probably because literate priests could read or explain the content to anyone who wished to know. In addition, in rural spaces, besides the churches, the doors of chapels represented spaces of gathering for people who lived on their farms and sugar mills most of the time. We can clearly see this in a *bando* launched by Jeronimo de Mendonça Furtado to be proclaimed at the "doors of the chapels of all the sugar mills so that it was acknowledged by all".[57] In doing so, De Mendonça Furtado tried to reach spaces of communication that went far beyond the town of Olinda, from where he issued the *bando*.

Sometimes, governors were personally instructed by the King and his ministers to publish *bandos* to communicate decisions taken by the high instances of Crown administration, making them acknowledgeable by people. In May 1733, for example, Diogo de Mendonça Corte-Real, Secretary of State,

54 Cosentino et al., "Governadores reinóis e ultramarinos", 300.
55 Cosentino et al., "Governadores reinóis e ultramarinos", 316–319.
56 Cardim and Baltazar, "A difusão da legislação régia (1621–1808)", 179–180.
57 AUC, CCA, cod. 31, fol. 170r.

ordered governors in Portuguese America to publish a *bando* in the name of King João V, explaining a new practice for sending official letters, petitions and correspondence to Portugal that determined that such papers should be sealed and handled directly to the captains of the ships, instead of being delivered by the hand of personal bearers.[58] In Pernambuco, the *bando* was launched by Governor Duarte Sodré Pereira in July 1736, replicating the exact content of the Secretary's order to the sound of drums.[59] This may be a good example of how interpersonal communications exchanged privately between the Secretary and the Governor in the first place, reached communities. *Bandos*, however, could replicate the full content of royal dispositions or also summarise them. We can see this very clearly in a *bando* launched in the Maranhão and Pará captaincies by Governor Francisco de Sá e Meneses in August 1682, in which he communicated that a royal letter received in that same month expressly prohibited the accumulation of public offices by settlers, who had to renounce one of the offices within six months or lose both.[60] While doing so, he did not replicate the full text of the royal letter, but merely the information it conveyed. Dozens of similar cases show that the summarisation of royal dispositions contributed to making them acknowledgeable by concentrating the oral transmission of the messages on the essential or most important parts of normative texts, highlighting the prohibitions or allowances conveyed by them.

In addition to the promulgation of royal normative production, governors used *bandos* to communicate their own dispositions to society. It is precisely here that my interests lie since I consider this specific kind of *bando* a tool to produce knowledge of local and regional normativity in a given space. I insist that the martial essence of *bandos* was never fully forgotten, and I have found some good evidence that their publication was remarkable for governors. This may explain why Luís Correia de Sá wrote down in his personal diary the day on which he launched his first *bando*,[61] or why some cautious voices advocated against their unnecessary use by governors, as stated by an anonymous paper, a sort of *alvitre*, addressed to Governor Félix José Machado in 1710, on the eve of his departure to Pernambuco. The author of the writing advised him clearly: "experience has shown that the overseas governors who ruled well, not failing in any matters concerning the Royal Service and common good, being loved by the settlers of the land, were those who issued few *bandos*, and just to a

58 *ABNRJ*, Informação Geral da Capitania de Pernambuco, 139.

59 AUC, CCA, cod. 32, fol. 520v.

60 BNPA, 51-V-43, fol. 20r.

61 *RIHGP*, Diário do Governador Luís Correia de Sá, 1746–1756, 37.

most needed few of them they gave execution".[62] In this sense, their use should be moderated, and their application tempered. This was only natural, in a legal culture that praised the construction of political authority through consent, pact and negotiation, and not by arbitrary imposition.[63] This evidence suggests that *bandos* were probably regarded as one of the most interventive forms of rule.

Were those cautions ever respected? Did the so-called "good governors" produced fewer *bandos*? It is hard to confirm this in a comparative approach, since we do not have complete records covering great periods of time for all territories. Félix José Machado himself seems to have ignored the advice that was given to him, producing no less than 91 *bandos* between his arrival in October 1711 and his departure in early June 1715.[64] Could this be casually associated with the very harsh circumstances he faced during his mandate? Perhaps. His mandate was indeed troubled by many tensions during the *Guerra dos Mascates* (1710–1711), during the wars against the *Janduís* in Açu and by the outcomes of the Spanish Succession War (1700–1714) with at least 56 of his *bandos* addressing military questions.[65] But should this not mean that political tensions enhanced these cautions? Probably this was not the case. His own father, António Félix Machado, second Marquis de Montebelo, signed at least 57 *bandos* when he governed Pernambuco between June 1690 and June 1693.[66] Those numbers are not so distant from the quantity of *bandos* published in Angola a century later, between 1790 and 1796, where Governor Manuel de Almeida de Vasconcelos issued 98 *bandos*.[67]

A minimum of 400 *bandos* were laid down by governors in Pernambuco between 1648 and 1746, according to the incomplete samples provided by the copy books of Governor Noronha e Brito.[68] A similar amount, however, is suggested by the official record book of *bandos* from the Government of Bahia that registers at least 196 launched between 1760 and 1800.[69] In absolute contrast, the Secretary record books of the newly created General Government of Azores registers merely 11 *bandos* issued between 1766 and 1797,[70] a period

62 Anonymous *lvitre* entitled "A respeito do Governo", BNP, PBA, cod. 526, fol. 265r.
63 Hespanha, "Por que é que foi 'portuguesa' a expansão portuguesa? Ou o revisionismo nos trópicos", 46–47.
64 BNP, Coleção Pombalina, cod. 115.
65 Mello, *A fronda dos mazombos*.
66 Curvelo, *Governar Pernambuco e as "capitanias anexas"*, 399.
67 AHU, cod. 1634, fols. 1r–23v.
68 Curvelo, *Governar Pernambuco e as "capitanias anexas"*, 401.
69 BNRJ, Livro de Bandos, ms. 07, 03, 009.
70 BPARLSR, CGA, liv. 49; BPARLSR, CGA, liv. 50.

that could be regarded as the peak of the government's attempts to implement a political repertoire based on the reformist practices in this archipelago.[71] Low numbers can also be identified in Madeira where, during the mandate of D. Lourenço de Almada (1688–1690), I barely found six *bandos* registered in his personal book of records.[72]

What could possibly explain this discrepancy between the quantity of *bandos* produced in the Angolan and American territories and the numbers found in Azores and Madeira? Though I do not present definitive answers to this question within the limits of this chapter, I would like to advance a hypothesis that will be further explored here and in future works. Within the politico-administrative architecture, governors were not as politically relevant in Madeira and Azores as they were in America and Africa, since their roles in the insular spaces resembled those of the *Governadores de Armas* of Portugal or, in other words, they had to restrict their duties to military questions. In addition to the archipelagic configuration of the territory, other difficulties related to weather and navigation limited communications between the islands, especially in Azores, making efforts of regional integration a serious challenge.[73] In the second half of the 18th century, attempts to establish a regional centralised government in Azores, with some resemblance to the governorships of Brazil, proved to be a failure, as demonstrated by José Damião Rodrigues, and royal governors had to deal with the fierce resistance of islanders and their local elites when implementing the reformistic repertoires aimed at by the Portuguese Crown.[74] All of this may have diminished the political importance of insular governors within the constellation of local powers, leading, henceforth, to a smaller role of the production of normativities that were publicly communicated to local communities. The main reasons for the discrepancy between the Atlantic Islands and other territories must also be examined within the complex social and economic configurations of the African and American territories. I will demonstrate that governors in different captaincies of Portuguese America used *bandos*, for example, to organise large scale operations of commerce and transference of goods between their captaincies and Europe, as well as to deal with the complex social configurations of a slave society. For now, these numbers suggest the hypothesis that the promulgation of *bandos* was not as unusual in colonial territories as it was in Portugal and its Atlantic islands in times of peace.

71 Rodrigues, "Para sossego e tranquilidade pública das ilhas", 144–170.
72 BNPA, 51-XI-34.
73 Rodrigues, "Com exorbitância inaudita", 215–225.
74 Rodrigues, "Para sossego e tranquilidade pública das ilhas", 166.

4.1 The Territorial Reach of *Bandos*

The amount of *bandos* is an interesting means of understanding their normative production, as I demonstrate in the next pages, but territorial reach may be a more coherent form of typifying them according to what we find in Ancient-Regime, political-administrative vocabulary. Through the cases of Portuguese America, for example, it is possible to identify two modes for the distribution of *bandos*: on the one hand, those that were proclaimed in determined towns or cities, with merely local effects and, on the other, the so-called "bandos circulares", as they were meant to "circulate", disseminated in all the towns and parishes of a given district.

The diffusion and supervision of *bandos circulares* posed some challenges to governors. In the capital city of each captaincy, *bandos* were read by military officers directly subordinate to the authority of governors and viceroys, such as the Lieutenant General (*Tenente General*) or the Aid-de-Camp (*Ajudante de Ordens*). However, in the most distant towns and parishes, it was always indispensable to have local intermediaries, not only to guarantee public proclamations to the sound of drums, but to supervise the effective application of the penalties imposed, and municipal councils, captain-majors and royal magistrates were the most recurrent. In previous works, based on the case of Pernambuco, we can observe that unipersonal authorities, either military or judicial, were preferred to receive and proclaim *bandos* in distant territories rather than corporative ruling bodies, such as the municipal councils. The main cause for this preference is that a majority of officers of the municipal council needed to be assembled to receive and open the *bandos* before their proclamation, which caused long delays.[75]

Besides local intermediaries, the territorial diffusion of *bandos circulares* implied some material challenges posed by distance and some costs related to the messengers who transported them. Until the very late 18th century there was no "professional", i.e., permanent and royally organised, land mail service in Portuguese America, and governors often relied on soldiers to deliver copies of the *bandos* to the more distant towns, making the Royal Treasury (*Fazenda Real*) pay them for this service.[76] In some cases, especially in long-distance voyages, governors delegated this task to Amerindians, trusting that the papers would reach their destination more quickly due to their knowledge of the

75 Curvelo, *Governar Pernambuco e as "capitanias anexas"*, 340.

76 Guapindaia, *O controle do fluxo das cartas e as reformas de Correio na América Portuguesa (1796–1821)*, 195–235; Salvino, *Correios dos governadores*.

terrain and routes.[77] Another practice for the territorial diffusion of *bandos*, quite similar to the *practica de cordillera* identified by Borah in New Spain,[78] was to take advantage of the political-administrative framework ordering that the first village that received the *bando* should register it and send a copy to the closest, which should replicate it and pass it on in the same way.[79] The judicial districts, *Comarcas*, were also privileged spaces for organising the circulation of *bandos*. A good example can be traced back to 1714, when the royal magistrate José da Cunha Soares, *ouvidor* in Alagoas, received an order from the governor to publish four *bandos* in the three towns and ten parishes under his jurisdiction, with the specific task of "carrying out their execution, imposing the penalties of the law on transgressors".[80] To diffuse a *bando* in the whole Ceará Captaincy in 1746, Governor Noronha e Brito used a similar measure, instructing its captain-major to produce and send copies to all the villages and parishes of his jurisdiction and, to ensure they were really promulgated at a local level, instructing all their captains to write back with a record of acknowledgement stating that it was published locally.[81] These were some ways of transferring the costs associated with territorial communications to the hands of local and regional administrative bodies, but also of guaranteeing the observation of the orders conveyed in the *bandos*.

Naturally, such material conditions affected the frequency in which Governors sent *bandos* to the more distant villages and parishes of their district. As shown in previous works, nearly 75% of the *bandos* issued by the governors of Pernambuco between 1648 and 1746 were confined to the surroundings of the governorship headquarters, i.e., Recife and Olinda and their rural parishes.[82] Merely 12% of the *bandos* were circulated in all the six or seven villages that existed in Pernambuco during this period.[83] In 18th-century Bahia, barely five among 196 recorded in the book of *bandos* between 1760 and 1800 brought with them specific instructions for circulation outside of Salvador.[84] It is still necessary to examine such trends in other territories, but the data currently compiled in my study suggests far less interventive actions carried out by governors over the peripheral areas of their districts. Rather, in the urban centres of each captaincy, where the harbour, the regular troops and most of the

77 Curvelo, *Governar Pernambuco e as "capitanias anexas"*, 330.
78 Borah, "Los lazos con la capital y con otras provincias", 208.
79 AUC, CCA, cod. 32, fol. 372r.
80 BNP, PBA, cod. 115, fol. 237v.
81 AUC, CCA, cod. 35, fol. 219r.
82 Curvelo, *Governar Pernambuco e as "capitanias anexas"*, 401–403.
83 Curvelo, *Governar Pernambuco e as "capitanias anexas"*, 401.
84 BNRJ, Livro de Bandos, ms. 07, 03, 009, fols. 46r–46v, 58v–59v, 87v, 106v, 146v.

population were concentrated, *bandos* were more often used as legal communication instruments.

4.2 Routine and Occasional *Bandos*

Although territorial reach can be regarded as an interesting way of looking at different types of *bandos*, it may not suffice to enable their categorisation. In this sense, based on my own research experience and not on any sort of Ancient-Regime categorisation, I suggest another typification method: dividing them, according to their regularity, into either routine or occasional *bandos*.

Among what I name "routine" *bandos*, we might include those whose regularity was defined by predicted circumstances, subjected to the requirements of the governor's responsibilities as defined by their royal instructions (*Regimentos*). In this type of *bando*, as prescribed by the abovementioned *Regimento das Fronteiras*, are those issued for military inspection (*bandos da mostra*) launched month by month, and which were intended to summon the armed forces for exercises and/or payment. At least 29 of the 57 *bandos* launched by the Marquis de Montebelo and 39 of the 91 laid down by Félix José Machado during their mandates in Pernambuco were related to this military purpose.[85] Beyond military obligations, royal instructions regarding commerce and the tax collection of tobacco in Bahia and Pernambuco, made in 1699, obliged governors and viceroys to launch one *bando* a year offering rewards for sailors or any other person who denounced illicit cargoes containing such commodity in ships bound for Lisbon.[86] We could also include in this category the *bandos* that needed to be dispatched every year in the main Atlantic port cities during preparation for the royal fleet's arrival, loading and departure. From the 196 recorded in Bahia between 1760 and 1800, at least 97 derived from routine circumstances.[87]

Moving on, we might call "occasional" *bandos* those that were launched in response to casuistic, specific and non-predicted circumstances without an established periodicity. An overwhelming variety of themes can be Included in this second, more common, category: the regulation of fiscal repertoires and the activities of small and large commerce; the restriction of the movement of people within the cities, especially free women and enslaved persons; sanitary issues; and, above all, issues related to the administration of justice, namely

85 BNP, PBA, cod. 239; BNP, PBA, cod. 115.

86 *ABNRJ*, "Regimento que se há de observar no Estado do Brazil na Arrecadação do Tabaco", Informação Geral da Capitania de Pernambuco, 363.

87 BNRJ, Livro de Bandos, ms. 07, 03, 009.

those meant for the coercion of social violence or for the criminal's persecution. Such thematic variety could also derive from the fact that many *bandos* were merely answers to local petitions or information received by governors. Having established this distinction of types, the next section observes the elasticity of *bandos* in the governance of overseas territories, exploring concrete cases of their production by the governors and captain-generals of Madeira, Azores, Maranhão, Bahia, Pernambuco, Goiás and Angola.

5 Thematic Diversity of *Bandos* in the Portuguese Atlantic

The diversity of the matters conveyed in *bandos* reflects the complexity of tasks and jurisdictions that colonial governors were obligated to carry out and that today are associated with what we may call "civil administration". As it is virtually impossible to contemplate all the matters expressed in the *bandos* of the 17th and 18th centuries, this section only concentrates on six of the most recurrent themes: justice; navigation and trade; economic production; settlement and movement of people; moral questions; and sanitary issues.

5.1 Justice

As suggested by Covarrubias' definition of *bando* as a *pregão* proclaimed to "call any delinquent that has run away", one of the most important uses of such dispositions was the persecution of criminals. *Bandos* of this nature formalised a cooperation that was most needed between magistrates and governors, both for the surveillance and punishment of crimes. As armed forces were necessary for the diligences of justice, one could eventually associate this sort of *bando* with the military obligations of governors. However, it was more important to announce that the crimes had been committed and to create the conditions for the denunciation of criminals, as dozens of cases reveal. One launched in Belém, captaincy of Pará, by Governor Francisco de Sá e Meneses in 1683, for example, declared that a man named João Soares da Costa, arrested for many "harsh" and "atrocious crimes", escaped the fortress' prison and ran away. This *bando* called for the populace to stay alert and denounce his whereabouts, threatening punishment to all those who helped him escape or hid him in their homes, with the exact same punishments that would be applied to the condemned.[88] To aid the search, Governor á e Meneses appealed specifically

88 BNPA, 51-V-43, fol. 73r.

to the enslaved people, Africans and Amerindians, encouraging them to denounce the prisoner's whereabouts in exchange for rewarding them with their freedom.[89]

Other crimes, such as theft, could also be announced to the populace through *bandos*, like one published by Duarte Sodré Tibão in Pernambuco in 1730, communicating that a lamp made of precious materials was stolen from the church of Our Lady of the Pillar the previous night. He thereby summoned the settlers to secretly denounce the whereabouts of this piece and receive a secret reward for the efforts.[90] The threat of punishments and the offering of rewards, in such cases, were the means used most often to encourage the denunciation of criminals before the authorities.

5.2 Navigation, Trade and Commerce

Bandos were also crucial for organising the rhythms of navigation and intercontinental trade in the great port cities of the Portuguese Atlantic World. Until the mid-17th century, Portuguese vessels could cross the Atlantic without restriction, but the demand for protection against enemy ships and pirates introduced a strict fleet regime that continued from 1649 to 1766.[91] While it endured, merchant ships would all sail together, in convoy, under the armed protection of war vessels, and no ship could cross the ocean alone without a royal provision granted by the *Conselho Ultramarino*. For practical reasons, the fleet was divided into three smaller convoys that anchored in Pernambuco, Bahia and Rio de Janeiro. Once they arrived in America, each convoy would continue on to its destination port and await the loading of goods and commodities, sometimes detaching themselves in smaller groups to load in the ports of the neighbouring captaincies and then return to the main ports. After loading, the convoy of Rio de Janeiro would follow north to Salvador to meet the convoy of Bahia and, after they joined at sea, they would continue up to encounter the convoy of Pernambuco, where the three of them would start their home-bound voyage to Lisbon. In theory, all of this had to respect a very strict sailing calendar that considered the weather and tides, as well as a large-scale cooperation between governors of those three captaincies, based on their correspondence, was necessary to fulfil this schedule. When the fleet anchored in each of the ports, each governor would immediately dispatch letters to the other two governors, informing them that the fleet had arrived and,

89 BNPA, 51-V-43, fol. 73v.
90 AUC, CCA, cod. 32, fol. 180r.
91 Boxer, *O império marítimo português (1415–1825)*, 224.

most importantly, they would promulgate a *bando* that scheduled an estimated date for the departure of the convoy, in accordance with the fleet's captain-general. These *bandos* ordered the merchant community and proprietors to proceed, negotiate and load their cargoes onto the ships. The penalty for not doing so was to spend a whole year anchored, waiting for the next year's fleet.[92] All goods had to be loaded on time. The news that the fleets had departed from one port and were on their way to another would only speed up this process, and new *bandos* with more accurate dates would then be issued. At least 10 out of 33 launched in Pernambuco in 1691 and 12 of the 21 *bandos* published in Salvador in 1763 dealt with questions related to the fleets, either with changes in scheduling or loading problems.[93] These numbers suggest their importance among the normative production of colonial governors alongside the very dynamics that sustained the economic relations between Portugal and the Portuguese America.

The logistics of arrival, loading and departure of fleets brought with them other kinds of problems, and the governors answered some of these with *bandos*. To fiscally control the flow of precious metals and precious stones during the 18th century, royal instructions required governors to issue *bandos* to guarantee that they were properly loaded and sent to Portugal. *Bandos* such as these stated that gold and diamonds could only be transported in the coffers of the king's flagship so that they could be transported safely and be more easily controlled by the Royal Customs (*Alfândega*), in Lisbon.[94]

Besides cargo, some concerns involved the administration of crews. Death was part of sea life and, to replace sailors and other officers who passed away during voyages, governors often published *bandos* offering positions to anyone who wished to embark and fulfil the necessary posts of a ship's crew. The Marquis de Lavradio in March 1760 did this when he laid down a *bando* in Salvador offering positions for sailors, gunners and cabin boys to embark, to Lisbon, on the service of the flagship *Nossa Senhora da Ajuda*.[95] Desertion was also a key problem, with many sailors and tripulants deserting their ships on the eve of departure and hiding from their captains with the purpose of remaining onshore and trying out a new way of life in America. To prevent this, governors often issued *bandos* forbidding settlers to hide them in their houses,

92 AUC, CCA, cod. 31, fol. 200v.
93 BNRJ, Livro de Bandos, ms. 07, 03, 009, fols. 37r–45v.
94 AUC, CCA, cod. 32, fol. 474v.
95 BNRJ, Livro de Bandos, ms. 07, 03, 009, fol. 7r.

under penalty of a fine for those who concealed the runaway sailors.[96] Violent episodes between sailors and the soldiers garrisoned in Recife, for example, also triggered a *bando* launched by Governor Sousa Coutinho in June 1672, expressly prohibiting them from engaging in duels and street fights, under penalty of receiving lashes and *suplício* on the strappado (*polé*).[97]

Fleets were an essential system for transferring wealth from the American territories to Lisbon, and the preservation of colonial markets in Portuguese hands was another. Navigation conditions often proved harsh and, eventually, the Brazilian ports were opened to ships of foreign allied nations who needed repair and food supplies. Naturally, the presence of foreign ships often provided opportunities for smuggling between settlers and tripulants, leading governors to issue *bandos* forbidding them to go onboard foreign ships. In Salvador da Bahia, between 1760 and 1782, at least 13 *bandos* were made to prevent people going onboard English, French and Dutch vessels or even communicating with the sailors, under death penalty for anyone caught disregarding these measures.[98] A *bando* made in 1782, forbade people from hiding English sailors in their homes under the same penalty.[99] In Pernambuco, some decades earlier, in 1732, the governor forbade people from going onboard a French slave ship, stationed on the shores of Itamaracá, with the hidden purpose to trade enslaved people with the foreigners, under penalty of publicly burning the boats and *jangadas* of anyone who tried to do so.[100]

Angola never directly engaged with the fleet system. Instead, navigation was mostly organised in bilateral flows between Africa and America.[101] But here, *bandos* had an important role in the organisation of the transatlantic slave trade. A procedure, established by a law regarding the transportation of enslaved persons in 1684, gave central importance to *bandos* and lasted until the 19th century.[102] Before departure, the ship masters were obliged to petition the governor in Luanda to launch a *bando* scheduling a date for their voyage, like the one done by Manuel de Medeiros, master of a corvette ship, when he asked the governor for a *bando* to announce his voyage on 30 September 1764.[103] *Bandos* issued in response to petitions like these scheduled the voyages

96 Among a few examples, see AUC, CCA, cod. 31, fols. 359v, 559v; BNRJ, Livro de Bandos, ms. 07, 03, 009, fols. 82r, 122v.
97 AUC, CCA, cod. 31, fol. 267v.
98 BNRJ, Livro de Bandos, ms. 07, 03, 009, fols. 10r, 51r, 65v, 70v, 90v, 96v, 99v, 101r, 122r.
99 BNRJ, Livro de Bandos, ms. 07, 03, 009, fol. 122v.
100 AUC, CCA, cod. 32, fol. 468r.
101 Alencastro, *O trato dos viventes*, 116.
102 *ABNRJ*, Informação Geral da Capitania de Pernambuco, 209.
103 ANTT, Condes de Linhares, ms. 47, d. 139.

and warned that anyone interested in carrying enslaved people should "order their catechisation", probably baptism, and "provide the necessary provisions" for the voyage.[104] To give an idea of the importance of this sort of *bando*, no less than 87 from a total of 93 that were registered during the mandate of Governor Almeida de Vasconcelos in Angola (1790–1796) are related to the scheduling of slave voyages to Bahia, Pernambuco, Rio de Janeiro and Pará.[105] Such data suggests that they were essential for port governance, to organise and tax the slave trade, but, apparently, this specific type served only to schedule these dreadful voyages, threatening no form of penalty, since there was no actual form of transgression nor strict schedule to fit into, as seen in the Brazilian case.

Baptism of enslaved persons was a paramount concern of the Portuguese authorities in Angola, since it was one of the strongest moral justifications for the transatlantic slave trade.[106] A royal decree made in 1697 established that any person should be baptised before embarking in Angola for the plantations of Portuguese America, and the governors' *bandos* regularly reminded slave traders of this obligation. In January 1792, the same Governor, Almeida de Vasconcelos, issued one *bando* in Luanda to reinforce this measure. According to him "with the lapse of time, and the laxity that infuses this climate, the execution of the wise, catholic and pious intentions of our Augustus sovereigns has been forgotten", making it necessary to remind the settlers and traders of their obligations. He then consulted the government archives and found and entirely replicated one *bando* launched in February 1761 by Governor António de Vasconcelos, ordering that any slave traders who purchased enslaved persons from local traders should be obliged to arrange their conversion to Catholicism and baptism within 24 hours after purchase, incurring a fine of 1,000 *réis* for each unbaptised slave found.[107] To discover such irregularities, Vasconcelos offered half of the fine's value to anyone who denounced the transgression of this order. After the entire replication of the 1761 *bando*, the Governor Almeida de Vasconcelos complemented it with another measure that ordered all slave traders to mark the bodies of their baptised slaves with a *carimbo*. He also predicted that if there was not time to baptise slaves before they embarked to America, a small semi-circle was required to indicate that they still needed the sacraments.[108] This case is interesting because it shows the validity of

104 AHU, cod. 1634, fol. 1r.
105 AHU, cod. 1634, fols. 1r–23v.
106 Alencastro, *O trato dos viventes*, 155–188.
107 AHU, cod. 1634, fols. 7v–8r.
108 AHU, cod. 1634, fols. 7v–8r.

bandos as legitimate sources of law and normativity even after decades of their publications.

Though the examples above show how *bandos* were essential to communicate normativities that regulated the very foundations of colonial trade between America, Europe and Africa, governors also used *bandos* to regulate commercial relations within their own jurisdictions. In backland captaincies, such as São Paulo, Goiás or Minas, controlling land routes that connected those spaces to the port cities was essential for fiscal reasons, namely, to avoid tax evasion. Therefore, it was frequent during the 18th century for the governors of São Paulo or Minas to expressly forbid, through *bandos*, settlers and miners from opening new roads and routes to connect themselves to other captaincies, such as Bahia, Maranhão or Pernambuco. One made in São Paulo by Governor António Luís de Távora in October 1732 established that the only official route to access the captaincy of Goiás should be the road that connected it to the village of Jundiaí through Mogi dos Campos.[109] No slaves, cattle herds or any other cargo could be transported outside this route, under penalty of confiscation and public sale. Diffusion and surveillance of *bandos* in backland areas, however, was much more difficult, because the population was more dispersed, making the territories less reachable by Portuguese local or royal authorities. Though most *bandos* were published in the most frequented spaces of urban districts and towns, in the case of the backland and non-urban areas of the gold captaincies, mining fields and *arraiais*, where miners and local settlers were concentrated, were the privileged spaces for the promulgation of such normative dispositions to the sound of drums.[110] Denunciation was one of the few available methods used to unveil the transgression of *bandos* such as these, and rewards were often offered to denunciators, in this case, half of the confiscated cargo.[111]

Beyond the organisation of sea and land commercial routes, governors often used *bandos* to regulate local trade relations. Between 1720 and 1739, at least seven *bandos* were laid down by governors forbidding black women from going outside the town of Ouro Preto in order to sell groceries to miners in mining fields.[112] In Pernambuco, for example, four *bandos* issued in 1679, 1693, 1707 and 1731 expressly forbade traders and salesman from raising the prices

109 AUC, CCA, cod. 23.

110 AUC, CCA, cod. 23.

111 AUC, CCA, cod. 23.

112 Nunes, *Comunicação e prática política nas monarquias ibéricas de Antigo Regime (1700–1750)*, 199.

of manioc flour during times of scarcity.[113] Some of them established the very prices of manioc flour, a competence that was, in principle, reserved to municipal councils. The penalties for disregarding these *bandos* varied, from imprisonment for three months in jail to the payment of a heavy fine. Very similar measures can be found in late 18th-century Azores, where the General Government issued at least five *bandos* to regulate the sale of wheat and barley flour in public granaries and counter the speculation practiced by merchants in the islands of Terceira and São Miguel.[114] In Bahia, a *bando* issued in April 1761 forbade salesman and *jangadeiros*[115] from purchasing fish and seafood from fishermen before they disembarked, in order to stop them from reselling it to the local populace for double the purchase price. To face the shortage of groceries in Luanda, and attributing it to the prices that were fixed by the town council, Governor Almeida de Vasconcelos issued a *bando* allowing salesman to arbitrate the prices at their will, just as practiced in the markets of Lisbon, but promising "contemplation" for those who were willing to sell at lower prices for the "public benefit".[116]

Regional commerce could also find itself in the hands of *bandos*, as can be demonstrated in several examples. In Pernambuco, eight *bandos*, launched between 1679 and 1738, strongly controlled and forbade the commerce of manioc flour, to other ports and towns, with the purpose of retaining it for local consumption. The harsher the circumstances of scarcity, the stronger the penalties applied in those *bandos*, ranging from monetary fines, lashes and even two years of exile (*degredo*) in Angola.[117] Similar measures were adopted in one *bando* of April 1707 which expressly forbade settlers from taking enslaved persons from Pernambuco by sea or land routes with the intention of reselling them in other captaincies, especially in the flourishing mining zones where the demand for an enslaved working force was growing.[118] Another, made in Salvador, in August 1761 prohibited people from breeding mules instead of horses as they were noble and essential animals and were indispensable not only to daily life in Bahia, but also to the slave trade with African ports.[119]

---

113 AUC, CCA, cod. 31, fols. 339r, 472v, 567r; cod. 32, fols. 23r, 65v, 457v.

114 BPARLSR, CGA, liv. 49, fols. 20r–21v, 107v–108v; BPARLSR, CGA, liv. 50, fols. 11v–12r.

115 Owners of a *jangada*, a sort of flat boat made of several cords of wood tied up.

116 AHU, cod. 1634, fol. 11r.

117 AUC, CCA, cod. 32, fol. 274v.

118 AUC, CCA, cod. 32, fols. 12r, 620v.

119 BNRJ, Livro de Bandos, ms. 07, 03, 009, fols. 23r–23v.

5.3 Economic Production

In addition to commerce, governors could eventually issue *bandos* to stimulate or interfere with the economic production of commodities that were exported in global trade. A fine example can be found in the late 17th-century Maranhão, where Governor Sá e Meneses issued a *bando* to improve the quality of the sugar that this captaincy exported to Portugal. In this *bando*, published in 1682, he expressly mentioned complaints regarding the irregularities in which the product was weighed and that the amount of sugar arriving in Lisbon was often lower than described. Then, he ordered that all *senhores de engenho* of Maranhão be obliged to replace all weights of stone for weights of metal that should be checked by the municipal council every six months. Another measure was to improve the quality of the sugar crates, making them out of better wood and letting them dry for over a year before they were loaded with sugar. Any *senhor de engenho* who did not purchase and replace the weights within four months would receive a fine worth 100 *cruzados* the first time. If caught a second time, he would not only pay double that value but would also be put in jail for an indefinite time, at the governor's discretion.[120] To ensure the observance of these determinations, the governor offered rewards to anyone who denounced transgressors.

Regulations could also target the section of economic production that supplied internal markets with subsistence genres. To counter the effects of one of the many food crises experienced in 17th-century Olinda and Recife, Governor Francisco de Brito Freire circulated a *bando* in all the towns and parishes of Pernambuco in May 1661 determining that at least twice a year all farmers (*roceiros*) were obliged to plant 1,000 *covas*[121] of manioc per slave they owned, and the sugar mill owners and sugar planters (*senhores de engenho* and *lavradores*) had to, in turn, guarantee at least 500 *covas* in their properties.[122] If they were caught or denounced disrespecting this *bando* they would receive a fine worth 100 *cruzados*. Similar measures can be found in 18th-century Bahia, as we can see in a *bando* issued by the Marquis de Valença in 1781, mentioning that a law of 1701 and a *bando* of 1750 regarding the planting of manioc flour by the manioc planters had both fallen into oblivion, and that each of their slaves should plant at least 500 *covas* per year to supply the city of Salvador. For disregarding this *bando*, planters would be arrested and only released after

120 BNPA, 51-V-43, fol. 21v.

121 One *cova*, or hole, being equivalent to one plant of this root.

122 AUC, CCA, cod. 31, fol. 53v.

the payment of a bail worth 100,000 *réis*.[123] In 1740 Goiás, a *bando* by Governor Luís Mascarenhas determined that miners were forbidden from rushing and exploring new gold deposits before they planted subsistence farms near the mining fields for the sustenance of labourers and slaves, under penalty of the confiscation of their black slaves. In addition, the *bando* disposed that they could only initially enter the mining zones with farm tools.[124] Therefore, these *bandos* targeted the specific needs of daily governance that were not covered by royal legislation repertoires, and we could suggest that they fulfilled some legal gaps with measures based on experience and need. Further, it is necessary to remember that food supply was not only a matter of health, but also of social order in the Ancient Regime.

If one considers commerce and navigation as two of the backbones that defined colonial relations in any given empire, the many examples shown above demonstrate the importance of *bandos* in the regulation of such activities, either on the global, regional or local level. By diffusing knowledge on normativities, they can be regarded as one of the legal tools available not only to organise, but also to make colonisation and its economic rules intelligible to local communities. Colonial relations, however, were not restricted to commercial and economic matters.

5.4 Settling, Migration and Mobility

Colonising often meant settling, and *bandos* could be used to foment migration, forced or voluntary, and to communicate the measures that favoured displacement and movement of people between different territories. Despite some efforts, no permanent form of occupation had thrived in the islands of Fernando de Noronha, in northeastern Brazil, until the decades of 1730 and 1740. Before that, the islands were described as the refuge of pirates and privateers. The Crown and governors managed to occupy them by sending convicts who were charged with major or minor crimes. In this regard, some *bandos* made in the 17th and 18th centuries established deportation as a penalty for disregarding the dispositions conveyed in them, like in 1654, for example, when Governor Francisco Barreto de Meneses issued a *bando* condemning anyone who hid runaway slaves in their homes to conviction in Fernando de Noronha.[125] However, an attempt by the French to establish a permanent base in the islands in 1735 led the Crown to take more effective measures to create

123 BNRJ, Livro de Bandos, ms. 07, 03, 009, fols. 117r–118r.

124 AUC, CCA, cod. 23, fol. 96v.

125 AUC, CCA, cod. 31, fol. 17v.

a permanent defensive base. After reconquering them in 1736 and implementing several orders to establish a garrison in the islands, it was with a *bando* laid down in February 1738 that Governor Henrique Luís Pereira Freire offered lands and enough groceries to any inhabitant of Pernambuco who wished to embark to Fernando de Noronha and settle with his family to produce the subsistence items that were necessary for the island's self-sufficiency.[126] No penalties, in this case, were applied and the *bando* merely communicated conditions to encourage migration. Another issued by the Governor General in Azores in 1774 encouraged islanders to migrate to Rio de Janeiro and enlist themselves in the regular infantry companies, promising several advantages in terms of wages and time of service.[127]

In the same way that *bandos* could sometimes foment the movement of people between different territories, they could also establish measures to restrict it, especially within urban spaces. In Pernambuco, for example, a *bando* issued in June 1730 forbade black people, freed or enslaved, from walking and selling anything on the streets after 9pm. Another, made in November 1740, reinstated this measure, and prohibited enslaved people from running away and sleeping away from their masters' homes. This *bando* also forbade them from having rented houses in Recife for this specific purpose, and they had to be arrested if caught by the night watches.[128] A *bando* launched by the viceroy in Salvador in October 1760 forbade women specifically from walking unaccompanied and masked through the streets of the city, under penalty of arrestment, and a later one, published in November, extended this prohibition also to men.[129] To avoid the formation of marron communities in the hinterlands of Salvador, the interim members of the General Government established some policies conveyed in a *bando* of October 1763 to control the movement of black people in and out of the city. This *bando* ordered that all black persons who walked outside of their homes had to bear either their manumission letters (*cartas de alforria*) to prove that they were free or, if they were slaves, they had to bring written papers declaring their names, the names of their masters and the lands and properties where they lived. All this information had to be inspected by officers of the militia, and the penalty for disregarding the *bando* would be 100 lashes for enslaved persons and 20 days in jail for freed people of colour.[130] Measures conveyed in this type of *bando* expressed one of the means

126 AUC, CCA, cod. 32, fol. 314r.
127 BPARLSR, CGA, liv. 50, fols. 11v–12r.
128 AUC, CCA, cod. 32, fol. 630v.
129 BNRJ, Livro de Bandos, ms. 07, 03, 009, fols. 12v–13r.
130 BNRJ, Livro de Bandos, ms. 07, 03, 009, fols. 44v–45v.

normatively available to socially regulate racial and gender relations targeting, mostly, the enslaved and freed populace, but also woman of either enslaved, freed or free condition. For this reason, they could be regarded as normative repertoires that created politics of difference in the Portuguese cities and towns, by putting restrictions on the social behaviour of the subaltern populace.

5.5 Moral and Behavioural Issues

This can also be demonstrated with *bandos* that regulated specific behavioural and moral questions, such as the behaviours that should be observed in public rituals or church festivities. In the 18th century, during vacancies in the viceroyalty in Bahia, the Chancellor of the Bahian High Court, the highest command of the military forces and the archbishop formed a kind of council, called a *junta*, that replaced the viceroy as the head of the General Government.[131] It is interesting to note that during such occasions some agents could use the prerogatives of the vacant post to advance their own interests and policies, including through *bandos*. It is not a mere coincidence that, between 1760 and 1800, five of the six *bandos* made in Salvador regulating moral practices and religious festivities were published in times of vacancy, when the archbishop himself was at the head of the Governorship or participated in the *junta*. Speaking as one voice, they declared that they issued one of these *bandos* "as Sons of the church and Governors of the State",[132] an unusual attitude that clearly reveals the use of the civil-military position proportioned by the occupation of the Governorship to address social and moral discipline matters. In this same *bando*, launched in January 1763, they tried to suppress a popular festivity devoted to Saint Gonsalo, marked by several acts of cultural expression of the African cults, expressly forbidding people from parading and following the image of the saint through the streets of Salvador, and from making "noises, [and using] *atabaques*, war drums and other excesses".[133] These prohibitions transport us to the soundscape that marked the feast with expressions of cultural resistance, principally from the Afro-descendent populace. For disregarding this *bando*, the *junta* recommended penalties of six months in jail for white people, 13 months on the galleys for *mulattos* and *pardos* and no less than 500 lashes for black people, either free, freed or enslaved.[134]

---

131 Mota Bezerra, "Os governos interinos no Império Português (séculos XVII–XVIII)", 23–25.
132 BNRJ, Livro de Bandos, ms. 07, 03, 009, fol. 44v.
133 BNRJ, Livro de Bandos, ms. 07, 03, 009, fol. 44v.
134 BNRJ, Livro de Bandos, ms. 07, 03, 009, fol. 45v.

The surveillance of moral questions was frequently associated with public order, as we can see in a *bando* published by Governor Noronha e Brito in the captaincy of Goiás in January 1751. In this *bando* he expressly forbade balls and *batuques* that were held in the houses of some inhabitants of Vila Boa with the pretext that they were frequented by "white men, black and *mulata* women, freed and enslaved" and that they often resulted in "turmoil, challenges and other unrests that disturbed the quietude of the People and the peaceful tranquillity of its residents, resulting in great harm to the republic".[135] He thus forbade all settlers from holding such balls and *batuques*, with the penalty of two months in jail and a fine worth 28 *oitavas* of gold for white people and if black or *pardo* the penalty would be accompanied by lashes in a public space.

To this, we could certainly add other examples, such as the prohibition of gambling in Salvador da Bahia through three *bandos* launched in 1755, 1768 and 1782[136] or another prohibiting the construction of small sugar mills that were built for the production of *aguardente* in the captaincy of Minas in 1732, considered to be a "pernicious" stimulation of morally deviant miners and settlers of that captaincy.[137] But what is most interesting to highlight is that such prohibitions often targeted enslaved or freed populations, working as an attempt to suppress leisure-based activities or cultural manifestations of their faiths.

5.6 Sanitary Questions

Hundreds of examples could be given to address the thematic diversity of *bandos*, but to conclude this section, I would like to mention those issued by governors to regulate sanitary questions, a matter that is usually commissioned to the responsibility of municipal councils.[138] Our best examples are taken from Pernambuco. In the last two decades of the 17th century, Olinda and Recife suffered from a harsh plague often associated with yellow fever due to its symptoms.[139] To overcome them, Governor Antônio Félix Machado, Marquis of Montebelo, himself a victim of the plague, advised by some physicians of his circle, launched four *bandos* to counter the pandemic. Later known as "Bandos de Saúde", literally "health *bandos*", they prescribed a series of measures that had to be adopted to clean and purge the streets of Recife of the

135 AUC, CCA, cod. 23.
136 BNRJ, Livro de Bandos, ms. 07, 03, 009, fols. 84r–84v, 121v–122r.
137 AUC, CCA, cod. 23.
138 Magalhães, *Concelhos e organização municipal na Época Moderna*, 23.
139 Andrade, *Montebelo, os males e os mascates*, 151–170; Constant, "Governar o lugar da peste", 17–28.

"infected airs", as they believed at that time. The first, published in May 1691, ordered the registration of any person, sailor or passenger who disembarked from the ships. It also disposed that if they showed any symptoms, they were to remain in quarantine. A second *bando*, issued on that same day, regulated the burial practices of anyone who died from the plague, expressly forbidding any burials inside the churches and chapels. The third, launched a day later, imposed seven measures for sanitation, urban cleaning and even purification of the airs, that involved street clearance, washing houses and streets, waste management measures, disposal of clothes worn by the ill and the continuous burning of aromatic herbs to purify the infected airs.

A fourth *bando* was driven towards moral purification of the city. This disposition regulated the "public scandals" related to prostitution and promiscuity among the inhabitants. All women who depended on prostitution to survive had to be enlisted, and brothels had to be closed to the public. Besides this, like other *bandos*, it forbade the women from wandering the streets after 6pm, with the extreme penalty of permanent exile in Angola. Finally, the *bando* condemned "all white people and black, slaves or freed" who "sung songs with dishonest lyrics, played sounds and danced at balls that aroused luxury and scandal among good Christian people" to a fine and to have their instruments broken. All these extraordinary measures, simultaneously moral and sanitary, had to be closely supervised by commissioned inspectors directly appointed by the governor, the *Superintendentes da Saúde*, who could denounce transgressors and impose fines and other penalties to anyone who disrespected the measures conveyed in the *bandos*.[140] Penalties were so heavily imposed by Montebelo that the Crown revoked them a few years later, ordering his successor, Caetano de Melo e Castro, to cancel the *bandos*, except the second one regarding the burial of people inside the churches, which proved to be a reasonable practice.[141]

One hundred years later, in the city of Luanda, similar measures were taken by Governor Almeida de Vasconcelos against a plague of grasshoppers that infested the city. Fearing the effects that the insects could have over the "corruption of the air", and consequently to prevent the harm that may be caused to "the health of the inhabitants", he promptly issued a *bando* in April 1793 ordering all dwellers of the city to sweep the insects off their houses and to gather as many of them as possible for burial in deep holes under the earth.[142] After this, all streets and houses were to be purged, perfumed and smoked with

---

140 BNP, PBA, cod. 239, fols. 97r, 100r, 101r, 104r.

141 AHU, cod. 256, fol. 199v.

142 AHU, cod. 1634, fols. 12v–13v.

tar in order to purify the air. In contrast with the case of Pernambuco, the surveillance of this *bando* was carried out by the officers of the municipal council and *almotacés*, who had the duty of walking through the streets and checking whether or not the dwellers were fulfilling its requirements.

Together, the examples mentioned here are surely not sufficient to encapsulate all the matters governors expressed in *bandos*, but they do provide an image of their elasticity. One of the reasons that can explain this is that many *bandos* not only resulted from royal instructions or from the concerns of governors to deal with casuistic problems of governance, but could also formalise answers to local petitions. In 1671, for example, the town council of Olinda and the merchant community of Recife presented complaints to Governor Sousa Coutinho against peddlers who were selling retail cloth and fabrics in Pernambuco, thereby harming local shops. Sousa Coutinho answered both petitions with a *bando* forbidding peddlers from selling retail cloth under penalty of confiscation of their possessions.[143] After receiving petitions from the settlers of Sirinhaém, Governor Duarte Sodré Tibão sent a *bando* to the village, suspending a local tribute charged in manioc flour by the town council in 1731.[144] In both cases, governors reinforced the powers of petitioners and contributed to enhancing local authority.

6 Conclusion

The scattered evidence gathered at the present time cannot confirm whether the social uses of *bandos* in Portugal during the 17th and 18th centuries were mostly confined to military questions or not, and only future research within local archives will test the validity of this hypothesis. I have, however, demonstrated in this exploratory chapter that *bandos* were very adaptative normative dispositions that evolved far beyond their martial origins and purposes of production, becoming one of the most important normative dispositions for conveying and communicating authority in the Portuguese Atlantic world. More importantly, they were one of the key legal instruments available that governors disposed to create normativities within their own jurisdictions, understood here in both the legal and territorial sense. As royal governors gained the highest military post with the civil command of their districts, we could suggest that *bandos* were an expression of a normativity that depended on a martial context of production marked with its own rituality but that

143 AUC, CCA, cod. 31, fol. 288v.
144 AUC, CCA, cod. 32, fol. 454r.

addressed many aspects of imperial governance, in other words, a martial way of conducting the governance of non-military questions that were nevertheless crucial for defining colonial relations and politics of difference. In the governance of port cities and urban spaces, they were an important legal tool through which governors could play an important role and interfere in the balances of local governance, often concurring with the powers of local councils, as shown in the examples of sanitary or urban commerce regulations.

Even though some *bandos* merely served to disseminate information, being the most usual means to publicise royal orders, a substantial number of them established penalties for offenders in cases of noncompliance, thereby enhancing governors' powers in penal matters. After observing the *bandos* from different Atlantic territories, it was possible to verify that there are at least four recurrent penalty modalities. The first, and simplest, are fines imposed, either in terms of money or the sequestration of assets. The second, found in more serious issues, involved the imposition of exile to remote or frontier regions, like Angola, Fernando de Noronha or Ceará. The third involved corporal punishment, ranging from lashes, to torture on the strappado (*polé*) or the mutilation of limbs, mostly applicable to enslaved people. The fourth and final, death penalty, was, with some exceptions, only applied in situations of war or for controlling revolts. The four types were applied accordingly to the different social and racial status of people, which made enslaved people, Amerindians and *peões* more susceptible to more severe punishments. From this perspective, *bandos* appear to be a flexible and essential normative tool for shaping and administrating the politics of difference within imperial territories of the Portuguese Atlantic World. This is particularly evident when we consider that *bandos* were used to convey normativities that targeted and framed indigenous and black persons specifically.

Were those mechanisms effective enough to guarantee the compliance of settlers? Could they not just be ignored? Nonconformity with norms is an obvious part of social dynamics in any part of the world, and we can always ask ourselves how the transgression of such normativities was acknowledged and sentenced by governors. Though the prosecution of transgressors remains an unanswered question in this chapter, the supervision of *bandos* and the effective enforcement of penalties were prescribed in the very content of these normative dispositions and depended on two mechanisms: denunciation and surveillance. On the one hand, when published, *bandos* often opened the opportunity, or even imposed the social obligation, to denounce offenders and provided rewards for those who did so. Surveillance, on the other hand, could be entrusted to town councils, magistrates, military corps, night watches and officers who patrolled the cities and towns or even to scouts (*olheiros*) recruited specifically for the purpose. When dispatched to distant locations, application of the *bandos* was charged to the very intermediaries who received and published them, such as the town councils, royal magistrates and officers of the militia. Resistance to *bandos*, moreover, remains a topic for future research.

As normative expressions of the authority and power of command of governors, could the effects of *bandos* be comparable to the effects of royal normative dispositions, such as decrees or *alvarás*? The first question one should ask while considering this is: were they meant to endure like royal legislation? Or did they lose effectiveness when one governor succeeded the other in the post? Could they be acknowledged as legal references over time and space? Although they all had an immediate effect from the moment of publication, most had no expiration date or established validity. For this reason, it is difficult to predict whether the effects of a *bando* laid down by one governor ended with the arrival of his successor or whether they endured long after they were published. If their duration was determined by a governor's mandate, what motivated, for example, Caetano de Melo e Castro to petition the King to put an end to the *bandos de saúde* laid down by the Marquis de Montebelo in Pernambuco? Apparently, there were no other normative dispositions capable of revoking or annulling the effects of a *bando* except for royal warrants and orders issued by the Crown. Thus, in theory, a governor could not revoke the *bandos* of his predecessor. An atypical attitude is to confirm all *bandos* of a predecessor, just as the bishop D. Matias de Figueiredo, interim Governor of Pernambuco in 1688, did with those that were issued by deceased Governor Fernão Cabral.[145] What we more often see, however, is the reedition of *bandos* or the repetition of their subjects as shown in many cases, as society regularly needed reminding of some topics, such as the prohibition of duels or certain types of weapons, through *bandos*.

Even though I have not found a satisfactory solution for the question of endurance, I suggest that the recording of *bandos* in specific books of the governorship's secretariat created the opportunity to invoke them as normative sources. Otherwise, for what purpose were these books kept in the archives of the governorships? We can see this very clearly in Bahia, where the governor launched a *bando* in 1781 regarding the sale of manioc flour quoting a law from 1701 and a *bando* from 1750 or, even in 1782, when he forbade illicit games, mentioning a previous *bando* made in 1755.[146] Another *bando* made in 1783 Salvador mentioned royal warrants of 1641, 1696 and 1707, as well as the chapters

145 AUC, CCA, cod. 31, fol. 467r.

146 BNRJ, Livro de Bandos, ms. 07, 03, 009, fols. 117r–117v; 121r–122v.

of the *Ordenações* that regulated the sale of meat and butchery.[147] In this sense, though perhaps not eternal, they could surely be regarded as a powerful legal instrument to remind people of and convey the communication of normativities, making them known and intelligible under a ritualised and originally martial atmosphere of promulgation.

Finally, I hope to have presented enough evidence to suggest that, among many other sorts of normativities, *bandos* reflected legal changes in the Portuguese Atlantic World, where they acquired greater plasticity as legal tools that regulated aspects of imperial governance far beyond the military contexts they originated from. Though this chapter has reflected those changes in a broad political and territorial sense, regional studies are still necessary to observe them across time, considering the forms and contents of *bandos*, and how they were shaped and reshaped under the administration of different viceroys, governors and captain-majors. Such studies may contribute to the understanding of their importance as pragmatic instruments of governance, indeed one of the most interventive expressions of Portuguese rule, that contributed to shaping the social and political landscapes of the Atlantic territories.

Bibliography

Manuscripts

Anais da Biblioteca Nacional do Rio de Janeiro (ABNRJ), Informação Geral da Capitania de Pernambuco (1746), Rio de Janeiro 1908: Officinas de Artes Graphicas da Bibliotheca Nacional, 117–496.

Arquivo da Universidade de Coimbra (AUC), Coleção Conde dos Arcos (CCA), cod. 23.

Arquivo da Universidade de Coimbra (AUC), Coleção Conde dos Arcos (CCA), Disposições dos Governadores de Pernambuco, cod. 31 (1648–1699).

Arquivo da Universidade de Coimbra (AUC), Coleção Conde dos Arcos (CCA), Disposições dos Governadores de Pernambuco, cod. 32 (1700–1746).

Arquivo da Universidade de Coimbra (AUC), Coleção Conde dos Arcos (CCA), cod. 35, fol. 219r.

Arquivo Histórico Ultramarino, Lisboa (AHU), cod. 256, fol. 199v.

Arquivo Histórico Ultramarino, Lisboa (AHU), cod. 1634, Livro de Registo de Bandos do Exmo. Sr. Manuel de Almeida de Vasconcelos (1790–1794), fols. 1r–22v.

147 BNRJ, Livro de Bandos, ms. 07, 03, 009, fols. 124r–125v.

Arquivo Histórico Ultramarino, Lisboa (AHU), CU, Bahia, Luísa da Fonseca, box 14, doc. 1688, fol. 1v.

Arquivo Nacional Torre do Tombo, Lisboa (ANTT), Arquivo da Casa dos Condes de Povolide, suplemento 1, no. 3.

Arquivo Nacional Torre do Tombo, Lisboa (ANTT), Condes de Linhares, ms. 47, doc. 139.

Arquivo Nacional Torre do Tombo, Lisboa (ANTT), Manuscritos da Livraria, Livro nº 2611, "*Livro que há de servir na vedoria de Pernambuco...*" (sem data/c.17–).

Biblioteca Nacional de Portugal, Lisboa (BNP), Coleção Pombalina (PBA), [Anon.,] *alvitre*, "A respeito do Governo", cod. 526, fol. 265r.

Biblioteca Nacional de Portugal (BNP), Coleção Pombalina (PBA), cod. 115, Livro de Assento da Junta das Missões, Cartas Ordinárias, Ordens e Bandos [...] (1711–1715).

Biblioteca Nacional de Portugal, Lisboa (BNP), Coleção Pombalina (PBA), cod. 239, Livro de Portarias, Ordens Bandos [...] (1690–1693).

Biblioteca Nacional de Portugal, Lisboa (BNP), Regimento dos Governadores das Armas das Províncias, 01.06.1678, miscelânea, cod. 105, fol. 396r.

Biblioteca Nacional do Palácio da Ajuda (BNPA), 51-V-43, Livro de Ordens, Bandos e Portarias de Francisco de Sá e Meneses (1682–1685).

Biblioteca Nacional do Palácio da Ajuda (BNPA), 51-XI-34, Livro do Governo da Madeira (1688–1690).

Biblioteca Nacional do Rio de Janeiro (BNRJ), Coleção Documentos Históricos, vol. 107, 160.

Biblioteca Nacional do Rio de Janeiro (BNRJ), Livro de Bandos expedidos pelos governadores e capitães-generais do Estado do Brasil e dos Governadores e Capitães-Generais da Bahia (1759–1821), ms. 07, 03, 009.

Biblioteca Nacional do Rio de Janeiro (BNRJ), Livro de registos, I-12-03-035, fol. 41v.

Biblioteca Pública e Arquivo Regional Luís da Silva Ribeiro, Angra do Heroísmo (BPARLSR), ALL, CMAGH, C-A, 005, 008.

Biblioteca Pública e Arquivo Regional Luís da Silva Ribeiro, Angra do Heroísmo (BPARLSR), Capitania Geral dos Açores (CGA), liv. 49, liv. 1 de Registo de Portarias e Ordens do Governo-Geral dos Açores (1766–1773).

Biblioteca Pública e Arquivo Regional Luís da Silva Ribeiro (BPARLSR), Capitania Geral dos Açores (CGA), liv. 50, liv. 2 de Registo de Livro de Portarias e Ordens do Governo-Geral dos Açores (1773–1799).

Revista do Instituto Arqueológico Histórico e Geográfico Pernambucano (*RIHGP*), Diário do Governador Luís Correia de Sá, 1746–1756, vol. 56, Recife 1983, 9–378.

Printed Sources

Coelho, Laranjo (ed.), *Cartas dos Governadores da Província do Alentejo a El-Rei D. João IV e a El-Rei D. Afonso VI*, vol. II, Lisboa 1940: Academia Portuguesa da História.

Coelho, Laranjo (ed.), *Cartas dos Governadores da Província do Alentejo a El-Rei D. Afonso VI*, vol. III, Lisboa 1940: Academia Portuguesa da História.
Bluteau, Rafael, *Vocabulario portuguez e latino* [...], vol. 2: *Letras B–C*, Coimbra 1712: Collegio das Artes da Companhia de Jesu.
Bluteau, Rafael, *Vocabulario portuguez e latino* [...], vol. 6: *Letras O–P*, Coimbra 1720: Collegio das Artes da Companhia de Jesu.
Covarrubias Orozco, Sebastián de, *Tesoro de la lengua castellana o española*, Madrid 1611: Sanchez.
Real Academia Española, *Diccionario de la lengua castellana* [...], vol. 1, Madrid 1726: en la imprenta de Francisco del Hierro, impressor de la Real Academia Española.
Regimento das Fronteiras» (1645), in: Mendonça, Marcus Carneiro Xavier de. *Raízes da Formação Administrativa do Brasil*. Tomo II. Rio de Janeiro: Instituto Histórico e Geográfico Brasileiro, Conselho Federal de Cultura, 1972, 631–656.
Xavier, Filippe Nery, *Collecção de Bandos e outras diferentes providências que servem de leis regulamentares para o governo económico e judicial das províncias denominadas Novas Conquistas*, Pangim 1840: Imprensa Nacional.

Literature

Alencastro, Luiz Felipe de, *O trato dos viventes. Formação do Brasil no Atlântico Sul, séculos XVI e XVII*, São Paulo 2000.
Andrade, Gilberto Osório de, *Montebelo, os males e os mascates. Contribuição para a história de Pernambuco na segunda metaâe do século XVII*, Recife 1969.
Borah, Woodrow, "Los lazos con la capital y con otras provincias", in Borah, Woodrow (ed.), *El gobierno provincial en la Nueva España (1570–1787)*, México 2002, 207–212.
Boxer, Charles R., *O império marítimo português (1415–1825)*, Lisboa 2015.
Cardim, Pedro and Miguel Baltazar, "A difusão da legislação régia (1621–1808)", in Monteiro, Nuno Gonçalo and João Fragoso (eds.), *Um reino e suas repúblicas no Atlântico: comunicações políticas entre Portugal, Brasil e Angola nos séculos XVII e XVIII*, Rio de Janeiro 2017, 161–207.
Constant, Bernardo Manoel Monteiro, "Governar o lugar da peste: disputas políticas e construções simbólicas sobre a epidemia dos males no Governo do Marquês de Montebelo (Pernambuco, 1685–1695)", in *Revista Ágora* 32, no. 2 (2021), 1–33.
Cooper, Frederick and Jane Burbank, *Empires in World History: Power and the Politics of Difference*, Princeton 2010.
Coronado Schwindt, Gisela, "La dimensión auditiva del poder en los ámbitos urbanos del reino Castilla entre la Baja Edad Media y la Temprana modernidad", in *Huarte de San Juan. Geografía e Historia*, no. 30 (2023), 139–160.
Cosentino, Francisco, Mafalda Soares da Cunha, António Castro Nunes and Ronald Raminelli, "Governadores reinóis e ultramarinos", in Monteiro, Nuno Gonçalo and

João Fragoso (eds.), *Um reino e suas repúblicas no Atlântico: comunicações políticas entre Portugal, Brasil e Angola nos séculos XVII e XVIII*, Rio de Janeiro 2017, 299–334.
Costa, Fernando Dores, *Insubmissão. Aversão ao serviço militar no Portugal do século XVIII*, Lisboa 2010.
Curvelo, Arthur, *Governar Pernambuco e as "capitanias anexas": o perfil de recrutamento, a comunicação política e as jurisdições dos governadores da Capitania de Pernambuco (c.1654–c.1756)* (Ph.D. Thesis), Lisboa 2019.
Duve, Thomas. "What Is Global Legal History?", in *Comparative Legal History* 8, no. 2 (2020), 7–115.
Garavaglia, Juan Carlos, "La cuestión colonial", in *Nuevo Mundo Mundos Nuevos* (2005), https://doi.org/10.4000/nuevomundo.441, 1–52.
Guapindaia, Mayra, *O controle do fluxo das cartas e as reformas de Correio na América Portuguesa (1796–1821)* (Ph.D. Thesis), Lisboa 2019.
Herzog, Tamar, "Colonial Law: Early Modern Normativity in Spanish America", in Tellkamp, Jörg Alejandro (ed.), *A Companion to Early Modern Spanish Imperial and Political Thought*, Leiden 2020, 105–127.
Hespanha, António Manuel, *Poder e instituições na Europa do Antigo Regime. Colectânea de Textos*, Lisboa 1984.
Hespanha, António Manuel, "Por que é que foi 'portuguesa' a expansão portuguesa? Ou o revisionismo nos trópicos", in Souza, Laura de Mello e, Júnia Ferreira Furtado, and Maria Fernanda Bicalho (eds.), *O governo dos povos*, São Paulo 2009, 39–62.
Hespanha, António Manuel, "Modalidades e limites do imperialismo jurídico na colonização portuguesa", in *Quaderni fiorentini per la storia del pensiero giuridico moderno*, no. 41 (2012), 101–135.
Kluger, Viviana, "Disciplinamiento familiar y social en el Rio de La Plata, Tucumán y Cuyo: amancebados, casados ausentes e hijos fujitivos en la mira de los bandos de buen gobierno", in *Revista de Historia del Derecho*, no. 33 (2005), 131–158.
Magalhães, Joaquim Romero, *Concelhos e organização municipal na Época moderna*, Coimbra, 2011.
Martins, Cínthya da Silva, *Ao rufar das caixas, leia-se o bando: estudo diacrônico da tradição discursiva Bando no Ceará (1670–1832)* (Master's Thesis), Fortaleza 2013.
Mello, Evaldo Cabral de, *A fronda dos mazombos. Nobres contra mascates, Pernambuco, 1666–1715*, São Paulo 2003.
Melo, Josemar Henrique, *A ideia de Arquivo. A secretaria do Governo da Capitania de Pernambuco (1687–1809)* (Ph.D. Thesis), Porto 2006.
Monteiro, Ana Rita, "Moçambique, 1750–1800: Os 'Bandos' na administração do território", in *Africana* 22 (2000), 7–32.
Monteiro, Nuno Gonçalo, *Elites e poder. Entre o Antigo Regime e o Liberalismo*, 3rd ed., Lisboa 2012.

Mota Bezerra, Naira Maria, “Os governos interinos no Império Português (séculos XVII–XVIII)”, in *Revista Ágora* 32, no. 3 (2021), 1–30.

Nieto Soria, José Manuel, “El pregón real en la vida política de la castilla Trastámara”, in *Edad Media. Revista de Historia* 13 (2012), 77–102.

Nunes, António Castro, *Comunicação e prática política nas monarquias ibéricas de Antigo Regime (1700–1750): Évora, Córdova, Ouro Preto e Quito* (Ph.D. Thesis), Évora 2016.

Rodrigues, José Damião, “‘Para sossego e tranquilidade pública das ilhas’”: fundamentos, ambições e limites das reformas pombalinas nos Açores”, in *Tempo* 11, no. 21 (2006), 144–170.

Rodrigues, José Damião, “‘Com exorbitância inaudita’: elites locais e magistrados régios na Horta em finais de Setecentos”, in Garrido, Álvaro, Costa, Leonor Freire, Duarte, Luís Miguel (orgs.), *Estudos em homenagem a Joaquim Romero Magalhães. Economia, instituições e império*, Coimbra 2012, 215–225.

Roque, Ricardo, “A voz dos bandos: colectivos de justiça e ritos da palavra portuguesa em Timor-Leste colonial (séculos XIX–XX)”, in A. B. Xavier and C. N. Da Silva (eds.), *O governo dos outros: poder e diferença no império português*, Lisboa 2016, 235–265.

Ross, Richard, “Legal Communications and Imperial Governance: British North America and Spanish America Compared”, in Michael Grossberg and Christopher Tomlins (eds.), *The Cambridge History of Law in America*, vol. 1, Cambridge 2008, 104–143.

Salvino, Romulo Valle, *Os correios dos governadores: sistemas de comunicação escrita administrativa e militar na América portuguesa,* Jundiaí 2024.

Sellers-García, Sylvia, *Distance and Documents at the Spanish Empire’s Periphery*, Stanford 2014.

Slemian, Andréa, “Estilos das relações: práticas fundacionais para o Tribunal de Pernambuco (1826–1831)”, in *LexCult. Revista eletrônica de direito e humanidades* 4, no. 2, (2020), 88–107.

CHAPTER 6

Legal Changes and Royal Officers in Portuguese America

The *Correições* in the Towns of Curitiba (1721) and Aquiraz (1729) and their Normative Power

Gustavo César Machado Cabral

1 Introduction

In Early Modern Catholic monarchies, such as Portugal, the idea of a universe created by God was strong enough to determine the foundations of the legal phenomenon. According to scholastic legal thought, human law was part of a natural order based on God's will; as a result, its enforceability depended on its conformity with natural order. A statute enacted by the proper authority was only enforceable if it was in accordance with natural law, since no human act against the natural order was allowed, no matter how the political power was organised in that community.

For these reasons, which I have explored elsewhere,[1] I am convinced that, in Catholic monarchies, during most of the Early Modern period, human law had a declarative role rather than a constitutive one.[2] Human law did not create an autonomously legal status; it only regulated specific situations following what was believed to be part of the natural order. This argument explains the mainstream Portuguese legal thinking that prevailed until the mid-18th century, after which new political ideas took shape and the Crown found other arguments besides the metaphysical ones to exercise its powers.[3]

This introductory remark is important for understanding the dynamics of the legal sources in the Portuguese Empire because of their belonging to an essentially Christian legal order highly dependent on the arguments of God's

1 Among others, see Cabral, "Os Jesuítas e a construção da ordem jurídica", 275–297; Cabral, "Jesuit Pragmatic Literature", 151–186; Cabral, *O Direito na América Portuguesa*.
2 From the same perspective, see Vallejo, "Acerca del fruto del árbol", 36–42.
3 Among others, see Torgal, *Ideologia política e teoria do estado na Restauração*.

© 2026 THE AUTHOR(S) | HTTPS://DOI.ORG/10.1163/9789004764422-007

will and divine providence.[4] While the possibility of human actions to interfere in social reality through legal instruments was quite limited and depended on conformity with that Christian legal order, we can clearly see a bunch of legal sources that share the same fundamental grounds. With this teleological aim to regulate human actions and to make people behave according to this idea of natural order, human law had an unequivocal rhetorical nature, considering its intention to persuade people to follow what was allegedly the right thing to do.[5]

Among this persuasive means, we find the argument of authority grounded in the classics (particularly Greek and Latin poetry) and moral theologians and jurists of the *ius commune* tradition, as well as Biblical allegories. Following the Aristotelean rhetoric and the appeal to the audience's emotions, fear became an outstandingly persuasive mode (1381a21–1383b11) for human law. In a legal text, such as a statute, the materialisation of the fear meant the possibility of a sanction. Alongside the description of the unwanted behaviour, criminal statutes, like Book 5 of the Portuguese Royal Laws (*Ordenações Filipinas*), indicated the utmost penalty the judge could rule, but it did not mean that the judges adjudicated those penalties very often. Literature demonstrates that the actual application of severe penalties was not that frequent, due to the possibility of the judge to choose the appropriate penalty for the case and due to the power of the king in forgiving or commuting it.[6] The very possibility of being punished for an undesired behaviour could persuade people to act according to legislation.

Bearing in mind the role of the Crown in shaping behaviours, aiming to create a Christian society in America, the officials held a prominent position. Not only were the Crown officials sent to the New World to deal with jurisdictional matters, such as the royal *ouvidores*, but the local ones, the so-called *oficiais da câmara*, were also appointed among the citizens of the local communities. By accomplishing their duties, these officials crucially contributed toward the implementation of a legal order based on the Catholic theological and *ius commune* traditions.

This chapter analyses the role of the *ouvidores* in this process, considering the relations between local realities and the Crown and their role in changes

4 The works of António Manuel Hespanha are particularly influent to this perspective. See, among others, Hespanha, *As vésperas do Leviathan*; Hespanha, "A constituição do império português".

5 Some of these ideas are developed in Cabral, "Uma teoria do direito para a América Portuguesa", 17–52.

6 On this topic, see Hespanha, "Da 'iustitia' à 'disciplina'", 493–578; Meccarelli, *Arbitrium*; Cabral, "Direito penal na literatura", 23–76.

in normative practices, under the influence of a perspective focused on the knowledge of normativity.[7] The individuals living in political communities of the Portuguese Empire, once they had accepted the authority of the king and the Catholic faith, were subjects of the Crown, but this did not mean a general success for every order that came from the Court in Lisbon. Though sometimes these relations were strained, inciting strong reactions from the Crown, at other times the geographical distance separating these communities and the centres of power resulted in a disagreement between local and general interests that had to be resolved by the action of royal officials who were to fulfil, as much as possible, the interests of the Crown.

Serving in office for only a three-year term, the *ouvidores* were not originally from the area in which they were acting. Economic and some personal relations with locals (for example, marriage and commercial partnerships) were forbidden. Studies, like Stuart Schwartz's classic book on the Court of Bahia, have demonstrated that close relations between royal judges and local elites did occur in a few cases,[8] but this happened more regularly with magistrates, who acted for longer periods. Since the terms of the *ouvidores* were shorter and their activities included expeditions to areas that were far away from the head of the circumscription, they were agents who were not part of local dynamics. As erudite judges (*letrados*), they were supposed to follow the laws enacted by the king in their two main activities: the judgement of civil and criminal claims and corrections (*correições*) in the towns under their jurisdiction. Their role in the corrections is the most relevant part of this study because, during this activity, the *ouvidores* were in contact with local institutions and local norms and decided, in many cases, which norms should be observed in the local sphere.

In short, the corrections were expeditions made by Crown officials around the area under their jurisdiction in order to supervise some issues, such as the administration of justice and the actions of local officials. In the Peninsular space of the Portuguese Monarchy, the officials in charge of the corrections in the areas that belonged to the Crown were the *corregedores*; overseas, the royal *ouvidores* were in charge of the corrections. As Roberta Stumpf pointed out, during the inspection the *ouvidores* consulted papers and books produced by the peripherical administration.[9] Among the duties of the royal *ouvidores* in Portuguese America was travelling around their *comarcas* to inspect those

7 Duve, "Legal History as a History of the Translation".
8 Schwartz, *Sovereignty and Society*.
9 Stumpf, "Correições baianas", 203–205.

areas, and after each inspection the *ouvidor* had to put in writing what the people of the inspected areas were supposed to do from then onwards. These instructions, known as *capítulos de correição*, are not so easy to find in contemporary archives, and maybe this is the reason why there are not many studies on the corrections, despite a growing interest in the last years.[10]

In the following pages, after dealing with the role of local law in the Portuguese Empire, I discuss the normative powers of the *ouvidores* during the *correições*. Two *correições* will be in the spotlight, both of which were carried out during the first half of the 18th century in the towns of Curitiba (1721) and Aquiraz (1729). As time went by, Curitiba and Aquiraz experienced different fortunes: while, today, the former is the capital of the state of Paraná, with one of the highest HDIs among Brazilian cities, the latter is a quiet, 80,000-inhabitant city that is highly dependent on tourism. By the first half of the 18th century, however, the similarities were big enough to spark a comparative study. While the provisions of the *correição* in Curitiba were published almost a century ago, the provisions of Aquiraz consist in a manuscript, part of a book of the municipal council of the town where royal legislation was written down, that can be found in the Public Archive of Ceará (APEP) in Fortaleza.

Comparative legal history[11] is a useful perspective to understand the similarities and the distinctions between these two cases. The sources analysed here have a common background, which is the autonomy of the local towns and the control the Crown had over them, but their experiences, from a legal historical perspective, were different. These differences can be better explained if we look precisely at the role of the local phenomenon, where the ideas of glocalisation and translation become useful: leaving behind the "binary division" of local and global, this chapter looks at the production of normativities from a local perspective,[12] since every global legal issue exists in a local reality. The aims of this chapter align with a perspective that understands legal history "as a process of translation of normative knowledge, integrating normative information stemming from other areas and converting them in the act of cultural translation into local knowledge".[13]

---

10 Mello, *Administração, justiça e poder*; Mello, *Magistrados a serviço do rei*; Paiva, *Justiça e poder na América Portuguesa*; Stumpf, "Correições baianas"; Atallah and Mota, "Justiça e bem-estar dos povos".

11 Among others, see Halpérin, "Histoire comparée du droit", 183–203.

12 Duve, "Legal History as a History of the Translation".

13 Duve, "What Is Global Legal History?", 113.

2 Local Law in the Portuguese Empire

Ibero-American legal historiography has shown a growing interest in an analysis that considers particular legal experiences focused on specific areas, and not on general viewpoints. Victor Tau Anzoátegui highlighted that what he referred to as local and provincial law must consider "every city, province or kingdom, observing from below the plot of the juridical life, realising its development and verifying its alternatives of apogee and decline".[14] Law has to be seen as "historically shaped, entangling with the culture and the mentality of the *ius commune*, with the particularity of having arisen in different places and circumstances from its European predecessors".[15]

The relevance of such studies, like the one published by Tau Anzoátegui, can be found in the emphasis on the local phenomenon, since traditional studies, particularly those on the so-called *derecho indiano*, were more concerned with general issues. One of the problems that arose from this traditional historiography is the risk of increasing the duality between centre and periphery, which should be avoided. Since the proposal of this chapter is more related to a perspective based on ideas of diversity, which features polycentric monarchies and empires, such as the Portuguese,[16] and also assumes that the legal phenomenon in Iberian monarchies is composed of somewhat local experiences linked to a common tradition, it seems to be a mistake to study the legal experience in Colonial Brazil as if there are two separate worlds, that is to say, the standard legal experience and the particular ones, as if they exist apart from each other. There were local communities connected to the Portuguese Crown that had to be organised following that tradition and royal law. The *ouvidores*, particularly due to the *correições*, acted as intersectional points among those communities and the Crown. For those reasons, this study is not interested in depicting peculiarities nor curious cases of political communities, but it intends to understand how this connection was maintained.

A starting point in this analysis is the division suggested by Alejandro Agüero for the studies of legal local experiences. The first category is what he calls 'local law', norms directly or indirectly produced by local authorities, such as municipal statutes (*posturas locais*, in Portuguese), customary law and privileges. The category 'localization' focuses on the interpretation of a general

14 Tau Anzoátegui, "La configuración del derecho Indiano", 25.

15 Tau Anzoátegui, "La configuración del derecho Indiano", 27.

16 Among many others, see Hespanha, *As vésperas do Leviathan*; Hespanha, "A constituição do império português"; Xavier and Nogueira da Silva (eds.), *O governo dos outros*; Cardim et al., "Introduction", 3–10.

legal order made by local authorities.[17] While 'local law' highlights a static perspective, 'localization' is more concerned with the dynamics resulting from the actions of Crown officials.

This idea is useful to understand what I call local law in a way that is immediately related to the spatiality of the legal phenomenon. Determining the legislator is one issue in the study of local law, but it can hardly be considered the only one. This chapter is more concerned with what is valid, what was believed as being endowed with normativity within a certain space, particularly the space of a town. Certainly, it has much in common with what traditional legal historians have studied under the name of *iura propria* or the *derecho municipal* in the studies on the *derecho indiano*, but those categories do not seem to be sufficient to explain the common points among local realities and royal law.[18] These interactions must be understood in a different way.

An important element for this study is that cities and towns were part of the Portuguese imperial structure, even if they were in remote areas. The very idea of a town, respecting its creational process, meant that those people living there shared and were part of the Portuguese tradition. As Maria Fernanda Bicalho and Nuno Monteiro have pointed out, the municipal councils, alongside the *ouvidorias*, the captaincies, the parishes and the *sesmarias*, were institutions that Portugal reproduced in the territories under its authority and its formal control,[19] and the Crown followed legally based proceedings to erect a town. The legal instrument that granted and, at the same time, limited the political autonomy of the town was the *foral*, a formal document enacted by the Crown and whose origins date back to the Middle Ages. A *foral* nominated both the powers acknowledged to the municipal councils and the matters under their competence in the government of the town.[20]

The *foral* had a role in granting and, simultaneously, limiting the powers of political communities whose autonomy was far from unrestricted. Under the influence of the Aristotelean idea of political community, scholasticism provided legal and theological frameworks for this autonomic discourse based

---

17 Agüero, "Local Law and Localization", 101–129.

18 Among many others, for the *ius commune*, the traditional perspective on this division can be found in Calasso, *Medio Evo del Diritto*. For a critical perspective, see Duve, "Von der Europäischen Rechtsgeschichte", 18–71. For criticism of the traditional perspective of the *derecho indiano*, including the notions of *derecho municipal*, see Hespanha, "O 'direito das Índias'", 43–83; Herzog, "Colonial Law", 105–127.

19 Bicalho and Monteiro, "As instituições civis", 209–236.

20 On the *forais* and their progressively decreasing relevance in Portugal, see Hespanha, *História das instituições*, 152–154; Hespanha, *Uma monarquia tradicional*, 229–249.

on the idea of 'republic', described by Francisco Suárez.[21] According to this view, towns were republics living under a regime of autonomy that, from a more radical perspective, was strong enough to legitimise the derogation of royal laws by local customs.[22] References to the expression "republica" were common in the documents dating from those years.[23] Far from prevailing, this argument illustrates how far the discourse of autonomy could go, but it did not completely convince the Crown, who only acknowledged these prerogatives under rigid control.

Charles Boxer's outstanding book on the municipal councils of Salvador, Luanda, Goa and Macau clearly demonstrated the similarities in the organisation of local powers in cities located in four areas very distant from one another within the Portuguese Empire.[24] There was no aprioristic difference in whether the city was placed in the Kingdom or overseas, because their legal regimes could still be (but not necessarily were) very much alike. Referring to political representation, for example, the cities that were the heads of the Portuguese overseas states (Brazil, Maranhão and India), Salvador da Bahia, São Luís and Goa, had representatives (*procuradores*) in the courts that took place after the 1640 Restoration.[25] This kind of political arrangement had an unquestionable impact on the creation of a sentiment of belonging, which we can clearly see in documents, like a letter from 8 September 1660 written by some citizens of Salvador to the King, asking for the edition of a law prohibiting the construction of new sugar mills on the coast of the captaincy,[26] among many others. Only citizens under the authority of the King, living in areas under his jurisdiction, could ask for similar measures.

Among the powers held by the municipal councils, the possibility of enacting norms is particularly relevant for this study. This power was not limitless, since it was part of the structure previously mentioned: a legal order based on the Christian tradition in which local authorities had few possibilities to

21 Suárez, *Tractatus de legibus*, 113–205.

22 For an example of this radical view, see "Apologia Pro Paulistis (1684)", 362–416.

23 Among many other examples, using the word "republic" to refer to an idea of common good for the community, there is a record of a session of the Municipal Council of Salvador, held on 9 February 1649, that mentions: "[…] in this way, His Majesty […] considers that it should not be sold, and even less as stated, as it is for the common good of this Republic […]". *Documentos históricos do Arquivo Municipal*, vol. 2, 38. In the same way: "Oath of office and sworn statement of the officials entering to serve in the Republic in this year of 1723". *Boletim do Archivo Municipal de Curityba*, vol. 10, 37–38.

24 Boxer, *Portuguese Society*.

25 Bicalho, Rodrigues and Cardim, "Cortes, juntas e procuradores", 101–135.

26 AHU, Bahia, Luísa da Fonseca, box 15, doc. 1778.

implement true innovative legal measures in local spaces, as Tamar Herzog pointed out when she analysed the case of Spanish America.[27] In order to determine the province of local normative powers, the *Ordenações Filipinas* stated, in the section dedicated to the municipal councils, the matters that corresponded to the competence of the towns. The *posturas*, as the statutes enacted by municipal councils were known, dealt with the use of common goods and the goods of the council and with charging taxes and fines, while the *almotacés*, who were local officials, dealt with the regulation of urban cleaning, weighing and measuring and neighbourhood rights.[28] Based on documents and other primary sources, historiography added further matters: food supply, organisation of the mechanical offices, organisation of fairs and markets and the administration of the wasteland in the town.[29]

In short, local law dealt with questions directly related to the ordinary life of those political communities, namely food supply and some commercial issues, particularly relating to the monopoly granted to the municipal council after a royal order. The so-called *estanco* was seen as a good of the council and was very often auctioned to a private person who explored the business. A comparative analysis of some municipal *posturas* exemplifies the matters previously mentioned; a statute enacted on 28 August 1655 by the Municipal Council of Salvador regulated fishing and the use of fishing nets around the town, prescribing a fine and imprisonment in cases of non-compliance.[30] On 2 January 1709, the Municipal Council of Curitiba forbade people who had no license from selling spirits, prescribing a fine in cases of non-compliance.[31] Some years before, the Municipal Council of São Paulo created, in a statute from 28 March 1702, a fine for the disobedience of the monopoly (*estanco*) in the selling of wine, olive oil and vinegar,[32] as well as forbidding, on 19 September 1705, the sale of some foodstuffs (wheat flour, beans, corn and cattle) outside the jurisdiction of the town.[33]

Enacting norms and providing a means to make people observe them was part of the police' power (*Gute Policey*), a wider concept that included the traditional idea of municipal administration and its activities, which was related

27 Herzog, "Colonial Law", 119–121.
28 *Ordenações Filipinas*, livro 1, tit. 66 and 68.
29 Monteiro, "Os concelhos e as comunidade", 283–287.
30 *Documentos históricos do Arquivo Municipal*, vol. 2, fols. 254v–255r.
31 *Boletim do Archivo Municipal de Curityba*, vol. 2, 93.
32 *Actas da Camara Municipal de S. Paulo*, 31–32.
33 *Actas da Camara Municipal de S. Paulo*, 86–87.

to a literature concerned with the good administration of the house.[34] In the curse of the 18th century, during its incorporation into Portuguese legal literature, police became even more related to the idea of public administration, a perception that was already clear in the ancient use of the word. The famous manuscript by the Vicomte da Lapa, written in 1813, refers to this traditional concept of *polícia*, which dates back to the Middle Ages, as the specific activities of the communal administration to maintain public order and public cleaning.[35] Most of the municipal *posturas*, both in the Kingdom and in America, can be understood through this concept, whose comprehension not only continued into the existence of the statute, the introduction of the norm in the social world, but can also be found in the means to guarantee that this statute would be enforceable. Most of these statutes punished non-compliance with fines, imprisonment or even exile to outside of the town's jurisdiction and, in ordinary life, a council's official (*almotacé*) was in charge of inspecting the observance of the legal determination on foods and fairs, for example.

Until now, this chapter has been concerned with one expression of local law, the statutes enacted by the municipal councils. Alongside the municipal statutes, which consist in the first material evidence of local law that legal historians mention, I have gathered three other possible species of local law. The local customs, understood as the legal norms that emerged from the uses of such a community, inducing tacit agreement about their content,[36] will not be discussed here, as well as what I call the royal norms registered by the municipal councils, which are instead the topic of a specific study under development.[37] There is a fourth expression, however, that I analyse in the following pages: the norms enacted by the *ouvidores* for the areas under their jurisdiction. This phenomenon is particularly interesting because the *ouvidores* not only enacted norms for specific areas, many of them directly dependent on royal law, but they also controlled the local norms enacted by the municipal councils. It is quite similar to what Agüero described as the 'localization' of law.

34 For an overview of the concept of *polícia* in Portugal and its latter relations with the idea of public administration, see Seelaender, *Polizei, Ökonomie*, 56–64. For a more complex analysis of the literature and the use of *Policey* in Germany, see Stolleis, *Geschichte des öffentlichen Rechts*, 334–365.

35 Seelaender, *Polizei, Ökonomie*, 74–75.

36 Hespanha, *Como os juristas viam o mundo*, 158.

37 The forthcoming study, "On letters and laws: Books of the Municipal Council in Portuguese America (18th century)", is based on a discussion during the conference "The Dynamics of Early Modern Colonial Law and Legal Literature at the University of Helsinki" (October 2022).

3 *Ouvidores* and their Normative Powers

The legal regime of the *ouvidores* in Portuguese Empire was complex due to many reasons, starting with the different uses of the name *ouvidor* for distinct offices. In mainland Portugal, there were the royal *ouvidores*, whose attributions were overall jurisdictional. They were in charge of adjudicating appeals of decisions taken by first grade judges, both ordinary judges and the *juízes de fora*,[38] who acted in the towns under their jurisdiction, but they also had the authorisation to judge (*de conhecer*) new legal suits, that is to say, first grade claims. *Comarca* was the name of the jurisdictional space of the *ouvidores*. The administrative control of the municipal councils in the *comarcas* was part of the duties of another official, the *corregedor*. Lisbon and Oporto have a different institutional organisation because of the existence of the courts, respectively the *Casa da Suplicação* and the *Tribunal da Relação do Porto*. Among the *desembargadores* of the *Casa da Suplicação*, there was an *ouvidor-geral* for the criminal claims, in charge of ruling the appeals.

There were also manorial *ouvidores*, appointed by the landlords who had the privilege to nominate appeal judges in an area under their jurisdiction. Their powers were essentially to adjudicate appeals but, since the privileges *de non appellando* were not very commonly granted to landlords in the Portuguese Empire, their decisions could be reviewed by courts like the *Casa da Suplicação*.[39] Manorial *ouvidores* had no correctional functions, therefore the *correições* were an attribution of the *corregedores*, an office that was not found overseas.

In Portuguese America, the royal *ouvidores* cumulated correctional and jurisdictional powers, reaching areas that were part of the lordships, which in Brazil were called *capitanias hereditárias*. Appointed by the Crown, from those who had a law degree and served a three-year term, the royal *ouvidores* had first level jurisdiction of some *léguas* around the place where they were (the so-called head of the *comarca*) and second level to rule appeals from the decisions taken by ordinary judges and, more rarely, the *juízes de fora*.[40] They were also in charge of the *correições* in all the areas inside the *comarca*, supervising

38 While the ordinary judges (*juízes ordinários*) were elected as members of the municipal councils and were not necessarily erudite, serving for a one-year term, the *juízes de fora* were appointed by the Crown and among them were those who had a law degree and would serve for three years.

39 On the manorial *ouvidores*, see Saldanha, *As capitanias do Brasil*, 215–280; Cabral, "Os senhorios na América Portuguesa", 65–86.

40 For an overview of the appeal system in civil matters in Portuguese America, see Cabral, "Recursos cíveis ultramarinos", 41–72.

the actions of the municipal councils at least once during the term they served. Supervision, in that context, meant analysing whether the municipal councils and the officers of the council proceeded according to the royal laws, particularly through verification *in loco* of the jurisdictional apparatus (such as the conditions of the public jail) and activities of the municipal councils.

The space of the *comarcas* did not necessarily overlap the other administrative circumscriptions in Portuguese America, the *capitanias*. As more *comarcas* were created by the Crown, amounting to 23 in the late 18th century,[41] there were captaincies with more than one *comarca*, such as the four in the Captaincy of Minas Gerais (Ouro Preto, Rio das Velhas, Rio das Mortes and Serro Frio) but, at the same time, there were *comarcas* whose jurisdiction reached more than one captaincy, such as the *Comarca* da Paraíba.[42] On the other hand, the *ouvidores* of Bahia and Rio de Janeiro would often become *desembargadores*, that is to say, judges of the courts (*tribunais de relação*) created in those cities in 1609 (and recreated in 1652) and 1751, respectively.

When they were appointed to office, the royal *ouvidores* received, alongside the royal provision, a statute (*regimento*) in which their powers were stated. The first *ouvidores* had very particular *regimentos* but, in the 17th century, the Crown standardised their contents. Yamê Paiva described the common points of these *regimentos*, which were, among others, where the *ouvidor* should live, the power of judging civil and criminal suits under their jurisdiction, the power of judging appeals (*apelações* and *agravos*) over the jurisdiction of the ordinary judges of the towns inside the *comarca* and performing the *correição* every three years.[43] Most of the *regimentos* are now lost, and Paiva used some of the surviving documents to reconstruct what would have been the standard attributions of the *ouvidores*.

Besides their own *regimentos*, the *ouvidores* were supposed to follow the royal laws, particularly Book 1, Chap. 58 of the *Ordenações Filipinas*, when they were acting as *corregedores*. Looking specifically at the issues that are more related to this study, we find some paragraphs that describe the inspection of jurisdictional activities of the ordinary judges (§5), the investigation of whether there were norms (*bandos*)[44] to be inspected (§9), the necessity of examining *in loco* the situation of the public jails (§14), the verification in practice of whether

41 Cunha and Nunes, "Territorialização e poder", 1–30.

42 Created in 1688, the *Comarca da Paraíba*, hosted in the town of Nossa Senhora das Neves, had, until the first decades of the following century, jurisdiction over the royal captaincies of Paraíba, Rio Grande and Ceará and the hereditary captaincy of Itamaracá, but this last case involved only correctional powers.

43 Paiva, "Os regimentos dos ouvidores".

44 For more on the changing character of the *bandos*, see Curvelo in this volume.

the legal regime granted by the *foral* was disrespected (§15) and if there were any local statutes (*posturas municipais*) against the interests of the people, the commonwealth or the *Ordenações do Reino* (§17), as well as the possibility of ordering the construction of public betterments (§43) or planting trees (§46). All these cases can be found in the corrections in Portuguese America during the 17th and 18th centuries.

Literature has shown a growing interest in the works of the royal *ouvidores*[45] and, as mentioned in the introduction, there is growing interest in their correctional activities by the specialised historiography, with a special regard for the circulation of agents in royal justice and relations (most of time, very controversial) between those magistrates and local authorities.[46] While in some cases these relations were quite close and even convergent, in others they were very troubled. This highly qualified historiography is helpful to understand the role the *ouvidores* had in practice in areas that were distant from the centres of the monarchy's power, notably the difficulties they faced when imposing what they considered to be the royal law and vehemently opposing the infringement of royal authorities. Despite the relevance of this topic, it is not exactly what this study is willing to focus on.

During the first half of the 18th century, despite the existence of specific *regimentos* and royal legislation ruling the activities of the *ouvidores*, many doubts about their legal regime persisted, like those related to the spatial limits of their jurisdiction. A letter written by the *ouvidor* of Ceará Vitorino Pinto da Costa Mendonça, from 6 June 1737, is an example. Mendonça transcribed a few passages of the *Regimento* of the *ouvidor-geral* of Pernambuco to ask the King and his Council about the limits of his power, for example, to adjudicate new claims he received during corrections in very distant areas, the so-called *sertões* (hinterlands).[47] Differing from the peninsular territory, in Portuguese America the spaces of the *comarcas* were, most of time, huge. The description made by the *ouvidor* of São Paulo, Rodrigo César de Menezes, during his expedition to mining areas at the western limits of the captaincy, regarding the establishment of the town of Cuiabá, on 12 March 1727, is an example of the extreme difficulties in moving due to the distance, the paths and the dangers of the journey.[48] For isolated areas, even if a royal town was formally established,

45 Among others, see Carvalho, *Governanças das terras*; Jesus, "Juízes letrados, vilas e julgados", 79–106; Mello, *Administração, justiça e poder*; Mello, *Magistrados a serviço do rei*; Paiva, *Justiça e poder na América Portuguesa*; Pegoraro, *Ouvidores régios*; Pegoraro, *Zelo pelo serviço real*.

46 Camarinhas, "O aparelho judicial", 84–102.

47 AHU, Ceará, Papéis Avulsos, box 3, doc. 181.

48 AHU, Mato Grosso, Papéis Avulsos, box 1, doc. 9.

the presence of an *ouvidor* during the *correição* was of one of the few moments those people came into contact with the Crown. This is the reason why the performance of the *ouvidores* could be very diverse considering the final objective of the *correição*, which was the maintenance of the authority of the Crown in all the areas of the Portuguese Empire.

Not even the 58 paragraphs of the *Ordenações Filipinas* regulating the *correições* in the Kingdom were sufficient to create an undoubtedly legal regime for corrections in Portuguese America, and this increased the importance of the specific *regimentos*, which were supposed to be concerned with the particularities of the New World. Paiva compares the surviving *regimentos* to explore the similarities among them and discusses the authorship of those norms, during which she realised that some of the acts were enforceable in areas they did not originally reach.[49] Considering three examples of surviving documents, the *Regimento* of the *Ouvidor-geral* of Rio de Janeiro (1658), the *Regimento* of the *Ouvidor-geral* of Pernambuco (1668) and the *Regimento* of the *ouvidores* of São Paulo (1700), we clearly see the equivalence of different parts of the normative texts, such as the paragraphs regarding the civil and criminal competences. Yet, at the same time, there are considerable differences. Referring to the main topic of this chapter, the *Regimento* of the *ouvidor* of Rio de Janeiro had an explicit reference to the *correições*,[50] while both the *regimentos* of Pernambuco and São Paulo did not explicitly regulate them.[51] However, this absence did not prevent the *ouvidores* of Pernambuco nor those who followed this *regimento* from making *correições*, considering other norms imposing this duty, particularly the previously mentioned chapter of the *Ordenações Filipinas*. On the contrary, since the *Ordenações Filipinas* provided the *ouvidores* with a relatively detailed legal regime, they could follow what royal legislation prescribed and their correctional activities.

---

49 Paiva, *Justiça e poder na América Portuguesa*, 116–125.

50 "Nas visitas e correições que fizerdes provareis o que conforme o direito vos parecer é necessário, e fazem os Corregedores das Commarcas; e vos informareis se os Donatarios usam de mais poderes e jurisdicções dos que lhe são concedidos por suas Doações, e Provisões minhas, e fórma da Ordenação, e não lhes consentireis o contrario, e me dareis conta do que nisso achardes, e do mais que vos parecer necessário provêr-se, dando as razões que para isso há, que remettereis á Mesa do Paço, ao Escrivão do despacho dela". Silva, *Collecção Chronologica*, 18.

51 The case of São Paulo only mentioned the authorisation of the *ouvidores* "to carry with them the signatures that the 'corregedores das comarcas' can carry to the good of their regiments and *Ordenação*" ("Levareis as assinaturas que podem levar os 'corregedoes das comarcas' por bem do seu regimento, e Ordenação"). Figueiredo and Campos (eds.), *Códice Costa Matoso*, 344.

Carefully reading all the paragraphs that deal with the *corregedores*, we do not find words nor expressions equivalent to a "normative power" for this office, and the *regimentos* did not explicitly grant this power to the *ouvidores*. However, the analysis of the decrees enacted by the *ouvidores* after the *correição* left no doubt about their normative nature, particularly in the sense Herbert Hart described as primary rules, which create obligations, regulate behaviours and have an imperative essence.[52] Those norms enacted by the *ouvidores* were in force in their area of application and could be followed by the receivers, otherwise the authority would apply a penalty for the fault. They were not fully autonomic norms, since, as I have already pointed out, there were no fully autonomic rules in Early Modern Catholic monarchies, not even those enacted by the king if we consider the argued dependence of natural order.

Therefore, the object of the correctional decrees depended on the issues the *ouvidor* faced during the *correição* or, in other words, depended on the matter that would be inspected during the *correição*. The receivers/subjects were mostly the local authorities whose acts were under inspection, such as the municipal councillors, the ordinary judge, the *almotacés* and other officials, but also the inhabitants who violated the royal laws. The issuer was the *ouvidor*, and the time of the enactment was the end of the *correição*. Finally, the materialisation of the norms was complete after the transcription of the decrees in the books of the municipal council (*livros da câmara*).

There were essentially two situations that called for the use of an actual normative power by the royal *ouvidores*: (a) when they were inspecting the conformity of local *posturas* with the royal legislation, and (b) when they were evaluating actions of the local officers or inhabitants. Situation (a) could lead to the invalidity of local norms since they were not allowed to damage people or the common interest of the community. This happened quite often during corrections; for example, on 6 August 1631, the *ouvidor* of Rio de Janeiro, Paulo Ferreira, ordered the reformation of local statutes for that reason.[53] As Manuel Álvares Pegas stated when he commented on the title of the *Ordenações* which ruled the *corregedores*, the king was not allowed to prescribe against the people, nor the people against the king.[54]

On the other hand, situation (b) could be analysed from two perspectives: (b1) original regulation, when the resolution of problematic cases was necessary, and the decree might be in accordance with royal laws, and (b2) the

52 Hart, *The Concept of Law*, 82–91.

53 *Autos de Correições de Ouvidores*, 21–22.

54 "Princeps non potest praescribi contra populum, nec populus contra Principem, & na seruitta praescribi possint". Pegas, *Commentaria ad Ordinationes*, 548.

decrees were directly inspired by the *Ordenações Filipinas*, that is to say, the norms of the *Ordenações* were transcribed/translated into the books of the municipal council. An example of situation (b1) is the decree by the *ouvidor* of Rio de Janeiro, João de Abreu e Silva, ordering, on 30 October 1671, and under the penalty of a fine in cases of non-compliance, the closure of all taverns on the route between the parishes of Nossa Senhora d'Ajuda and Nossa Senhora do Bom Parto and the place known as Carioca, because these establishments were used to guard stolen things.[55] The best example of situation (b2) is the *correição* held by the *ouvidor* Rafael Pires Pardinho of the town of Curitiba in 1721, which will be detailed below.

4 Analysing *Correições* during the 18th Century

In this section, I analyse two correctional experiences held in the towns of Curitiba and Aquiraz. There are good reasons to analyse them together, starting with their chronological proximity, as the *correição* in Curitiba happened in 1721 and the one in Aquiraz in 1729. Both towns were created in a similar context (Curitiba in 1693 and Aquiraz in 1699 but settled in 1713). Curitiba was located on the hinterland of the Captaincy of São Paulo, in an area that, in 1723, became part of the *Comarca* of Paranaguá. Aquiraz, in turn, was a shore town in the Captaincy of Ceará and, at the time of the 1729 correction, was the head of the *Comarca* of Ceará.

Despite the objective difference between a town that hosted the *ouvidoria* and another one who did not, as well as the huge distance (more than 3,000 kilometres) between them, since one is located in the north and the other in the extreme south of Colonial Brazil, Curitiba and Aquiraz were towns of a similar size in the early 18th century, with the latter having perhaps a slight advantage over the former, and they both faced quite similar challenges, to be discussed in the following sections. Their corrections were almost contemporaries of one another and regulated similar problems. Chronological and circumstantial similarities are reliable reasons for a comparative study of two ordinary towns' images in Portuguese America during the 1720s.

4.1 *Correição* of the town of Curitiba (1721)

On 20 January 1721, the *ouvidor* of the *Comarca* of São Paulo, Rafael Pires Pardinho, enacted a long decree after the *correição* he made in the town of

55 *Autos de Correições de Ouvidores*, 64.

Curitiba.[56] Pardinho had an important role as a *letrado* in the administration of justice in Portuguese America. He served as *ouvidor* of São Paulo between 1717 and 1721 and, afterwards, as *intendente* of the Diamantino District in Minas Gerais between 1734 and 1740. In 1743, he was appointed member of the overseas council, the most relevant council for administrative affairs regarding overseas possessions.

The documents testify to the efforts of the *ouvidor* Pardinho for the regulation of many aspects of ordinary life in the community, particularly those relevant to legal aspects. At the beginning of the decrees, Pardinho stated his intention to enact a large and complete document because it was the first *correição* ever made in the town. According to him, such a document would avoid "the disorders that until now some people made due to ignorance, and the malicious people will not have the excuse of being ignorant".[57] After recommendations of divine worship and religious processions,[58] he reaffirmed the geographical limits of the term of the town since nobody had previously done so.[59] Other questions related to the organisation of the town were also discussed in the *correição*, such as the power of the municipal council to order the owners of houses in bad condition to reform them according to a deadline of one year, as well as the obligation of "cleaning the creek that goes through the middle of the town in order to have current and to receive the rainwater of the streets, and then avoid quagmires in the town".[60]

The *correição* also determined the repair and the opening of a new path connecting Curitiba to Paranaguá, in an explicit reference to the necessity of improving communication with the most relevant town in the southern area of the Captaincy. As Paranaguá hosted an important harbour, the new path would improve the circulation of foodstuffs, consequently avoiding higher prices.[61] Some paragraphs ruled food supply as one that imposed the enactment of municipal *posturas* to force the cultivation of foodstuffs by the

56 Before the creation of the *Comarca* of Paranaguá, in 1723, the town of Curitiba was one of the areas under the jurisdiction of the *ouvidor* of São Paulo. Only after the installation of the new *comarca* did the jurisdictional and correctional competences over the term of the town of Curitiba change.

57 "[…] as desordens em que athe agora alguns tropeçavam por Ignorancia, e os maliciosos, não tenhão já a desculpa de ignorantes". *Boletim do Archivo Municipal de Curityba*, vol. 8, §3, 6. Translated by the author.

58 *Boletim do Archivo Municipal de Curityba*, vol. 8, §5–6, 7.

59 *Boletim do Archivo Municipal de Curityba*, vol. 8, §11–12, 8–9.

60 "[…] limpar o Ribeiro que corre por meyo da villa para ter boa correnteza, e a fação ter as aguas das chuvas nas mais ruas para que não aja charquos na villa". *Boletim do Archivo Municipal de Curityba*, vol. 8, §43, 17. Translated by the author.

61 *Boletim do Archivo Municipal de Curityba*, vol. 8, §51, 19–20.

inhabitants of the town[62] and others prohibited the transportation of cattle to outside the limits of the town.[63] The necessity of organising the commerce of foodstuffs was also easily realised in the decrees, when, for example, they ordered the acquisition of instruments for weighing and measuring.[64]

Other issues that very often concerned Crown officials can also be found in these *correições*, such as the regulation of mining and gold,[65] the prohibition of entering the hinterlands to capture indigenous people to turn them into slaves[66] and the issue of escaped slaves.[67] One paragraph prohibits people from collecting the eggs of partridges and other birds or hunting them "during the time of their breeding, which in this land is during the months of September until December".[68] The explicit reason for this prohibition was the prevention of the extinction of these birds, and that norm, which imposed fine and imprisonment penalties in cases of non-compliance and was related to a survival concern of the community, clearly reveals what is nowadays seen as an environmental concern.

A substantial part of the *correições* was addressed to the council's officials, namely to their competence and jurisdiction. In many topics, Pardinho emphasised that the officials (municipal councillors, ordinary judges, the council's attorney and *almotacés*) should observe their regiments in the *Ordenações Filipinas*, in a clear reference to the necessity of respecting royal legislation. As a *letrado*, Pardinho was aware of the obligation every official had to observe the royal laws, particularly those dealing with justice and the administration of public affairs. However, as he realised during the *correição*, ignorance was a strong argument, whose credibility was justified by the isolation of the town and the difficulties faced by the officials in accessing those laws.

---

62 *Boletim do Archivo Municipal de Curityba*, vol. 8, §56, 20.

63 *Boletim do Archivo Municipal de Curityba*, vol. 8, §54, 20, §64, 23.

64 *Boletim do Archivo Municipal de Curityba*, vol. 8, §57, 20–21.

65 *Boletim do Archivo Municipal de Curityba*, vol. 8, §67–68, 24.

66 *Boletim do Archivo Municipal de Curityba*, vol. 8, §72, 25.

67 *Boletim do Archivo Municipal de Curityba*, vol. 8, §119–120, 41–42.

68 "Proveo que nenhuma pessoa com pena de 2000rs pagos da cadea apanhem ovos de perdizes ou de outras aves, nem ande a cassa delas no tempo da sua criação que nesta terra hé nos mezes de Setembro athe Dezembro, e os juízes ordinários procederão contra os q o contrario o fizerem na forma da Ord. Lb. 5º ttº 88 pois tem ele Ouvidor Gl emformação que muitas pessoas de proposito andão no dito tempo a cassa dos ovos e creações das ditas aves, como qu se hirão extinguindo sobre o q os Juizes e off.es da Camera ferão suas posturas e acórdãos, para se quartar [*sic*, por coartar] este danno", *Boletim do Archivo Municipal de Curityba*, vol. 8, §66, 23–24. Translated by the author.

Bearing this context in mind, Pardinho decided to write down in the books of the municipal council many dispositions found in the *Ordenações Filipinas*, probably aiming to provide easier access to their content, including explicit references to the *Ordenações* and even transcribing some excerpts. As his intention was to facilitate access to norms that already existed and, in some cases, the regulation was long, Pardinho preferred to summarise the content of the regulation in the *Ordenações*. When he regulated the duty of the ordinary judges to take *devassas*, he mentioned the necessity of observing the eight paragraphs of the *Ordenações* on that issue,[69] and then he focused on the topics he considered the most relevant, using the strategy of epitomising to make it easier and clearer for the readers to know what they should do in those cases. The matters Pardinho detailed that way were, among others, the *devassas*, the *corpus delicti*, the *cartas de fiança*, imprisonment, seizure of goods, judicial deposits after a conviction of capital punishment[70] and the legal regime of the notaries[71] and the judges of orphans.[72]

Considering the topics in which Pardinho managed offices regarding the administration of justice and jurisdictional proceedings, which starts in paragraph 73 and continues until the end of the decrees, we find a significant number of explicit references to articles of the *Ordenações Filipinas*. The table below shows the correspondence between the topics and the *Ordenações Filipinas*, as well as other royal laws, revealing that the structure of Pardinho's text reinforced the mandatory nature of the royal dispositions on those topics.

TABLE 6.1 Matters regulated in the Correctional Decrees and the references to royal legislation

Matters	**Normative reference**
Election and competence of judge of *vintena* for the *freguesia* of São José (§73)	Ord. Fil., book 1, tit. 65, §74
Election of a scribe for the wills of the *freguesia* of São José (§74)	Ord. Fil., book 1, tit.78, §20
Devassas ex officio by the ordinary judges (§§76–78)	Ord. Fil., book 1, tit. 65, §§31–38
Devassas gerais by the ordinary judges (§79)	Ord. Fil., book 1, tit. 65, §§39–69 *Lei* (10 January 1692)

69 *Boletim do Archivo Municipal de Curityba*, vol. 8, §76, 26.
70 *Boletim do Archivo Municipal de Curityba*, vol. 8, §76–83, 26–29.
71 *Boletim do Archivo Municipal de Curityba*, vol. 8, §90–93, 31–33.
72 *Boletim do Archivo Municipal de Curityba*, vol. 8, §98–115, 34–40.

TABLE 6.1 Matters regulated in the Correctional Decrees and the references to royal legislation (*cont.*)

Matters	Normative reference
Devassas for murders (§81)	Ord. Fil., book 1, tit. 65, §33
Imprisonment and surety letters (§§82–83)	Ord. Fil., book 1, tit. 127, §11
	Ord. Fil., book 1, tit. 133
Public notaries and their legal regime (§§87–94)	Ord. Fil., book 1, tit. 20,
	Ord. Fil., book 1, tit. 78–80
	Carta régia (2 October 1701)
Judges of Orphans and proceedings of succession (§§95–118)	Ord. Fil., book 1, tit. 88, §32
	Ord. Fil., book 1, tit. 89
	Ord. Fil., book 1, tit. 95–97
Ordinary judges and special proceedings (§§121–124)	Ord. Fil., book 1, tit. 83
	Ord. Fil., book 1, tit. 85
	Ord. Fil., book 1, tit. 88, §49
	Ord. Fil., book 1, tit. 89, §9
	Ord. Fil., book 1, tit. 90
	Ord. Fil., book 3, tit. 94
	Carta régia (19 December 1699)
	Provisão (20 August 1703)

A careful view of some provisions left no doubt about the primary intention of the enactment of these rules. In the paragraph dedicated to the *juízes de vintena* and the scribes of wills, Pardinho refers to the norms in the *Ordenações Filipinas* and thereafter clarifies the powers and the jurisdiction, as well as the form of some acts they would perform. Pardinho did not create a legal regime for those officials; he translated that regime, which was primarily found in the *Ordenações*, into an easier language and, more importantly, into a text that was available to the citizens of Curitiba, since it had to be archived in the municipal council in order to be consulted by the local officials. At the same time, these norms regulated situations particularly related to the context of the town, such as the creation of an office of *juiz de vintena* in a *freguesia* (São José) located inside the term of the town of Curitiba.

The next table compares the text of the norms in the correctional decrees with the part of the *Ordenações Filipinas* mentioned by the *ouvidor* Pardinho:

TABLE 6.2 Comparing the norms about the *juízes de vintena*

Decrees of the 1721 correction	***Ordenações do Reino***
Due to the distance between this town and the *freguesia* of São José, the judges and the officials of the Council will elect each year, at the beginning of January, in the form of the Ord., book 1, tit. 65, 74, a good man of the very *freguesia* to serve as judge in the district of the same *freguesia*, and they will take the oath in the Council to serve well the occupation and will take note in the Council. He can determine the disputes between the inhabitants until the limit of 400 *réis*, arrest the defendants and the criminals that were there, and he bring them to the jail of this town and will do what more the Law provide him. They will elect an able person that can act in governance of this town. (§73)[a]	We order that in every hamlet where there are 20 neighbours or more, until 50, and which is one *légua* or more far from the city or town, in whose term it is located, the Judges alongside the councillors and attorney should choose each year a good man of this very hamlet to be judge, and they will take the oath in the Council, in order to know well and truly and determine verbally the disputes among the inhabitants of this very hamlet until the limit of 100 *réis*. (…) And if there are 200 or more neighbours he will know until the limit of 400 *réis*, without appeals and verbally, and he will not make a process. (…) (Ord. Fil., book 1, tit. 65, §73)[b]

a "Proveo que vista a distancia, que desta Villa fica a freguesia de Sam Joseph os Juizes e Off.es da Camera todos os anos no principio do mês de janeiro na forma da Ord. Lb.º 1º 65 §74 elegerão hum homem bom dá dª freguesia o qual sirva de Juiz no descricto da dª freguesia, ao qual darão juramento em Camera para que bem sirva a dita ocupação de q farão termo em Camera; o qual poderá determinar as contendas, que entre aquelles moradores houver athe a valia de coatro centos reis, prender, os réos, e criminosos que nella achar, q trará logo para a cadea desta Villa, e o mais que na dita Ley se lhe concede. E lhes adverte que fação elyção de pessoa capaz, e que costume, e possa andar na Governança desta Villa". *Boletim do Archivo Municipal de Curityba*, vol. 8, §73, 25. Translated by the author.

b "Mandamos, que em qualquer aldêa, que houver vinte visinhos, e d'ahi para cima até cincoenta, e for uma legoa afastada, ou mais da cidade, ou villa, de cujo termo for, os Juizes da dita cidade, ou villa, com os Vereadores e Procurador, escolham em cada hum anno hum homem bom da dita aldea, que seja nella Juiz; ao qual darão juramento em Camera, que bem e verdadeiramente conheça e determine verbalmente as contendas, que forem entre os moradores da dita aldea, de quantia até cem réis. E sendo a aldea de cincoenta visinhos até cento, conhecerá de quantia de duzentos réis. E se for de cem visinhos até cento e cincoenta, conhecerá da quantia de trezentos réis. E se for de duzentos visinhos, e d'ahi para cima, conhecerá até quantia de quatrocentos réis e das ditas quantias todas sem appellação, nem aggravo, e verbalmente, sem sobre isso fazer processo. E da mesma maneira conhecerão, segundo as posturas dos Concelhos, das coimas e danos, e isto entre os moradores d'essa aldêa, e darão a execução com effeito as ditas sentenças. E não conhecerão de contenda alguma, que seja sobre bens de raiz". *Ordenações Filipinas*, livro 1, tit. 65, §73. Translated by the author.

TABLE 6.2 Comparing the norms about the *juízes de vintena* (*cont.*)

Decrees of the 1721 correction	*Ordenações do Reino*
	And they will not know about crimes. However, they are allowed to arrest malefactors caught doing mischiefs in the hamlet and in its limits, or if it is required by the parts, they must be arrested, but the warrants and quarrels must be shown to them. After the imprisonment, they will send the malefactors to the Ordinary Judges of the town, in whose term the hamlet is located. (Ord. Fil., book 1, tit. 65, §74)[c]

c "E não conhecerão sobre crime algum. Porém poderão prender os malfeitores, que forem achados commettendo os maleficios na aldea e seu limite, ou lhes for requerido pelas partes, que os prendam, sendo-lhes mostrados mandados, ou querelas, per que o devam ser. E tanto que forem presos, os mandarão entregar aos Juizes ordinarios, de cujo termo for a dita aldea". *Ordenações Filipinas*, livro 1, tit. 65, §74.

The rules about the public notaries are an example of how the correctional decrees regulated, in an easier and shorter way, an office whose legal regime was longer in the *Ordenações*. Pardinho summarised, in around 30 lines, 20 paragraphs in which many issues were discussed, particularly the procedure for the making of the deeds about contracts, wills and sales and the rules about the public form. The *Ordenações Filipinas* are clear in the announcement of the primary activity of the notaries ("And they shall write in a book, which each one shall have for this purpose, all the notes of the contracts. And as they are written, the notaries shall immediately read them before the parties and witnesses, of whom there shall be at least two. If the parties agree, they will sign, as well as the witnesses"),[73] but the other paragraphs carefully detail the rules. On the other hand, the correctional decrees opted for compiling rules that were dispersed in the same section of the *Ordenações* and in other parts of the statute.

73 "Escreverão em hum livro, que cada hum para isso terá, todas as Notas dos contractos, que fizerem. E como forem scriptas, logo as leam perante as partes e testemunhas, as quaes ao menos serão duas. E tanto que as partes outorgarem, assinarão ellas e as testemunhas". *Ordenações Filipinas*, livro 1, tit. 78, §4. Translated by the author.

> The public notary will observe his statutes for the public and notes which are in the Ordenações, book 1, tit. 78, and will always have a well-bound, initialled and numbered book and there he will write the deeds of the contracts and conventions made by the parties, he will be warned about the notes, accordingly the conventions made by the contractors, and after writing them he will read them before two or three witnesses that will soon sign them, and when the contractor's wives need to grant in the same deed they will be required to assist the reading and the signing, in order to avoid nullity, and the notary will be punished due to the forgery, and after the conclusion of the writing of the deed in the book, if the parties do not sign it, the notary will issue a warning saying it had no effect. And he will provide public faith to the deeds after their signing by the parties and witnesses, and when some person asks him to write down in his book information about credits or other papers or documents, he will transcribe them into the very book, as they really are, and above the very transcription on the same book the party will sign. And the notary is warned that in the very Book of Notes he will write down all the contracts made by the parties and give them the transcriptions in public form. And he is not allowed to do what some notaries previously did, to receive the contracts in a single sheet on which the parties and the witnesses sign and thereafter transcribe the Book of Notes, because it is against the Law.[74]

It is indisputable that Pardinho did not create norms out of nothing, but he opted for the incorporation of normative content, originally found in the

---

74 "Proveo que o Tabalião guardará o seu regimento do publico e notas, que he na Ord. Do Lb.º 1º tt. 78 e terá sempre hum livro bem emcadernado, rubricado e numerado para nelle lançar as escrepturas dos contratos e convençais q as partes fizerem, e será advertido de as lançar e notar, comf.e a convença dos contraentes, e depois de escriptas as lerá sendo presentes as mesmas partes e duas ou três testemunhas que logo assignarão todos, e quando as mulheres dos contraentes ajão de outrogar, na dita escreptura, serão também presentes ao ler, e assignar delas porque, de outra sorte ficará nulla a escreptura e o taballião será pugnido como falçario, e quando depois de notada e lançada a escreptura no livro se não assignar pelas partes por se terem desavindo, lhe porá logo o Tabalião hua cota, em que se diga: não teve efeito. E das notas depois de assinadas as escrepturas pelas partes e testemunhas dará os treslados em publica fórma, e quando alguas pessoas lhe requeirão lançe no seu livro de notas alguns créditos, ou outro quais quer papeis, ou documentos o farã Tresladandoos no dito Livro, como na verdade forem, e ao pé do dito treslado no mesmo Livro asignará sempre a parte de como torna a receber o dito crédito, ou papeis. E Advert ao tabelião que no mesmo e Livro das Notas hade escrever, e Lançar todos os contratos que as partes fizerem, e do dito livro dar as partes os treslados em publica forma: E não façã o que algú tabalião fasia, que tomara o contrato das partes em hua folha de papel avulsa em que as partes e testemunhas asignavão e despois os Tresladava nos livros das notas, o que hé contra direito". *Boletim do Archivo Municipal de Curityba*, vol. 8, §90, 31. Translated by the author.

Portuguese royal legislation, into the local sphere. Taking the useful distinctions between significant (acoustic image) and signifier (its concept), to use Ferdinand de Saussure's terms,[75] or between norm (content) and normative formulation (signal or symbol used to enunciate the norm) if we opt for Georg Henrik von Wright's contribution,[76] we can clearly understand that the correctional decrees enacted by Pardinho mediated access for a population living in the confines of Portuguese America to a normative content that had to be observed. The decrees, in this case, were a medium for normative circulation and used traditional juridical ways to persuade people to behave accordingly. The registration of this normative content allowed the officials and other inhabitants of the town to have access to those norms.

4.2 *Correição* in Aquiraz (1729)

Unlike the previous case, the *correição* in Aquiraz in 1729 was not the first one to take place in the town, as the introduction of the decrees clearly mentions. The infringement of orders enacted by the former *ouvidor* provided a reason for the *correição* discussed here. The decrees start with the notice that,

> Because I have been informed that the provisions that my predecessors left with such zeal and care were not executed, I order that they be observed in whatever is not altered by the change of themes so requested, with the same penalties imposed on them that will invariably be executed on the transgressors.[77]

The officer in charge of this *correição* was Antônio de Loureiro de Medeiros, the second *ouvidor* of the *Comarca* of Ceará, who was appointed in 1728 and served between 1729 and 1731. Like in other areas of Colonial Brazil, to act as *ouvidor* in this *comarca* was not an easy task. His term was particularly troubled, due to the numerous conflicts with local authorities (the offices of the municipal council), the Governor of Pernambuco, Duarte Sodré Pereira and especially with his successor in office, Pedro Cardoso Novais, as well as with part of the elites in the hinterland of the Captaincy of Ceará. These controversies resulted

75 Saussure, *Cours de linguistique générale*, 97–100.

76 Wright, *Norm and Action*, 93.

77 "Porque sou informado q os prouimentos que com tanto zelo e cuidado deixárão meus antecessores não foram executados, mando que se observem no q por estes não for alterado pela mudança dos temas assim o pedir, com as mesmas penas nelles impostas que invariavelmente se executarão nos transgressores". APEC, Fundo Câmaras Municipais, box 3, book 8 (1728–1737), fol. 18v. Translated by the author.

in his imprisonment as part of the *residencia*[78] against him, and he was still in jail in 1738, the year of the last-known document about him.[79] Differing from the *ouvidor* Pardinho, who finished his career as a member of the overseas council, the trajectory of Medeiros ceased after his months as *ouvidor* of Ceará.

The provision enacted on 1 August 1729 is shorter than the decrees described in the previous sections (20 paragraphs against 125). It was an essentially critical correction against the measures taken by local authorities. Medeiros enacted a tough decree that regulated the main issues of ordinary life in the town, aiming to propose rules according to royal laws. Among the matters faced by Medeiros we find provisions on food supply, public cleaning, orphans, council's offices, and others.

Land cultivation opens the decrees. Medeiros used the verb 'to order' (*mandar*) to enact an obligation for the inhabitants to plant trees that were useful to that place, such as coconut palms, orange trees and banana trees. The inhabitants who had their own lands or *aforadas* were obliged to plant at least two trees, under the penalty of 6,000 *réis* for the municipal council in cases of non-compliance.[80] There is no explicit justification for this order, but the list of trees seems to be related to food supply, and not to ornamental or environmental reasons, observing the passage of the *Ordenações* which regulated the cultivation of trees as a competence of the *corregedor*.[81] This topic is directly associated with the discussion on the *sesmarias*, since their foundation by late medieval statutes, which were based on the idea of land cultivation.[82] Medeiros emphasised that all the *sesmarias* in the entire *comarca* were donated as royal lands and therefore should respect the cultivation that required concession and maintenance. In the following, after saying that he was informed about the reduced level of cultivation in many areas because of the lack of manure, Medeiros ordered the landowners to fertilise properly, because "the *sesmarias* act (*lei das sesmarias*) orders the council's attorney to be informed

78 *Juízo de residências* was a proceeding against an *ouvidor* due to the misconducts he had committed in office. For more information about this proceeding, see Camarinhas, "As residências dos cargos", 161–172.

79 For more information about the conflicts involving Antônio de Loureiro de Medeiros, see Carvalho, *Governanças das terras*, 121–127. Medeiros' trajectory in the *ouvidoria* of Ceará was the subject of nine documents in the Arquivo Histórico Ultramarino (AHU).

80 APEC, Fundo Câmaras Municipais, box 3, book 8, fol. 18v.

81 *Ordenações Filipinas*, livro 1, tit. 60, §15.

82 The literature about *sesmarias* in Colonial Brazil is large. From a legal historical perspective, see, among many others, Alveal, *Converting Law into Property*; Varela, *Das sesmarias*; Motta, *Direito à terra no Brasil*.

about how these lands are fertilised and cultivated", under a fine penalty (3,000 *réis*) in cases of non-compliance.[83]

Food supply also appears in other paragraphs, most of them combined with other topics. Medeiros ordered the people who used to fish in the rivers or in the sea to sell some of the fishes in the town and in other places where the inhabitants needed them, but he emphasised the necessity that the price charged had to be reasonable.[84] Despite the theological nature of the discussion,[85] fair pricing was also an issue that concerned the Crown, particularly due to the economic impact of high prices. It was not related to any kind of economic planning but rather to the idea that governing the community required an adequate offer of food for the people, and high prices damaged this. Another provision determined that butcheries had to offer meat in abundance, but the price of the public auction had to be maintained, and the meat had to be clean and well cut.[86] As in the first case, food supply here is related to price control, aiming to keep the terms of the so-called *contrato das carnes*, which is representative of the monopoly on some items that was held by the municipal councils. At the same time, this provision deals with public cleaning, which was, alongside price control and food supply, a very relevant topic for the laws of police during the Early Modern period, as well as weighing and measuring, which prompted the *ouvidor* to order that a specialist would act as controller of the weights in the region of the *Cariris Novos*, in the southern part of Captaincy of Ceará.[87]

The protection of public goods and the goods of the councils are the subject of some parts of the decrees, starting with a prohibition to people of "any quality" to sleep in the house of the council and jail (*casa de câmara e cadeia*), imposing a fine penalty (6,000 *réis*) to those who infringed it and to the officials who allowed this.[88] Within this topic, we also find a decree ordering maintenance of the paths to the town so that they remain in good condition, ensuring one is "able to walk over them and to ride a horse without inconvenience". As the decree made known, the main receivers of this order were the landlords, who needed to clean the front parts of their possessions, under the penalty of paying the cost of opening those paths.[89]

83 APEC, Fundo Câmaras Municipais, box 3, book 8, fol. 20v.
84 APEC, Fundo Câmaras Municipais, box 3, book 8, fol. 19r.
85 See Decock, *Theologians and Contract Law*.
86 APEC, Fundo Câmaras Municipais, box 3, book 8, fol. 19v.
87 APEC, Fundo Câmaras Municipais, box 3, book 8, fol. 20r.
88 APEC, Fundo Câmaras Municipais, box 3, book 8, fol. 19r.
89 APEC, Fundo Câmaras Municipais, box 3, book 8, fol. 19r.

Questions of general interest were also ruled, such as the regulation of some public offices. Council's officials, particularly judges and councillors, were obliged to live in the town, paying 30,000 *réis* in cases of non-compliance.[90] The *almotacés*, who oversaw many issues relayed here, were required to observe the correctional decrees entirely.[91] The municipal council had to enact *regimentos* for the offices that required one and also had to deal with offices (here in the sense of mechanical offices), including the election of judges for them.[92]

Another topic that reveals a common concern of the Crown is the 'indigenous problem'. Two norms are directly related to this, and the first one ordered indigenous people to cultivate manioc, beans, pumpkin (*jerimum*), fruits and cotton. The penalty for negligence was ten days labouring in community work,[93] documenting one of the only cases of non-financial penalties in these decrees. In the following paragraph, Medeiros prohibited the commerce of alcoholic drinks inside indigenous towns, under the penalty of a fine (6,000 *réis*). Collaboration with the indigenous people was mandatory for the success of this measure, therefore the norm stated that an indigenous person of "good reputation" ("hum dos indios de melhor nota") should be informed of the delicts, and each report should be testified by two witnesses.[94]

Among the topics of local interest relevant to the specific local context of the Captaincy of Ceará, cattle affairs were centre stage. Cattle raising was the most important economic activity in that captaincy during all of the colonial period and was one of the leading reasons for the occupation of that territory.[95] Throughout the 18th century, two of the most important towns of Ceará were created with immediate dependence on cattle raising: Icó (1738), where the raisers met for commercial transactions, and Aracati (1748), which was the final destination of the cattle, along a road on the riverside of Jaguaribe, before being slaughtered and before the dry beef was transported from that harbour to other areas of Portuguese America. The norms enacted by the *ouvidor* Medeiros aimed to protect the patrimony of the cattle owners, keeping in mind the relevance of the economic activity and the necessity to observe legal provisions.

Medeiros forbade any person from guiding cattle (*vaquejar*) through a land without the agreement of the owner, under the penalty of 6,000 *réis*, and the landlord, accompanied by a trustful witness, could do the *coima*.[96] Cattle

90 APEC, Fundo Câmaras Municipais, box 3, book 8, fol. 21r.
91 APEC, Fundo Câmaras Municipais, box 3, book 8, fol. 21r.
92 APEC, Fundo Câmaras Municipais, box 3, book 8, fol. 19r.
93 APEC, Fundo Câmaras Municipais, box 3, book 8, fol. 20r.
94 APEC, Fundo Câmaras Municipais, box 3, book 8, fol. 20r.
95 On this topic, see Nogueira, *Às margens do império*.
96 APEC, Fundo Câmaras Municipais, box 3, book 8, fol. 19v.

slaughter would only be allowed if the owner of the cattle consented, no matter if the reason behind it was to sell or eat the meat.[97] Slaughtering cattle was only permitted when the slaughterer could provide a written license from the legitimate owner, with a fine of 10,000 *réis* and the possibility of creating a *devassa* to investigate and punish the crimes in cases of non-compliance.[98] In a shocking but coherent (with the legal system of Portuguese America) decree, Medeiros equated the situation of cattle with slaves who had escaped and entered someone's property, and their owners did not know how strange cattle had entered the land. The provisions ordered that the landowner of the land where the cattle or slaves were had to inform the *Provedor* of the Royal Treasure to pay the appropriate amount;[99] the clear intention was to avoid illicit advantage.

Like any other Crown official, Medeiros wanted his provisions to be observed. However, like most of his fellows, he could not fully achieve this aim, not only because of the misfortune in his career, but also due to difficulties in providing his decrees with any real force of the law. In 1731, just before leaving office, he enacted new correctional provisions that, among other things, applied a fine of 12,000 *réis* to the municipal council because of the non-compliance of the correctional provisions of 1729. He literally affirmed that "the provisions of the last correction must be maintained inviolably with the imposed penalties",[100] a phrase that proves the inefficacy of the norms he enacted because an actual enforceable norm does not need to have its efficacy reaffirmed. At the end of the correctional provision, he stated that the municipal statutes written in the books of the council were made null because they were against the law.[101]

5 Conclusions

Royal *ouvidores* were external agents acting in local communities during an age when those towns experienced a particular situation: they were subjects of the Portuguese Crown and therefore shared a tradition based on the *ius commune* and Catholic theologian principles. However, distance from the centres of power had an impact on the practice of the limited (but existing) autonomy

97 APEC, Fundo Câmaras Municipais, box 3, book 8, fol. 19v.

98 APEC, Fundo Câmaras Municipais, box 3, book 8, fol. 21r.

99 APEC, Fundo Câmaras Municipais, box 3, book 8, fol. 19v.

100 "Os provimentos da Corr.cam. passada se goardarão inviolavelmente com as penas nelles impostas". APEC, Fundo Câmaras Municipais, box 3, book 8, fol. 52v. Translated by the author.

101 APEC, Fundo Câmaras Municipais, box 3, book 8, fol. 53r.

of political communities. The *ouvidores* played a relevant role in controlling this autonomy when they compared the conformity of the local law and the local practices with the royal legal order and discovered a divergence, defending the prevalence of the royal law. Localisation of the legal phenomenon did not mean full autonomy but rather, on the contrary, the possibility of controlling local powers and, in an incipient but progressive way, the centralisation that became a tendency a few decades later. However, there were many empirical challenges to the real implementation of this kind of centralisation, such as the structural and logistical difficulties the *ouvidores* suffered when travelling inside their jurisdictions. All this contributed to the localism and relative autonomy of the communities.

In some ways, royal *ouvidores* were agents of change, a change that meant the maintenance of the ties with the Portuguese Crown both in structural matters (such as the matters of general interest like food supply, mining, slavery or relations with indigenous people) and even in the details of the life of those communities, like the organisation of the space of the towns.[102] When they tried to control these norms, the *ouvidores* tried to alter reality and then to guarantee the adherence of those communities to the Portuguese normative order.

Despite the mandatory nature of those actions – and the normative essence of the decrees enacted by them reinforces this argument – this process was, overall, simply an attempt, because its success was not guaranteed. As the 1731 correction clarifies, *ouvidor* Medeiros failed in his attempt to change some points of the local law in the town of Aquiraz. The introduction of new norms, particularly those which come from outside, is always an attempt whose outcomes are uncertain and depend on many factors. The very existence of mechanisms like the *ouvidores'* correctional decrees proves that changing reality through the enactment of norms was a tool used by Crown officials in their attempts to the control the Empire.

Bibliography

Manuscripts

Arquivo Histórico Ultramarino, Lisboa (AHU), Bahia, Luísa da Fonseca, box 15, doc. 1778.

Arquivo Histórico Ultramarino, Lisboa (AHU), Ceará, Papéis Avulsos, box 3, doc. 181.

102 On this topic, see Cabral, Costa and Sá, "Fontes do direito e planejamento urbano", 224–243.

Arquivo Histórico Ultramarino, Lisboa (AHU), Mato Grosso, Papéis Avulsos, box 1, doc. 9.
Arquivo Público do Estado do Ceará, Fortaleza (APEC), Fundo Câmaras Municipais, box 3, book 8 (1728–1737).

Printed Sources

Actas da Camara Municipal de S. Paulo, vol. 8: *1701–1719*, São Paulo 1916: Archivo Municipal de São Paulo.

"Apologia Pro Paulistis (1684)", in *Clio – Série Revista de Pesquisa Histórica* 26, no. 2 (2008), 362–416.

Autos de Correições de Ouvidores do Rio de Janeiro, vol. 1: *1624–1699*, Rio de Janeiro 1929: Off. Graphicas do "Jornal do Brasil".

Boletim do Archivo Municipal de Curityba: Documentos para a História do Paraná, vol. 2: *Cartas régias, provimentos, alvarás, resoluções, vereanças de Curytiba*, Curytiba 1906: Impressora Paranaense.

Boletim do Archivo Municipal de Curityba: Documentos para a História do Paraná, vol. 8: *Provimentos de correições, 1721 a 1812*, Curityba 1924: Livraria Mundial.

Boletim do Archivo Municipal de Curityba: Documentos para a História do Paraná, vol. 10: *Resoluções, ordens e provisões e termos de vereanças, 1721 a 1736*, Curytiba 1924: Livraria Mundial.

Documentos históricos do Arquivo Municipal. Atas da Câmara, vol. 2 (1641–1649), Salvador 1949: Prefeitura do Município do Salvador-Bahia.

Figueiredo, Luciano Raposo de Almeida, Maria Verônica Campos (eds.), *Códice Costa Matoso: Coleção das notícias dos primeiros descobrimentos das minas na América que fez o doutor Caetano da Costa Matoso sendo ouvidor-geral das do Ouro Preto, de que tomou posse em fevereiro de 1749, & vários papéis*, vol. 1, Belo Horizonte 1999: Fundação João Pinheiro.

Ordenações Filipinas, livro 1, Lisboa 1985: Fundação Calouste Gulbenkian.

Pegas, Emmanuelis Alvarez, *Commentaria ad Ordinationes Regni Portugalliae, Tomus Quintus*, Ulyssipone 1680: Antonii Leite Pereyra.

Silva, José Justino de Andrade e, *Collecção Chronologica da Legilação Portugueza, 1657–1674*, Lisboa 1856: Imprensa de F. X. de Souza.

Suárez, Francisco, *Tractatus de legibus, ac Deo legislatore*, Moguntiae 1619: Mylius Birckmannus.

Literature

Agüero, Alejandro, "Local Law and Localization of Law. Hispanic Legal Traditions and Colonial Culture (16th–18th centuries)", in Meccarelli, Massimo and María Julia Solla Sastre (eds.), *Spatial and Temporal Dimensions for Legal History. Research Experiences and Itineraries*, Frankfurt am Main 2016, 101–129.

Alveal, Carmen, *Converting Law into Property in the Portuguese Atlantic World, 16th–18th Century* (Ph.D. Thesis), Baltimore 2007.

Atallah, Claudia C. Azeredo and Maria Sarita Mota, "Justiça e bem-estar dos povos: as correições do primeiro ouvidor do Espírito Santo na vila de São Salvador da Paraíba do Sul (1742–1745)", in *Almanack* 35 (2023), 1–31.

Bicalho, Maria Fernanda and Nuno Gonçalo Monteiro, "As instituições civis da monarquia portuguesa na Idade Moderna: centro e periferia do império", in Xavier, Ângela Barreto, Federico Palomo and Roberta Stumpf (eds.), *Monarquias Ibéricas em perspectiva comparada (sécs. XVI–XVIII). Dinâmicas imperiais e circulação de modelos administrativos*, Lisboa 2018, 209–236.

Bicalho, Maria Fernanda, José Damião Rodrigues and Pedro Cardim, "Cortes, juntas e procuradores", in Fragoso, João and Nuno Gonçalo Monteiro (eds.), *Um reino e suas repúblicas no Atlântico. Comunicações políticas entre Portugal, Brasil e Angola nos séculos XVII e XVIII*, Rio de Janeiro 2017, 101–135.

Boxer, Charles R., *Portuguese Society in the Tropics. The Municipal Councils of Goa, Macao, Bahia, and Luanda, 1510–1800*, Madison 1965.

Cabral, Gustavo César Machado, "Os senhorios na América Portuguesa: o Sistema de capitanias hereditárias e a prática da jurisdição senhorial (séculos XVI a XVIII)", in *Jahrbuch für Geschichte Lateinamerikas* 52 (2015), 65–86.

Cabral, Gustavo César Machado, "Direito penal na literatura de *Decisiones* em Portugal (1578–1660)", in Cabral, Gustavo César Machado, Francesco Di Chiara, Óscar Hernández Santiago and Belinda Rodríguez Arrocha, *El derecho penal en la Edad Moderna: Nuevas aproximaciones a la doctrina y a la práctica judicial*, Madrid 2016, 23–76.

Cabral, Gustavo César Machado, "Os Jesuítas e a construção da ordem jurídica: uma contribuição ao estudo da normatividade dos catecismos e confessionários na América Portuguesa (séculos XVII–XVIII)", in *Nomos* 39:2 (2019), 275–297.

Cabral, Gustavo César Machado, "Jesuit Pragmatic Literature and Ecclesiastical Normativity in Portuguese America (16th–18th centuries)", in Duve, Thomas and Otto Danwerth (eds.), *Knowledge of the Pragmatici: Legal and Moral Theological Literature and the Formation of Early Modern Ibero-America*, Leiden 2020, 151–186.

Cabral, Gustavo César Machado, "Recursos cíveis ultramarinos: apelações e agravos cíveis da América Portuguesa à Casa da Suplicação de Lisboa (1754–1822)", in *Revista do Instituto Histórico e Geographico Brasileiro* 182:486 (2021), 41–72.

Cabral, Gustavo César Machado, "Uma teoria do direito para a América Portuguesa (séculos XVI–XVIII)", in Cabral, Gustavo César Machado, Delmiro Ximenes de Farias and Sarah Kelly Limão Papa (eds.), *Fontes do direito na América Portuguesa: estudos sobre o fenômeno jurídico no período colonial (séculos XVI–XVIII)*, Porto Alegre 2021, 17–52.

Cabral, Gustavo César Machado, *O Direito na América Portuguesa: fundamentos, jurisdições, normas e práticas no Brasil Colonial (1530–1800)* (forthcoming).

Cabral, Gustavo César Machado, "On letters and laws: Books of the Municipal Council in Portuguese America (18th century)" (forthcoming).

Cabral, Gustavo César Machado, Ana Carolina Farias Almeida da Costa and Matheus Silva de Sá, "Fontes do direito e planejamento urbano na Capitania do Ceará: os casos das vilas de Icó e Aracati", in Cabral, Gustavo César Machado, Delmiro Ximenes de Farias and Sarah Kelly Limão Papa (eds.), *Fontes do direito na América Portuguesa: estudos sobre o fenômeno jurídico no período colonial (séculos XVI–XVIII)*, Porto Alegre 2021, 224–243.

Calasso, Francesco, *Medio Evo del Diritto*, vol. I: *Le fonti*, Milano 1954.

Camarinhas, Nuno, "O aparelho judicial ultramarino português: o caso do Brasil (1620–1800)", in *Almanack Brasiliense* 9 (2009), 84–102.

Camarinhas, Nuno, "As residências dos cargos de justiça letrada", in Stumpf, Roberta and Nandini Chaturvedula (eds.), *Cargos e ofícios nas Monarquias Ibéricas: provimento, controlo e venalidade (séculos XVII e XVIII)*, Lisboa 2012, 161–172.

Cardim, Pedro, Tamar Herzog, José Javier Ruiz Ibáñez and Gaetano Sabatini, "Introduction", in Cardim, Pedro, Tamar Herzog, José Javier Ruiz Ibáñez and Gaetano Sabatini (eds.), *Polycentric Monarchies. How did Early Modern Spain and Portugal Achieve and Maintain a Global Hegemony?*, Sussex 2012, 3–10.

Carvalho, Reinaldo Forte, *Governanças das terras: poder local e administração da justiça na Capitania do Ceará (1699–1748)* (Ph.D. Thesis), Recife 2015.

Cunha, Mafalda Soares da and António Castro Nunes, "Territorialização e poder na América portuguesa. A criação de comarcas, séculos XVI–XVIII", in *Tempo* 39:22 (2016), 1–30.

Decock, Wim, *Theologians and Contract Law. The Moral Transformation of the Ius Commune (ca. 1500–1650)*, Leiden 2013.

Duve, Thomas, "Von der Europäischen Rechtsgeschichte zu einer Rechtsgeschichte Europas in globalhistorischer Perspektive", in *Rechtsgeschichte – Legal History* 20 (2012), 18–71.

Duve, Thomas, "What Is Global Legal History?", in *Comparative Legal History* 8:2 (2020), 73–115.

Duve, Thomas, "Legal History as a History of the Translation of Knowledge of Normativity", in *Max Planck Institute for Legal History and Legal Theory Research Paper Series*, no. 2022–16 (2022) (https://ssrn.com/abstract=4229323), 1–12.

Halpérin, Jean-Louis, "Histoire comparée du droit", in Krynen, Jacques and Bernard d'Alteroche (eds.), *L'Histoire du droit en France. Nouvelles tendances, nouveaux territoires*, Paris 2014, 183–203.

Hart, Herbert L. A., *The Concept of Law*, 2nd ed., Oxford 1994.

Herzog, Tamar, "Colonial Law: Early Modern Normativity in Spanish America", in Tellkamp, Jörg Alejandro (ed.), *A Companion to Early Modern Spanish Imperial Political and Social Thought*, Leiden 2020, 105–127.

Hespanha, António Manuel, *História das Instituições. Épocas medieval e moderna*, Coimbra 1982.

Hespanha, António Manuel, "Da 'iustitia' à 'disciplina': textos, poder e política penal no Antigo Regime", in *Anuario de Historia del Derecho Español* 57 (1987), 493–578.

Hespanha, António Manuel, *As vésperas do Leviathan. Instituições e poder político, Portugal, Séc. XVII*, Coimbra 1994.

Hespanha, António Manuel, "A constituição do império português. Revisão de alguns enviesamentos correntes", in Fragoso, João, Maria Fernanda Bicalho and Maria de Fátima S. Gouvêa (eds.), *O Antigo Regime nos Trópicos. A dinâmica Imperial Portuguesa (séculos XVI–XVIII)*, Rio de Janeiro 2001, 163–188.

Hespanha, António Manuel, *Como os juristas viam o mundo. 1550–1750. Direitos, estados, pessoas, coisas, contratos, ações e crimes*, Lisboa 2015.

Hespanha, António Manuel, "O 'direito das Índias' no contexto da historiografia das colonizações ibéricas", in Duve, Thomas (ed.), *Actas del XIX Congreso del Instituto Internacional de Historia del Derecho Indiano*, Madrid 2017, 43–83.

Hespanha, António Manuel, *Uma monarquia tradicional. Imagens e mecanismos da política no Portugal Seiscentista*, Lisboa 2019.

Jesus, Nauk Maria de, "Juízes letrados, vilas e julgados: a ouvidoria e os ouvidores em Cuiabá e Vela Bela (1728–1822)", in Bicalho, Maria Fernanda, Virgínia Maria Almoêdo de Assis and Isabele de Matos Pereira de Mello (eds.), *Justiça no Brasil Colonial: agentes e práticas*, São Paulo 2017, 79–106.

Meccarelli, Massimo, *Arbitrium. Un aspetto sistematico degli ordinamenti giuridici in età di diritto comune*, Milano 1998.

Mello, Isabele de Matos Pereira de, *Administração, justiça e poder: os ouvidores gerais e suas correições na cidade do Rio de Janeiro (1624–1696)* (Master's Thesis), Niterói 2009.

Mello, Isabele de Matos Pereira de, *Magistrados a serviço do rei: a administração da justiça e os ouvidores gerais na comarca do Rio de Janeiro (1710–1790)* (Ph.D. Thesis), Niterói 2013.

Monteiro, Nuno Gonçalo, "Os concelhos e as comunidade", in Hespanha, António Manuel (ed.), *História de Portugal*, vol. 4: *O Antigo Regime (1620–1807)*, Lisboa 1998, 283–287.

Motta, Marcia, *Direito à terra no Brasil. A gestação do conflito, 1795–1824*, 2nd ed., São Paulo 2012.

Nogueira, Gabriel Parente, *Às margens do império: a pecuária das carnes e o comércio nos portos da porção oriental da costa leste-oeste da América Portuguesa nas dinâmicas de um império em movimento (século XVIII)* (Ph.D. Thesis), Fortaleza 2021.

Paiva, Yamê Galdino de, "Os regimentos dos ouvidores de comarca na América portuguesa, séculos XVII e XVIII: esboço de análise", in *Nuevo Mundo Mundos Nuevos* [*Online*] (2017) (http://journals.openedition.org/nuevomundo/71578).

Paiva, Yamê Galdino de, *Justiça e poder na América Portuguesa: Ouvidores e administração da justiça na Comarca da Paraíba (c.1687–c.1799)* (Ph.D. Thesis), Lisboa 2020.

Pegoraro, Jonas Wilson, *Ouvidores régios e centralização jurídico-administrativa na América Portuguesa. A comarca de Paranaguá (1723–1812)* (Master's Thesis), Curitiba 2007.

Pegoraro, Jonas Wilson, *Zelo pelo serviço real: ações de ouvidores régios nas comarcas de São Paulo e de Paranaguá (primeira metade do século XVIII)* (Ph.D. Thesis), Curitiba 2015.

Saldanha, António Vasconcelos de, *As capitanias do Brasil. Antecedentes, desenvolvimento e extinção de um fenómeno atlântico*, Lisboa 2001.

Saussure, Ferdinand de, *Cours de linguistique générale*, Paris 1917.

Schwartz, Stuart B., *Sovereignty and Society in Colonial Brazil. The High Court of Bahia and its Judges, 1609–1751*, Berkeley 1973.

Seelaender, Airton L. Cerqueira Leite, *Polizei, Ökonomie und Gesetzgebungslehre. Ein Beitrag zur Analyse der portugiesischen Rechtswissenschaft am Ende des 18. Jahrhunderts*, Frankfurt am Main 2003.

Stolleis, Michael, *Geschichte des öffentlichen Rechts in Deutschland*, vol. 1: *Reichspublizistik und Policeywissenschaft 1600–1800*, München 1988.

Stumpf, Roberta, "Correições baianas: uma sondagem da fiscalização sobre as Câmaras", in Souza, Evergton Sales, Ana Paula Medicci and Pedro Cardim (eds.), *Salvador da Bahia: escravidão, economia, poderes e representações (séculos XVI–XIX)*, Salvador 2022, 201–226.

Tau Anzoátegui, Victor, "La configuración del derecho Indiano provincial y local: cuestiones metodológicas y desarollo de sus fases históricas", in Tau Anzoátegui, Victor and Alejandro Agüero (eds.), *El derecho local ena la periferia de la Monarquía Hispana: Río de La Plata, Tucumán y Cuyo, siglos XVI–XVIII*, Buenos Aires 2013, 13–90.

Torgal, Luís Reis, *Ideologia política e teoria do estado na Restauração*, 2 vols., Coimbra 1981–1982.

Vallejo, Jesús, "Acerca del fruto del árbol de los jueces. Escenarios de la justicia en la cultura del ius commune", in *Anuario de la Facultad de Derecho de la Universidad Autónoma de Madrid* 2 (1998), 19–46.

Varela, Laura Beck, *Das sesmarias à propriedade moderna: um estudo de história do direito brasileiro*, Rio de Janeiro 2005.

Wright, Georg Henrik von, *Norm and Action. A Logical Inquiry*, London 1963.

Xavier, Ângela Barreto and Cristina Nogueira da Silva (eds.), *O governo dos outros. Poder e diferença no império português*, Lisboa 2016.

CHAPTER 7

A Gendered Penalty

Adultery, *Recolhimentos* and Legal Change in Portuguese America (18th Century)

Vanessa Massuchetto

1 Introduction

In 1792, in Salvador, Ana Maria Joaquina da Purificação was accused by her husband, Jacinto Tomas de Faria, of engaging in adultery with the canon (*cônego*) of that city. In the situation, "forgetting [...] the faith, and loyalty, that she should always keep to her lawful husband, she gave consent to the torpid desires of the canon" who, in turn, "tried to ruin the honour, and credit of the supplicant committing the detestable crime of treason and treachery".[1] This betrayal, as perceived by Jacinto, inflicted a grave wound upon his honour, prompting him to sue both Ana Maria and the canon. Seeking to mitigate the public scandal, Jacinto requested the Secretary of State of the Navy and Overseas Territories to confine Ana Maria in a *recolhimento*.

This case underscores a recurring theme in historiography concerning the societal perception of cloistered institutions as a form of castigation, or penalisation,[2] of women who deviated from moral normativities. Influenced by theological discourses, society often viewed women as particularly susceptible to sinful temptations, thereby necessitating strict control over their behaviour and thoughts. Consequently, the confinement of women in such

1 "esquecida [...] da fé, e lealdade, que deveria sempre guardar a seu legítimo marido, deu consentimento aos torpes desejos do cônego"; "intentou arruinar à honra, e crédito do suplicante cometendo o detestável crime de traição, e aleivosia". AHU, Bahia, Papéis Avulsos, box 58, doc. 11067, fol. 3v. With regard to quotations from sources, my translation has been inserted into the text while the original in Portuguese can be found in the footnotes. All quotations from the same source have been gathered into one footnote for each page. If the quote is from printed sources, the spelling has been respected, and when it is from manuscript sources, the spelling has been updated.

2 Castigation and penalisation are perceived as two methods of punishment, differing in terms of the range of normativities to which they related. Castigation stems from the concept of theological punishment, administered within the internal forum of individuals. Penalisation, on the other hand, pertains to prescribed penalties within legislation, addressing the external forum of individuals.

institutions was perceived as a corrective measure aimed at maintaining social order and upholding Christian values.[3]

The analysis of female sexualities in the modern period demands a focus on the social dynamics that relied on binary concepts. Historical actors articulated and enacted their expressions within these ideas, highlighting the interplay between perceptions and their agencies. Some examples of these notions are clemency and cruelty, forgiveness and punishment, virtue and sin. They were often manipulated by the Catholic Church and the Crown to enforce behavioural normativities to maintain social order.[4] In this universe, sexual practices were perceived through the lenses of crime and sin, often hybrids because they brought in their core a double prohibition: they simultaneously supposed legislative fraud (by violating the normative written order) and attacked moral and religious normativities.[5] For jurists of the time, matters of moral conduct were connected to both the external and internal forums of people. Thus, royal law acted in the external forum when temporal laws were broken, whereas ecclesiastical law acted in the internal forum for the breaking of spiritual laws. In theory, not every sin constituted criminal behaviour, but every crime was the result of sinful conduct.[6] In these cases, in addition to castigation applied by canon law, the punishment could also include the imposition of a penalty by royal law.

The research developed in this chapter begins by examining the conceptual frameworks underpinning the practice of sending women who deviated from moral normativities to *recolhimentos*. Specifically, it aims to elucidate how actors, particularly female actors as documented in the sources, perceived this practice. It seeks to determine whether they viewed it primarily as a form of castigation or penalisation. The inquiry questions whether the disciplinary bias was evident in the cases analysed, representing a tool used by domestic authorities to correct those under their power, thus constituting one of the potential punitive measures within the domestic sphere.

To do so, an understanding of the development of the practice within normativity frameworks is important, with the aim to grasp the social perspectives regarding cases of moral transgressions, particularly those related to sexual behaviours. The objective is not solely to examine the treatment within

3 Lopes, "Dominando corpos e consciências", 99.
4 Undurraga Schüler and Gaune, "Diálogos y propuestas historiográficas", 21.
5 Torremocha Hernández, "El estupro en el Informe jurídico de Meléndez"; Blanco Carrasco, "¿Adónde irán los secretos?"; Martínez Llorente, "Una notación histórica sobre el delito de estupro".
6 Bazán Díaz, "El estupro", 13.

specific institutions of female confinement but to grasp more broadly which normativities surrounded the practice of sending women to such institutions. Before delving into cases of the daily lives of women within the cloisters, this chapter explores external issues, such as conflicts, responses to conflicts and perceptions of punishment (penalisation and castigation), as well as the social functions of these institutions.

Furthermore, this chapter also focuses on the legal changes throughout the 18th century, aiming to understand the diachronic nuances of the practice from the perspectives of women and their families, and of secular and ecclesiastical authorities. It centres on the structural changes within various normativities, aiming to uncover the construction of knowledge of normativity through processes of cultural translation between global and local normativities. The dynamics of transformation are discerned through the exploration of local normative production encompassing practices, rules, discourses, norms and principles derived from archival sources spanning different regions of Portuguese America.[7]

Within this theoretical framework, attention is directed towards two main aspects. Firstly, the motivation driving historical actors to engage in such practices, including the moral and religious factors that encouraged them, the impacts they pursued, and the values they upheld. Secondly, the focus extends to the institutional changes that both influenced and were influenced by the exchange of knowledge of normativity within the social context. That is, the research seeks to understand the range of normativities that shaped a certain stability in the legal scenario and in which ways this stability underwent transformations, detecting the agents that motivated the changes and, above all, their perspectives, especially those of women, on the legal changes. The primary manuscript sources are the documents housed at the Lisbon Overseas Archive on cases of adultery in the Captaincies of Bahia, Pernambuco, Grão Pará, Rio de Janeiro and São Paulo.

The mentioned captaincies were characterised by distinct contexts, and the women residing in them were subjected to different realities. This study does not seek to homogenise these contexts. The colonisation processes in the Northeast and North regions differed from those in the Southeast. While in the South the settlements commenced in the late 16th century, in the Northeast and North the colonisation processes started earlier. During the first half of the century, these areas of Portuguese America held significant economic importance, a status maintained until the 18th century. Cities, such as Recife,

7 Duve, "Historia del derecho como historia del saber normativo"; "What is global legal history?"; "Legal History as an Observation of Historical Regimes of Normativity".

Olinda and Salvador, were renowned for their sugar cane production, which integrated them into the transatlantic trade network. This not only facilitated commercial exchanges but also spurred population growth, increased the movement of people and brought the arrival of a larger number of enslaved Africans, the construction of colonial administrative structures, and the initial influx of colonisers eager to exploit the land. Salvador served as the capital of colonial administration until 1763, maintaining a crucial role in the colonial political system by virtue of its connections to the kingdom and other parts of the empire.[8]

The mining activities in the region of Minas Gerais drew significant attention from the Crown and colonisers, prompting considerable changes in that society. The decision to relocate the capital to Rio de Janeiro was motivated not only by these activities, but also by political colonisation strategies aimed at the southern territories. Over time, the harbour of Rio de Janeiro gained prominence within the colonial scenario of the Portuguese worlds, facilitating increased movement of people throughout the region. As a consequence, there was a notable surge in economic activities already underway in the region, accompanied by population growth, expanded trade networks, a larger influx of enslaved people, attraction of more colonisers and the spreading of strategies for enslaving indigenous peoples.[9]

Despite the impossibility of homogenising the mentioned captaincies, it was possible to detect similarities in how women acted and how they were treated by their families and local institutions. Sending adulterous women to the *recolhimentos* seemed to have similar characteristics in these analysed regions. As will be shown in the next sections of this chapter, the practice changed mainly during the late 18th century until its consolidation as a gendered penalty. The practice brought meanings from the penalty of *degredo* together with normativities that were specific to the local social order along with the prevalence of shame, revenge and tolerance. In this sense, the practice was related to the social responses it could provide, responding much more to the husband's needs and concerns with honour than to the wife's.

The next section of this chapter introduces some of the contexts regarding the *recolhimentos* in Portuguese America and the meanings they held

8 Puntoni, "Bernardo Vieira Ravasco, secretário do Estado do Brasil", 163–164.

9 Privately administered (*administrado particular*) was a social-legal category developed in colonial society. The full prohibition of indigenous slavery existed in Portuguese legislation as early as 1596, however, breaches of these norms were pervaded by normativities that meant the category was widespread throughout the 18th century. See more in: Brighente, "Entre a Liberdade e a administração particular".

throughout the 18th century. Afterwards, the cases found in the collection of the *Arquivo Histórico Ultramarino*[10] are presented in order to understand the patterns of behaviour, thought and procedure of the historical actors, the authorities and the institutions involved in the cases. Finally, some ideas will be presented to explain such patterns, interweaving local and global normativities, mainly the practices, the meanings of the penalty of *degredo* and the laws of shame and revenge, inquiring to what extent sending women to *recolhimentos* could be related to this form of punishment.

2 *Recolhimentos* in Luso-Iberian Worlds of the Modern Period, Women's Daily Lives and Legal Change

The female cloistered institutions fulfilled several functions within the Portuguese colonies. On the one hand, the convents were designed to shelter those who wished to follow religious life and who took permanent vows of obedience, chastity and poverty. The *recolhimentos*, on the other hand, sheltered lay women for various reasons, either for charity, education, correction or punishment. It was common that these institutions received single women and orphans for their protection, housed married women during the absence of their husbands and accommodated widows in a temporary or permanent way, offering them a daily life based on Catholic religious values from temporary vows.[11]

Raphael Bluteau, during this period, conceptualised *recolhimentos* as "the preserver of honesty" (*pregoeiro da honestidade*) for women – "seclusion of young women is the best preservative of their honesty" – accompanying also the notions of "house of religion or retreat from the world, without religious vows; confinement, without conversations, outings, walks and other distractions; withdrawal of the spirit, abstraction from things that distract it or meditation and deep reflection, without distraction".[12] From this, one could think

10 First created in 1604 by King Filipe II under the name of *Conselho da Índia* following the model of the *Consejo de Indias*, the Overseas Council (*Conselho Ultramarino*) was the royal apparatus in charge of governing the colonies. The 17th and 18th centuries were marked by intense activity by the Overseas Council for Portuguese America due to the progressive population increase in colonial society, the foundation of new villages and cities, sugar production, the discovery of gold in the Minas Gerais region, intensification of the slave trade from Africa and designation of colonial institutions.

11 Algranti, *Livros de devoção, atos de censura*, 30.

12 "o recolhimento nas donzelas é o melhor preservativo da sua honestidade"; "casa de religião ou retiro do mundo, sem votos religiosos; encerramento, sem conversações,

of the institutions of confinement as places of no social contact, to "not talk" and "not be seen". More than just a contemplative life and devotion to God, the confinement maintained a link with the idea of withdrawal from society. *Recolhimentos* also had to be, at least theoretically, regulated by statutes that governed daily life and directed desired feminine behaviours, and they had to maintain this direction in the production of normativity in terms of the religious-moral order.

Usually, the focus of the *recolhimentos* for single women was the contraction of advantageous marriages upon leaving, as it was an institution that aimed to educate women according to Christian values. For married women and widows, it could be a place in which they would be able to preserve their honour when their families were in the process of impoverishment. Also, women who were mistreated by their husbands used to ask the ecclesiastical judge to be "deposited" there when they petitioned for marriage dissolution. However, when women – single, married or widowed – were sheltered by force, the motivation was mainly to "correct" their behaviours according to the terms seen as right by their families, especially their husbands and fathers. In this sense, *recolhimentos* represented (but not only) spaces for the preservation and restoration of the honour of those belonging to elite families and, in these cases, the goal of sending them to confinement was not marriage, but rather to avoid the dishonour of the family.[13]

Honour, in the colonial context, corresponded to the values given to one by the society with which one interacts, directly guiding the value given to oneself.[14] Its apprehension and its loss, thus, are related to the way individuals were seen by their peers regarding the qualities they possessed – arising from the status in which they were born and in the titles they might receive – and their virtuous behaviours.[15] For this reason, virtues were also a means of construction, conservation or destruction of honour for men and women, a situation that implied the observation of the social practices of individuals. This range of desired behaviours was based on Catholic moral doctrine

saídas, passeios e outras distrações; recolhimento do espírito, abstração das coisas, que o distraiam, ou meditação e ponderação profunda, sem distração". Bluteau, *Vocabulario Portuguez e Latino*; *Diccionario da Lingua Portugueza*, lib. VII. Translated by the author.

13 Almeida, *O sexo devoto*; Lopes, "Transgressões femininas".

14 Braga, "A bigamia em Portugal na Época Moderna", 63–64. And, also, Ruff, "Violence in Early Modern Europe".

15 Garnot, "Justiça e sociedade na França do século XVIII".

and controlled by the strategies of social discipline. There were distinctions between the genders, differentiating what was expected of women and of men.[16]

Male honour was usually associated with courage, righteousness and loyalty to one's word, while female honour was linked to a series of representations from moral-religious thought and medicine of the period, especially honesty. The main attribute of honesty was chastity, and virginity was understood as fundamental proof by which it was possible to achieve this.[17] Consequently, the honour attributed to women was correlated to sexual behaviour because it was based on the biological differences between the sexes. It could be ascertained whether women had engaged in active sexual behaviour – pregnancy and offspring were difficult to conceal – but not men. Female honour ended up being controlled by reproduction; their sexual behaviour was the motive for them to be honourable. Thus, conceiving only legitimate children was one factor that ensured honour.[18]

The individual social value of women was thus essentially tied to their reputation. Without social confirmation, the individual claim was groundless and untenable. One's value needed to be defended and socially affirmed, otherwise it could also jeopardise the family's social standing. The main issue of honour, therefore, seems to involve the publicity of qualities and behaviours that expressed the desired virtues. Honour had a public nature, representing much more than a set of rules for behaviours. Namely, in the colonies, it constituted the very social organisation, permeating everyday life and defining a series of social ("public") roles to men and women, especially to those belonging to the elite.[19]

The ideal of honour did not impact all women in the same way and, in colonial society, the differences between legal statuses and privileges guided the demands of different female groups. Enslaved black and indigenous women were considered to be women without honour, which is why it was believed that sexual abuse committed against them by their masters would not solely be liable in a legal complaint. Although only the women considered non-white

16 Braga, "A bigamia em Portugal na Época Moderna", 64; Johnson and Lipsett-Rivera, "Introduction", 3–4; Spurling, "Honor, Sexuality, and the Colonial Church", 45.

17 Lopes, "Estereótipos de 'a mulher' em Portugal", 34; Braga, "A bigamia em Portugal na Época Moderna", 64; Twinam, "The Negotiation of Honor", 81.

18 Braga, "A bigamia em Portugal na Época Moderna", 12, 64–65; Braga, "Punir a Violação, perdoar os Violadores", 171; Algranti, *Honradas e devotas*, 111–112.

19 Johnson and Lipsett-Rivera, "Introduction", 6–7; Twinam, "The Negotiation of Honor", 83.

were enslaved, non-white women who were free, freed or bonded could be still seen by whites as without honour and, consequently, without virtue.[20]

Women tended to be more protected due to the fear that the loss of their honour would mean tarnishing the family's honour. That is, the female honour symbolised the male honour of the father or husband, even of the brother, denoting a special impact on matrimonial economic issues. The contract of *arras* was one of the ways in which this could be verified, bearing in mind that it meant payment, from the husband to the wife, for her honesty and virginity at the time of marriage. Dowries, in turn, proved to be a strategy for social reproduction through the accumulation, concentration and donation of wealth through marriage, resulting in political alliances between the elite, territorial implications and, to a certain extent, family endogamy. Typically, issues concerning the virginity of young women ended up becoming a family priority, due to the patrimonial and social impacts it would have on them all.[21]

Following this line of thought, although the cloister, in general, existed for both men and women, the institutions for female confinement had a greater emphasis on inviolability. The rules specifically placed on female cloisters had a specific sexual meaning and can be exemplified by the differences between exit permissions granted to abbots for male monasteries while for women decisions on this fell to the discretion of the bishop. These spaces were subject to greater hierarchisation and the necessary subjection of the residents to male advice, whether from bishops or the pope.[22]

Thus, the female cloister was much more related to the condition of women than to their devotion, and in this characteristic is included the permissibility of the entrance of lay women who sought protection and asylum under the guise of preserving their virtues. The idea of the cloister was that women needed to be away from the bad influences of the outside world so that they could achieve spirituality, and it became a basic principle of female religious life. In Portuguese America, the first religious communities emerged at the end of the 17th century with small groups of women confined to devotion and, over the decades, they acquired a reputation for being pious by welcoming orphans

20 Algranti, *Honradas e devotas*, 121–122, 129.

21 Braga, "A bigamia em Portugal na Época Moderna", 67; Vandenbogaerde, "(Wo)Men in legal history", 16–17. The dowry had multiple facets in the modern period; it was also used by women for their own living and, in some cases, interests and negotiations. Especially in the 17th and early 18th centuries, it used to correspond to a major part of a couple's patrimony, which kept them both linked to the wife's family and gave her weight in the matrimonial pact, providing her with the power of negotiation in specific matters. Nazzari, *O desaparecimento do dote*, 268.

22 Algranti, *Livros de devoção, atos de censura*, 24–25.

and impoverished women. In theory, these institutions had to be authorised by the royal power and have statutes that regulated the activities carried out. Some of them started operating without such a concession, due to the needs of the region, and not all of them, as far as records show, had statutes.

The major institutional motive for allowing the entry of laywomen was in accordance with the mentality that the condition of misery would inevitably lead them to the corruption of good manners and, consequently, to prostitution. The charity practices of these institutions, as well as of religious sisterhoods, attracted orphans, beggars and impoverished women seeking shelter. After the Council of Trent, charity began to have a moral, condemnatory, rather than religious, conception, and these types of institutions began to have more of a welfare than doctrinal nature. That is, assistance to the miserable was accompanied by forms of discipline and punishment since in some measure they represented a series of dangers to social order. The religious motivation remained but sprouted with strategies of control.[23]

According to Leila Algranti, the cloister for women, whether convents or *recolhimentos*, represented a place of normalisation, control of sexuality, preservation of honesty and maintenance of woman's status. They were places whose purpose was to preserve virtue and chastity through distance from family and urban sociabilities, besides representing an alternative for women so as not to suffer the consequences of poverty and misery, situations that put at risk the preservation of their condition. At the same time, being *recolhidas* could give more prestige to women than being married, especially for non-white women. Michelle McKinley discovered that, in 16th- and 17th-century Lima, religious education provided by cloister institutions offered freed women more privilege than marriage did. According to her, monasteries were also key institutions to Spanish colonisation and represented places of normatisation.[24]

As a result of the ideal of preservation of honesty, it is well known that, in Portuguese America, women who committed crimes against the religious-moral order – such as consensual rape,[25] concubinage, incest and adultery

23 Algranti, *Livros de devoção, atos de censura*, 25–26.

24 Algranti, *Honradas e devotas*, 109–120; McKinley, *Fractional Freedoms*, 149–150.

25 In the Portuguese and Spanish legal traditions from the early modern period, two types of behaviour were identified as rape: one with the woman's consent and one without. Consensual rape typically occurred when virgin women and men entered relationships and had sex without being married. In Portuguese legislation, the terms most widely used in the book V of the Philippine Ordinances are "to sleep with" and "to sleep by force with," describing the presence or lack of consent by the presence of force. Therefore, the first behaviour was termed "with consent", and the second, "with force". The literal translation from Portuguese results in the terms "consensual rape", and "rape by force" or

– were often sent to *recolhimentos* or convents as a kind of, roughly speaking, punishment for their bad behaviour. These crimes were socially perceived as between the logic of crime and sin, holding at their core the complexity of this double prohibition. Thus, the women were liable to be castigated and, at the same time, penalised. Although royal law had widened the contours of some of these crimes and modified the requirements for committing them and included other forms of punishment throughout the 18th century, the secular and ecclesiastic legislation did not foresee the imprisonment of the convicted as a form of penalty.[26]

The resolution of conflicts regarding sexuality was part of a strategy to discipline the behaviours in the colonies, and sending female transgressors to *recolhimentos* or convents seems to point in this direction. This is because, according to Algranti and Suely Creusa de Almeida, the *recolhimentos* and convents meant spaces of normatisation for the *recolhidas*, with a privileged focus on the maintenance of honour and on the practices of devotion. However, the Portuguese Crown's strong incentives of matrimony in the colony resulted in several measures to prohibit – or at least obstruct – the opening of female convents. Faced with what Algranti calls the "resistance" of the colonists – that is, a series of requests for royal grants and negotiations with the Overseas Council – the impediments were gradually relaxed and resulted in permission for the funding of a few convents and *recolhimentos*.[27]

The royal policy of instrumentalising marriage as a tool to populate Portuguese America was reported in 1551 by Father Manuel da Nóbrega through a [famous] letter in which he requested the King to send white, orphaned women to marry the Portuguese. In 1603, the priest reinforced the request, arguing that he did it so that the Portuguese could be removed from the sin in which they lived, noting that "white women here are so desired that they will do much good to the land and they will be won over and the men here will

---

"violent rape". However, the terminology for these offenses was not consistent throughout the early modern period, leading to frequent confusion between the terms. Portugal, *Ordenações Filipinas*, lib. V, tit. XVIII, tit. XXIII, § 2º; Braga, "Punir a Violação, perdoar os Violadores".

26 In the early modern period, imprisonment was not perceived as a way of penalising criminal cases. Consequentially, it was not defined in legislations as a penalty to be applied. At the time, it served the purpose of preventing people accused of committing crimes from fleeing after they had been pronounced in a *devassa* (the "investigative" process), making it possible for the offended party to present the accusatory libel in the condemnatory process and give rise to the imposition of a penalty.

27 Algranti, *Honradas e devotas*, 62–108; Almeida, *O sexo devoto*.

depart from their sins".[28] Sharing the same idea, the Royal Letter of 2 September of the same year prohibited the foundation of convents in the captaincies of Bahia and Pernambuco because they needed to "increase the population of that State, to be populated with main and honourable people, that is the intention, with which, from the beginning of its discovery, are sent to it every year young orphan women of good fathers, to be married there".[29] This belief apparently continued throughout the next century, expressed in an authorisation for the operation of a *recolhimento* founded without royal authorisation but that could have some function considering that "he believes that if in Brazil there were some *recolhimentos* where young women were created to marry they would be useful for the population of that state, and concubinage would largely cease".[30] Marriage constituted, then, a royal policy for the settlement of Portuguese America.

According to the royal norm of 1603, the women of the colony were mostly destined to confinement in institutions in Portugal, since there was only one convent in Olinda, created at the end of the 16th century and, due to the limited number of women that could be placed in this convent, the option was to request royal authorisation to go to the metropolis. This was perpetuated until the beginning of the 18th century and is usually exemplified by the Royal Charter of 10 March 1732, which attempted to contain the migration of colonial women within the kingdom under the pretext of becoming nuns not only on the grounds of the need to increase the population of Portuguese America, but also because many young women sent to the kingdom did not come by choice, but were sent by their families.[31] This measure was understood as a way to force elite women who wished to follow religious life to contract marriages due to the absence of convents. To the metropolitan authorities, it did not seem convenient to have convents in the colony so, over the decades, a preference was shown for the foundation of *recolhimentos*, especially those

28 "são tão desejadas as mulheres brancas cá que quaisquer farão cá muito bem a terra e elas se ganharão e os homens de cá apartar-se-ão dos pecados". Biblioteca Nacional de Portugal (BNP), Nóbrega, [Cartas,] 192. Translated by the author.

29 "acrescentamento d'aquelle Estado, povoar-se de gente principal e honrada, que é o intento, com que, do principio do seu descobrimento, se enviam e elle cada anno donzelas órfãs de bons paes, para alli se casarem". Portugal, *Collecção Chronologica da Legislação Portugueza*, 22. Translated by the author.

30 "entende ele conselheiro que se no Brasil houvessem alguns recolhimentos em que se criassem donzelas para casarem seriam úteis para a povoação daquele estado, e cessariam em grande parte as mancebias". AHU, Pernambuco, box 66, doc. 5560, fols. 2v–3r. Translated by the author.

31 Portugal, *Collecção Chronologica de Leis Extravagantes*, 431.

that did not economically depend on the Crown but were under its authority so that they would not become houses of nuns. Throughout the 18th century, the colonial society gradually found ways to avail itself of the "devotional" desires through requests and the granting of mercies, and some convents were founded, but mainly *recolhimentos*, in various places in Portuguese America.[32] Thus, the increase in these institutions ended up becoming, depending on the region, an issue of dispute between the wishes of the monarch and the colony's inhabitants.

For example, in 1724, the council officials of Olinda sent a letter to the King informing him about the population increase in that town and, for this reason, requested the conversion of the *Recolhimento* of *Nossa Senhora da Conceição* into a convent. They said that it was in the interest of the many noble people who lived in the village, as well as the honourable women of these families, and that the place already had all the necessary structures to receive professed novices, and that they only needed the royal grace to do so.[33] In 1725, the officials sent another request with the same content, answered in 1726 with a negative response.[34] Regarding this same *recolhimento*, in 1725 there were express orders from the deans of Olinda directed to the regent, Ana Nunes, to work to avoid disorder and dishonesty in that house, not receiving women of "depraved customs" or who had "minimal note in their customs".[35] In this same sense the functioning of the *Recolhimento* of Igarassu, founded without a royal licence, was authorised to continue through rules, such as not building a church, not exercising any function for the community of that village, not receiving more women than those already gathered and keeping them in complete confinement. The apparent belief, in this letter of authorisation, was for the existence of women who had actually converted among those who were already confined, so there would be some function in keeping this institution active.[36]

The case of *Dona* Isabel Maria is perhaps more elucidative of the disputes not only between the villagers and the royal representatives but also with regard to the ecclesiastical authorities and among the colonists themselves. Isabel, along with other women, established a *recolhimento* in the village of

---

32 Almeida, "A clausura feminina no mundo ibero-atlântico", 97, 108–109; *O sexo devoto*, 95–96.

33 AHU, Pernambuco, box 30, doc. 2720, fols. 1r–1v.

34 AHU, Pernambuco, box 32, doc. 2924, fols. 1r–3r.

35 "depravados costumes"; "mínima nota em seus costumes". AHU, Pernambuco, box 32, doc. 2926, fol. 1r. Translated by the author.

36 AHU, Pernambuco, box 66, doc. 5560, fols. 2v–3r.

Bom Sucesso, in Bahia, aiming to "apply themselves in what is neither forbidden by divine nor human law". In July 1753, the archbishop received news of a *recolhimento* in which a priest was confessing ten women through their dowries without, however, requesting permission for the erection of the chapel, the statutes and the rules for living. Thus, he ordered that diligence should be carried out in the chapel and the *recolhimento*, consequently closing the activities of the place if there was no licence, and ordering the relatives of the sheltered women to go there and take them away.[37]

Isabel, in a request addressed to the archbishop in March 1754, described the activities she was developing in her house and stressed that her intention was to help women who lived in poverty. She expressed knowledge that though she could not receive a licence from the vicar general to build the *recolhimento*, she claimed that he could not prevent her from receiving in her house the women she had been helping. She claimed dissatisfaction with the information that the archbishop had sent to the governor of the captaincy about how the women behaved under her tutelage, pointing out that "I have no doubt that the successes of the world in the feminine state will make the deliberation with which some find themselves seem frivolous, but this is not the general rule". She added that those statements were motivated by envy, and that "nor should anyone who wants to serve his creator be cold on the path he has started because of such suspicion, because the machines of the devil, our ancient enemy, are like clouds that quickly form and suddenly disappear". She also sent certificates of the notary public faith with more than 25 signatures of people (mostly men) from the neighbourhood attesting that she was a serious, honest and devout woman, and that the women under her guard were applied to "women's work of sewing, lace and [...] to praise God in the spiritual exercise of honour, and zeal for the same Lord in continuous mental prayer".[38]

In the report responding to questions made to Isabel, she added that she had the trust of the parents of the girls that she kept in her house, "because

37 "se exercitarem no que não é proibido nem por lei divina nem humana". AHU, Bahia, Papéis Avulsos, box 8, doc. 1193, fols. 2r, 8v. Translated by the author.

38 "não duvido que os sucessos do mundo no estado feminino farão parecer frívola a deliberação com que algumas se acham mas isso não é regra geral"; "nem por tal suspeita deve quem quer servir a seu criador esfriar no caminho principiado porque as máquinas do demônio nosso inimigo antigo são como nuvens depressa se armam de repente se desfazem"; "trabalho mulheril de costura, renda, e [...] de louvar a Deus em exercício espiritual da honra, e zelo do mesmo Senhor em contínua oração mental". AHU, Bahia, Papéis Avulsos, box 8, doc. 1193, fols. 2r, 5r. Translated by the author.

they thought she could educate them – [and] had sent them so she could teach them to read, write, sew and embroider, and have good manners, things that she was doing for the love of God". The same questions were asked to some of the women and they answered – signing the document themselves – that they were there due to their families and the friendship they had with Isabel and her cousin, claiming that they were happy to learn to read, write, sew and embroider. In the end, the vicar general decided not to evict the residents from the house because the premises of the judge commissioner's warrant were not flawed and he mentioned that Isabel and her aggregates – not *recolhidas* – could continue in that house because her assertion was true.[39]

The activities and forms of education mentioned by Isabel were, basically, what filled the daily lives of women in most of the *recolhimentos* in Portuguese America. Theoretically, the day-to-day activities had to be established by the statutes, which contained the basic norms and principles for female behaviour, reflecting some of the social dynamics and expectations regarding the conduct seen as ideal for women of the period.[40] The statutes of the *Recolhimento* of *Nossa Senhora da Glória do lugar da Boavista* in Pernambuco, written by bishop Joaquim da Cunha de Azeredo Coutinho, is an example.[41] This *recolhimento* was founded for adult women in the absence of their husbands or when they wanted to correct their bad behaviour, and this document detailed what should be taught, and which behaviours should be disciplined, repressed and controlled, symbolising a kind of pedagogical educational project. Almeida has identified that, throughout the 18th century, the *recolhimentos* provided to women without permanent vows the possibility of performing the functions of educators, called reading masters. By providing this service, many were able to develop their means of subsistence.[42]

The advice by Azeredo Coutinho in the statutes led to female education that fulfilled what, for the bishop, was women's primordial role: the care of the domestic economy and children. He considered that women had some social influence, being able to act both for the good and bad of society, even though they were not able to occupy ecclesiastical or official positions. The functions of caring for the home and mentoring the children within the virtues

39 "por julgarem as poderia ela dita educar – bem lhes tinham entregue para as ensinar a ler, escrever, cozer e bordar, e bons costumes, o que tudo fazia pelo amor de Deus". AHU, Bahia, Papéis Avulsos, box 8, doc. 1193, fols. 10v, 11r. Translated by the author.

40 Algranti, *Honradas e devotas*, 51; *Livros de devoção, atos de censura*, 49.

41 Coutinho, *Estatutos do Recolhimento*.

42 Almeida, *O sexo devoto*, 19.

were enough for the bishop to warn his peers about the importance of their education.[43]

For the education in the *recolhimento*, the bishop guided an instruction on the principles of religion, so that the young girls would be cautioned early on about the "ordinary defects of their sex". He considered that the feminine nature involved simulation, artifice and vanity, had the habit of talking a lot and sought after "pleasures of the spirit and body". According to him, the general principle of the instruction was employment in the different occupations available. Those destined for religious life would be required to learn Latin and music, and those who would live for their husbands and children would progressively learn to read, write, count, sew and embroider. They would be trained to be wives and mothers, and to "capture their husbands and children, as if by magic, without them realising the hand that directs them", and it would be women's responsibility to maintain the honour of their homes and strategies to prevent their husbands from seeking outside amusement. Literacy, therefore, was an educational proposal for all women entering the institution, and it was to be taught to prevent other "feminine defects", such as prolixity and errant imagination. In sewing and embroidery classes, they were allowed to sing "innocent songs to keep them always happy and amused".[44]

Uncovering these ideas, the *recolhimentos* were called "houses of correction" by Algranti if they received women with bad behaviour. Maria Antónia Lopes, working with the statutes and *devassas* of the *recolhimentos* from Porto and Coimbra, discovered a quite violent daily life, with penalties commonly applied through humiliation. The author describes some of the passages, such as women left with a rope around their necks and with a piece of wood, bone or gag in their mouths, being forced to ask for forgiveness on their knees while proclaiming their faults, having to kiss the feet of the community members and being imprisoned in a cell or dungeon, all of which were punishments applied at the discretion of the confessors.[45]

According to historians of Portuguese America, daily life in colonial *recolhimentos* seemed to have had a less violent facet. They were part of an attitude of correction. However, this did not mean that the confinement always symbolised punishment. Almeida and Algranti state that, in general, there were

---

43 Silva, *Vida privada e quotidiano*, 23.

44 "defeitos ordinários do seu sexo"; "agrados do espírito, e do corpo"; "prender a seus maridos e filhos, como por encanto, sem que eles percebam a mão que os dirige"; "cantigas inocentes, para as ter sempre alegres, e divertidas". Coutinho, *Estatutos do Recolhimento*, 80, 84, 106, 109. Translated by the author.

45 Algranti, *Honradas e devotas*, 105–106; Lopes, "Dominando corpos e consciências", 109.

several women who wanted to go to *recolhimentos* by vocation or the cultural process of naturalisation, what was called *recolher-se*. The education given to the girls from an early age was oriented towards religion, in order to qualify them for their societal circumstances, and going to a *recolhimento* or to a convent was not a forced or shocking decision as many had already been prepared for it. For some, it could represent a stimulus, such as an alternative to marrying a much older man, a better alternative to the monotony of confinement in the home or a way of subsistence in the absence of family members.[46]

In the cloisters, the coexistence among the multiplicity of women who were sheltered was filled with daily religious and feminine practices. Although the statutes regulated the religious life of the residents, the daily practices and the maintenance of certain norms were reproduced by those same women. Professed religious women, laywomen, orphans, widows, daughters, relatives and maids all shared those spaces and maintained sociability dynamics that allow us to affirm the expression and reproduction of an essentially feminine religious culture, supported by models of social and family organisation.

Even though the representation of socially idealised behaviours was present in the daily control and discipline, focused on Christian values, the *recolhidas* brought with them a series of customs, habits and entertainments that they enjoyed before their imprisonment, such as dance, theatre, music, making decorations and sharing culinary skills. This filled the enclosure, in the practices of daily life, with dynamics of symbolic exchanges and experiences among women involving elements both learned inside and outside of seclusion. Among these elements of exchange was, also, instruction – and not only religious instruction. *Recolhimentos* and convents were spaces in which reading and writing were encouraged, for the sake of a literate female religious cultural expression.[47]

3 Adulterous and Seduced Women, Repentant and Converted Women

In 1727, the archbishop of Bahia sent representation to the Secretary of State of the Navy and Overseas Territories regarding the need for a *recolhimento* for

46 Almeida, "A clausura feminina no mundo ibero-atlântico", 97, 110–113; *O sexo devoto*, 26, 97–98.
47 Algranti, *Livros de devoção, atos de censura*, 43, 49–50.

converted women[48] in the city of Bahia to avoid "offences to God and spiritual harm to many souls". The archbishop visited the cathedral and the parishes of the city, got to know the common practices in the regions and concluded that "there is a relaxation of the customs with which the people of one sex and the other generally live in this city, which results in very serious offences against God, and notable damage to souls". He reported that he personally admonished some people during his visit and noticed that they were "inwardly moved, and with the desire to distance themselves from the occasions, especially women", but theoretically they could not take refuge because there was no *recolhimento* in the city that could receive them. It is common to find in the sources reports describing that "the people in these faraway places live, and everywhere they are harassed by the impudent, who live at their own will doing what they do, as the cries of the complainers everywhere are public", generalising the behaviours seen as immoral of the inhabitants of several villages in Portuguese America, focusing mainly on women as the agents of the biggest problems.[49]

In this same sense, we can shed light on the manifestation of the bishop of Rio de Janeiro regarding the dishonourable practices of the inhabitants in a letter sent to the Overseas Council in 1756. He mentioned that the city suffered from the increase in death crimes against adulterous women, and that there was the "continuation of the sin of these depraved women" through an excuse made by women about not having any means of support – most likely referring to prostitution. Additionally, he said that "with this same excuse they intend to get rid of the corrections of the parish priests, who at every step call me for remedy".[50]

---

48 The term "converted women" is employed meaning those women in penance, who had undesired behaviours according to Christian values in their past but, when joining the *recolhimentos*, manifested regret and, theoretically, began to live their lives according to the church precepts. The term was translated from the Portuguese "convertidas".

49 "ofensas a Deus e de se ocorrer dano espiritual de muitas almas"; "relaxam de costumes, com que geralmente vivem nesta mesma cidade as pessoas de um, e outro sexo de que se seguem gravíssimas ofensas de Deus, e notável prejuízo das almas"; "interiormente movidas, e com desejo de se separarem das ocasiões principalmente mulheres". AHU, Bahia, Papéis Avulsos, box 38, doc. 3443, fol. 6r. "vivem os povos nestes lugares longes, e em toda a parte vexados dos atrevidos, que vivem a sua vontade fazendo o que fazem, como é público os clamores dos queixosos em todas as partes". AHU, Bahia, Papéis Avulsos, box 74, doc. 14326, fol. 1r. Translated by the author.

50 "continuação do pecado destas deprava[das]"; "com esta mesma desculpa pretendem livrar-se das correções dos Párocos, que a cada passo me clamam pelo remédio". AHU, Rio de Janeiro, Papéis Avulsos, box 50, doc. 5067, fol. 1r. Translated by the author.

The bishop affirmed that he had contact with women who wanted to "get rid of their guilt", but the absence of a shelter made them go to "hidden and remote locations" to escape the dangers they suffered in their husbands' homes and in the urban environment. One place he mentioned where he had seen repentant women was at "a house adjoining the Church of *Nossa Senhora do Parto* in this city, where there are 12 of them living with great *recolhimento*, honesty and virtue, giving a good example" and this, for him, meant "a great incentive for many others to want to keep them company". However, the size of the house was a limiting factor, besides the poverty in which they lived, since they survived by begging. According to the bishop's perspective, the existence of this format of *recolhimento* added to the objectives of recovering the virtues of the women, converting them from sin and making them live in honesty. He also claimed that "it would also serve to gather married women, who I am obliged to help, either to save them from death, or for their husbands to save them from continuing to offend them".[51]

The maintenance of active sexual behaviour, which implied loss of virginity and absence of chastity, as well as the existence of sexual relations outside marriage, were two of the main social harms to women which would end up sacrificing not only themselves but also their families.[52] However, within the culture of honour existing in Portuguese America, the historical agents rarely saw a stain on honour as an immutable characteristic. That is, they usually believed that honour could be reestablished. For dishonest women, it was possible to abandon the dishonourable practices, repent and atone for their guilt and turn away from sin, resuming virtue. Despite the presence of discourses about the ruin of honour, the sources suggest that it was common to attempt, and succeed in many cases, to make reparation. Honour was something to be acquired, and, in many situations, it could even be negotiated.[53]

---

51 "se livrar de suas culpas"; "lugares ocultos e retirados"; "uma casa contígua à Igreja de Nossa Senhora do Parto desta cidade, onde se acham doze vivendo com grande recolhimento, honestidade, e virtude, dando com o seu bom exemplo"; "um grande estímulo, para que outras muitas pretendam fazer-lhes companhia"; "também serviria para nele se recolherem as mulheres casadas, o que eu estivesse obrigado acudir, ou para as livrar da morte, ou para seus maridos as livrarem, de que continuem em ofendê-los". AHU, Rio de Janeiro, Papéis Avulsos, box 50, doc. 5067, fol. 2r. Translated by the author.

52 Braga, "A bigamia em Portugal na Época Moderna", 65, 68, 77.

53 Twinam, "The Negotiation of Honor", 72, 96–97.

In this regard, the *recolhimentos* of converted or repentant women were seen as a form of restoration of the virtuous behaviours of women who had deviated from the moral normativities, and consequentially there was the belief that they involved tools of reparation of honesty and honour. The credence in such reparation was not something that ended in the field of virtuous behaviour; it was something that also affected medicinal techniques and was included in the arsenal of healing practices. For example, it is worth mentioning a curious document found in a trunk in a church in the village of Curitiba, of anonymous authorship and whose date of production is 1703:[54] a *Formulario Medico* with a compilation of various prescriptions for cures for many health conditions, including *quebranto*[55] and melancholy. There is no date to indicate when this document was found, but the handwriting on the cover suggests it was in the late 19th or early 20th century. The place in which it was found was a church attached to a building that was supposed to have been a monastery in the 18th century, but which was never completed.

The most interesting prescription for the analysis of this chapter is the one for the restoration of virginity. Simply described in 15 lines, without any additional arguments by the author who recorded it in the *Formulario*, it reveals to a great extent the contours of the meanings and the layers of acceptability around the issue of virginity and chastity. The fact that it was found in a church that should have been part of a monastery, and that it is the only prescription in the book that contains a Latin passage – all the rest were written in vernacular language – sheds light on who, in theory, would be directed to use it. That is, maybe it was not a prescription that was widely circulated in society and, even if it was, the writing of the main application of the remedies on women's bodies was in Latin, preventing a large part of the literate population from understanding the guidelines. One can also think, however, that the recording of such a prescription meant that it was a common practice taken from social knowledge and written in the book for the use of surgeons and barbers at the

54 [Anon,] Formulário Médico. The document is held in the collection of the Fiocruz Library and the information indicating its discovery is handwritten on its first page. Although it has been identified as characteristic of 18th-century handwriting, the authorship remains undetermined. The content of the prescription is descriptive, meaning it describes the ingredients and their usage. It does not contain considerations of when and why it should be applied.

55 Raphael Bluteau's description of *quebranto* in his dictionary describes physical conditions. It involved an impression of an evil and deadly quality for the person who had contracted it, and some physicists of the period believed that it created an internal poison in the body. Bluteau, *Diccionario da Lingua Portugueza*, lib. II, 273.

time. The source does not cover the uses for the prescriptions it carried, but the use of these kinds of techniques could have happened in the *recolhimentos* of converted women. Since the main belief was that they would restore honesty, perhaps such prescriptions would end in some unwritten promise to family members in specific cases.

The *recolhimentos*, then, were institutions that carried the ideal of conversion of sinners and restoration of their honour. For this to be achieved, Lopes argues that they embraced strategies of punishment, penance and scourging, corresponding to practices of repulsion on the body whose goal was to reach the internal forum so that there would be repentance and conversion. Sending sinners to the convents would be a more effective attitude than any other type of penalty or punishment for the purpose of placing them in the social role they were believed to be in, restricting them to the social understandings of female behaviour. It would be a way, affirms Lopes, of applying representations to those who transgressed the norms, especially of social justice, much more than institutional justice.[56]

According to the sources analysed, the *recolhimentos* mainly directed at converted women started without a previous royal licence. Apparently, their function was the aggregation of women in a house led by some other woman or by a priest in order to protect, welcome and educate them in terms of Christian values. It was in this way that the *Recolhimento* of Igarassu emerged, in the captaincy of Pernambuco, in the first half of the 18th century. This information is accessible in a letter from the governor of the captaincy to the Secretary of State of the Navy and Overseas Territories in 1768, reporting the existence of a *recolhimento* "of women instructed by Father Gabriel de Malagrida", in charge of "reforming these women".[57] Despite not having a royal licence, the creation of this house had the support of the town council officers. In their letter to the King, they explained that the place "of converted prostitutes" left them in the "exercise of the most praiseworthy penance" and, for this reason, asked for confirmation for the continuity of its operation.[58] Note that this institution was located in a region far from the city of Recife, along with the *São Raimundo*

56 Lopes, "Dominando corpos e consciências", 99.

57 "de mulheres instruídas pelo padre Gabriel de Malagrida"; "reformar estas mulheres". AHU, Pernambuco, box 106, doc. 8206. AHU, Pernambuco, box 105, doc. 8187. AHU, Pernambuco, box 62, doc. 5292. Translated by the author.

58 AHU, Pernambuco, box 66, doc. 5560, fol. 1r. "de meretrizes convertidas"; "exercício da mais louvável penitência". AHU, Pernambuco, box 63, doc. 5376, fol. 1r. Translated by the author.

e de Santa Maria Madalena, founded in 1759 in the region outside the walls of Salvador. Both were, evidently, suitable places to receive the repentant women, and it is common that the sources mention them followed by their function, that is, it was a place "where some women gather, who lived without that honesty and decorum due to sex".[59]

Even though the letter from the council officials of Igarassu stated that the *recolhimento* would be for "converted prostitutes", the most recurrent accounts are about the reception of adulterous women. In this regard, José Fernandes Portugal, a royal official travelling to Bahia in 1800, gives an overview – however, rather biased to his beliefs – of how this type of house might have been developed at the time. He expressed to the Overseas Council that the married men of Salvador lived in a "disgraceful situation [...] due to the lassitude and infidelity of women, which has resulted in the greatest offence against God and public scandal". Once discovered, their fate could be prison and *degredo*, or the *Recolhimento de São Raimundo e de Santa Maria Madalena*, the "only one there is for such criminals". When sentenced to *degredo*, says the official, there was an absence of punishment due to the favour of the courts, by which the punishment applied to convicted women was *degredo* for a few years in Ceará, although for adulterers it was permanent to much more distant places. For this reason, the women could return to Salvador, to continue "in their wretched life", and the husbands would retire to farms or mills in places far from the city because they did not want to live with the unwanted behaviour.[60]

Women who deviated from the moral normativities were sent to the *Recolhimento de São Raimundo*, in the words of José Fernandes Portugal, "because the Reverend Archbishop did not want them with just cause in the case of young women". He stated that, in theory, they "persuade that their husbands are rich (which easily connects, as the treatment there is excessive in almost all possessions) to give them large amounts of food, finding justice always willing to arbitrate them".[61] Moreover, he accused the house of keeping

59 "em que se recolhem algumas mulheres, que viveram sem aquela honestidade e decoro devido ao sexo". AHU, Bahia, Papéis Avulsos, box 95, doc. 18520, fol. 3v. Translated by the author.

60 "desgraçada situação [...] pela lassidão, e infidelidade das mulheres, de que se tem seguido a maior ofensa de Deus, e escândalo público"; "único que ali há de semelhantes criminosas"; "na sua péssima vida". AHU, Bahia, Papéis Avulsos, box 108, doc. 21086, fol. 1r. Translated by the author.

61 "por não as querer com justa causa do reverendo arcebispo nos de donzelas, fazem persuadir que os maridos são abundantes (o que liga facilmente, por ser ali o tratamento em quase todos excessivo as posses) para lhes darem grandes alimentos, achando a justiça

alcoviteiras,[62] citing the name of "Ana de tal", a woman who would welcome in her household those women who ran away from the *recolhimento* "to live off their interests". He mentions having heard from one of these women that they were acquainted with the conduct of married women who were confined in the *recolhimentos*. Consequently, they were aware of potential escape routes and would congregate in houses in nearby towns and parishes and "the women seek to live in greater freedom, when their husbands deprive them of the opportunities for their wickedness, and such is the misery that in the parish of São Pedro alone [...] live more than 40 divorced women, and of these only one is honest". In addition to the *recolhimentos*, he cited other places headed by women and that were supposedly sheltering married women who had separated from their husbands or, also, who had run away from the *recolhimentos*. Regarding this practice, it is noteworthy to mention the house owned by *Dona* Ana Quitéria Cardosa, who harboured two women under her guardianship in such circumstances. Married women, accompanied by their husbands, would use this specific house when threatening their escape in cases of mistreatment.

According to José Fernandes Portugal's perspective, sending women to *recolhimentos* and processing them through justice institutions were not solutions to conflicts generated by adulterous relations. Apparently, for this historical agent, the resolution that meant punishment was to send the woman away to distant places for a long time, which would cause her civil death. The separated woman who lived honestly was not enough proof to believe in the resumption of the adulteresses' honour while criticising the management of the *recolhimentos* to which they could enter. In this case, castigation would mean penalty.

The fear of leaving free the married women who were separated from their husbands was the social disorder, especially in terms of moral and religious norms. The consequences of these practices, continues the author of the letter, would be "the disturbance of most families, and the lack of marriages of white men, which follows not only the perdition of many maidens, but also the death of many foetuses, that the daughters kill in the wombs, for fear of their fathers".[63]

sempre disposta para lhos arbitrar". AHU, Bahia, Papéis Avulsos, box 108, doc. 21086, fol. 1r. Translated by the author.

62 *Alcovitaria* was the term used to describe the practice of financially benefitting from the exploitation of the bodies of women under guardianship.

63 "para viver dos seus interesses"; "as mulheres buscam para viverem em maior liberdade, quando os maridos lhe privam as ocasiões das suas maldades, sendo tal a miséria que só na freguesia de São Pedro [...] moram mais de 40 desquitadas, e destas só uma com

This perspective can be seen in the argument of José Gomes Pereira to keep Mariana Maria de Jesus, his wife, in the *recolhimento* in Salvador in 1801. He manifested that "a woman who is adulterous, free without someone to dominate her, has more occasion to communicate with her lover and to give even more scandal, until what usually happens in these cases, such women become prostitutes".[64] This perspective was, apparently, common throughout at least the late 18th century. For example, in the mid-18th century, *Dona* Angela Maria de Souza e Fragoso expressed the fear, carried by many in society, that a woman with socially considered dishonest behaviour could influence others. José Pires dos Santos, Angela's husband, made requests in 1755 in Rio de Janeiro, to have her *recolhida* so that "she would not continue in her scandalous behaviour", nor would "her bad example be harmful".[65] The source suggests that in the domestic unit in which the couple resided, there were probably other women, perhaps younger than Angela, who accompanied her in her conduct. The desire that the husband expressed was to extract her from the daily life of people she could influence, and not necessarily from his acquaintanceship, and he did not expose in detail the circumstances of the occurrence. The letter only hints, in a very subtle way, that it was probably a case of adultery, since Joseph claimed that he did not want to make a "complaint" against Angela, which refers to possible judicial requests through quarrels to secular justice. However, any legal proceedings would bring the case into greater publicity and thus further tarnish Joseph's honour, which he explicitly wished to avoid.

In another case, the offence to João Pinto Coelho's honour did not allow him to maintain daily interaction with his daughter – whom he called his goddaughter. He had placed her, in 1799, in the *Recolhimento dos Perdões* in Salvador, even without the archbishop's permission, because he did not want her in his household anymore, after having placed his wife in the *Recolhimento da Misericordia* "because he considered himself offended in his honour".[66] The

---

honestidade"; "a perturbação da maior parte das famílias, e a falta de casamentos de homens brancos, de que se segue não só a perdição de muitas donzelas, como também a morte de muitos fetos, que as filhas famílias matam nos ventres, por temor de seus pais". AHU, Bahia, Papéis Avulsos, box 108, doc. 21086, fols. 1r–1v. Translated by the author.

64 "uma mulher que é adúltera, ficando na sua liberdade, sem pessoa que a domine, fica em ocasião mais ampla de se comunicar com seu amasio, e de dar ainda maior escândalo, até o que costuma nestes casos acontecer, é que semelhantes mulheres se façam prostitutas". AHU, Bahia, Papéis Avulsos, box 221, doc. 15408, fol. 1r. Translated by the author.

65 "não continuasse no seu escandaloso procedimento"; "prejudicial o seu mau exemplo". AHU, Rio de Janeiro, Papéis Avulsos, box 49, doc. 4916, fol. 1r. Translated by the author.

66 "por se julgar ofendido na sua honra". AHU, Bahia, Papéis Avulsos, box 96, doc. 18732, fol. 1r. Translated by the author.

fact that the document by the archbishop of Bahia includes in parenthesis the information that João considered his daughter to be his goddaughter seems to suggest that the girl was not biologically his daughter, but probably his wife's daughter. The document does not leave any information that would allow us to definitively conclude in this direction, however, it is very possible if not highly likely.

Another case of adultery that occurred in the same period but with some different elements is the one involving Luisa Josefa. In the village of Viçosa do Cametá, located in Pará, Manuel da Silva de Carvalho, Luisa's husband, sent a request to the King in 1768 to issue an order so his criminal appeal complaining about her adultery with Manuel Gomes, subdeacon, would be received in the *Casa da Suplicação de Lisboa*. The *junta das justiças* had been sentenced in favour of the accusation, but with the acquittal of Luisa because Manuel da Silva had also committed adultery. For being "notoriously offended, and insulted and affronted" the husband understood that "even if the adultery of the petitioner were true, it could not be compared with that of the adulteress because according to the resolutions of law, and the opinion of men, the adultery of the husband is not insulting and affronting to the wife but the latter's is, on the contrary".[67] That is, even if the adultery was proven, Manuel da Silva knew that, at least according to the knowledge of normativity, the normativities expressed by the royal and canon law were applicable to adulterous women, and not to men, considering that the husband would be much more reviled than the wife. According to canon law, both male and female adultery had to be equally punished, but for the Philippine Ordinances[68] the penalty was directed mainly at women.

Regulated by titles XXV and XXVI of book V, adultery, according to the Ordinances, meant sleeping with a married woman. However, for Bluteau, the practice's denomination was valid for both sexes, adding that it was a "sin of the

67 "notoriamente ofendido, e injuriado, e afrontado"; "nem o adultério do suplicante fosse verdadeiro se podia comensurar com o da dita adúltera porque segundo as resoluções de Direito, e opinião dos homens, o adultério do marido não é injurioso e afrontoso à mulher sendo o desta pelo contrário". AHU, Pará, box 63, doc. 5496, fol. 1r. Translated by the author.

68 The *Ordenações Filipinas* was the main legislative compilation produced in Portugal for the period in this research, published in 1603 in the context of the Iberian Union (1580–1640) by King Filipe II. This format of normative body was one of the written normativities within the range of documents that throughout the 18th century were called "direito pátrio". It was not produced at the time with the purpose of marginalising or reducing the applicability of common law and preexisting normativities.

flesh that violates conjugal fidelity".[69] Domingos Vieira conceptualised it in the same way, pointing out that according to the Roman Catechism it constituted an insult to the legitimate *toro*, be it that of the married man or of the married woman.[70]

The First Constitutions of the Archbishopric of Bahia[71] defined adultery as a crime "against the faith of Matrimony" which had to be punished in an exemplary way, especially for the clerics. However, the ecclesiastical justice would only take this crime upon itself if it was practiced continuously, with perseverance, infamy and scandal, thus entering into the normativities relative to concubinage. In these cases, adulterers would be prosecuted in the manner of paragraph 990 of title XXIII, a rule that specifically dealt with women, married or single, who were involved in sexual situations. In other words, adultery, within the canonical legislation, was understood as a subspecies of concubinage and should be prosecuted by ecclesiastical institutions if the illicit relationship met the requirement of continuity over time.[72]

Regarding the involvement of adulteresses with clergymen, there is an interesting range of cases. The case that opened this chapter, between Ana Maria and Jacinto in 1782, offers very detailed accounts. The news of the occurrence came to the attention of the Secretary of State of the Navy and Overseas Territories when Jacinto, a mill owner, "seeing his honour seriously offended",[73] sent a petition requesting the resolution of the case of Ana Maria's involvement with José da Silva Freire, canon of the cathedral in that city. The cause was being processed under secular and ecclesiastical jurisdiction; in the secular court, the ombudsman of the crime since 1780 was in charge of the complaint against Ana Maria, but for more than six months it was held in the hands of the magistrate without a decision. In the ecclesiastical court, Jacinto filed a libel against the canon who, in opposition, defended himself by denying having

69 "peccado da carne violador da fidelidade conjugal". Bluteau, *Vocabulario Portuguez e Latino*, lib. I, 141; *Diccionario da Lingua Portugueza*, lib. I, 31. Translated by the author.

70 Vieira, Domingos, *Grande diccionario portuguez*, 174–175.

71 The *constituições* of the overseas dioceses was a juridical-pastoral compilation of tridentine dogmas, canon law, church tradition and local practices that aimed to distribute among the colonial possessions the Catholic matrixes of institutional organisation and behavioural regulation. The *Constituições Primeiras do Arcebispado da Bahia*, although written for the diocesan jurisdiction of Bahia, were also used in the bishops of Olinda and Rio de Janeiro and had to be sent to all the existing parishes.

72 Vide, *Constituições Primeiras*, lib. V, tit. XIX, § 966–968; Silva, *Sistema de casamento*, 40; Goldschmidt, *Convivendo com o pecado*, 130.

73 "vendo-se gravemente ofendido na honra". AHU, Bahia, Papéis Avulsos, box 58, doc. 11067, fol. 1r.

illicit dealings with Ana Maria.[74] The final decision in this case, however, had not been issued due to procedural debates about the correct jurisdiction for filing the suit. In both cases, Jacinto claimed to be at a loss because he was paying daily maintenance to support Ana Maria, who, however, was still in a state of adultery – and with it, public scandal.

Jacinto and Ana Maria had been married for approximately 16 years, and the canon had become a spiritual relative of the couple as a result of their daughter's baptism, which is why he started to visit their house and Ana Maria's parents' house, where she used to spend more time than at Jacinto's mill. The husband, Jacinto, argued that, from the visits, the canon "began to have a libidinous affection for the wife of the supplicant, and to request her love either through herself or through third parties, it was easy to obtain her correspondence".[75]

Ana Maria's father, according to Jacinto's narrative, upon discovering his daughter's relationship with the cleric was also indignant and seeing "the honour of his house outraged by a traitor, and treacherous man, the father ended up dying". Blaming Ana Maria for the death of her father with the addition of an emotional tone to capture the mercy of the readers of his petition, Jacinto claimed that "this daughter, being the one who, with her mischief, deprived of life the man who had given her life. The offence of honour can do so much in an honourable breast." Honour issues appear in this case as fundamental points in the experiences of the men involved in the case and, in this regard, Jacinto expressed, following the same emotional tone, that "she came to hate him, and made him *mofa* and made fun of him among her friends, boasting that the supplicant did not deserve her". He described some of the lines that, according to him, Ana Maria had said to her friends and, in this way, the source lets us glimpse at least some of her personality traits, as well as the social understandings and levels of permissibility of the context in which she lived: she said that "She would rather be a clergyman's concubine, than the lawful wife of a good man. [...] live with infamy than honour. [...] live with public disrepute, and that of her husband, than to restrain herself within the limits of honesty according to divine law".[76]

---

74 AHU, Bahia, Papéis Avulsos, box 70, doc. 11367, fol. 5r. AHU, Bahia, Papéis Avulsos, box 79, doc. 15422, fol. 1r. Translated by the author.

75 "entrou a receber uma libidinosa afeição a mulher do suplicante, e passando a solicitá-la de amores já por si, já por terceiras pessoas, fácil foi o conseguir a sua correspondência". AHU, Bahia, Papéis Avulsos, box 58, doc. 11067, fol. 3v. Translated by the author.

76 "assim ultrajada a honra da sua casa por um traidor, e aleivoso, que veio a morrer"; "Sendo esta filha a que com as suas desenvolturas privou da vida a alguém que lhe tinha dado

This excerpt highlights a number of normativities that are indispensable to understanding women's experiences in the colonial context. Besides it being possible to see something of her personality traits (biased by the melancholic and aggressive tone of the husband), it is possible to ascertain at least some of the sociabilities of colonial women and the knowledge of normativity expressed by Ana Maria. This is in line with previous research conducted by me as well as work by Luisa Stella de Oliveira Coutinho Silva, who concluded that women in the Captaincy of Paraiba had knowledge about various normativities in their contexts and, moreover, knew which activities to employ to achieve their interests.[77] Specifically about crimes and deviations, they understood – quite consciously – the extremes of the social and juridical norms: the scandalous and the tolerated, the illicit and the licit.[78] Thus, they had notions of what to do with their neighbours so as not to exceed the limits of what was tolerated, and what to say when taken to court so as not to exceed the limits of what was legal. From what the source shows with reference to the supposed statements by Ana Maria, there was clear knowledge that, according to the normativities and to canon law, to relate to clergymen was something that went beyond the limits of what was tolerated and licit.

In this same way, this knowledge can be seen in the passages in which Jacinto mentioned that Ana Maria had rented a house in the urban area of Salvador with an entrance through the house of prostitute women to be able to cover up the canon's visits. Since she was living alone and in an urban area, where the eyes of the neighbourhood closely watched the daily life of other families, she did not want to attract attention when she received such visits. When she was at her mother's house, located on a farm, the visits were apparently less covert since the only people who would see the canon's attendance at the house were those who were part of the household.

---

o ser. Tanto pode em um peito honrado a ofensa da honra"; "de sorte que o chegou a aborrecer, e a fazer dele mofa, e zombaria entre as suas amigas, jactando-se de que o suplicante a não merecia"; "Queria antes ser manceba de um clérigo, que legítima mulher de um homem de bem. Queria antes viver com infâmia, do que com honra. Queria antes viver com público descrédito, e de seu marido, do que conter-se nos limites da honestidade conforme a lei divina". AHU, Bahia, Papéis Avulsos, box 58, doc. 11067, fols. 5r–5v. *Mofa*, as described by Bluteau, meant the mocking of another person, using irony to make a joke, i.e., making fun of someone. Bluteau, *Vocabulario Portuguez e Latino*, lib. V, 536. Translated by the author.

77 Coutinho Silva, *Nem teúdas, nem manteúdas*; Massuchetto, *Mulheres, conflitos e normatividades*.

78 Mantecón Movellán, "Desviación, disciplina social e intervenciones judiciales".

When Jacinto discovered the relationship between Ana Maria and the canon through the confessions of one of the enslaved women that had accompanied her over the previous years, he requested the governor to send her to the *Recolhimento de São Raimundo e de Santa Madalena* which would be granted by a normative instrument ensuring the financial support of Ana Maria by Jacinto. He also explained that he was outraged by the lack of punishment on the part of Ana Maria's family, who, he argued, would rather see her in public scandal than "in a cloister of virtue acquired through repentance". He sent Ana Maria to the *recolhimento* causing the discontentment and opposition of her mother, her brother, her brother-in-law and the canon. Her family sent petitions to recognised people of the city requesting her release, seeking, finally, the governor, who allowed her to leave the cloister. After leaving the institution, Ana Maria went to meet Jacinto,[79] who described that "having violated the most sacred laws of Holy Matrimony with scandalous offence of the Republic, Politics and Christianity, she was loose, free and unpunished by an absolute discretion not regulated by laws".[80]

Ana Maria, in turn, had filed for divorce against Jacinto also claiming alimony, which is why he was imprisoned. In the course of this lawsuit, Ana Maria was deposited in the household of her brother-in-law and his sister as determined by the archbishop. With this situation, recounted Jacinto, the case took on greater fame and public scandal, requiring once again that the vicar order her to go back to the *recolhimento* as a deposit house since at her brother-in-law's house she had the freedom to move around the city and go to her mother's house. Ecclesiastical officials went to the house to execute this request, but Ana Maria's brother had obtained an order from the same authority suspending the warrant because he had complained about the canon.[81]

---

79 The contours of this situation are not clear, but it is possible to think Ana Maria went to Jacinto's house to collect her belongings, to confront him or to negotiate the conflict resolution.

80 "em um claustro da virtude adquirida pelo arrependimento"; "havendo violado as mais sagradas leis do Santo Matrimonio com escandalosa ofensa da República, Política, e Cristã, se achava solta, livre, e impunida por um arbítrio absoluto não regulado pelas leis". AHU, Bahia, Papéis Avulsos, box 58, doc. 11067, fols. 6r, 9r. Translated by the author.

81 AHU, Bahia, Papéis Avulsos, box 58, doc. 11067, fols. 11r–27v. Jacinto also exposed the canon's infamy, calling him "one of those pampered men of fortune"; he was used to soliciting women. He had a relationship with the wife of an apothecary who, upon learning of the illicit affair, beat her and wanted to kill her. Another case he had was with the wife of a diamond miner who, upon hearing of the adultery, sent her to the *Recolhimento dos Perdões*, but when her husband left, the archbishop authorised her to leave the *recolhimento*. When the governor heard of the case, he ordered her to be found and sent back to the *Recolhimento de São Raimundo e de Santa Madalena*, where the woman had been for ten

In 1789, in a new letter, Jacinto stated that he had obtained the conviction of his wife for the crime of adultery to be deported for ten years to Ceará – where "there was already a general and notorious fame of the adulterous and incestuous trade"[82] – but that he had not obtained a conviction for the canon in ecclesiastical justice. In a request made by Ana Maria to the governor of the captaincy to be given permission to enter a *recolhimento*, Jacinto was called to make a concession but "to enter under my conditions of remaining in the same cloister as long as she lives, and that if she wanted to leave under any pretext, she would at all times serve the *degredo* in the form of the sentence given by the *Relação*".[83] In December of the same year, the archbishop wrote to the same Secretary of State reporting about the sentencing of the canon to a one-year *degredo* to one of the villages of the *comarca* of Ilhéus, in the same archbishopric, based on book V, § 966 of the First Constitutions of the Archbishopric of Bahia. This case brought with it many details that are not largely explored in other cases. Similar situations occurred with Ana Joaquina de São José, Ana Clara de Freitas, Mariana Maria de Jesus and Luisa Francisca do Nascimento, as will be described below.

We can begin with José Francisco da Costa, Ana Joaquina's husband, who requested in 1793 that she be sent to the *Recolhimento de São Raimundo* or to the *dos Perdões* because he accused her of having, soon after their marriage, "such scandalous conduct that she prostituted herself publicly". José wanted to rid himself of the "shame she caused him", so he filed a suit of adultery against her. This case leads us to think that the plea for prostitution was an argumentative strategy by José. In addition to the fact that prostitution was not a crime in the 18th century, proof of adultery could not be based on occasional events, but rather on relationships that lasted over time.[84]

The case of Manuel Francisco de Olivera, whose wife is not known by name in the consulted source, can be referred to along the same lines of difficulty in proving relationships that took place in intimate environments and when the husbands were away. In 1800, in Salvador, Manuel suspected that his wife was

---

years at the time of the record. AHU, Bahia, Papéis Avulsos, box 58, doc. 11067, fols. 13r–14r. Translated by the author.

82 "já havia fama geral, e notória do adulterino, e incestuoso comercio". AHU, Bahia, Papéis Avulsos, box 70, doc. 11367, fol. 5r. Translated by the author.

83 "para entrar debaixo das minhas condições de se conservar na mesma clausura enquanto viva fosse, e que havendo de querer sair com qualquer pretexto, fosse em todo o tempo cumprir seu degredo na forma da sentença dada pela relação". AHU, Bahia, Papéis Avulsos, box 69, doc. 13305, fols. 1r–2r. Translated by the author.

84 "tão escandalosa, que se prostituía publicamente"; "vergonha que ela lhe causa[va]". AHU, Bahia, Papéis Avulsos, box 196, doc. 14223, fol. 1r. Translated by the author.

having an illicit relationship with an officer because he frequently visited her house. For this reason, he sent his wife to the *Recolhimento da Misericórdia* and, in a letter in which he reported the case to the Overseas Council, the governor stated that finding evidence of "facts of this nature", although possible, for it to be made judicial would be difficult, "however, as it is public and constant that this woman did not live honestly, and is discredited, and her husband who is a good man, intends to have her *recolhida* and to support her".[85] In other words, apparently, having women convicted of the crime of adultery was not something easy, nor proven only on the basis of rumours in the neighbourhood. As a crime that necessarily involves a hidden practice, evidence from eyewitness testimonies was considerably rare, which would make the conviction difficult. For husbands, the easiest attitude, and at the same time the one that would cost the least resources, was to send their wives to the *recolhimentos* for life, supporting them in the same way they already, theoretically, did.

Returning to the accusations that relate to Ana Maria's case, those of Ana Clara and Mariana are even closer in theme because they also, allegedly, had been involved with clergymen. José Machado Pimentel, Ana Clara's husband, requested, to the Queen in 1784, that she be moved from the *Recolhimento de Nossa Senhora da Conceição* in Olinda to another "of the reformers" in the kingdom. Ana Clara had been seduced by the priest Antonio Borges Veloa and committed adultery with him in treachery against her husband, which is why José filed specific lawsuits seeking the punishment of both. The priest was convicted and imprisoned in the ecclesiastical prison (*aljube*), and Ana Clara was sent to the *recolhimento*. However, José argued that he had no assurance that she would be definitively locked up, that her conversion would be assured or, consequently, that the insult he had suffered would be suppressed. He probably had news that she was seeking her release by contacting procurators and sending petitions to the competent authorities, both the ecclesiastical judge and the archbishop, as well as the governor of the captaincy and, finally, the Queen. Thus, he believed it was safer for him that Ana Clara be removed to the metropolis as a way to definitively distance her from the priest who had seduced her, imposing on her not only a permanent cloister, but the definitive removal of all her social ties.[86]

In the other case, in 1801, José Gomes Pereira, Mariana's husband, requested to the governor that she be kept in the seclusion to which he had sent her

85 "porém como é público, e constante que esta mulher não vivia honestamente, e está desacreditada, e o marido que é bom homem, pretende que esteja recolhida sustentando-a". AHU, Bahia, Papéis Avulsos, box 108, doc. 21063, fol. 1r. Translated by the author.

86 AHU, Pernambuco, box 154, doc. 11072, fols. 1r–5r.

because of her adultery with Father Bernardo de Melo Brandão in "public scandal". He had already assumed the obligation to financially support her in her confinement in order to avoid the consequences of divorce proceedings. José was a merchant and was warned, most likely by a neighbour, that when he was away from home Mariana used to receive Bernardo both day and night. In his petition to the prince regent, José described Mariana as having a "proud temper" that had affronted "his honour, credit and reputation", which was why he was in the process of suing the couple to remove this stain from his name.[87]

In the same year, Manuel José Froes, Luisa's husband, requested that she be kept in the convent of *Nossa Senhora da Lapa* in Salvador due to her "disorders". Luisa had been kept there since 1789 as a result of Manuel's previous request, in which he argued that she was prostituting herself, wanting more freedom and "resourcefulness" and that, furthermore, he was unable to go out and take care of his business due to the public humiliation he was going through. He claimed that, at first, he hoped that "the increase in age and the example of those good religious women would inspire her with honest and honourable thoughts", however, he had news that Luisa was in contact with people outside the convent, especially with prosecutors who had helped her get a licence to leave the cloister. Due to the very existence of Manuel's request, we can conclude that Luisa did not go looking for him and, most likely, took refuge in the households of relatives or, ultimately, in houses with other women in the same condition.[88]

We find all these cases, however, concentrated at the end of the 18th century, and practices are likewise rare to find in the first half of the century. The first case found is of *Dona* Helena de Lima in 1718 in Salvador. Helena was accused of concubinage with a religious person and, for this reason, the archbishop sent her two daughters against their will to the convent of *Desterro* to be educated. Helena had tried to remove her daughters from the cloister by means of a request to the chapterhouse, but "as he and the religious sisters themselves were aware that this tyrant mother was removing her daughters to imitate her bad examples, they tried to stop her in every possible way". She had tried to ask a brother and an uncle for help, both clerics, but she was unsuccessful because they suspected that she had made "arrangements" for the daughters to be the concubines of a cleric and a secular person. Thus, the viceroy and

87 "orgulhoso gênio"; "sua honra, crédito, e reputação". AHU, Bahia, Papéis Avulsos, box 221, doc. 15408, fol. 1r. Translated by the author.

88 "desembaraço"; "o aumento da idade e o exemplo daquelas boas religiosas, lhe inspirassem honestos e honrados pensamentos". AHU, Bahia, Papéis Avulsos, box 222, doc. 15466, fol. 1v. Translated by the author.

governor-general of Brazil issued an order stating that, as soon as the daughters were removed from the convent, they were to be sent to a convent in order to "always preserve their honesty" a decision that brought Helena disgust and dissatisfaction.[89]

Therefore, it does not seem that the practice of sending women to *recolhimentos* was as common at the beginning of the 18th century as it was at the end. According to the sources, the practice was consolidated to the extent that most husbands wished to separate from their wives, as well as to end the adulterous relationship that they were probably in. At the end of the 18th century, there are cases of family members, such as brothers and fathers, requesting the *recolhimento* of women, but most of them refer to requests with no expression as to what the woman was doing, so the family constated some lack of honesty. Most of the petitions only explained the interest of the petitioner and the request to grant a licence, without further details. The conflicts in which family relations are more prominent seem to bring with them a wider range of normativities that are not explicitly expressed in the consulted documents. That is, it seems that the true reasons for what was alleged in the letters and requests addressed to the authorities are veiled, while in the case of adultery the husbands seem to have had to more explicitly expose why they wanted their wives to remain imprisoned – even though they still hid their violence towards their wives and their motives which used to go beyond the "culture of honour". Perhaps fathers and brothers did not need to state their reason for wanting the licence, since, in addition to their daughters and sisters being unmarried, it could be implied that they wished for them to maintain honourable behaviour and, consequently, ensure the family honour. The husbands' requests, on the other hand, would have to demonstrate sufficient reasons for the women to remain in confinement, even if said reason was to prevent themselves from mistreating them at will should they be released.

In what concerns the requests made by women, the great majority refer to cases of abuse (*sevícias*) and divorce, a situation that would mean the ecclesiastical authorities, as already mentioned, could deposit them in the *recolhimentos*. Although a detailed analysis of this part of the research has to be done another time due to the specific focus of this chapter, and also due to space limitations, it is important to mention that in these cases the *recolhimentos*

89 "constando-lhe a ele, e as mesmas religiosas que esta tirana mãe tirava as filhas para a imitarem nos seus maus exemplos trataram de lho impedir pela maneira possível"; "conservar sempre a sua honestidade". AHU, Bahia, Papéis Avulsos, box 22, doc. 1972, fols. 1r–1v. Translated by the author.

acquired another complexity of meanings for the women. While it was confinement, these women often simultaneously required this situation because they were being severely abused in their own homes, thus it represented a place of security where their husbands could not bother them. Perhaps this same logic could also be applied to adulteresses, especially considering the networks of sociability and support ties that they created by going into confinement with other women in similar conditions. As the sources analysed are very much interpolated by the views of men, they do not allow us to glimpse the dynamics of these specific women inside the institutions and do not allow concrete conclusions in this direction. Therefore, the reflection of "plausible reality" remains.[90]

4 Penalisation, Normativities and Legal Change: Recolhidas Women, Degredadas Women

The royal and ecclesiastical norms regarding adultery, seen in the aforementioned cases, were intrinsically intertwined with the normativities from the social order, so as to compose the range of normativities that corresponded to the order of colonial jurisdiction in Portuguese America. To begin a more detailed treatment of what was stated in the legislation and from the perspectives of doctrine jurists of the modern period, it might be interesting to refer to an excerpt from Jacinto's extensive petition to the Overseas Council regarding the penalties for the crime committed by his wife and the canon, namely, incestuous adultery:

> This crime has challenged the strength of penalties among all nations. The laws seem brief in their description of its abomination. Among the Portuguese, the most sensitive nation in this matter, the laws entrust to the husband himself the execution of the death penalty against the wife caught with the adulterer, even allowing him the power to summon relatives and friends to help him in the execution of the just penalty with compensation for their persons. Such is the concept, which the laws form, of the living for and feeling of innocent husbands, in the considerable loss of honour, to which good men sacrifice their own lives with contempt of goods.[91]

---

90 Ginzburg, *O queijo e os vermes*.

91 "Crime este, que tem desafiado entre todas as Nações o vigor das penas. Parecem curtas as Leis na descrição que fazem da sua abominação. Entre os Portugueses, Nação mais

In this excerpt, Jacinto exposed the general absence of a penalty application for adulterous women,[92] just as José Fernandes Portugal argued, in 1800 when he went to Bahia, in disbelief that the secular and ecclesiastical justice systems could respond to his desire, or rather what he believed he was entitled to because of the stain to his honour, but did not. The delegation of the act of justice to the husband himself was, in fact, a mechanism foreseen in the Philippine Ordinances that derived from the logic that the royal power could not meddle in matters exclusive to the domestic authority.

In favour of the family power, title XXXVI of book V of the Philippine Ordinances stated that royal justice had to withdraw and "penalties shall have no place" when violence was used to punish women. Pascoal José de Melo Freire, in trying to define what the "right to impose penalties" would mean, argued that the rule was exclusive detention by royal power. He did, however, exclude cases involving the dominion of parents over children, of masters over slaves and of husbands over wives, as he recognised the existence of the power of the former over the latter. The husband's power over his wife was understood as originating from natural law and gave him "the faculty to drive his wife's actions", but it was not recognised by the legislation as unlimited; castigation was determined by the application of certain punishments and, still, only in a light and moderate way "when the woman was unruly".[93]

Along this line of thought, the Ordinances extended the penalty if the husband found his wife in adultery so that he was allowed to kill her without being penalised. For this, it was mandatory to prove both the marriage according to the Council of Tridentine and the situation of the crime and the flagrancy, otherwise the husband would be condemned and banned from access to the dowry.[94] However, pardon and acquittal of the adulteress was possible even if she became pregnant from the illicit relationship. Manuel Barbosa, in the first

---

melindrosa nesta matéria, confiam as Leis do próprio Marido a execução da pena capital contra a mulher apanhada com o adúltero, até lhe permite o poder convocar parentes, e amigos, para o ajudarem na execução do justo castigo com indemnidade de suas pessoas. Tal é o conceito, que as Leis formam da viva for, e sentimento dos inocentes maridos, na considerável perda da honra, a que os homens de bem sacrificam com o desprezo dos bens a própria vida". AHU, Bahia, Papéis Avulsos, box 58, doc. 11067, fol. 3v. Translated by the author.

92 Penalty application, in this passage, means institutional enforcement of a condemnation. Portugal, *Ordenações Filipinas*, lib. V, tit. XXXVIII; Barbosa, *Remissiones Doctorum ad Contractus*, 303–304.

93 "penas não haverão lugar". Portugal, *Ordenações Filipinas*, lib. V, tit. XXXVI. "direito de impor penas"; "faculdade de digirir as acções da mulher"; "quando desregrada". Freire, *Instituições de direito criminal português*, 60–61. Translated by the author.

94 Portugal, *Ordenações Filipinas*, lib. V, tit. XXXVIII.

half of the 17th century, expressed that, although lawful under royal law, killing the wife would mean a sin for the internal forum of the husband, and at this point there would have been the express link that in the theological field, and canon law, causing someone's death would always have a spiritual consequence, referring to the "forum of the soul".[95]

António Manuel Hespanha explains that the penalty for adultery came from one branch of Roman law and another of canon law. In the Roman tradition, the violation was of the "conjugal law" and it was penalised due to its patrimonial consequences and the possibility of transferring the patrimony to a child considered legitimate due to being born within the matrimonial bond but who did not belong to the husband's blood inheritance. In the canonical tradition, the transgression was against marital fidelity, which is why it could be committed by either the man or the woman. The Ordinances followed the definitions of Roman law because of how the penalty was applied and the fact that male adultery was usually not punished.[96]

Joaquim José Caetano Pereira e Sousa classifies the offence in the field of moral crimes, stating that this crime can be committed by both husband and wife and was performed through contempt for the conjugal faith of the married person. It could be committed in three ways: by two married people, representing a "double" crime; by an unmarried man with a married woman; and by a married man and an unmarried woman.[97] When the crime was committed between Christians it was "simple" – whereby the adulteress could be forgiven by her husband and be free of all penalties – and it was "double" when committed with a Moor or Jew – by which the extent of the husband's forgiveness would be limited and the penalty for having sinned with infidels would remain. The offence would be qualified when it was committed in conjunction with abduction – either by the will of the woman or by force – an element that excluded all possibilities of forgiveness and penalty mitigation for the adulterer.[98]

Pereira e Sousa explains that it was not considered a crime of public accusation and, for this reason, the husband was the only one competent to file a complaint, "without the public prosecutor getting involved", except in cases of major scandal.[99] For Pereira e Sousa, the scandal – therefore a deviation

---

95 Barbosa, *Remissiones Doctorum*, ad Ord. lib. V, tit. XXIII, § III, tit. XXXVIII. Amaral, *Liber utilissimus*, lib. I, verbo mulier. Portugal, *Ordenações Filipinas*, lib. V, tit. XXV, § 4, tit. LV.

96 Hespanha, *Como os juristas viam o mundo*, 639–640.

97 Sousa, *Esboço de hum Diccionario Juridico*, lib II, 18.

98 Portugal, *Ordenações Filipinas*, lib. V, tit. XXV, § 2, § 4.

99 "sem que nisso se intrometta o ministério público". Sousa, *Classe dos crimes*, 210. Translated by the author.

from social order – seems to be the element that made the practice illicit to the point of institutional intervention. Thus, regulated by § 3º of title XXV of book V of the Ordinances, Melo Freire defends that the exclusivity of the accusation in the secular court occurred because the insult of the crime was made against the husband in particular. In these terms, fathers, brothers, relatives or any other persons were not admitted, nor was the judge *ex officio* or on request. In the accusation, the husband had to prove the marriage through witnesses who had heard their vows, seen the couple at the door of the Church before the clergyman or had received them on their return home, living with the voice and fame of marriage. The exceptions were given in paragraphs 2 and 3 of title XXV – namely, double adultery, committed by Christians with infidels, and adultery coupled with incest – however, the *Alvará* of 26 September 1769 excluded all powers of complaint and initiation of criminal proceedings other than the husband's.[100]

Before, it was possible to denounce someone else's adultery *sub judice* of concubinage. According to the fundament of the *Alvará* of 26 September 1769, it was apparently common for there to be "greater confusion, and abuse" due to the imprecision of criminal processing, making it possible for enemies to falsely denounce and testify against women. Arrested and imprisoned, these women were then mistrusted by their husbands and the neighbourhood, ruining their honour and that of the other women in their family, especially their daughters.[101] This description in the *Alvará* suggests that this was a common practice, at least within the realm, that the King wanted to curb by issuing such a rule, aiming to "eliminate private discord and defend the honour of families".[102]

According to title XXV, the penalty was death for both adulterers – this was the ordinary penalty – except if the man was of a higher quality than the husband.[103] If the crime was committed with someone from the husband's house, the adulterers would be condemned to death; the same penalty would be given to the one who took the woman by force and against her will, in addition to

100 Portugal, *Ordenações Filipinas*, lib. V, tit. XXV, § 8. Freire, *Instituições de direito criminal português*, 192–193.

101 Portugal, *Collecção da Legislação Portugueza*, 432–433.

102 "eliminar as discórdias particulares e defender a honra das famílias". Freire, *Instituições de direito criminal português*, 192–193. Portugal, *Ordenações Filipinas*, lib. V, tit. CXVII. It follows, therefore, that if the husband died before the plea was entered, the accusation would be cancelled; if death occurred after the plea was entered, the title CXVII of Book V of the Ordinances allowed the continuance of the accusation by his father or brothers. Translated by the author.

103 What Pereira e Sousa calls cumulation with incest. Sousa, *Classe dos crimes*, 210.

the duty to compensate her husband pecuniarily. If the crime occurred with the connivance of the husband, the couple would be flogged with "wreaths of horns"[104] and deported to Brazil while the adulterer would be condemned to *degredo* to Africa for all her life. Other cases of extraordinary penalties, reducing the severity and gravity of the ordinary penalty, listed by Melo Freire would occur in situations where the adulterer had abandoned the adulteress, the husband who accused his wife of adultery was committed for the same delict or the betrayed spouse had long been suffering from an illness that prevented him from fulfilling his marital duty.[105]

The ecclesiastical judge was exclusively responsible for the practice of sending women to *recolhimentos* in these situations.[106] In terms of the Tridentine Council, in cases of continuous adulterous concubinage even after three admonitions, the punishment given to the women was to be sent "outside the place, or out of the Diocese, if it so appears to the same Ordinaries, invoking for this, if necessary, the Secular arm".[107] The power of discretion attributed to the ecclesiastical authorities to send women "outside the place, or out of the Diocese", using the royal institutions denotes the penalty of *degredo*, applied by secular justice, closer to ecclesiastical justice.

According to Hespanha, the debates about the definitions of *degredo* and cases of application encompassed the death penalty, often referred to throughout book V of the Philippine Ordinances, and the absence of its application was predicted by the Ordinances. One of the interpretations made for this absence can be found in the differentiation between what was natural and what was civil, which was recurrent in common law theory. Thus, death could be natural, meaning the physical death of the subject, or civil, indicating *degredo* for more than ten years, removing one from one's community and consequently causing one's death in relation to the political group to which one belonged. Some scholars of the period, such as Manuel Barbosa, understood that civil death meant a permanent *degredo*, equivalent to exile. From the same perspective, Domingos Antunes Portugal asserted that where there was a "death penalty" in the text of the Ordinances, it should be interpreted as a sentence of *degredo*. Also, the judge Manuel Lopes de Oliveira, in the 18th century, argued that when in the Ordinances there was the commination of the death penalty through the

104 "senhas capellas de cornos". Portugal, *Ordenações Filipinas*, lib. V, tit. XXV. Translated by the author.

105 Freire, *Instituições de direito criminal português*, 190.

106 Amaral, *Liber utilissimus*, lib. I, verbo adulterium.

107 "fóra do lugar, ou da Diocese, se assim parecer aos mesmos Ordinarios, invocando para isso, se for necessario, o braço Secular". Catholic Church, *O sacrosanto, e ecumenico Concilio de Trento*, lib. II, sec. XXIV, cap. VIII. Translated by the author.

expression "morra por ello", this would mean the civil death penalty, and only the specification of the natural death penalty would indicate physical death. Furthermore, "On this basis, this author dubbed the judges who applied the natural death penalty indiscriminately as 'inexperienced pragmatists' (*imperiti Pragmatici*) and 'monstrous butchers' (*immanissini carnífices*)".[108]

Although this conception was not the most reproduced one by jurists of the period, it should be noted that there was no opposition from the social order to this logic. That is, at no time during the debates raised about these meanings was there any other jurist who accused Lopes de Oliveira of relapsing into negligence or who affirmed that this opinion represented a threat to the social order. The dissenting arguments were based on the magistrate's discretion in adjusting sentences to the circumstances of the crime and the guilty party. In any case, both opinions were legal explanations for the existing social practice.[109]

The *degredo* was one of the most common penalties imposed in judicial proceedings, as the central form of penalty of the political-legal-administrative apparatus of the Portuguese Empire throughout the modern period, considering that the book V of the Ordinances indicated it as the penalty applicable to 256 offences. It represented the removal of the transgressor from the locale in which he lived, often determining his civil death within the community to which he belonged. It was based on a double motive, which to some extent may explain its wide scope: on the one hand, the desire was to remove those considered undesirable while, on the other hand, it was useful in terms of work and occupation in distant lands.[110]

If these meanings are intertwined with the norms of canon law, the sacrament of marriage could only be dissolved by the death of one of the spouses; however, the First Constitutions of the Archbishopric of Bahia inserted the possibility of permanent separation in cases of adultery.[111] Note that dissolution of marriage and separation were different notions, not corresponding to one another; that is, separation did not represent the dissolution of marriage but rather the separation of the *torus*, the cohabitation of the consorts. Therefore, permanent separation did not involve the dissolution of marriage, but rather the separation of bodies. Since the penalty for adultery was linked to adulterous concubinage and, for this reason, the passage which specifically punished women considered them to be the concubines of adulterous men

108 Hespanha, "Da 'iustitia' à 'disciplina'", 297–310.
109 Hespanha, "Da 'iustitia' à 'disciplina'", 310–311.
110 Toma, "A pena de degredo", 438; Pieroni, *Os excluídos do reino*, 24–37.
111 Vide, *Constituições Primeiras*, lib. I, tit. LXXII, § 305.

and there was no discussion of the dissolution of marriage by separation of the consorts.

The practice of sending women to *recolhimentos*, thus, seems to have had a double function: at the same time as carrying out the separation of the couple, it had a restorative educational nature. With *recolhimentos* it was then possible to emulate the idea of *degredo*, but with an additional element: the possible reinsertion of the women into society. That is, in addition to condemnation and imputation of guilt, the focus of criminal law in the modern period, the educational ideal imprinted an objective of effectiveness in controlling the behaviour of women so that it would then be possible for them to live once more in society. Even if, in some cases, permanent separation from the husband with the removal of women from the social contexts in which they had ties and relations of reciprocal influence could mean their civil death, the idea of reintegration into the community was not completely taken from them. This perspective meets the notion that, in 18th-century criminal law, the penal provision was equated with the logic of penalty and, as Pereira e Sousa explains, represented a form of atonement for the crime with the purpose of reparation for the offence.[112] It had to thus be measured proportionally against the scandal caused by the offence, and it seems the practice of female confinement was a response to this.

Specifically regarding penalties applied to women, the criminal law of the modern period was based on convictions in which the penalisation had to be mitigated. Rui Gonçalves defended that penalties directed at women had to be more lenient because they were "naturally less daring".[113] This provision was supported by *ius commune* and Christian doctrine, often directed towards the recommendation for penal mitigation, but on the grounds of natural weakness.[114] The less daring – a notion perhaps used by the author in an interesting attempt to soften the words with which the feminine gender was normally described by jurists – implied that women would not be fully mentally apt to commit crimes, perhaps due to natural weakness, which would explain the lesser punishment due to the nature of the crimes themselves and, also, the perspective that sending them to the *recolhimentos* would provide a valid and effective punishment. That is, punishment was to be mitigated by considering the absence of intellect to understand the behaviour. The theology doctrine, on the one hand, seems to point to both *imbecilitas* in the act of delinquency

---

112 Sousa, *Esboço de hum Diccionario Juridico*, lib. II, 358.

113 "naturalmente menos ousadas". Gonçalves, *Dos privilegios e praerrogativas*, 96. Translated by the author.

114 Goldschmidt, *Convivendo com o pecado*, 52.

and feminine weakness in the reception of punishment. The weakness of essence would then be considered not only according to the mental facet and world perceptions, but also under corporal bias, adding reasons for why the punishment should be milder.

On the other hand, this penalty seems to have served the husbands as a strategy to minimise the humiliation caused by the "law of shame" in their daily lives.[115] Present in the colonial range of normativities, this "law" complexified social norms and, by imposing a series of requirements, or expectations, of behaviour, ended up creating a network of reciprocal social surveillance. For men who suffered adultery by their wives, the dishonour attributed to them could affect them in all areas of their lives, as highlighted by the cases analysed in this chapter. In one of the cases above, Manuel José Froes, specifically, could no longer exercise his profession as a merchant and carry out his business in his village because of the humiliation he suffered from his wife's adultery.[116] Employing socially acceptable measures to solve the case, according to the law of shame, was a way to, in addition to obtaining institutional support that would consider his reasons true, express a quest for revenge, which became quite a fundamental obligation for the restoration of honour.

These ideas are in line with the logic that criminal justice in Portuguese America was greatly shaped by society, according (or not) to normativities from the Portuguese Empire. The sources allow us to visualise that the resolution of the cases desired by the parties was sometimes not assured by the institutions of justice but rather by a kind of justice from society. This leads to the idea that the responses sought by the historical actors who claimed in the courts were not ones that the institutions could provide, but ones that social elements could and did bring to their daily lives. Therefore, the criminal justice system was, in reality, social criminal justice, and was undertaken in terms of normativities from social order through laws of shame, humiliation and tolerance.[117]

5 Conclusions

The presented cases carry many key issues that are not only important to understanding women in colonial contexts but also concerning the range of

115 Muchembled, *História da violência*, 27–28.
116 AHU, Bahia, Papéis Avulsos, box 222, doc. 15466, fol. 1r.
117 Massuchetto, *Mulheres, conflitos e normatividades*.

normativities and worldviews in the 18th century. It is possible to verify in the sources, even if only in subtle ways, the knowledge of normativity and the understanding of local normativities, which held a lot of influence from Christian and moral values, but – in the social order, taking into consideration the social consensuses and the notions of tolerance and scandal – they were fluid.

Considering the above, it is possible to conclude that sending deviant women to *recolhimentos* was a legal change gradually consolidated as a gendered penalty practice, especially in the second half of the 18th century. This practice of castigation and penalisation is related to perspectives concerning which punishments were valid to achieve the social responses desired by the historical actors. Such answers, in the presented cases, were desired by the family authorities, that is, the husbands, responding much more to their needs and concerns with honour than paying attention to the woman's needs. The woman's condition and the consequent restoration of honesty were necessary elements for the restoration of the honour of the husbands, together with the attitudes employed for the satisfaction of revenge.

The punishment was constituted in between institutional penalty and domestic castigation, complexifying the existence of control in the households. The punishments applied by husbands in the exclusively domestic sphere were concentrated on corporal castigation and death threats, which provided the women with enough arsenal to complain about their mistreatment to the ecclesiastical authorities and, thus, achieve their separation from their husbands. Apparently, the husbands sent them to *recolhimentos* so that, besides removing them from their daily lives and validating their claims, they could avoid being denounced to the ecclesiastical courts, thus avoiding a greater loss of honour and a greater stain on the family's honour. Once the cases were brought to social knowledge, these elements were the focus of rumours and would probably be spread throughout the villages making reparation of the situation even more difficult.

For the women, moving away from the social practices of which they were used to was something negative, but it is possible to wonder if it was not also somewhat of a solution for them. To wear themselves out by filing claims to the secular or ecclesiastic courts against their husbands and suffering daily violence from them and, possibly, from the family would not have presented them with the most positive living situation. The sources do not allow concrete conclusions along these lines, but almost exclusive coexistence with other women could, in some ways, have offered them a far safer situation with greater freedom of expression and independence than their previous experiences with their husbands.

Bibliography

Manuscripts

[Anon.,] Formulário Médico, [no place,] [no publisher,] 1703.
Arquivo Histórico Ultramarino, Lisboa (AHU), Bahia, Papéis Avulsos, box 8, doc. 1193.
Arquivo Histórico Ultramarino, Lisboa (AHU), Bahia, Papéis Avulsos, box 22, doc. 1972
Arquivo Histórico Ultramarino, Lisboa (AHU), Bahia, Papéis Avulsos, box 36, doc. 3239.
Arquivo Histórico Ultramarino, Lisboa (AHU), Bahia, Papéis Avulsos, box 38, doc. 3443.
Arquivo Histórico Ultramarino, Lisboa (AHU), Bahia, Papéis Avulsos, box 58, doc. 11067.
Arquivo Histórico Ultramarino, Lisboa (AHU), Bahia, Papéis Avulsos, box 66, doc. 5551.
Arquivo Histórico Ultramarino, Lisboa (AHU), Bahia, Papéis Avulsos, box 69, doc. 13305.
Arquivo Histórico Ultramarino, Lisboa (AHU), Bahia, Papéis Avulsos, box 70, doc. 11367.
Arquivo Histórico Ultramarino, Lisboa (AHU), Bahia, Papéis Avulsos, box 74, doc. 14326.
Arquivo Histórico Ultramarino, Lisboa (AHU), Bahia, Papéis Avulsos, box 79, doc. 15422.
Arquivo Histórico Ultramarino, Lisboa (AHU), Bahia, Papéis Avulsos, box 95, doc. 18520.
Arquivo Histórico Ultramarino, Lisboa (AHU), Bahia, Papéis Avulsos, box 96, doc. 18732.
Arquivo Histórico Ultramarino, Lisboa (AHU), Bahia, Papéis Avulsos, box 108, doc. 21063.
Arquivo Histórico Ultramarino, Lisboa (AHU), Bahia, Papéis Avulsos, box 108, doc. 21086.
Arquivo Histórico Ultramarino, Lisboa (AHU), Bahia, Papéis Avulsos, box 196, doc. 14223.
Arquivo Histórico Ultramarino, Lisboa (AHU), Bahia, Papéis Avulsos, box 221, doc. 15408.
Arquivo Histórico Ultramarino, Lisboa (AHU), Bahia, Papéis Avulsos, box 222, doc. 15466.
Arquivo Histórico Ultramarino, Lisboa (AHU), Pará, box 63, doc. 5496.
Arquivo Histórico Ultramarino, Lisboa (AHU), Pernambuco, box 30, doc. 2720.
Arquivo Histórico Ultramarino, Lisboa (AHU), Pernambuco, box 32, doc. 2924.
Arquivo Histórico Ultramarino, Lisboa (AHU), Pernambuco, box 32, doc. 2926.
Arquivo Histórico Ultramarino, Lisboa (AHU), Pernambuco, box 62, doc. 5292.
Arquivo Histórico Ultramarino, Lisboa (AHU), Pernambuco, box 63, doc. 5376.
Arquivo Histórico Ultramarino, Lisboa (AHU), Pernambuco, box 66, doc. 5560.

Arquivo Histórico Ultramarino, Lisboa (AHU), Pernambuco, box 105, doc. 8187.
Arquivo Histórico Ultramarino, Lisboa (AHU), Pernambuco, box 106, doc. 8206.
Arquivo Histórico Ultramarino, Lisboa (AHU), Rio de Janeiro, Papéis Avulsos, box 49, doc. 4916.
Arquivo Histórico Ultramarino, Lisboa (AHU), Rio de Janeiro, Papéis Avulsos, box 50, doc. 5067.
Biblioteca Nacional de Portugal (BNP), Nóbrega, Manuel da, [Cartas,] [no place,] [no publisher,] 15–, Cota 2008389.

Printed Sources

Amaral, Antonio Cardoso do, *Liber utilissimus judicibus et advocatis* [...], lib. I, Coimbra 1729: Antonij Simoens Universitatis Typographi.
Barbosa, Manuel, *Remissiones Doctorum ad Contractus, ultimas voluntates, et delicta spectantes* [...], Lisboa 1618: Officina Petri Craesbeeck.
Bluteau, Raphael, *Vocabulario Portuguez e Latino* [...], lib. I, Coimbra 1712: Collegio das Artes da Companhia de JESU.
Bluteau, Raphael, *Vocabulario Portuguez e Latino* [...], lib. V, Lisboa 1716: Officina de Pascoal da Sylva, Impressor de Sua Magestade.
Bluteau, Raphael, *Vocabulario Portuguez e Latino* [...], lib. VII, Lisboa 1720: Officina de Pascoal da Sylva, Impressor de Sua Magestade.
Bluteau, Raphael, *Diccionario da Lingua Portugueza* [...], lib. I, Lisboa 1789: Officina de Simão Thaddeo Ferreira.
Bluteau, Raphael, *Diccionario da Lingua Portugueza* [...], lib. II, Lisboa 1789: Officina de Simão Thaddeo Ferreira.
Catholic Church, *O sacrosanto, e ecumenico Concilio de Trento em latim e portuguez* [...], lib. II, Lisboa 1781: Officina Patriarcal de Francisco Luiz Ameno.
Coutinho, José Joaquim da Cunha de Azeredo, *Estatutos do Recolhimento de Nossa Senhora da Glória do lugar da Boavista de Parnambuco* [...], Lisboa 1798: Tipografia da Academia Real das Ciências.
Freire, Pascoal José de Melo, *Instituições de direito criminal português*, trans. Miguel Pinto de Menezes, in *Boletim do Ministério da Justiça*, no. 155–156 (1966 [1794]), 5–202 and 69–168.
Gonçalves, Rui, *Dos privilegios e praerrogativas q[ue] ho genero feminino te[m] por direito comu[m] & ordenações do Reyno mais que ho genero masculino*, Lisboa 1557: Jobanné Barreiú Regium Typograpbum.
Portugal, *Collecção Chronologica de Leis Extravagantes posteriores à nova compilação das Ordenações do Reino, publicadas em 1603*, lib. II, Coimbra 1819: Real Imprensa da Universidade.

Portugal, *Collecção da Legislação Portugueza desde a ultima compilação das Ordenações, redegida pelo desembargador Antonio Delgado da Silva*, Lisboa 1829: Typografia Maigrense.

Portugal, *Collecção Chronologica da Legislação Portugueza compilada e annotada por José Justino de Andrade e Silva bacharel formado em Direito. 1603–1612*, Lisboa 1854: Imprensa de J. J. A. Silva.

Portugal, *Ordenações Filipinas*, lib. V, 14th ed., Rio de Janeiro 1870: Typographia do Instituto Philomathico.

Sousa, Joaquim José Caetano Pereira e, *Classe dos crimes, por ordem systematica, com as penas correspondentes, segundo a legislação actual*, Lisboa 1803: Regia Officina Typografica.

Sousa, Joaquim José Caetano Pereira e, *Esboço de hum Diccionario Juridico, Theoretico, e Practico, remissivo ás leis compiladas, e extravagantes*, lib. II, Lisboa 1827: Typographia Rollandiana.

Vide, Sebastião Monteiro da, *Constituições Primeiras do Arcebispado da Bahia*, lib. I–V, Coimbra 1720: Real Collegio das Artes da Companhia de JESU.

Vieira, Domingos, *Grande diccionario portuguez ou Thesouro da lingua portuguesa* [...], Porto 1871: Ernesto Chardron, Bartholomeu H. de Moraes.

Literature

Algranti, Leila Mezan, *Honradas e devotas: mulheres da colônia. Condição feminina nos conventos e recolhimentos do Sudeste do Brasil. 1750–1822*, Rio de Janeiro 1993.

Algranti, Leila Mezan, *Livros de devoção, atos de censura: ensaios de história do livro e da leitura na América portuguesa (1750–1821)*, São Paulo 2004.

Almeida, Suely Creusa Cordeiro de, *O sexo devoto: normatização e resistência feminina no Império Português – XVI–XVIII* (Ph.D. Thesis), Recife 2003.

Almeida, Suely Creusa Cordeiro de, "A clausura feminina no mundo ibero-atlântico: Pernambuco e Portugal nos séculos XVI ao XVIII", in *Tempo* 18:32 (2012), 95–113.

Bazán Días, Iñaki, "El estupro: sexualidad delictiva en la Baja Edad Media y primera Edad Moderna", in Charageat, Martine (ed.), *Matrimonio y sexualidad*, Madrid 1992, 13–45.

Blanco Carrasco, José Pablo, "'¿Adónde irán los secretos?' Reflexiones en torno el estupro y el mercado matrimonial en la Edad Moderna", in Torremocha Hernández, Margarita and Alberto Corada Alonso (eds.), *El estupro: Delito, mujer y sociedad en el Antiguo Régimen*, Valladolid 2018, 133–163.

Braga, Isabel Drumond, *A bigamia em Portugal na Época Moderna. Sentir mal do sacramento do matrimónio?*, Lisboa 2003.

Braga, Isabel Drumond, "Punir a Violação, perdoar os Violadores: entre a justiça e a clemência no Portugal Moderno", in Torremocha Hernández, Margarita and Alberto Corada Alonso (eds.), *El estupro: Delito, mujer y sociedad en el Antiguo Régimen*, Valladolid 2018, 165–187.

Brighente, Liliam Ferraresi, *Entre a liberdade e a administração particular: a condição jurídica do indígena na vila de Curitiba (1700–1750)* (Masters Dissertation), Curitiba 2012.

Coutinho Silva, Luisa Stella de Oliveira, *Nem teúdas, nem manteúdas: História das Mulheres e Direito na capitania da Paraíba (Brasil, 1661–1822)*, Frankfurt 2020.

Duve, Thomas, "What is global legal history?", in *Comparative Legal History* 8:2 (2020), 73–115.

Duve, Thomas, "Historia del derecho como historia del saber normativo", in *Revista de Historia del Derecho* 63 (2022), 1–60.

Duve, Thomas, "Legal History as an Observation of Historical Regimes of Normativity", in *Max Planck Institute for Legal History and Legal Theory Research Paper Series*, no. 17 (2022), 1–11.

Garnot, Benoît, "Justiça e sociedade na França do século XVIII", in *Textos de História* 11:1/2 (2003), 13–27.

Ginzburg, Carlo, *O queijo e os vermes: o cotidiano e as ideias de um moleiro perseguido pela Inquisição*, São Paulo 2006.

Goldschmidt, Eliana Maria Rea, *Convivendo com o pecado na sociedade colonial paulista (1719–1822)*, São Paulo 1998.

Hespanha, António Manuel, "Da 'iustitia' à 'disciplina'. Textos, poder e política penal no Antigo Regime", in Hespanha, António Manuel, *Justiça e litigiosidade: história e prospectiva*, Lisboa 1993, 493–578.

Hespanha, António Manuel, *Como os juristas viam o mundo. 1550–1750. Direitos, estados, pessoas, coisas, contratos, ações e crimes*, Lisboa 2015.

Johnson, Lyman and Lipsett-Rivera, Sonya, "Introduction", in Johnson, Lyman and Sonya Lipsett-Rivera (eds.), *The Faces of Honor: Sex, Shame, and Violence in Colonial Latin America*, Albuquerque, NM 1998, 1–17.

Lopes, Maria Antónia, "Dominando corpos e consciências em recolhimentos portugueses (séculos XVIII–XIX)", in Rubio Pérez, Laureano (ed.), *Instituciones y centros de reclusión colectiva. Formas y claves de una respuesta social (siglos XVI–XX)*, León 2012, 99–130.

Lopes, Maria Antónia, "Transgressões femininas no Recolhimento da Misericórdia do Porto, 1732–1824", in Santa Casa da Misericórdia do Porto (ed.), *Saúde, Ciência e Património – Atas do III Congresso de História da Santa Casa da Misericórdia do Porto*, Porto 2016, 95–123.

Lopes, Maria Antónia, "Estereótipos de 'a mulher' em Portugal dos séculos XVI a XIX (um roteiro)", in Rossi, Maria Antonieta (ed.), *Donne, Cultura e Società nel panorama lusitano e internazionale (secoli XVI–XXI)*, Viterbo 2017, 27–44.

Mantecón Movellán, Tomás, "Desviación, disciplina social e intervenciones judiciales en el Antiguo Régimen", in *Studia Historica: Historia Moderna* 14 (1996), 223–243.

Martínez Llorente, Félix, "Una notación histórica sobre el delito de estupro hasta la codificación penal", in Torremocha Hernández, Margarita, Alberto Corada Alonso (eds.), *El estupro: Delito, mujer y sociedad en el Antiguo Régimen*, Valladolid 2018, 17–37.

Massuchetto, Vanessa, *Mulheres, conflitos e normatividades: a justiça criminal e o feminino nas vilas de Curitiba e Paranaguá (1750–1800)* (Ph.D. Thesis), Curitiba 2021.

McKinley, Michelle A., *Fractional Freedoms. Slavery, Intimacy, and Legal Mobilization in Colonial Lima, 1600–1700*, Cambridge 2016.

Muchembled, Robert, *História da violência: do fim da Idade Média aos nossos dias*, Rio de Janeiro 2012.

Nazzari, Muriel, *O desaparecimento do dote: mulheres, famílias e mudança social em São Paulo, Brasil, 1600–1900*, São Paulo 2001.

Pieroni, Geraldo, *Os excluídos do reino: a Inquisição portuguesa e o degredo para o Brasil colônia*, Brasília 2000.

Puntoni, Pedro, "Bernardo Vieira Ravasco, secretário do Estado do Brasil: poder e elites na Bahia do século XVII", in Bicalho, Maria Fernanda and Vera Lúcia Amaral Fernili (eds.), *Modos de governar: idéias e práticas políticas no império português. Séculos XVI–XIX*, São Paulo, 2005, 157–178.

Ruff, Julius R., *Violence in Early Modern Europe 1500–1800*, Cambridge 2001.

Silva, Maria Beatriz Marques Nizza da, *Sistema de casamento no Brasil colonial*, São Paulo 1984.

Silva, Maria Beatriz Nizza da, *Vida privada e quotidiano no Brasil na época de D. Maria I e de D. João VI*, 2nd ed., Lisboa 2004.

Spurling, Geoffrey, "Honor, Sexuality, and the Colonial Church: The Sins of Dr. González, Cathedral Canon", in Johnson, Lyman and Sonya Lipsett-Rivera (eds.), *The Faces of Honor: Sex, Shame, and Violence in Colonial Latin America*, Albuquerque, NM 1998, 45–67.

Toma, Maristela, "A pena de degredo e a construção do império colonial", in *Métis: História & Cultura*, 5:10 (2006), 61–76.

Torremocha Hernández, Margarita, "El estupro en el Informe jurídico de Meléndez Valdés. Una visión ilustrada de un delito contra el honor familiar (1796)", in Torremocha Hernández, Margarita and Alberto Corada Alonso (eds.), *El estupro: Delito, mujer y sociedad en el Antiguo Régimen*, Valladolid 2018, 91–131.

Twinam, Ann, "The Negotiation of Honor. Elites, Sexuality and Illegitimacy in Eighteenth-Century America", in Johnson, Lyman and Sonya Lipsett-Rivera (eds.), *The*

Faces of Honor: Sex, Shame, and Violence in Colonial Latin America, Albuquerque, NM, 1998, 68–102.

Undurraga, Verónica and Rafael Gaune, "Diálogos y propuestas historiográficas desde un espacio de disciplinamiento", in Undurraga, Verónica and Rafael Gaune (eds.), *Formas de control y disciplinamiento*, Lima 2014, 21–45.

Vandenbogaerde, Sebastiaan, "(Wo)Men in legal history: Possibilities and challenges for gendered legal historical research", in Vandenbogaerde, Sebastiaan, Iris Lellouche, Hélène Duffuler-Vialle, Sébastien Dhalluin and Bruno Debaenst (eds.), *(Wo) Men in Legal History*, Lille 2016, 1–19.

CHAPTER 8

Normativities of Freedom

Suing for the Possibility to Self-Purchase in São Paulo during the Second Half of the 18th Century

Felipe Garcia de Oliveira

1 Introduction

Manumission was a legally recognised form for changing the legal status of an enslaved person[1] to that of someone free. It could be obtained through a will (*post-mortem*), at the moment of baptism (known as *Ad Pias Causas*), acquiring and receiving a manumission letter (which could be registered in a notary office or be a private letter) or even through legal procedures. The practice of manumission was widely disseminated and assumed distinct characteristics depending on the location, the historical period and the growing number of freed individuals in the colonies.

Differences can be found in the ways the Crowns dealt with manumissions in the early modern period. The French Crown, for instance, introduced the *Code Noir* (Black Code) in 1685, which not only constrained manumission to the owner's discretion but also established that only men over the age of 20 could free a slave without the authorisation of a local agent. However, in 1724, in Louisiana, this policy shifted to require approval from the local government for granting manumissions. In Virginia, governed by the British Crown, the manumission was dependent on the owner's will until the beginning of the 18th century. After that, meritorious service needed to be demonstrated, and approval from local authorities was also required. This situation only changed with the Manumission Act of 1782, which instituted manumission as a private act that did not require any governmental approval and enabled the enslaved persons the right to sue for their freedom.[2]

1 In this chapter, I use "enslaved person/people" to reinforce the idea that slavery of African peoples was not natural, but rather a social and historical construction. The word "slaves" will be used only when I quote or make references to the sources as they often refer to these historical subjects as slaves.

2 Fuente and Gross, *Becoming Free, Becoming Black*, 19–20, 49–50, 60–61; Helg, *!Nunca Más esclavos!*. See also, Health, "The Meaning of Freedom", 342–359.

The Spanish Crown took a different route. Since the compilation of *Siete Partidas* in the 13th century, which was composed under the influence of Roman and canon laws (*ius commune*), ways to grant freedom to slaves were provided in cases of mistreatment and denunciation by masters, and it was also possible to receive manumission by prescription. While the purchase of freedom or self-purchase was never properly regulated by the Spanish Crown, there are also no records of acts aiming to restrict the granting of manumission. However, since the 16th century, some royal cedulas (*cedulas reai*s) indicated that enslaved peoples could request judicial intervention to litigate for their freedom.[3]

Like Spain, the Portuguese Crown has never regulated the right to buy or sell manumission, with the Royal Decree of 24 December 1734 being the only exception to this rule. According to this Decree, slaves who delivered a diamond of 20 carats or higher to *Casa de Fundição* could receive a manumission letter issued by the King himself. The same Decree stipulated that slaves who reported individuals carrying such diamonds could also obtain their freedom. While this decree marked the peak of interference from the Crown in the practice of manumission, it was suspended in 1750,[4] which aligned with a historical understanding in Portugal that manumission was a donation given by the owner of the slave and not a practice under the control of the Crown. This was expressed in the *Ordenações Filipinas* which was the second version of the Portuguese legal compilation published in 1603. According to its Book 4, Title 63, manumission was categorised as a donation and not as a purchase.[5] It also mentioned the possibility of revocation in cases of ingratitude on the part of the recipient.[6] This situation was resolved in 1871, when *Lei do Ventre Livre* in Brazil regulated the practice of purchasing freedom.[7] Even though at that moment Brazil was already independent from Portugal, some historians argue that this law represented a turning point in what had been a large and

3 For example, we know for Cuba that a royal cedula from 1526 questioned the possibility of slaves being freed based on their length of service or through payment. Furthermore, another cedula from 1540 determined that slaves who claimed to be free could be heard in *audiencias* to discuss it. Fuente and Gross, *Becoming Free, Becoming Black*, 45–46; Lucena Salmoral, *Los Códigos Negros de la América Española.*

4 *Lei de 24 de dezembro de 1734*, in Lara, "Legislação sobre escravos africanos na América portuguesa", 291.

5 Almeida, *Ordenações Filipinas.*

6 On the re-enslavement of a manumitted enslaved person in court, see Pinheiro, *Em defesa da liberdade*; Oliveira, "Da Liberdade ao Cativeiro", 175–190.

7 Manuela Carneiro Cunha was the first to draw attention to this point. Cunha, "Sobre os silêncios da Lei", 123–144. For a review about it, see Silva Júnior, *História, direito e escravidão.*

complex means of granting and conquering manumissions in the colonies, as the self-purchase of freedom had been the subject of customary law and was situated under the master's authority. Thus, manumissions were a respected social practice, in which enslaved people were able to achieve freedom through financial accumulation (*pecúlio*), donation, negotiation and lawsuits.

Although some aspects related to manumission were systematised in these *diplomas*, manumission by self-purchase was never regulated. In other words, the interference of the Crown in regulating ways to liberate enslaved people was a topic of debate, particularly due to the unease expressed by political elites concerning the growing population of freedmen within Brazilian colonial society throughout the 18th century. This regulation did not occur because it could have imposed risks to a colonial system based on the notion and exercise of paternal power by masters, which involved a combination of concessions and punishments.[8] Other historians, however, pointed out that freedmen were an integral part of the colonial system, as they could become owners of enslaved people themselves, which would make manumission part of the logic of slavery in the Brazilian society, strengthening its structures instead of breaking its chains.[9]

Therefore, this chapter focuses on the freedom of enslaved people who sought justice through the judicial system in order to purchase their freedom. It aims to answer the following questions: what is the normative potential of lawsuits of manumission by self-purchase? How did the judicial system deal with this practice? What was the legal change produced by lawsuits judged in the *Juízo ordinário* and the *Ouvidoria* of São Paulo?

To address these questions, I will present the arguments I found in lawsuits involving enslaved individuals claiming freedom in 18th-century São Paulo. The region gained greater political importance and a demographic increase in the enslaved African population. In this sense, it is interesting to observe how enslaved individuals interacted with the courts. Thus, I will focus on cases where self-purchase was central to the issue, as I have already mentioned, since the Portuguese Crown did not regulate this. I will analyse three cases from different periods and courts. One case occurred in the *Juízo ordinário*, which was the first instance of the colonial court. Their judges were locally elected by the Government and were members of the elite, although they normally did not hold a degree. The other two cases occurred in the *Ouvidoria*, which was the superior court. The *Ouvidor* (superior magistrate) was appointed by the Crown and normally held a degree in law. Among their functions were

8 Lara, *Campos da Violência*; Lara, *Fragmentos Setecentistas*.

9 Marquese, "A dinâmica da escravidão", 107–123.

receiving appeals from other courts; overseeing courts; administering elections in municipal councils and receiving complaints from officials.

In line with Thomas Duve's theoretical and methodological framework, which defends that legal history can be understood as a process of cultural translation, this chapter explores and discusses how the demands of enslaved people resulted in normativities capable of judicially defining and changing their legal status, giving them the possibility to buy their freedom.[10] To understand this process of cultural translation, I analyse how the lawyers mobilised the pragmatic normative literature; which conceptions of slavery and freedom they defended; how they could prove their arguments and how they enforced their conceptions about self-purchase. Therefore, I consider the making of the law as a product of a certain social and cultural environment, in which the enslaved people, freedmen and masters, through their attorney, were producing agents of law whilst also being products of colonial law. In this sense, lawsuits can be considered "concrete law" in practice.[11]

The process of translation of social conceptions in the legal argumentation proceedings was intense and complex. During these proceedings, conceptions could be reiterated, reappropriated and recreated locally. In other words, enslaved people, accompanied by their lawyers and sometimes legitimised by the authorities, produced normativities of freedom and slavery, in which the power masters held over them could be questioned. On the other hand, masters mobilised normativities to reinforce their dominance and ownership. I argue that these lawsuits tried to create norms that could expand or reduce the possibility of freedom for these individuals. Through creative legal mobilisation, enslaved people not only challenged the authority of their masters but also established and reinforced what could be perceived as fair and unfair within the relationship between master and slave, using the judicial system to do so.

2 The Legal Statuses of Enslaved People and the Possibility of Suing for Freedom in São Paulo in the 18th Century

The study of the interaction between historically subalternised groups and judicial instances in diverse geographical and temporal frame has gained

10 Duve, "Pragmatic Normative Literature and the Production of Normative Knowledge in the Early Modern Iberian Empires (16th–17th Centuries)"; Duve, "Legal History as a History of the Translation of Knowledge of Normativity".

11 Duve, "Global Legal History".

increased attention over the past decades as recent historiography has highlighted the diversity of the "uses of justice" by many people.[12] When examining individuals who experienced Early Modern slavery, of which the historiographic production is vast in several parts of the world, countless accounts discussing the active role these subjects played in the fight for their freedom can be found, even though they were subjected to many processes of violence and political, legal and social exclusion.

Since the 1980s, in Brazilian historiography, scholars have been analysing lawsuits involving enslaved people.[13] However, these studies have not focused on specific legal terms or the production of normativities. In fact, not much has been done regarding this topic concerning the 18th century. The study conducted by Fernanda Pinheiro is an interesting exception since it analyses how the choice of arguments and the type of lawsuit provided the foundation for deepening the strategic actions of enslaved people from Africa and their masters in the courts of Mariana and Lisbon. This research also demonstrates that interactions with the law shaped, questioned and placed limits on the authority of masters.[14]

Early Modern society was understood as naturally unequal, in which individuals could have representation in justice according to the place (*statutes*) they occupied in the social body, since duties derived from this place. The king was considered the head of society. He had the power to distribute jurisdiction for the maintenance and harmony of the body. The agents of the Crown received jurisdiction, the act of dictating and declaring what was right and fair.[15]

Therefore, different social groups in society had limited access to justice depending on their status within it and their socio-cultural and material conditions. Thus, it is important to think about the ways in which an enslaved person accessed the judicial system. Firstly, according to extensive Early Modern pragmatic normative literature, slaves were classified both as a chattel (*coisa*) and a person (*pessoa*). According to Antônio Manuel Hespanha, slaves represented the most interesting case for examining the relationship between chattel and person, and this fact should not be taken as ambiguous or a contradiction. The concept of nonpersons (*coisa*) was expanded, and included

12 Fortea Pérez, Gelabert and Mantecón Movellán (eds.), *Furor et rabies*; Benton and Ross (eds.), *Legal Pluralism and Empires, 1500–1850*; Vermeesch, Heijden and Zuijderduijn (eds.), *The Uses of Justice in Global Perspective, 1600–1900*.

13 Chalhoub, *Visões da liberdade*; Mattos, *Das cores do silêncio*; Grinberg, *Liberata*.

14 Pinheiro, *Em defesa da liberdade*.

15 Xavier and Hespanha, "A representação da sociedade e do poder", 113–140; Garriga, "Gobierno y Justicia: el Gobierno de la Justicia".

individuals, rights, legal statuses and actions.[16] Under civil law, the legal capacity of slaves was denied, resulting in a range of limitations and restrictions imposed upon them. They were unable to be witnesses, own property or write a will, even though some enslaved people could own slaves themselves and possess some property as has been shown by the historiography.[17] They needed a representative or authorisation from their master or judge to start legal proceedings.[18]

The option to change a slave's legal status via the courts had long been in place. Since the enslavement of the Moors in the Iberian Peninsula, lawsuits for changing one's legal status existed in the Early Modern world. For instance, the book on judicial practice (Book 3, Title 18 – On Holidays, paragraph 8) of the *Ordenações Filipinas* established that cases of captivity and freedom had an exception when it came to the restrictions of judicial acts on days of court vacations without the consent of the parties. In the same sense, the *Ordenações Filipinas* pointed out that "many things could be granted against the general law in favour of freedom", when referring to the liberation of the Moors.[19] The *ius commune* provided the possibility of changing masters and the viability of starting a lawsuit, considering situations of violence suffered by slaves or the possession of freedom after 20 years of service.[20]

Even in the Portuguese jurisprudence of the 16th century, lawsuits initiated by enslaved people were not uncommon. One example, from as early as the 16th–17th centuries, is the practice of giving an enslaved person three days in a week to deal with their court cases. A reference to this common practice, called *estilo*,[21] is found in the *aresto* of the *Casa de Suplicação*. According to Belchior Febo's *Decisiones*, when questioned in a lawsuit whether a master was obliged to pay the costs of his slave's lawsuit or claim for manumission, the decision was that he was "obliged" to give the slave time to go to court to request his justice and to attend hearings and that for "*estilo* he is given three

16 Hespanha, *Como os juristas viam o mundo. 1550–1750*, 207, 213–218, 309–311 and 576–577.

17 Reis, "Slaves Who Owned Slaves in Nineteenth-Century Bahia, Brazil".

18 Seixas, *Pessoa e Trabalho no direito português (1750–1878)*, 85–87.

19 Almeida, *Ordenações Filipinas*.

20 Premo, *The Enlightenment on Trial*. On emancipation by prescription, see Dias Paes, "Sobre origens, continuidades e criações", 1379–1406; Oliveira, "A posse da liberdade nas ações cíveis de escravos e libertos na justiça em São Paulo, século XVIII", 288–318.

21 In Portuguese legal practice, a customary practice that was not legalised was called *estilo*, which denoted an important action even though not sustainable as a law in the courts. From now on in this chapter, I refer to it in Portuguese without trying to translate the meaning of the word.

days in the week".[22] Other examples can be evoked to show that the practice of enslaved people suing and being sued was supported by the pragmatic normative literature.[23] These legal norms reflected the complexities and exceptions inherent in the legal landscape concerning freedom and slavery.

Despite the absence of formal regulations, conditional or self-purchase manumission was not only prevalent but also particularly frequent in the Iberian Peninsula during the 18th century.[24] It is well documented that enslaved people pursued and secured their freedom through various means. One of them, *coartação/coartacíon* in legal terms, was a type of contract in which enslaved people negotiated their freedom in instalments with their masters, a practice commonly observed in many urban centres, such as Mariana,[25] São Paulo[26] and Salvador.[27] According to Alejandro De la Fuente and Ariela Gross, in Cuba, *coartação* had its origins in customary practices, but had shaped the legal practice of paying for freedom. This was possible because freedom was favoured both in the customs and *ius commune*.[28]

Furthermore, the boundaries between slavery and freedom were more complex and nuanced. In an urban space, an enslaved person could have less or more autonomy and live socially "like a freedman", whereas some freedmen could still live under the authority of their masters as aggregates and be considered as enslaved people by their society. How individuals obtained their manumission could directly interfere in the way they experienced their freedom. If an enslaved person obtained freedom gratuitously, the reciprocal ties between them and their master could be more frequently asserted. On the other hand, if they bought it, such as self-purchase, relationships could be different, sometimes better for the freed person.[29] It is worth mentioning that

22 Febo, *Decisiones Senatus Regni Lusitaniae*, pt. 2, arestum 35, 425–426.

23 Caminha, *Tratado da forma dos libelos*, 213–214. For Canon Law and ways of achieving freedom, see Bremeu, *Universo Jurídico ou Jurisprudência Universal, Canônica e Cesárea.*

24 De la Fuente and Gross showed that in Havana "self-purchases represented about 80 percent of all manumissions": Fuente and Gross, *Becoming Free, Becoming Black*, 45–46.

25 Paiva, "Coartações e alforrias nas Minas Gerais do século XVIII: as possibilidades de libertação escrava no principal centro colonial", 49–57; Pinheiro, *Em defesa da liberdade.*

26 Goldschmidt, "A carta de alforria na conquista da liberdade", 114–125.

27 Souza, "Nos caminhos do cativeiro, na esquina com a liberdade", 103–135.

28 Lucena Salmoral, "El derecho de coartación del esclavo en la América Española", 357–374; Fuente, "Slaves and the Creation of Legal Rights in Cuba: Coartación and Papel", 659–692; Undurrraga, *Esclavos y esclavas demandando justicia*; Premo, *The Enlightenment on Trial*, 80–82, 193–194.

29 Diório, *As Marcas da Liberdade*, 51; Fioravante and Mathias, "A liberdade condicionada", 151–187; Almeida, *Escravos e libertos nas minas do Rio de Contas – Bahia, século XVIII*, 177–178; McKinley, *Fractional Freedoms.*

the forms of social mobility and the life of the freedmen in the Spanish and Portuguese Crowns were marked by norms that restricted the way they dressed and the access they had to public office, for example. In addition, several rules regulated and tried to limit the punishment and marriage of enslaved people.[30]

In the second half of the 18th century, the African enslaved population increased in São Paulo. The city was characterised by the composition of small slaveholders in the houses, since 67.8% of the houses had between 1 and 5 slaves and many owners shared the same living space with their slaves.[31] Thus, having a slave was a social and economic distinction. This explains why many masters fought to retain possession of their only slave. At that point, the enslaved population represented one-fifth of the regional population. The 1790 census shows that the entire region of São Paulo (which had 25 villages at the time) had approximately 140,858 inhabitants; in 1798, 32,491 were slaves – not including the city of São Paulo. In 1800, the population growth was 169,544 and, even though there is no data on slaves for this year, in 1808 they totalled 37,843 slaves.[32] Slave labour comprised 80% of agricultural activities, cultivation of foodstuffs for subsistence and plantation of rice, corn and beans, among other activities.[33] Their food excess was sold locally on the streets of the villages, alongside free family labour, generating competition between them.

In São Paulo, according to manumissions data collected by Eliana Rea Goldschmidt, 265 manumission letters were recorded between 1729 and 1804. From this number, 116 were unconditional manumissions, when the masters did not ask for any conditions or restrictions, such as a specific number of years of work or favours. Of these, the majority were self-purchases (37%), while the others were given by testament/will.[34]

For the city of São Paulo, I examined a total of 29 court cases that adjudicated changes in the legal status of slaves during the 18th century. Out of these cases, 21 were initiated by slaves seeking their freedom. The arguments mobilised in these cases were diverse. For example, eight argued the promise and the will of their masters and seven evoked that their master had "opened the price" (*aberto o preço*), an expression that appears in lawsuits when slaves claimed their masters were willing to sell them and had set a price for their freedom. Therefore, they sustained that they had acquired the right to pay for their freedom; three asserted indigenous descent as the basis for their claim;

30 Marquese, *Feitores do corpo, missionários da mente.*

31 Luna, Costa and Klein, *Escravismo em São Paulo e Minas Gerais*, 389.

32 Marcílio, *A cidade de São Paulo*, 129.

33 Luna, Costa and Klein, *Escravismo em São Paulo e Minas Gerais.*

34 Goldschmidt, "Alforrias e propriedade familiar em São Paulo colonial", 31–38.

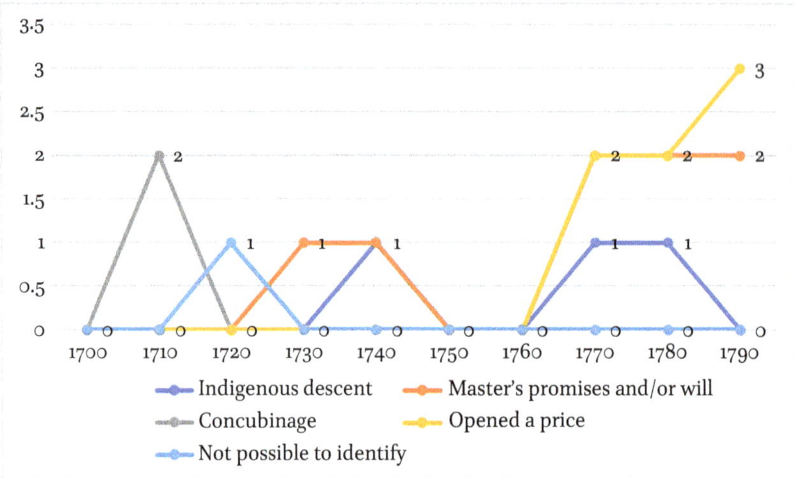

CHART 8.1 Arguments used in 29 lawsuits for freedom in São Paulo during the 18th century. (source: Arquivo Público do Estado de São Paulo)

two argued for their right to freedom due to being former concubines of their masters or having children with them and, in one case, it was not possible to ascertain the specific argument.[35]

The argument that masters had "opened the price" can be traced back to 1770, and it became recurrent as an argument in lawsuits in São Paulo. During a short period (1770–1800), seven cases in São Paulo mobilised this argument when suing for freedom, whereas before, over the longer period of a century (1700–1800), only eight cases argued the masters' willingness and/or promise of freedom. Significantly, this type of claim was accepted and led several owners to engage in legal disputes against their slaves in the courts. Additionally, it was an argument that challenged the master's prerogative in granting manumission. Although my research focuses on the courts of São Paulo, similar arguments can be found in other parts of the colonial space during the same period.[36] In the following pages, I analyse in more depth three cases that use the argument that the master had "opened the price" to claim the possibility of self-purchase.

35 Oliveira, *Cultura jurídica da liberdade*.

36 For Bahia, see Almeida, *Escravos e libertos nas minas do Rio de Contas – Bahia, século XVIII*, 193. For Minas Gerais, see Lima, *De libertos a habilitados*, 58, 101–108.

3 The Argument that Masters had "Opened the Price": (Re)creating Normativities of Freedom

Lawsuits had a logic and a procedure. This does not mean they could not be altered by the actions of those involved during the progress of their proceedings. A process could take diverse paths. A petition initially sent to the Governor could be later sent to the *Juízo ordinário* and even to the *Ouvidoria*. To initiate their lawsuits or petitions, enslaved people had to rely on a support network, in which lawyers and *solicitores de causas* played a fundamental role. In the 18th century, Portuguese America lacked law universities, so lawyers were trained at the University of Coimbra. While lawyers were trained in Portugal and held a degree, *solicitadores de causas*, on the other hand, received their training via practice and experience. Both were important translators and intermediaries between the legal literate and the enslaved people. They formed a considerable network responsible for the dissemination of legal provisions for suing someone.

In one of the dispatches about evaluating slaves in court dated 1774, the Governor of São Paulo determined that it was important to observe Conde da Cunha's *bando*, which established that attorneys should not "persuade slaves of others".[37] Thus, both the *bandos* and the fact that the Governor, years later, remembered this regulation, are indicators that rumours could circulate and that proxies, through wanting to earn some money, could induce and encourage enslaved people in their lawsuits.[38]

Regarding the moment of initiation of a lawsuit, data shows that more than 90% of cases began either after the death of their master, with the possibility of being sold; during some financial instability; or after agreements were not respected.[39] Overall, it seems the lawsuits emerged at times when a master's power had weakened. In other words, it was not just at any time that enslaved people took their demands to the public arena, as the analysis of the following three cases shows.

---

37 Arquivo Público do Estado de São Paulo (Hereafter APESP), Autos Cíveis, C03416, auto 3317, fol. 20r. I have not been able to find the mentioned *bando* of the Conde da Cunha. The mentioned Conde was D. Antonio Álvares da Cunha, Governor of Rio de Janeiro from 1763–1765.

38 *Bandos* were a local normativity, published by the Governor, concerning a variety of subjects, including slaves. On this, see Curvelo, *Governar Pernambuco e as "capitanias anexas"*. See also, Arthur Curvelo's chapter in this volume.

39 Oliveira, *Cultura jurídica da liberdade*.

3.1 The Willingness to Sell in the Event of the Master's Death

On 30 June 1770, the blacksmith Manoel *pardo*[40] sent a petition to the *Ouvidoria-Geral* of São Paulo. Manoel was the slave of Mestre de Campos Diogo Pereira do Rego. After his master passed away, Manoel started a petition using a notification of freedom, (*notificação de Liberdade*) and highlighted two important arguments. The first one was that his master's last wish was to make him a freedman for "good services", at the cost of one-third of his price, which could be proved by the fact that his master had made his desire known by telling it to himself and other several people. Even if this was, as Manoel argued, the master's "last wish" (*última vontade*), it did not happen due to a "disturbance" by *Dona* Isabel Caetana de Araújo, Diogo's wife. Manoel had continued serving the widow with continued "obedience" and "fidelity" after his master's death, but she had informed him he would only be freed upon her death. Manoel then used a second argument: he would pay for his freedom for "mercy in favour of freedom".[41] This principle of "favor libertatis" (favouring freedom) was derived from the *ius commune* and it was present in pragmatic normative literature in Iberia.[42] Manoel asked for a *curador* (guardian) to be appointed and for his worth in money to be evaluated by the court. *Ouvidor* Salvador Pereira da Silva granted permission to summon the owner to court and appointed João de Sampaio Peixoto as his *curador*. Perhaps to Manoel's benefit, the *curador* was someone who had great knowledge about freedom suits, as he had worked on similar cases in São Paulo since 1748. This experience could have offered some advantages for Manoel.

As a woman and a widow, *Dona* Isabel was not allowed to take part in the proceedings on her own.[43] Therefore, the lawsuit was referred to her son-in-law, but he abstained from his inheritance, informing the court that he would not take part in the lawsuit. The alternative found by *Dona* Isabel was to give power of attorney to José Correia da Silva and Luís de Campos. The attorneys argued that the deceased master had not left a will freeing the Manoel, and that he had "kept himself as a freedman" by working with horses,

40 The term *pardo* meant that Manoel was an enslaved boy born in the colony, not somewhere in Africa. On the different uses of *pardo*, see Oliveira, "Pardo".

41 APESP, Autos Cíveis, C03577, auto 2502.

42 Velasco, *Allegationum super varias materias: primus tomus*, alegatione 99°, no. 7, 597; Pinheiro, *Em defesa da liberdade*, 217; Almeida, *Escravos e libertos nas minas do Rio de Contas – Bahia, século XVIII*, 204, 214; Seixas, "Escravidão e favor libertatis no Brasil de oitocentos", 181–198.

43 On the legal status of women, see Menezes, *Sem embargo de Ser Femea*; Coutinho Silva, *Nem teúdas, nem manteúdas*. Also, see Ana Mafalda Pereira Lopes' chapter in this volume.

which gave him a small amount of income at times. In fact, Manoel was what was known as an *escravo de ganho*, an enslaved person who worked outside his master's house, selling things and also working for others. This situation enabled him to broaden his knowledge, allowing him to experience relative autonomy at the moment of his master's passing, which made it possible for him to go to the courts even though he lived in a society regulated by asymmetrical powers and violence.

However, *Dona* Isabel claimed that Manoel had been "insolent" since her husband died.[44] Despite this, she agreed to give him his letter of manumission as long as he delivered the amount that had been documented in the inventory, which was 200,000 *réis*,[45] so that she could settle her debts with her creditors. Upon being evaluated by the master's inventory, the enslaved Manoel saw the chance to pay for his manumission. However, he disagreed regarding his worth in money, since the master had attested he would be exempt from paying two-thirds of his price, which would make it approximately 66,000 *réis* instead. Manoel claimed that this was what his deceased master had desired, and though it is very clear that the widow agreed to sell him his freedom, the matter in question remained the amount to be paid. A lawsuit would then be required to resolve the evaluation of the enslaved person.

In another petition, Manoel's *curador* (guardian) requested that he be evaluated at half the price of 200,000 *réis*. According to attorney João de Sampaio Peixoto, the request to be evaluated by the Court was based on "reason and justice", particularly emphasising what the judge needed to pay attention to because the lawsuit was about "matters of freedom that are favoured by the law",[46] an argument that was based on a doctrinal notion that freedom should have priority according to the law. The *ouvidor* then determined that the enslaved person should be evaluated and his worth in money be given, since the master had "opened the price" by informing him he could have given 200,000 *réis* for his freedom.[47]

The defendant appointed the widow's son-in-law to evaluate the slave, but before proceeding with the evaluation, the owner objected to the evaluation request. Her lawyer, De Campos, alleged that proceeding with a new evaluation without respecting the amount documented in the inventory was null,

44 APESP, Autos Cíveis, C03577, auto 2502, fol. 5r.
45 *Réis* was the currency used in Portugal and Brazil during the colonial period.
46 APESP, Autos Cíveis, C03577, auto 2502, fol. 5v.
47 APESP, Autos Cíveis, C03577, auto 2502, fol. 5v.

and that her creditors could not be harmed "in respect of freedom" because his freedom could not be given in "fraud of creditors".[48]

The *curador* of the enslaved person responded to the judicial embargoes alleging that their matter carried no legal relevance, as had already been pointed out by Mendes de Castro, an important Portuguese jurisconsult from the 17th century.[49] Moreover, the creditors would not be at a loss, since the plaintiff would pay for his freedom and the couple had many other assets to pay off the debts. At the next hearing, the widow's attorneys started to quit the case. The judge did not accept the embargo in the evaluation alleging that it had been done to prevent freedom, which should not be admitted.[50]

The first person to bring up the idea of "opening the price" in this lawsuit was the *ouvidor*. Until then, the words had not appeared. The slave's *curador*, however, went on using it recurrently during his defence, claiming the price had been opened and the widow should be forced to accept the new evaluation. Moreover, the *curador* claimed that the couple did not have many debts. To prove it, he requested a survey of the couple's debts and was informed that they owed 54,000 *réis*, but credits were owed to them too. The owner appealed this judgement at the Court of Appeal of Rio de Janeiro. The appeal was accepted, but the judge also determined that a new evaluation of Manoel should take place.

The *ouvidor* ordered the evaluation under the allegation that Manoel's freedom should not be jeopardised due to its "inestimable" importance and the decision should not be delayed any longer and should be given priority as Manoel, considered a "miserable person" (*miserbilis persona*)[51] in the eyes of the law, had already suffered enough to the point of seeking a remedy for his sorrows in the courts.[52] This court's sentence was clear regarding two important aspects. Firstly, the need for a new evaluation to set a price, so the slave

48 APESP, Autos Cíveis, C03577, auto 2502, fol. 10r.

49 Castro, Prima, et secunda pars Practicae lusitanae advocatis.

50 APESP, Autos Cíveis, C03577, auto 2502, fol. 12r.

51 Hespanha, *Imbecillitas*; Duve, "La Condición Jurídica del Indio y Su Consideración como Persona Miserabilis en el Derecho Indiano", 3–33; Cunill, "El indio miserable: nacimiento de la teoría legal en la América colonial del siglo XVI", 229–248; Oliveira, "Escravos, forros e as estratégias jurídicas em São Paulo (séc. XVIII): pessoa miserável, rústica e ignorante no direito", 58–74. On widows as miserable people, see Ana Mafalda Pereira Lopes' chapter in this volume.

52 "devia prejudicar o direito que tem o escravo a sua liberdade por ser esta de inestimável valor, e privilegiada e o seu êxito sumario sem a demora o que se dirigiam os ditos embargos tudo em ódio do miserável buscando o remédio as vexações e rigorosidades com que pela agravante é tratado, que bastava esta circunstância para ser admitido a dar o seu valor", APESP, Autos Cíveis, C03577, auto 2502, fol. 31r. Translated by the author.

could buy his manumission. Secondly, it also highlighted the fact that *Dona* Isabel had already agreed to sell Manoel at the price of 200,000 *réis*. The *ouvidor* considered the fact that the owner claimed that the slave could pay 200,000 *réis* as clear proof of her willingness to sell his manumission. According to the *ouvidor*, freedom was something priceless and the slave had the right to self-purchase his freedom. Furthermore, despite the master's rights as a landlord, justice was established as the legitimate arena in which a fair valuation of the slave could be determined and litigated in the courts.

This kind of argumentation and outcome inspired other lawsuits judged later on. Arguing the same, but using different evidence and strategies, the enslaved Esperança addressed herself to the *Ouvidoria*, as described below.

3.2 The Willingness to Sell using a Private Note in a Moment of Financial Crisis

Taking advantage of a moment of financial crisis for her master Antônio Fernandes Nunes, in 1773 Esperança went to the *Ouvidoria-Geral* of the city of São Paulo with a note from her master. This note sent to Lourenço dos Reis read:

> As for the private matter that Your Grace spoke to me about, I tell you that I have no intention of selling the girl Esperança; however, since Your Grace is pointing me in the direction of buying her, I say that nothing less than 16 *doblas*[53] will do, as there is no lack of people who would be willing to give me this amount.[54]

The enslaved woman claimed she should be evaluated in court so that she could buy her freedom, since her master had "opened the price", as was proved by the attached note and, as someone had given her "alms" to pay for the "fair value for her freedom and manumission", her master should be "obliged" to receive the amount determined by the evaluation of that court. She argued that she had fled her master's house the day before she submitted the petition for "fear" of punishment, and since she could not leave the house without a court order, she asked the *ouvidor* to appoint a depositary, suggesting the name of De Campos or Francisco Coelho Aires.[55] *Ouvidor* José Gomes Pinto de

53 *Doblas* was an amount of money equivalent to 12,800 *réis*.

54 "No que respeita ao particular que vossa mercê me falou, nesta lhe digo que não tenho [in]tenção de vender a rapariga Esperança; porem visto a vossa mercê me apontar compra, digo que semederem dezesseis doblas menos nada, que não falta quem as queira dar", APESP, Autos Cíveis, C03416, auto 3317, fol. 3r. Translated by the author.

55 APESP, Autos Cíveis, C03416, auto 3317, fol. 3r.

Morais agreed with the request, instituting Aires as depositary and preparing an evaluation report. Even though De Campos had been working as the attorney of enslaved people in the city of São Paulo since 1720, he was not appointed to this case. Therefore, both the attorney and Esperança knew exactly who they had indicated a preference for. In addition, it is worth mentioning that De Campos was the attorney of *Dona* Isabel in the case mentioned above.

Esperança was evaluated by João Dias Cerqueira and Bernadinho de Sena at the amount of 150,000 *réis*. According to the evaluation, she was a "white *mulatto* woman", was single, 20 years old or a few years older, and knew how to sew, lace and perform other household services, but, despite all this, had a *Papo*.[56]

Well guided by her attorney João de Sampaio Peixoto, Esperança did not request for her master to be cited in the first petition of the lawsuit that would later be called a civil case of notification of freedom (*auto civil de notificação de liberdade*). It seems that the enslaved woman wanted to ensure she would be evaluated and judicially deposited first, which she succeeded in doing. In these kinds of lawsuits, enslaved people would appear in court with an attorney, and Esperança did not ask for a *curador* to be set up, probably because she could afford to pay for an attorney. It is worth mentioning that Esperança's attorney was the slave's *curador* in the previous case.

After being judicially deposited, which means she was placed under the protection of her depositary,[57] and after being evaluated, a few days later, the enslaved woman strategically delivered another petition requesting Nunes, her master, to be cited to receive the amount of 150,000 réis, which would be deposited by her judicially, and to write her a letter of manumission.[58] The *ouvidor* granted this, requesting, however, the master be summoned to appear in court if he wanted.[59] The issue was resolved quickly. João de Sampaio Peixoto had at least the experience from the previous case and he knew that the argument of "opening the price" was possible and could force an evaluation in court.

Nunes made the decision not to directly defend himself in the *Ouvidoria* and instead petitioned the Governor. In his petition, the master claimed that

---

56 *Papo* was the common name for *bócio/bronchocele*, a tumour that grew in the throat area. Bluteau, *Vocabulario portuguez e latino*, vol. 10, pt. 2, 138; APESP, Autos Cíveis, C03416, auto 3317, fol. 3v.

57 The legal deposit was a proceeding to place a property or chattel which was being litigated under the custody of someone, a depository. Pereira e Sousa, *Esboço de hum diccionario juridico, theoretico, e practico, remissivo ás leis compiladas, e extravagantes*, lib. I.

58 APESP, Autos Cíveis C03416, auto 3317, fol. 2r.

59 APESP, Autos Cíveis C03416, auto 3317, fol. 2r.

"without malice" he had communicated the price that Dos Reis could pay for the slave, which he would have done because he was full of debts, with six pledges that needed payment. Esperança had then taken the note and taken shelter in the house of Aires (who was later appointed as her depositary) and was evaluated by the court at an amount below what he, the master, would have asked for. He stressed he did not doubt she could buy her freedom, as long as she paid the amount he asked for, without the need for another evaluation as the judge had requested. He then requested the amount of 16 *doblas* (204,800 *réis*) to be judged as the correct and fair amount, or that the enslaved woman be returned.[60] As evident, in this case, the master agreed with the purchase but again disputed the price. The owner decided to go to the Governor as a matter of economy since his intervention would be quicker and less costly. The creditors were already at the door, and Nunes, who was facing attachment proceedings, wanted to receive the highest possible amount for his property.

The Governor of the captaincy of São Paulo agreed that the *ouvidor* should inform him about the case. In a mixture of explanation and information, the *ouvidor* replied that his decision was based on the practice "in favour of freedom". He affirmed that common practice was "that when the master of a slave has opened the price", "the slave may request the courts to have her appraised, and deposit her appraisal", and since the master confessed "that he has opened the price", he saw justice in her being appraised and deposited. In addition, he pointed out that he would have determined the master to be summoned to a hearing to learn about the whole situation and to take advice or "request any right".[61] In other words, the practice of self-purchasing when the master was interested in selling was endorsed by the *ouvidor* as something recurrent.

The Governor, Dom Luís Antônio de Sousa Botelho Mourão, was also called to mediate a conflict between the enslaved person and her master, determining that the master should be heard in the evaluation. The mentioned Governor, also known as Morgado de Matheus, was appointed by the Crown when the captaincy of São Paulo regained its autonomy in 1765. From 1711 until 1765 São Paulo was governed by the captaincy of Rio de Janeiro.

Having the Governor's order in hand, Nunes addressed himself to *Ouvidoria* to verify the notification of Esperança.[62] However, after a few hearings to pre-

60 APESP, Autos Cíveis, C03416, auto 3317, fols. 8r–8v.

61 "em favor da liberdade", "que quando o senhor de alguma escrava lhe abre preço" pode "o dito escravo requerer as justiças que a mandem avaliar, depositar a sua avaliação", APESP, Autos Cíveis C03416, auto 3317, fol. 9r. Translated by the author.

62 APESP, Autos Cíveis, C03416, auto 3317, fol. 10v.

sent the arguments of the parties, Nunes wrote again to the Governor claiming he could not respond to the lawsuit because he was "poor" and "owed many". He also claimed he had made the paper for the "sale" of the slave and not for her release. The Governor then allowed the enslaved woman to pay 200,000 *réis* at once, an amount he had offered in another situation.[63]

With the dispatch, Nunes went to the *ouvidor*, who established that Esperança should pay in cash the amount determined by the governing act.[64] As we can see, two judicial paths – ordinary justice and governing justice – could be related. But it was not only the master who used this expertise. A few days after the master had his order issued by the Governor, Esperança sent a long petition again defending that Nunes had "opened the price" and the court had followed "with all the more solemnities in law required". The enslaved person went on saying "there was neither law nor right" that allowed her to pay "a higher price" than "her fair value" and that to determine otherwise was to go "against good reason and equity for which reason it seems that the said respectable order of Your Excellency".[65] Finally, the petition stressed that Esperança was a "miserable person" who suffered from a neck tumour, which did not justify the high amount requested.[66]

It is noticeable that the enslaved woman had the support of some people who mobilised to help her. One of them was her godmother, the wife of the depositary appointed as such by the *ouvidor*. This was the reason Esperança suggested Aires as her depositary and she had been sheltered in their house since the first petition. In fact, the alms of 150,000 *réis* to buy her freedom were given to her by her godmother.

The Governor ordered a new evaluation[67] and this decision changed the lawsuit. These overlapping jurisdictions were also a result of the dynamics of the relationships of those involved in the case, which was not particular to this lawsuit. The *ouvidor* again tried to follow the Governor's orders. He appointed a *curador* for the slave. The Governor ordered that the depositary should also be the *curador*, Aires.

The *ouvidor* asked the parties to present who they would indicate as evaluators, each of whom could indicate one person. A few weeks later, Esperança's attorney embargoed the new evaluation. He defended the nullity that was

---

63 APESP, Autos Cíveis, C03416, auto 3317, fol. 20r.

64 APESP, Autos Cíveis, C03416, auto 3317, fol. 21r.

65 "aberto preço", "com todas as mais solenidades em direito requeridas", "lei nem direito", "contra a boa razão e equidade por cuja causa parece que aquele dito respeitável despacho de Vossa Excelência", APESP, Autos Cíveis, C03416, auto 3317, fol. 22r. Translated by the author.

66 APESP, Autos Cíveis, C03416, auto 3317, fol. 23r. Translated by the author.

67 APESP, Autos Cíveis, C03416, auto 3317, fol. 21r.

processed with the "intervention of the dispatches" since it ended up harming all the "good order of the lawsuit" and the intervention of a person who did not have the same "jurisdiction".[68] I believe, however, that it seems possible to suggest that the change in strategy was a result of the assurance that Esperança and her attorneys could win their case; either because the master did not have the money to pay for the lawsuit and/or it was "what was practiced" in similar situations. The first decision by the *ouvidor* endorsed the practice. Esperança did in fact have a note that evidenced the owner's willingness to sell her.

On 30 January 1776, the parties requested a *Termo de amigável* (terms of amicable composition). Nunes said that he had received from the enslaved woman 14 *doblas*, which was the equivalent of 179,200 *réis*. After the oath of amicable terms, the judge decided that the parties should divide the amount of the lawsuit costs.[69] Letters could serve as strong evidence for requesting an evaluation. In Spanish America, *Papel de venta* (a selling's paper, written by the owner attesting the willingness to sell the slave) was a common practice, whereas in São Paulo it was common to find private letters or notes.[70] As has been presented in this case, a private note was used by the enslaved woman to initiate her lawsuit against her master in court.

3.3 The Willingness to Sell is Proved by the Master's Inventory and Promises

In another lawsuit, the enslaved Pedro decided to claim the right to self-purchase through the courts, taking advantage of the death of his owner. On 2 August 1792, he presented a petition and a civil libel (*libelo civil*) to the *Juízo ordinário* of the city of São Paulo requesting that Maria Cardosa de Gusmão, the daughter of his recently deceased owner, be served to answer his civil libel in which he claimed his freedom. Manoel Eufrásio de Azevedo, Pedro's attorney, was very well acquainted with how to use lawsuits to change one's legal status, as he had been involved in at least ten lawsuits for freedom during

68 APESP, Autos Cíveis, C03416, auto 3317, fols. 30v–32r. The attorney quoted a short sentence from chapter II, Regimento dos Governadores das armas (…), § 11: "Mando que daqui em diante se não intrometam os Generais nem Governadores por qualquer via nas matérias tocantes a minha fazenda Real, como são Alfandegas, Portos Secos bens do concelho e outros feitos semelhantes que em tribunais separados donde tocam deles se conhece"; Ferreira, *Pratica criminal*, 450.

69 *Termo de amigável* (legal settlement) and sentence: APESP, Autos Cíveis, C03416, auto 3317, fols. 45v–47v.

70 Undurraga, *Esclavos y esclavas demandando justicia*; Premo, *The Enlightenment on Trial*; Fuente and Gross, *Becoming Free, Becoming Black*.

the 18th century.[71] The power of attorney was given on 14 June 1792 and it is important to mention that the venia license (*licença de venia*), or license, was a document that allowed the enslaved person to bring his owner to court. In this case, the enslaved Pedro had a proxy with power of attorney issued in the *Juízo ordinário*. While it is challenging to explain or comprehend what happened during this period, it is noteworthy that the first petition was only filed two months after De Azevedo was instituted as his attorney. This was not a common practice in the cases analysed here. Typically, a petition would be filed within two or three days of the power of attorney being given.

The libel (*libelo*) was a document in which the arguments had to be presented clearly and organised into items. So, in civil libel lawsuits (*ação civil de libelo*), after the libel was presented, the judge requested the defendant to reply. According to pragmatic normative literature,[72] the judge had to schedule two hearings for the defendant's defence, allowing the defendant a ten-day period to respond. Documents could be attached to the libels to substantiate the claims. Before countering the libel, the defendant had the option to request an oath of calumny and to post bail. When responding to the libel, the parties had the option to provide declarations addressing the individual articles point by point, through denial, or a combination of both. Following the procedure, the enslaved person and the attorney presented the petition and the libel to be opposed at the same time and took the oath of libel.[73]

The argument in the first libel was direct. Pedro was the enslaved man of the deceased couple, the parents of the defendant. Since he had been valued at seven *doblas* (totaling 89,600 *réis*) in the couple's inventory, he wanted to pay this amount for his freedom. Maria Cardosa's (mother) husband had died a few years before her, and Pedro was left to Maria Cardosa, her daughter. The mother and daughter had the same name. Considering that he had been in "laborious captivity and total subjection" since his childhood and that he had always served with fidelity and "as a good slave", his lawyer argued that Pedro could buy his manumission now that he possessed the full amount of his worth in money. He also pointed out that seven years before the lawsuit started, the

71 APESP, Autos Cíveis, C03650, auto 3532, fols. 4r–5r.

72 Duve and Danwerth (eds.), *Knowledge of the Pragmatici*.

73 Under the *Ordenações Filipinas*, the oath of calumny was to be taken by both plaintiff and defendant to prove that the action was not malicious, Almeida, *Ordenações Filipinas*, lib. 3, tit. 39. The *libelo* was a document in which the party presented in the form of items what it was requesting before the court. It had to be clear and present the reasons for the action and who should respond. Gomes, *Manual practico judicial, civel e criminal*; Cabral, *Pratica judicial, muyto util, e necessaria para os que principiaõ os officios de julgar, e advogar e para todos os que solicõ causas nos auditorios de um, e outro foro*, 12, 17–18.

enslaved Pedro had managed to gather the amount of five *doblas*, of which the deceased masters were aware, and that he had only been unable to buy his freedom because he was two *doblas* short. Finally, he noted that the enslaved man was "very tired and crippled" and could no longer "fulfil exactly the obligations of a laborious captivity and incessant service". However, he claimed that since his owner did not want to resolve the question of the self-purchase of freedom without a "judicial dispute", he asked for a resolution using a civil lawsuit. The owner had to be summoned to court and forced to accept the amount of the seven *doblas* and to give the letter of freedom since she had "opened the price".[74]

The narrative and rhetoric that the attorney constructed for the defence of the slave's freedom evoked categories of what was expected of a "good slave", going through the possibility that a master might be forced to sell the manumission when the price was opened, since freedom was invaluable and that, at some point, the master would have had such a desire.

When served to answer the libel, the defendant Maria Cardosa had difficulties finding a lawyer. She presented a petition to the judge requesting he order someone to be her attorney, and mentioned, more specifically, the name of Joaquim José de Sampaio Peixoto, who had accepted the role, but, with no explanation, had given up on the case. She asked that for "mercy's sake", considering she was a "poor orphan by father and mother", the judge appoint Joaquim José de Sampaio Peixoto to accept his role as her attorney in the case.[75]

Joaquim José de Sampaio Peixoto was at this time a *solicitador de causas*, which meant he was just at the beginning of his training to become a lawyer. Therefore, he did not hold a degree in Law. However, he was the relative of João de Sampaio Peixoto, the attorney of the enslaved person from Esperança's case. Although there is no specific study on the lawyers in São Paulo, it is not wrong to argue that a network of attorneys was in place.[76] Therefore, Joaquim José de Sampaio Peixoto had experience in lawsuits for freedom. From procedural practice, I observed that *solicitadores de causas* were involved in the bureaucratic procedures of presenting petitions and evidence at hearings. For instance, *solicitadores de causas* did not always sign the libel. Possibly, Joaquim José de Sampaio Peixoto was completing an apprenticeship. In this case,

74 "trabalhoso cativeiro e total sujeição", "como bom escravo", "muito cansado e estropiado", "cumprir exatamente com as obrigações de um laborioso cativeiro e incessante serviço", "contenda judicial", "aberto o preço". The term "open price" was first quoted in this case in the second libel filed by the defence. APESP, Autos Civeis, C03650, auto 3532, fol. 17r.

75 APESP, Autos Cíveis, C03650, auto 3532, fol. 6r.

76 Antunes, *Espelho de cem faces*.

however, he was responsible for arguing. This was the reason why the owner insisted he become her representative. I believe she knew he had extensive legal knowledge since he had acted as a lawyer in other lawsuits during the same period. Up to this very moment, I could not find a clear reason as to why he at first refused to represent her.

The judge ordered Joaquim José de Sampaio Peixoto to be the attorney in the case, and he answered the slave's libel by reaffirming that the defendant was a "miserable orphan". He pointed out that the slave "had been running away" and should return home to serve and be in the "power" of Maria Cardosa. According to him, the slave would have three days to deal with his lawsuit for freedom. The attorney also requested proof that the enslaved person possessed the amount to pay for bail or was able to appoint a guarantor.

The strategy of asking for bail was a means of stalling the case that often worked, and bail requests were relatively common. The judge ordered the slave to return to the owner's "domain" but did not accept the request for bail. After a few months, Maria Cardosa requested a hearing and presented her response to the slave's libel. It was simple and straightforward: she denied all the items in the first libel and asked for the posting of evidence on time. It is not very clear where Pedro was during the action, there is no information about whether he returned to the master's house or stayed in public jail.

Pedro presented four witnesses, all of whom were free people. The testimonies revealed interesting points of the story. All of them claimed that Pedro had worked and collected money for a long time to buy his freedom. They all affirmed that he was a good slave and served with fidelity. Joana Barbosa de Lima, the wife of Maria Cardosa's deceased brother, claimed that Pedro had gained from the masters "all the facility" to earn and work on Holy Days and Sundays. She stressed, however, that she knew the couple had never wanted to receive the amount offered by Pedro. Jeronimo Nogueira said he knew the slave wanted to pay the amount for himself because he had sometimes asked him to talk to the deceased couple about his freedom. He also claimed the couple wanted to sell his freedom for 12 *doblas*, but Pedro only had eight *doblas* at the time.[77] All of the witnesses were unanimous in confirming that it was "public" that the enslaved person had been valued by the inventory. However, they were not unanimous about the amount reported. Some claimed it was seven *doblas*, while others defended that it was seven and a half *doblas*. Only one witness claimed that "mistreatment" was the reason why Pedro wanted to buy his freedom.[78]

77 APESP, Autos Cíveis, C03650, auto 3532, fols. 12r–12v.
78 APESP, Autos Cíveis, C03650, auto 3532, fol. 15v.

After the inquest, Pedro's attorney presented another libel to make the rejoinder. Much of what he claimed is reproduced below before discussing what I understand as normativity creation. The libel reads:

1. Freedom is one of the attributes and predicates of human nature, the most appreciable and esteemed. This is what the *Alvará de lei* of 16 January 1759 declares, conforming to all divine and human rights and the law of all nations, for which reason it has also always been worthy of the greatest favour, as can be seen in another *Alvará* of 16 January 1773, where it is considered that the reasons in favour of liberty are stronger and more important than those that can make captivity just and for this reason the jurisconsult Gaius says in the law 122 ff Dig. reg. Ibi = *Libertas omnibus rebus favorabilior est.*
2. However, it is not only based on that favour of which freedom has been made worthy by all divine and human law that the Plaintiff asks for his freedom from the defendant, his owner, because he does not want the defendant to give him a free gift, nor yet remuneration for said freedom for the many good services that from his childhood to an advanced age he has done for his parents and his spouse, but he wants her to sell him his freedom at a reasonable price, that same freedom that by natural law was granted to him as soon as he appeared among the living.
3. In these skilful and ponderous terms is that the favour of the laws takes place together, because the defendant is not deprived of the profit [it] could have in serving the Plaintiff or in selling him for his fair price, and the Plaintiff keeps his freedom.
4. From here arises the style always practiced that, supposing any slave cannot absolutely oblige their master to sell them their freedom against their will, yet when circumstances occur in which the masters have promised them and have offered them a price, then they are obliged not only to confer upon him his freedom for the price which they stipulate, and in these terms and circumstances there is no doubt that the masters can be bound, obliged and condemned to receive the fair value of the slave for his freedom, as is commonly known, and has been decided in the district court, and in many courts in America.[79]

79 "1° A liberdade é um dos atributos e predicados da natureza humana o mais apreciável, e estimável. Assim o declara o Alvará de lei de 16 de janeiro de 1759 conformando se com todos os direitos divinos e Humanos e lei de todas as Nações, por cujo motivo igualmente foi ela sempre digna do maior favor como se vê do outro Alvará de 16 de janeiro de 1773 onde se pondera serem mais forte e de mais consideração as razões que há a favor da liberdade, do que as que podem fazer justo o cativeiro e por isso diz o jurisconsulto Gaio na lei 122 ff Dig. reg. Jur. Ibi = Libertas omnibus rebus favorabilior

As already mentioned, De Azevedo was well versed in lawsuits involving changing one's legal status. In his rejoinder, he quoted two different *alvarás* and evoked the juridical brocade that freedom was the most "appreciated" and "inestimable" good of mankind, in which, according to him, the laws, the *alvarás* and the divine, civil and natural laws concurred.

In general, before being appealed, the lawsuits had to undergo an evaluation to determine the court to which they would be forwarded. The *Alvará* of 16 January 1759 was produced precisely from a procedural misunderstanding, because if freedom could not be estimated, how could or should the cases centred around it be evaluated? This *Alvará* pertains to a consultation made to the Overseas Council, which was an institution created to solve conflicts and questions from Portugal's seaborne empire in 1642, to inquire about the possibility of evaluation for appeal or interlocutory appeal in lawsuits that judged freedom. In other words, it was published to clarify the doubt about whether, in cases where freedom was the issue, the appeal should be evaluated before going to another jurisdiction or whether it fit the jurisdiction of the *Tribunal da Relação*. In his response, the King mentioned a case in which the Higher Portuguese Court, called *Casa da Suplicação*, consented that the *Tribunal da Relação da Bahia* accepted a lawsuit that had been evaluated for appeal. Therefore, he determined that the cases about freedom could be evaluated to know whether to admit the appeal and the bill of review. Furthermore, the *alvará* clarified that the *Tribunal da Relação* was to be the final instance if the ruling

est. 2° Contudo não é só fundado naquele favor de que se fez digna a liberdade por todos os Direitos divinos e Humanos que o Autor pede a sua liberdade a ré sua senhora, porque ele não pretende que a ré lhe faça doação graciosa, nem ainda remuneratório da dita liberdade pelos muitos e bons serviços que desde a sua infância até uma avançada idade há feito a seus pais e casal mas ele pretende que ela lhe venda por preço razoável a sua liberdade, aquela mesma liberdade que por direito natural lhe competiu logo que apareceu entre os viventes. 3° Nestes hábeis e ponderosos termos é que juntamente tem lugar o favor das leis, porque a ré não fica privada do lucro [que] poderia ter em servisse do Autor ou em o vender pelo seu justo preço, e o Autor fica com a sua liberdade. 4° Daqui tem o estilo sempre praticado que suposto que qualquer escravo não possa absolutamente obrigar a seu senhor a vender lhe a sua liberdade contra sua vontade, contudo quando se dão as circunstâncias dos senhores lhes terem prometido e lhes abrirem preço, então ficam obrigados não só a conferir lhe a liberdade pelo preço que estipularem, se não como ainda também pelo justo preço, que o Escravo mostrar que ele vale, e nestes termos, e circunstâncias não padece a menor dúvida que os senhores podem ser adstrictos, obrigados, e condenados a receberem pela liberdade o justo valor do escravo como é vulgarmente sabido, e se tem decidido na relação do distrito, e em muitos juízos da América", APESP, Autos Cíveis, C03650, auto 3532, fols. 17r–17v. Translated by the author.

was in favor of freedom.[80] In this case, the lawyer only selected parts in which freedom was something that by "nature does not admit estimation".

The second *Alvará*, already well known by the historiography on slavery, dealt with the freedom of enslaved people in Portugal. The *Alvará* from 16 January 1773 determined that children of female enslaved people who were slaves at that time would continue to be slaves. However, the next generation of children born from enslaved mothers would be born free.[81]

The terms used in the items of the libel are the same ones from both *alvarás*. For instance, "the case about freedom, which by its nature does not admit estimation", "worthy freedom", "feelings of humanity and religion" and "divine or human law". Pinheiro showed how freedom suits from enslaved people and brotherhoods in Lisbon began to evoke the privilege of freedom based on the *alvarás* of 1761 and 1773.[82] Luiz Geraldo Silva also demonstrated how these *alvarás* were read by freedmen, raising questions about becoming free in Portuguese America.[83] The norms were read out in public by local officials, mainly so that no one could claim ignorance.[84]

Analysing the terms used, it is possible to argue that the lawyer made a cultural and selective translation, creating a normative attempt to endorse the favour that freedom would have. His reading was selective and reappropriated, as he highlighted the privilege that freedom had. In fact, this notion was, from his conception, already present in the *Digesta of* the Roman jurisconsult Gaius, who stated that "Freedom is the most coveted of all things".[85] The conception that freedom had greater favour was widespread in pragmatic normative literature and was a recurrent topic in legal lawsuits in Iberian normativities.

Another point that deserves attention is the fact that the lawyer established that the requested manumission would not be a "gracious donation" and the owner would not be "deprived of the profit". According to him, Pedro was establishing a "remunerative" agreement for the long service rendered. It would be a purchase, in other words, a purchase in terms of what was considered a "fair

80 *Alvará de 16 de janeiro de 1759*. In Lara, "Legislação sobre escravos africanos na América portuguesa", 337.

81 *Alvará com força de lei de 16 de janeiro de 1773*. In Lara, "Legislação sobre escravos africanos na América portuguesa", 359. See also, Pimentel, *Viagem ao fundo das consciências*.

82 Pinheiro, *Em defesa da liberdade*.

83 Silva, "Esperança de liberdade", 107–149. See also, Pimentel, *Viagem ao fundo das consciências*; Falcon, *A época pombalina*; Silva and Grinberg, "Soil free from slaves", 431–446; Rodrigues, "Escravos, senhores e vida marítima no Atlântico", 145–177.

84 Baltazar and Cardim, "A difusão da legislação régia (1621–1808)", 161–207.

85 Gaius, in *Digest*, lib. 50, tit. 17, fragment 122 – Libertas omnibus rebus favorabilior est. Translated by the author.

price". Freedom was a 'thing' (immaterial) and, as a 'thing', it could be bought. In this negotiation, the enslaved person acted as the buyer and the owner as the seller. The lawsuit aimed to legally empower the enslaved person as a full individual to self-purchase their freedom and, as a result, be recognised as a legally liberated person.

In his somewhat performative speech the lawyer retrieved the argument that it was a "manner always practiced" and presented in many "Courts of America" that slaves could pay for their freedom without the master wanting to sell it. In fact, the practice of buying manumission was a widespread reality in colonial America.[86]

For the lawyer, the fact that Maria Cardosa (mother) had "opened the price" was proven by the disclosure of the enslaved person's worth in money and a promise that she had made when she was still alive. In the first libel, freedom was supported by the argument that the price was set by the amount in the inventory. At this point, the promise of the deceased owner was also retrieved as an argument. The promise indeed provided a fundamental weight in legal trials and was a topic present in the 1800s as pointed out in the graph earlier in this chapter.[87] Speeches, comments and conversations could be interpreted and taken to the courts as promises. The promise was linked to the enunciation of the wishes of the owners. In this sense, the master's intentions, when perceived and proven by his actions, opened an important breach enabling one to question his authority. It seems to me that the reasoning was to prove that the master, at some point, had the willingness to sell the manumission.

The judicial ways of proving the "opened price" argument were the most diverse. In this case, according to the lawyer, Pedro's price was opened long before his deceased owner died, because she said she would sell his freedom for 12 *doblas*, as witnesses claimed. The public and notorious hearsay and the knowledge by hearing could substantiate the expression of this desire when taken to court.

At this point, the lawyer pointed out that one witness testified she had been the "mediator" of the possible sale of the manumission by the deceased Maria Cardosa as she had engaged in conversations with her on Pedro´s behalf. Based on Agostinho Barbosa´s argument about the weight of witnesses in legal procedures, the lawyer argued that this witness should be considered "full proof" of

86 "Estilo sempre praticado", "tribunais da Americas". Translated by the author. Meriño Fuentes and Perera Díaz, *Estrategias de libertad*; Premo, *The Enlightenment on Trial*; Fuente and Gross, *Becoming Free, Becoming Black*, 19–20, 49–50, 60–61; Helg, *!Nunca Más esclavos!*.

87 Oliveira, *Cultura jurídica da liberdade*.

the owner's desire to sell.[88] Finally, he argued that there was no sense or reason for the enslaved man to have worked so hard on Holy Days to gather the money if the promise to sell his freedom made by the deceased was not real. In other words, the rhetoric was simple: it made no sense for a Pedro to work and gather money with no hope of freedom on the horizon. The lawyer ended his defence by saying that it should be considered the "maxim" that Pedro had worked and served the deceased owner as a "good slave" with "fidelity" since his childhood. All the favour of the laws and the "right" in favour of freedom should therefore be considered, which Pedro was seeking "without prejudice" from Maria Cardosa (the daughter), and she should be "obligated" to receive his payment.[89]

As has been argued, attorney De Azevedo used various topics to legitimise the right of self-purchase and that the owner should be forced to receive the specified amount. The predisposition of the deceased owner to give Pedro his freedom, added to the privilege of freedom, was proof enough for this lawsuit.

The owner's attorney presented their arguments. He postulated that the daughter had the full master's authority and, no matter how much the slave begged, no law from the *ius commune* or local law could force her to free him "against her will".[90] According to him, since the Roman Emperor Antoninus Pius, it was only possible for the master to be forced to sell slaves who were treated "cruelly".[91] Still, according to the lawyer, the *Ordenações Filipinas* also stressed that the argument "in favour of freedom" did not fit the case, according to his interpretation of what was written in Book 4, Title 11, Paragraph 4, as it referred to Moorish captives, not enslaved Africans.[92]

To this end, he argued that if freedom was an "act" that "depends on the mere whim, consent and will of the master", because the master himself had dominion over the slave, he could not be forced to sell or free him against his will, and it did not matter if the parents had promised freedom.[93] Thus, he

88 He references Almeida, *Ordenações Filipinas*, lib. 3, tit. 54 and quotes verbatim from the commentary in Barbosa, *Collectanea doctorum tam veterum, quam recentiorum, qui super*, De testibus, & attestation, no. 26, 491.

89 APESP, Autos Cíveis, C03650 auto 3532, fols. 19r–19v.

90 "por mais que o autor implora[sse] a favor da liberdade não há de assinar lei alguma de direito comum ou pátrio pelo qual a ré contra a sua vontade seja obrigada a libertar", APESP, Autos Cíveis, C03650, auto 3532, fol. 21r. Translated by the author.

91 *Institutas do Imperador Justiniano*, lib. 1, tit. 8 – His qui sui vel alieni juris sunt. Excerpt mentioned: Ideoque cognosce de querelis eorum, qui ex família Juli Sabini ad statuam consungerunt; & sivel duris hábitos, quam aequum est, vel infami injuria affectos esse congnoveris, venire jube, ita ut in potestatem domini non revertantur. APESP, Autos Cíveis, C03650, auto 3532, fol. 21r. I use the translation by Bini, 2001.

92 Almeida, *Ordenações Filipinas*, lib. 4, tit. 11, § 4.

93 "depende do mero arbítrio, consentimento, e vontade do senhor", APESP, Autos Cíveis, C03650, auto 3532, fol. 22v.

considered that the change of master did not entail the fulfilment of promises that the previous one may have made.

According to the lawyer, the slave was property and part of the "general denomination of the class of goods of livestock" and since there was "no law that deprives the owner of the domain of the goods that they have as a member of the State", the master could not be forced to dispose of their property.[94] He claimed that if the son could not emancipate himself against his father's will, the slave could not force his master to "involuntarily" grant him his freedom, which would be provided for in the Institutes and Justinian's Codex. Still, he continued, no type of judicial action in civil law gave information on father and son and master and slave.[95]

Therefore, the defendant, having come into "possession and dominion" of Pedro, would have acquired all rights over him. He also pointed out that Pedro's money would, by common law (*direito comum*), belong to his mistress, since "everything he [the slave] acquires belongs to his master".[96] The way in which Joaquim José de Sampaio Peixoto recovered the common law to legitimise the lordly authority makes it possible to observe how the conceptions that the Crown should not and could not touch the power of the *pater familias* was the basis of colonial slavery. If, on the one hand, the enslaved person wanted this judicial intervention, the owner defended that such intervention could only occur in cases of violence. In the absence of any homeland normativity on the issue, the *ius commune* was mobilised as an important source to legitimise authority, even at a time when it sought to limit the application and interpretation of the law to the homeland.

Judge José Arouche de Toledo ruled that the case was based on two facts: the fact that the owner had "opened the price" when the slave was evaluated by the couple's inventory and the fact of the deceased couple's permissiveness that the enslaved man could buy his freedom. For the judge, Pedro had not

94 "denominação geral a classe dos bens semoventes", "lei alguma que prive ao proprietário do domínio dos bens que elas lhes facultam como membro do Estado", APESP, Autos Cíveis, C03650, auto 3532, fol. 21v.

95 He refers to the following texts: Institutas, lib. 1, tit. 12 – De Quibus modis jus patriae potestatis solvitur. *Institutas do Imperador Justiniano*, Trad. e notas de Bini, 2001, Codex of Justinian, lib. 7, tit. 1; and *Digest*, lib. 35, tit. 1, fragment 92; APESP, Autos Cíveis C03650 auto 3532, fol. 22r.

96 Justinian's Institutes, lib. 2, tit. IX – By means of which persons we can acquire, 3° We also acquire that which is obtained through tradition by our slaves, whether they do so by stipulation or for any other cause (...). *Institutas do Imperador Justiniano*, Trad. e notas de Bini, 2001; APESP, Autos Cíveis, C03650, auto 3532, fol. 23r.

proven "there was some contract by which himself and his heirs were bound to manumit him" and, without this, such an obligation could not be passed on to the heiress.[97] The "general rule" of *Ordenações Filipinas*, Book 4, Title 11 had to be observed, "which absolutely inhibits that anyone can be forced to sell his inheritance or property in which slaves are included under the name of chattels".[98] To the judge, it was inadmissible that an enslaved person could force a master to sell his freedom. In this case, the judge considered the need for a contract obligating it.

Also, according to the judge, it was not possible to apply to the circumstances the limitation provided in paragraph 6 of that same title, which stated that "in favour of liberty many things are granted against the general rules", since it "limited" the Moorish slaves and their right to ransom themselves.[99] With that, he acquitted the defendant and condemned Pedro to continue in slavery.

While reading the lawsuit, it is interesting to notice that the judge engaged directly with allegations through his marginal notes. In the libel where the Pedro's attorney mentioned the *alvarás* of freedom for the children of enslaved people in Portugal and Algarve, the judge wrote on the side that "this *Alvará* is not for our case".[100] When the Pedro's attorney claimed that there were "laws in favour of freedom", the judge questioned this, adding "where are these laws?"[101] When the same lawyer insisted that one of the witnesses had proved the promise of manumission, the judge wrote "and not for this should the defendant be compelled to forbear."[102]

The judge in question was an important character in the history of São Paulo. He was a Coimbra-trained judge just after Pombal's university reform, and his interpretation of this case was based on what the *Ordenações Filipinas* stated. He worked as a judge's assistant in the ordinary court of the city of São Paulo and as a lawyer.[103] He was a literate man with extensive knowledge, if we consider that some ordinary judges had no training, and it might be possible to argue that his decision could have been impacted by the Enlightenment when he tried to impose the applicability of the Portuguese law on to this particular case.

97 APESP, Autos Cíveis, C03650, auto 3532, fol. 24r.
98 APESP, Autos Cíveis, C03650, auto 3532, fol. 24v.
99 APESP, Autos Cíveis, C03650, auto 3532, fol. 24v.
100 APESP, Autos Cíveis, C03650, auto 3532, fol. 17r. Translated by the author.
101 APESP, Autos Cíveis, C03650, auto 3532, fol. 17v.
102 APESP, Autos Cíveis, C03650, auto 3532, fol. 18v.
103 He was assessor to the judge Alferes José da Cunha de Abreu between 1785 and 1786.

Pedro was held in the public jail to be delivered to his owner. He appealed to the *Ouvidoria* of São Paulo. The fact that Pedro was in prison certainly made things difficult for him; his lawyers began to withdraw from the case, claiming that they had no information.[104] After more than six months in prison, in June 1794, a petition was delivered by him claiming that he was out of money to pay the attorneys and asking that the proceedings be concluded. The *ouvidor* ruled that the case was well sentenced in the first instance. Thus, Pedro should return to the domain of his owner and pay the costs of the lawsuit. This sentence was issued in November 1794. In May 1795, Pedro delivered a new petition requesting the commendation (evaluation) and citation of Maria Cardosa because he was appealing to the *Tribunal da Relação* of Rio de Janeiro. The case was evaluated at 35,000 *réis*. Although Pedro was well informed, had some support for his argument regarding the fair amount concerning his worth in money and went to great lengths to mobilise all means possible to compel his owner to accept the payment for his self-purchase and grant him his freedom, a year later, on 31 May 1796, there was an agreement on the case that described it as being considered deserted (*deserta*) at the request of the owner.[105]

In this chapter, I argued that, from the beginning of the second half of the 18th century, the possibility of self-purchasing appears to have increased in São Paulo. The lawsuits of individuals in various judicial instances further established the norm that an enslaved person could compel the owner to sell their freedom through the judicial system because freedom had favour in law. This notion received various reactions from different perspectives. Of the seven freedom suits that used the argument that the owner had "opened the price" in São Paulo, in three of them the master was compelled to sell the enslaved person's freedom; in three further cases I could not determine the outcome and in one case the petitioner remained enslaved.

4 Conclusions

Esperança, Pedro and Manoel, along with many others, initiated legal proceedings in an effort to compel their masters to recognise the amount determined by the courts for their manumission. In a deeply unequal and violent society, challenging the authority of masters was only possible when it had been

104 First, Manoel Eufrásio de Azevedo and then João Moreira da Rocha.

105 APESP, Autos Cíveis, C03433, auto 3547.

weakened in some way. These enslaved people knew how to seize opportunities during moments of crisis or changes in ownership to apply pressure for their possibility to self-purchase.

The courts were spaces where lawyers and enslaved people created the "opened the price" argument based on the willingness of masters to sell their property. Through the use of letters, appraisals in inventories or promises, masters were brought into the public sphere. The "opened the price" argument was a legally constructed one that encompassed numerous possibilities, based on different evidence concerning the master's willingness to sell. The normativities were created when enslaved people, attorneys and masters alike resorted to the extensive framework of the *ius commune* to assert their own interpretations and arguments. Breaking away from the authority of the *pater familias* was no easy feat, even though pragmatic normative literature favoured freedom. Selective interpretation of norms allowed the creation of local rights that gained legitimacy with the authorities. The endeavour to broaden the concepts of fairness within the various dynamics of slave relationships was a daily occurrence in the courts. Law, as a social practice, was somewhat permeable in accommodating diverse interpretations and disputes. It is not new in historiography to recognise that judicial courts served as an arena of conflict. However, what must be understood is how the actions of these individuals who experienced slavery influenced the formation and changing of norms concerning freedom and enslavement, opening possibilities to use law to change their statuses.

In this context, the possibility of an enslaved person to self-purchase using the "opened the price" argument was a conceptual creation driven by the action of enslaved people. It was constructed through the active involvement of these individuals. Through their representatives, they utilised legal concepts to demonstrate their ability to secure their freedom. The willingness of slave owners played a crucial role in determining the right to freedom, and it was through legal proceedings that the enslaved individuals were able to establish this intention, employing speeches, promises, evaluations or documents that might not have originally been intended to be used to secure their freedom. In the absence of regulations regarding the right to manumission, enslaved people and their representatives created norms that opened up opportunities and challenged the authority of their masters, altering their daily lives. While they could not completely overhaul the system, the analysis of these freedom suits demonstrates that legal notions, practices and norms were influenced and established through the participation of the enslaved people who fought for legal change, despite it being an individual freedom.

Acknowledgements

This research was supported by a Foundation for Science and Technology (FCT) scholarship 2021.05777.BD (https://doi.org/10.54499/2021.05777.BD), and the project "RESISTANCE: Rebellion and Resistance in the Iberian Empires, 16th–19thcenturies", funded by the European Union's Horizon 2020 research and innovation Marie Skłodowska-Curie Grant Agreement no. 778076. Special thanks to Professor Rossana Pinheiro-Jones for her invaluable assistance with its translation.

Bibliography

Manuscripts

Arquivo Público do Estado de São Paulo (APESP), Autos Cíveis, Ordem C03416, auto 3317.

Arquivo Público do Estado de São Paulo (APESP), Autos Cíveis, Ordem C03433, auto 3547.

Arquivo Público do Estado de São Paulo (APESP), Autos Cíveis, Ordem C03577, auto 2502.

Arquivo Público do Estado de São Paulo (APESP), Autos Cíveis, Ordem C03650, auto 3532.

Printed Sources

Almeida, Cândido Mendes de, *Ordenações Filipinas*, Rio de Janeiro 1870: Typographia do Instituto Philomathico.

Barbosa, Agostinho, *Collectanea doctorum tam veterum, quam recentiorum, qui super* […], vol. 1, Roma 1626: Ex typografia reverendae câmera apostolicae.

Bluteau, Raphael, *Vocabulario portuguez e latino.* vol. 10, Coimbra 1728: Collegio das Artes da Companhia de Jesus.

Bremeu, Antônio Cortez, *Universo Jurídico ou Jurisprudência Universal, Canônica e Cesárea* […], Lisboa 1749: Na Officina de Domingos Rodrigues.

Cabral, António Vanguerve, *Pratica judicial, muyto util, e necessaria para os que principiaõ os officios de julgar, e advogar e para todos os que solicõ causas nos auditorios de um, e outro foro*, Coimbra 1730: Na Officina de Antonio Simoens Ferreira.

Caminha, Gregório Martins, *Tratado da forma dos libelos*, Coimbra 1764: Oficina dos Irmäos e Sobrinho Ginioux.

Castro, Manuel Mendes de, Prima, et secunda pars Practicae lusitanae advocatis, et judicibus, utroque foro quotidie versantibus admodum utilis, & necessaria: quae que in quinque libros divisa ... : opus celeberrimum ab eodem auctore Archiepiscopo, Ulysipponensi singulari Principi liberalíssimo, Ulysippone 1641: ex Officina Typographi Regii Antonii Alvarez.

Digest of Justitian, lib. 35, tit. 1, fragment 92.

Febo, Melchior, *Decisiones Senatus Regni Lusitaniae*, Lisboa 1619: Tipografia Ferreiriana.

Ferreira, Manoel Lopes, *Pratica criminal expendida na forma da praxe observada neste nosso reyno de portugal, e illustrada com muitas ordenaçõens, leys extravagantes, regimentos, e doutores* [...], Porto 1767: Na officina de Antônio Alves Ribeiro Guimaraens.

Gaius, in *Digest of Justitian*, lib. 50, tit. 17, fragment 122.

Gomes, Alexandre Caetano, *Manual practico judicial, civel e criminal* [...], Lisboa 1748: Na Officina de Miguel Manescal da Costa.

Institutas do Imperador Justiniano, Trad. e notas de Edson Bini, Bauru 2001.

Pereira e Sousa, Joaquim José Caetano. *Esboço de hum diccionario juridico, theoretico, e practico, remissivo ás leis compiladas, e extravagantes*, lib. I, Lisboa 1825: Na Typographia Rollandiana.

Velasco, Tomás. *Allegationum super varias materias: primus tomus*, In ciuitate Portugalensi 1612: ex Officina Fructuosi Laurentij de Basto.

Literature

Almeida, Kátia Lorena Novais, *Escravos e libertos nas minas do Rio de Contas – Bahia, século XVIII* (Ph.D. Thesis), Salvador 2012.

Antunes, Álvaro de Araújo, *Espelho de cem faces: o universo relacional de um advogado setecentista*, São Paulo 2004.

Baltazar, Miguel and Pedro Cardim, "A difusão da legislação régia (1621–1808)", in Fragoso, João and Nuno Gonçalo Monteiro (eds.), *Um reino e suas repúblicas no Atlântico: comunicações políticas entre Portugal, Brasil e Angola nos séculos XVII e XVIII*, Rio de Janeiro 2017, 161–207.

Benton, Lauren and Richard J. Ross (eds.), *Legal Pluralism and Empires, 1500–1850*, New York, NY 2013.

Chalhoub, Sidney, *Visões da liberdade: uma história das últimas décadas da escravidão na corte*, São Paulo 1990.

Coutinho Silva, Luisa Stella de Oliveira, *Nem teúdas, nem manteúdas: História das Mulheres e Direito na capitania da Paraíba (Brasil, 1661–1822)*, Frankfurt am Main 2020 (http://dx.doi.org/10.12946/gplh15).

Cunha, Manuela Carneiro da, "Sobre os silêncios da Lei: lei costumeira e positiva nas alforrias de escravos no Brasil do século XIX", in Cunha, Manuela Carneiro da, *Antropologia do Brasil: mito, história, etnicidade*, São Paulo 1987, 123–144.

Curvelo, Arthur, *Governar Pernambuco e as "capitanias anexas": o perfil de recrutamento, a comunicação política e as jurisdições dos governadores da capitania de Pernambuco (c.1654–c.1756)* (Ph.D. Thesis), Lisboa 2019.

Dias Paes, Mariana Armond, "Sobre origens, continuidades e criações: a posse da liberdade nos decisionistas portugueses (sécs. XVI–XVIII) e no direito da escravidão (séc. XIX)", in Duve, Thomas (coord.), *Actas del XIX congreso del Instituto Internacional de Historia de Derecho Indiano*, vol. 2, Madrid 2017, 1379–1406.

Diório, Renata Romualdo, *As Marcas da Liberdade: trajetórias sociais de libertos em Mariana na segunda metade do século XVIII* (Master Thesis), São Paulo 2007.

Duve, Thomas, "La Condición Jurídica del Indio y Su Consideración como Persona Miserabilis en el Derecho Indiano", in Losano, M. (ed.), *Un giudice e due leggi. Pluralismo normativo e conflitti agrari in Sud America*, Milano 2004, 3–33.

Duve, Thomas, "Global Legal History – A Methodological Approach", in *Max Planck Institute for European Legal History Research Paper Series*, no. 2016–04 (2016), 1–22 (https://ssrn.com/abstract=2781104).

Duve, Thomas, "Pragmatic Normative Literature and the Production of Normative Knowledge in the Early Modern Iberian Empires (16th–17th Centuries)", in Duve, Thomas and Otto Danwerth (eds.), *Knowledge of the Pragmatici: Legal and Moral Theological Literature and the Formation of Early Modern Ibero-America*, Leiden 2020, 1–39.

Duve, Thomas, "Legal History as a History of the Translation of Knowledge of Normativity", in *Max Planck Institute for Legal History and Legal Theory Research Paper Series*, no. 2022–16 (2022), 1–12.

Duve, Thomas and Otto Danwerth (eds.), *Knowledge of the Pragmatici: Legal and Moral Theological Literature and the Formation of Early Modern Ibero-America*, Leiden 2020.

Falcon, Francisco José Calazans, *A época pombalina. Política econômica e monarquia ilustrada*, São Paulo 1982.

Fioravante, Fernanda and Carlos Leonardo Kelmer Mathias, "A liberdade condicionada: senhores, escravos e suas orientações valorativas no contínuo reinventar da escravidão e da liberdade nas terras do ouro no decurso do Setecentos", in Guedes, Roberto, Cláudia Rodrigues and Marcelo da Rocha Wanderley (eds.), *Últimas vontades: testamento, sociedade e cultura na América Ibérica (séculos XVII e XVIII)*, Rio de Janeiro 2015, 151–187.

Fortea Pérez, José Ignacio, Juan E. Gelabert and Tomás Mantecón Movellán (eds.), *Furor et rabies: Violencia, conflicto y marginación en la Edad Moderna*, Santander 2002.

Fuente, Alejandro de la and Ariela J. Gross, *Becoming Free, Becoming Black: Race, Freedom, and Law in Cuba, Virginia, and Louisiana*, Cambridge, MA 2020.

Fuente, Alejandro, de la, "Slaves and the Creation of Legal Rights in Cuba: Coartación and Papel", in *Hispanic American Historical Review* 87, no. 4 (2007), 659–692.

Garriga, Carlos, "Gobierno y Justicia: el Gobierno de la Justicia", in Lorente, Marta (ed.), *Cuadernos de Derecho Constitucional, Consejo General del Poder Judicial. VII*

(*La jurisdicción contenciosa-administrativa en España. Una historia de sus orígenes*), Madrid 2008.

Goldschmidt, Eliana Rea, "Alforrias e propriedade familiar em São Paulo colonial", in *Reunião da Sociedade Brasileira de Pesquisa Histórica* 8 (1989), 31–38.

Goldschmidt, Eliana Rea, "A carta de alforria na conquista da liberdade", in *Ide* 33, no. 50 (2010), 114–125.

Grinberg, Keila, *Liberata: a lei da ambiguidade: as ações de liberdade da Corte de Apelação do Rio de Janeiro, século XIX*, Rio de Janeiro 1994.

Health, Elizabeth A., "The Meaning of Freedom: Slave Self-Purchase and the Making of Free Labour in Martinique", in *French History* 34:3 (2020), 342–359 (https://doi.org/10.1093/fh/craa048).

Helg, Aline, *!Nunca Más esclavos! Una historia comparada de los esclavos que se liberaron en las Américas*, Bogotá 2018.

Hespanha, António Manuel, *Imbecillitas. As bem-aventuranças da inferioridade nas sociedades de Antigo Regime*, São Paulo 2010.

Hespanha, António Manuel, *Como os juristas viam o mundo. 1550–1750. Direitos, estados, pessoas, coisas, contratos, ações e crimes*, Lisboa 2015.

Lara, Silvia Hunold, *Campos da Violência. Escravos e Senhores na Capitania do Rio de Janeiro, 1750–1808*, Rio de Janeiro 1988.

Lara, Silvia Hunold, "Legislação sobre escravos africanos na América portuguesa", in Andrés-Gallego, José (ed.), *Nuevas Aportaciones a la Historia Jurídica de Iberoamérica*, Madrid 2000.

Lara, Silvia Hunold, *Fragmentos Setecentistas: escravidão, cultura e poder na América portuguesa*, São Paulo 2007.

Lima, Priscila, *De libertos a habilitados. Interpretações populares dos alvarás antiescravistas na América portuguesa (1761–1810)* (Master Thesis), Curitiba 201.

Lucena Salmoral, Manuel, "El derecho de coartación del esclavo en la América Española", in *Revista De Indias* 59, no. 216 (1999), 357–374.

Lucena Salmoral, Manuel, *Los Códigos Negros de la América Española*, Alcalá de Henares 2000.

Luna, Francisco Vidal, Iraci Costa and Herbert S. Klein, *Escravismo em São Paulo e Minas Gerais*, São Paulo 2009.

Marcílio, Maria Luiza, *A cidade de São Paulo: povoamento e população, 1750–1850*, São Paulo 1973.

Marquese, Rafael de Bivar, *Feitores do corpo, missionários da mente: senhores, letrados e o controle dos escravos nas Américas, 1660–1860*, São Paulo 2004.

Marquese, Rafael de Bivar, "A dinâmica da escravidão: resistência, tráfico negreiro e alforria, séculos XVII a XIX", in *Novos estudos CEBRAP*, no. 74 (2006), 107–123.

Mattos, Hebe, *Das cores do silêncio: os significados da liberdade no sudeste escravista, Brasil século XIX*, 3rd ed., São Paulo 2013.

McKinley, Michelle, *Fractional Freedoms: Slavery, Intimacy and Legal Mobilization in Colonial Lima 1600–1700*, Cambridge, MA 2016.

Menezes, Jeannie da Silva, *Sem embargo de Ser Femea. As mulheres e um Estatuto Jurídico em Movimento no século XVIII*, São Paulo, 2013.

Meriño Fuentes, María de Los Ángeles and Aisnara Perera Díaz, *Estrategias de libertad: un acercamiento a las acciones legales de los esclavos en Cuba (1762–1872)*, 2 vols., La Habana 2015.

Oliveira, Felipe Garcia de, *Cultura jurídica da liberdade: autos cíveis e petições envolvendo escravos e forros na cidade de São Paulo, século XVIII* (Master Thesis), Guarulhos 2020.

Oliveira, Felipe Garcia de, "A posse da liberdade nas ações cíveis de escravos e libertos na justiça em São Paulo, século XVIII", in *Outros Tempos: Pesquisa Em Foco – História*, 19:33 (2022), 288–318 (https://doi.org/10.18817/ot.v19i33.917).

Oliveira, Felipe Garcia de, "Da Liberdade ao Cativeiro: A Reescescravização nos Autos Cíveis da Cidade de São Paulo (Século XVIII)", in Costa, Wilma Peres, Joana Monteleone, Fernando Victor Aguiar Ribeiro, Fernanda Sposito (org.), *Histórias de São Paulo. Construções e Desconstruções*, vol. 1: Colonial Period, São Paulo 2023, 175–190.

Oliveira, Felipe Garcia de, "Escravos, forros e as estratégias jurídicas em São Paulo (séc. XVIII): pessoa miserável, rústica e ignorante no direito", in Beraldi, Nicolas, María Sol Calandria, and Luis González Alvo (coords.), *Avances y nuevas perspectivas iushistoriográficas: 10 años de las Jornadas de Jóvenes Investigadoras/es en Historia del Derecho, 2009–2019*, vol. 1, San Miguel de Tucumán 2023, 58–74 (https://dialnet.unirioja.es/servlet/libro?codigo=969964).

Oliveira, Felipe Garcia de, "Pardo", in Xavier, Ângela Barreto, Graça Borges, Mafalda Soares da Cunha and Miguel Dantas Cruz (eds.), *Lexicon of Resistance in the Iberian Empires, 1500–1850*, Évora 2023 (https://doi.org/10.60469/73dm-z683).

Paiva, Eduardo França, "Coartações e alforrias nas Minas Gerais do século XVIII: as possibilidades de libertação escrava no principal centro colonial", in *Revista de História*, no. 133 (1995), 49–57.

Pimentel, Maria do Rosário, *Viagem ao fundo das consciências. A escravatura na época moderna*, Lisboa 1995.

Pinheiro, Fernanda Domingos, *Em defesa da liberdade. Libertos, coartados e livres de cor nos tribunais do Antigo Regime Português (Mariana e Lisboa, 1720–1819)*, Belo Horizonte 2018.

Premo, Bianca, *The Enlightenment on Trial. Ordinary Litigants and Colonialism in the Spanish Empire*, New York, NY 2017.

Reis, João José, "Slaves Who Owned Slaves in Nineteenth-Century Bahia, Brazil", in *Mecila Working Papers*, no. 36 (2021), 1–23 (https://mecila.net/wp-content/uploads/2021/05/WP_Joao_Reis_36.pdf).

Rodrigues, Jaime, "Escravos, senhores e vida marítima no Atlântico: Portugal, África e América portuguesa, *c.*1760–*c.*1825", in *Almanack*, no. 5 (2013), 145–177.

Seixas, Margarida, "Escravidão e Favor libertatis no Brasil de oitocentos:Tradição Romanista na obra de Perdigão Malheiro", in *Interpretatio Prudentium: Direito romano e tradição romanista em revista* 1, no. 1 (2016), 181–198.

Seixas, Margarida, *Pessoa e Trabalho no direito português (1750–1878): escravo, liberto e serviçal*, Lisboa 2016.

Silva, Cristina Nogueira da, Keila Grinberg, "Soil free from slaves: slave law in late eighteenth- and early Nineteenth-Century Portugal", in *Slavery & Abolition* 32, no. 3 (2011), 431–446.

Silva, Luiz Geraldo, "Esperança de liberdade: interpretações populares da abolição ilustrada (1773–1774)", in *Revista de História* 144 (2001), 107–149.

Silva Júnior, Waldomiro Lourenço da, *História, direito e escravidão: a legislação escravista no Antigo Regime ibero-americano*, São Paulo 2013.

Souza, Daniele Santos de, "Nos caminhos do cativeiro, na esquina com a liberdade: alforrias, resistência e trajetórias individuais na Bahia setecentista", in Reis Sampaio, Gabriela dos, Lisa Earl Castilho, and Wlamyra Albuquerque (orgs.), *Barganhas e querelas da escravidão: tráfico, alforria e liberdade (séculos XVIII e XIX)*, Salvador 2014, 103–135.

Undurrraga, Carolina González, *Esclavos y esclavas demandando justicia. Chile 1740–1823. Documentación judicial por carta de libertad y papel de venta*, Santiago de Chile 2014.

Vermeesch, Griet, Manon van der Heijden and Jaco Zuijderduijn (eds.), *The Uses of Justice in Global Perspective, 1600–1900*, Abingdon 2019.

Xavier, Ângela B. and António Manuel Hespanha, "A representação da sociedade e do poder", in Hespanha, António Manuel (ed.), *História de Portugal*, vol. 4, Lisboa 1993, 113–140.

CHAPTER 9

Dealing with the Normative Complexity of the Colony

Policey, Legal Change and Paths of New Meanings of Law in the Administration of the Diamond District (1771–1808)

Nathaly Mancilla-Órdenes

1 Introduction

Located where the county of Serro do Frio once was, Minas Gerais, the Diamond District, became the main overseas economic space for the Portuguese Empire during the 18th century. Discovery of the diamonds forced the Portuguese to set up and adapt a judicial, administrative and economic structure in order to obtain the benefits of the resource. Meanwhile, the local circumstances and local practices also needed to be dealt with.

It was no accident that during the period when the Portuguese Crown explored the diamonds in the region (1729–1845), they attempted three distinct systems of administration. Indeed, the task of administering the diamond lands was a relentless challenge for the metropolitan power. Initially, in 1730, a diamond mining regiment similar to the existing gold regulations was implemented, allowing free mining with a "head tax" and designating the Royal Magistrate (*ouvidor*) of Vila do Príncipe as the *Superintendente* of mining activities. However, the need to stabilise diamond prices in the international market and control unauthorised movements prompted significant administrative changes, enhancing control of both the people's circulation and the jurisdiction of mining activities. By 1734, mining was temporarily stopped, and the *Intendência dos Diamantes* was established, replacing the *ouvidor* of Vila do Príncipe as *Intendente*, and the district was formally demarcated within that year.

Between 1740 and 1771, mining was resumed under a system of administration in which the Crown would make a contract with one or more individuals who would then oversee this activity. This regime, however, did not function well according to the Crown's perception. As the sources and historiography show, the problems were many.[1]

1 See, among others, Furtado, *O livro da capa verde*.

© 2026 THE AUTHOR(S) | HTTPS://DOI.ORG/10.1163/9789004764422-010

In sum, the region developed organisational issues that were not being dealt with in the way the central power desired and, to remedy this situation, the Crown implemented the *Real Extração dos Diamantes* (or Royal Extraction) in 1771. This institution would act as a direct hand of the Crown overseas, with the *Intendente* as its head in Brazil functioning alongside a corresponding institution in Portugal. In this way, the *Alvará* of 2 August 1771 established mining as a royal monopoly. But, more importantly, it concentrated even more administrative and judicial powers in the *Intendente dos Diamantes* and the *Real Extração*, some of which had previously been in the hands of the *camêra municipal* or even the governor of captaincy.

In this chapter, I analyse the transformation of law that took place within the Diamond District, from 1771–1808. I specifically concentrate on the complex communicative process triggered by the creation of the *Real Extração dos Diamantes* and how it paved the way for new concepts of law. Furthermore, I demonstrate how colonial law related to this case could be conceptualised as a type of "police" regulation.

Regulation of the administration in the Diamond District has been usually described by Brazilian historiography as a hierarchical imposition of law: from the top (the Portuguese Crown) to the bottom (the local level).[2] Besides this, the tendency to ignore the multiplicity of normative spheres by perceiving the law in the *Ancien Régime* as a phenomenon constricted to the legislative activity of the Crown is still latent.[3] Generally, this reductionist conception of the legal landscape of early modernity results in an underestimation of the impact of social agency in the process of normative production.[4]

---

2 See, for instance, Furtado, *O livro da capa verde*; Furtado, "Relações de Poder no Tejuco"; Furtado, "Distrito Diamantino".

3 For more information on this subject, see Hespanha, *Caleidoscópio do Antigo Regime*. Recently, social historians have started to focus on the relationship between social realities and the statutes (legislation) related to the Diamond Demarcation. For instance, Joelmir Cabral Moreira's study (Moreira, *Legislação régia em terras minerais*) on the administrative systems of the district and their connection with general mining legislation between 1720 and 1771 aims to comprehend the Portuguese Crown's administrative framework in the region, considering the particularities of this social reality. However, this perspective is still insufficient when trying to understand the role of local complexities in the process of normative production during early modernity.

4 On the one hand, some social historians tend to reduce law to a mere political or economic instrument in the colonial process (see Souza, *O sol e a sombra*). On the other hand, even when social historians have the sensibility to recognise that the royal legislation may not have been central in this legal context, they are habituated to evaluate the social efficacy of said legislation in relation to how much of it was enforced or applied. The royal legislation is described then as completely ineffective, disappearing in the face of the network of

Taking a step away from these perspectives, the emphasis here relies on the importance of colonial institutions for legal change during early modernity, seeing this interaction as a constant process of social and cultural construction.[5] The argument here is that the legislation, in this case, can be interpreted as a source that enables us to understand how the Crown observed local complexities and attempted to address them using the best *remedios* available.

Rather than merely being a legal command, royal legislation from this period may be better understood as the outcome of a communicative process involving different normative expectations and social agents.[6] This understanding begins with the acknowledgment that the Iberian Empires were, unquestionably, informational empires.[7] Indeed, the legislation needs to be read alongside other sources that were involved in this communicative process, such as reports and letters, that had an impactful role as a decisive media for configuring "politics"[8] and, as it is possible to observe in the following section, in the normative production of the Portuguese Empire.

2 Colonial law as *Policey*

The expansion of the seaborne Portuguese Empire also meant the spread of the legal tradition that the agents of the Empire carried with them. However, this does not mean that it was a peaceful or even one-way movement. The normative production that this expansion entailed was not only a "westernalization"[9]

---

local powers and interests. See Furtado, *O livro da capa verde*; Furtado, "Relações de Poder no Tejuco", 2.

5 Duve, "Rechtsgeschichte als Geschichte".

6 Hespanha, "Southern Europe"; and also Hespanha, *Filhos da Terra*. For the specific case of police regulations as a complex communicative process that interconnected authorities, groups, institutions and subjects, the work of Karl Härter is fundamental. Härter, "Gesetzgebungsprozess".

7 For decades now, the theme of Empire and communication has been a topic of interest. From many possible examples, Arndt Brendecke's characterisation of the Spanish Empire as an "informational Empire" is synthetic and useful here also for the Portuguese Empire, Brendecke, *Império e Información*. For similar and complementary ideas, see Biedermann, *(Dis) connected Empires*; and Langfur, *Adrift on an Inland Sea*. Also noteworthy is the relevance that Hespanha gave to the subject in the preface of Fragoso and Monteiro (eds.), *Um reino e suas repúblicas no Atlântico*, 9–11.

8 Cardim, "Nem tudo se pode escrever".

9 Pihlajamäki, "The Westernization of Police Regulation".

of law, but also a decentralised process in which colonial institutions and the normativities of the colony had a relevant role.

As pointed out by António Manuel Hespanha, if we analyse the complex flux of this bidirectionality, it is possible to notice that, rather than an imposition from "above", legal transactions took place. They may be described as translations where each part uses the law of the other according to their own cultural models (and interests). In this context, the conditions and models of the political domain needed to be flexible enough according to the social reality that was extremely multifaceted.[10]

In other words, there was no unified colonial legal construction associated with a possible "imperial project".[11] The configuration of law itself during early modernity made this unfeasible. The legal pluralism of the *Ancien Régime*, and the coexistence of various normative spheres, made it impossible for the legislation/statute (*lei*) to be unequivocally applied in the kingdom, much less in the colony.[12] Furthermore, the very structure of some of these normative orders (for example, the *ius commune*) facilitated their localisation.[13]

In this scenario, the various localities and their normative expectations were extremely relevant in terms of creating law if compared to the figure of the prince, who had a primarily jurisdictional function.[14] On the other hand, at a political level, relations were not built radially either: material conditions, distance, communication channels, etc., made establishing decision-making centres a complex task. Rather, what existed were multiple centres connected between themselves and the King.[15]

In this context, to speak of colonial law means not allowing oneself to be enchanted by the mistaken (and anachronistic) idea of the existence of a unified normative body of laws enacted, consistently, by the Crown for its overseas domains – in this case, Portuguese America.[16] However, in most cases of urbanised settlements, the law applied overseas was Portuguese law. In this

---

10 Hespanha, "Uncommon Laws"; Duve, "The School of Salamanca".

11 Hespanha, "The Legal Patchwork of Empires", 305.

12 Hespanha, "Porque é que existe".

13 Agüero, "Las categorías básicas de la cultura jurisdiccional"; Benton, "Colonial Law and Cultural Difference".

14 Grossi, *A ordem jurídica medieval.*

15 The concept of polycentric monarchy is especially useful here; see Cardim et al. (eds.), *Polycentric Monarchies.*

16 See Cabral, "Case Law in Portuguese Decisiones in the Early Modern Age"; and Cabral, *Uma teoria do direito.*

sense, colonial law and European law are inseparable.[17] This situation cannot be confused with colonial law from the 19th century[18] that attends to different political structures from those of the *Ancien Régime*, because it is fundamentally anchored in the national State.[19]

Moving away from these perspectives, it is possible to speak of "colonial law" during early modernity in two senses. Both, albeit in different ways, are connected to the eminently pragmatical nature of law during that period. The first of them refers to the capacity of local normativities (for example, local customs) to fill legal gaps, which is typical of the *ius commune*. This direction, developed by Hespanha in his already classic text "porque é que existe e em que é que consiste um direito colonial brasileiro", emphasises how practices (mainly those occurring at border areas, such as colonies) that are divergent or even contrary to the statutes of the kingdom become nonetheless part of the law.[20]

The second sense refers to the use of *Policey* ordinances as a colonial law. In this case, the emphasis is placed on the use of a legislative tool as a way of coping with the needs of the administration to continuously and quickly adapt itself to a social reality that was considerably unfamiliar to royal officials and that was rapidly changing.[21] Although at first glance they may seem like two ideas that oppose each other, a careful look shows that both are intertwined through their casuistic nature.

In his work *El jurista en el nuevo mundo*, Víctor Tau Anzoátegui underscores the extent to which the diversity of situations influences legal conceptions. Specifically, in his analysis of Juan de Solórzano Pereira's *Política Indiana*, Tau Anzoátegui highlights the role the legislator should play in responding to the diversity that "sprouted from Indian reality".[22] In this context, the "good legislator" must possess the ability to adapt his precepts to the specific "regions

17 Among others, see Hespanha, "Porque é que existe"; Cabral, *Uma teoria do direito*; Camarinhas, "O aparelho judicial ultramarino português".

18 Pihlajamäki et al., "Comparing Early Modern Colonial Laws".

19 For the case of the African colonies from 19th-century Portugal, see Silva, *Constitucionalismo e Império*.

20 Cardim et al. (eds.), *Polycentric Monarchies*; Hespanha, "Porque é que existe"; Hannula et al., "Unpacking Early Modern Colonial Law"; Herzog, "How to Approach Colonial Law".

21 Pihlajamäki, "The Westernization of Police Regulation".

22 Tau Anzoátegui, *El jurista en el nuevo mundo*, 219. Although Tau Anzoátegui analyses how normative variety makes it impossible to create laws with a claim to universality in the context of the so-called *derecho indiano* (understood here casuistically and not as a monolithic body of laws), these remarks are equally applicable to Portuguese America. Regarding this point for Portuguese America, it is important to draw attention to the expression "sem embargo de ordenação em contrário", which was used to characterize exceptional treatment or so that the norm would not be followed in a particular case without affecting

and peoples" they are intended for. This attribute of the legislator is closely associated with the virtue of 'prudence', understood as respect for the inherent nature of things.[23]

In the lines that follow, I want to focus on the argument that colonial law could be conceptualised as a type of "police" regulation.[24] It is obvious that this does not mean that the *Policey* of early modernity had "colonial origins" or even that the term 'police' had a univocal meaning during early modernity. The concept of *Policey* here refers to the wider meaning of the word, which relates to general notions of "good order" or "good order of the city".[25] The relevant point is that the concept of "police" became, especially in the 18th century, one of the main vehicles for conceptualising law as an instrument of change and political steering in different European continental monarchies.[26]

Initially, the main goal of *Policey* was conserving society. However, halfway through the 18th century, the understanding of this concept changed.[27] Not only did the matters under the supervision of the "police" significantly increase, but its essence was no longer conservative: it was directed at changing social conditions. The amplification of tasks and the substantial review of "police" reflected the monarchies' continuous attempts to expand its activities and the struggle to deal with territorial disputes in continental Europe.[28] But, as I argue in the following, it also had to do with the colonial experience of these empires.

First, many of the matters regulated in the colonies were essentially matters that would be framed as police matters (this is valid not only for Portuguese, but also for British and other colonies).[29] Second, awareness of the discussion

---

its validity in the face of all others. Wehling and Wehling, "'Sem embargo da ordenação em contrário'", 40.

23 Tau Anzoátegui, *El jurista en el nuevo mundo*, 220.

24 Pihlajamäki, "The Westernization". See also Pihlajamäki et al., "Comparing Early Modern Colonial Laws".

25 Nitschke, "Von der Politeia zur Polizei"; Iseli, *Bonne Police*, 14–15; Knemeyer, "Polizei".

26 See Simon, *Gute Policey*, 546–562. It must be made clear that the concept of "Policey" was already present, but the point here concerns the structural transformations that occurred in the 18th century.

27 In the context of a corporative society, the concept of police was strongly connected to the concept of "domestic economy" (*oikonomos*). The monarch had the paternal prerogative of disciplining and ordering the subjects inside his territorial domain. As such, "police" designated a whole range of activities, matters, functions and duties that were connected to the notion of "good government" (from weights and prices in commerce, to orphans and vagrants, to urban and sanitary infrastructure). See Stolleis, *Storia del diritto pubblico in Germania*.

28 See chapter 9 of Stolleis, *Storia del diritto pubblico in Germania*.

29 See Seelaender, *Polizei, Ökonomie und Gesetzgebungslehre*.

about "police" and police science had expanded in the second half of the 18th century in Portugal – therefore, the royal officials were much more inclined to frame economic and social issues as "police matters". Third, even the institutional design of "police" started to be used in the colony, as can be seen in the figure of the intendant.

The argument here is that "police" is a useful category to analyse colonial normative production, namely because it pushes the perspective towards a comparative dimension.[30] *Polícia* was, no doubt, an essential device for managing the colonial administration of a "new world" with "new problems" because it offered sufficient flexibility in attempts to understand, process and reduce the complexity that the colonial world represented within the normative framework of the Ancient Regime.[31]

3 Types of Regulation between 1729 and 1771

In the Portuguese legal tradition, the discovery, demarcation, exploration and granting of privileges (*mercês*) associated with the mines was regulated by two titles of book II of the *Ordenações Filipinas*: *Título XXVI* "Dos Direitos Reais" and *Título XXXIV* "Das Minas e dos Metais". Nevertheless, the application of the *Ordenações* and the functioning of the normative structure in the Portuguese Empire were extremely casuistic. This not only implied an eminently jurisdictional nature, but also the relevance of *diplomas* for the local authorities.[32] These normative tools had the objective to manage the diverse and specific situations of daily life in the different places that composed the seaborne Portuguese Empire.

On 27 July 1727, the governor of the captaincy of Minas Gerais, D. Lourenço de Almeida, sent D. João V, the King of Portugal, an official notification of a fact that by then was already an "open secret" in the Portuguese court: that

30 See Pihlajamäki et al., "Comparing Early Modern Colonial Laws". The fact that "police" circulated all around Europe and beyond, even the northern and eastern corners, considered as distant from a central European perspective, has already been duly noted. See Kotkas, *Royal Police Ordinances in Early Modern Sweden*; Raeff, *The Well-Ordered Police State*.

31 Pihlajamäki, "The Westernization"; and Pihlajamäki, *Law in Spanish and Portuguese America*.

32 For an explanation of the different legislative types of the Portuguese Crown, see Cardim and Baltazar, "A difusão da legislação régia (1621–1808)".

diamonds had been discovered in the Region of Serro do Frio.[33] This piece of news was the concretisation of an old goal for the Portuguese, to find "precious stones" in America. The royal authorities quickly advanced to set up and adapt a judicial, administrative, military and economic structure destined to obtain the benefits of this resource. In the pursuit of this goal, this institutional structure would also need to deal with the local circumstances and practices.

Instructed to do so, the Governor of Minas Gerais took the first measure on 2 December 1729: through a *portaria*, he annulled all the *cartas de data* granted by *Guardas-Mores* that allowed their holders to mine in rivers where diamonds had been found. Later, the Royal Decree (*carta régia*) of 8 February 1730 declared the Crown's control over the exploration of diamonds but provided Governor D. Lourenço de Almeida with full powers to regulate such matters.[34]

Subsequently, a series of *cartas, bandos* and *portarias* were issued, intending to settle the normative shape of the administration of the activity in the region. Shortly after, on 25 June 1730, the first Regiment to "desbravar as minas de diamantes inteiramente" by D. Lourenço de Almeida was enacted, and land sales and provisions of *cartas de datas* were restricted.

Between 1730 and 1771, it is possible to distinguish two periods regarding the regulation of diamond exploitation in the Diamond District.[35] The first one was a short-lived experience, lasting only until 1734, initiated by the Regiment of 26 June 1730. This Regiment determined that exploitation was open to anyone who wished to dedicate themselves to it, granted that they paid a tax (the royal fifth) and got permission.

The Regiment of 1730 appointed two officers to mainly be in charge of the new activity: the '*Doutor*' *Superintendente* (in this case, the *Ouvidor-Geral* of the *comarca* of Serro do Frio, Antonio Ferreira do Valle e Mello, was nominated

33 BNP, cód. 1612, fols. 113v–114. "Foi me presente a vossa carta de 22 de julho passado em que me dais conta do descobrimento que se fez na Comarca do Serro do Frio, de umas pedras brancas de que remeteis amostras, referindo a opinião que corre de serem diamantes, e as razões, porque até agora, não me participastes esta notícia, e porque sou informado, que ela se divulgou nessas minas há alguns anos e que há já dois, que nas frotas se remetem várias pedras semelhantes com a certeza de serem diamantes vos estranho muito a indesculpável omissão que tivestes em não averiguar logo no seu princípio uma novidade de tanta importância.".

34 ANTT, cod. Manuscritos do Brasil.

35 The exact date of discovery of the diamonds is uncertain. The official date is the year 1729, when the then governor of the captaincy of Minas, D. Lourenço de Almeida, informed the Crown of the discovery of "a few white pebbles that are understood to be diamonds", ANTT, ordinance of 2 December 1729. Historiographical research points out, however, that as early as 1714 there was awareness of the existence of the stones in the region of Serro do Frio. See Furtado, "Distrito Diamantino".

as Superintendent) and the *Guarda-Mor*. They had to summarily judge all the disputes "between the miners", with the possibility of appeal to the *Superintendente*. Also, the *Superintendente* was to be responsible for overseeing the allocation of the permissions for land use, which would then be registered by the *Guarda-Mor*. The Regiment's provisions had to be implemented "safe-guarding all the equity of the miners; and making them observe the proper way in which their royal fifths should be paid" ("guardando toda equidade dos mineiros").[36]

The meagre income obtained in these circumstances, in addition to the high evasion of the tax, forced the Crown to change the administration strategy. In 1734, the Intendant of Diamonds was established. Meanwhile, to gain order in the region, all exploration was brought to a halt until 1739.[37] In essence, this carried a separation of jurisdictions, and the new Intendant of Diamonds absorbed all the competences of the former Superintendent of Diamonds, with the addition of a few more functions.

Once the quantity of stones circulating in the market was fairly under control, the Crown ordered the Governor José Gomes Freire de Andrada[38] to reopen the mines with "prudence and zeal". The new method of administration was based on contracts formed between one or more individuals and the Portuguese Crown, intensifying the monopoly of the services in a way that meant the Crown could in theory better oversee things.[39]

This model of contracts lasted until 1771. By then, the administrative irregularities of the contracts were considered to be so many "that they could not fit onto any paper".[40] In order to put an end to both the "scandalous and excessive loss of diamonds" and "the big disorder" caused by "the unlimited amount

---

36 ANTT, cod. Manuscritos do Brasil, fol. 8r.

37 BNL, seção de reservados, Avulsos, cód. 7167, fol. 10r.

38 The appointment of Gomes Freire de Andrada (1733) as governor and captain-general of the captaincy of Rio de Janeiro and the captaincy of Minas Gerais was part of an attempt to integrate the mining region into the centre-south axis in which Rio was the core. The union of the two areas through the same Governor also shows efforts to implement greater administrative rationality and cohesiveness into Portuguese institutional actions in America, even before the time of Pombal. Ribeiro, "'Razão de Estado' e pombalismo", 97.

39 The option for the monopoly was justified by the fact that the other "mercantile nations of Europe" had also adopted this for the case of diamonds: "Conhecido, que, as Naçoes mercantis da Europa tinhão absorvido em si, e feito monopólio dos Diamantes Occidentais, por serem fechada a fonte de donde emanarão a espalhar esos q' erão os milhores do Universo". Noticias das Minas de Diamantes. BNL, seção de reservados, Avulsos, cód. 7167, fol. 11r.

40 *Carta do Intendente Tomás Robi de Barros Barreto dirigida ao secretário de Estado em 25 de abril de 1755*, AHU, box 67, doc. 43, fol. 1r.

in leased Blacks [slaves]",[41] the *Alvará* and *Regimento* from 2 August 1771 was enacted. According to it, the contractor's system had to cease and the extraction transfer to the exclusive hands of the Royal Treasury.

The *Alvará* of 2 August 1771 established a new administration system named "Royal Extraction". With this, the Crown resumed the production of diamonds, leaving it in the hands of royal institutions and their officials, with the aim of rationalising the activity. It sought to control and increase production, while at the same time minimising its time and costs. The new model had as its primary goal the implementation of an efficient organisation for augmenting revenue. Accounting methods capable of ensuring greater control over the accounts, collections and frauds (contraband) were put into practice. As an accounting method, for example, the use of "double entries" and annual balances was determined, which had to be forwarded to the directors in Lisbon.[42]

The Crown's greater control over the general direction of activities meant, at the same time, an expansion of the powers of the Intendant of Diamonds. The *Alvará* granted even more specialisation to the police procedures: all matters in the district were supposed to be tried through a summary judgement, while it was only possible to make an appeal to the King himself. This is expressly stated in § XV of the *Alvará*:

> The General Intendant, and the administrators, who ocularly testify the facts, which constitute the causes of evictions, are the ones who can judge them more competently: I determine, that the jurisdiction of the same Intendant is in these cases of evictions, private and exclusive of any and all other jurisdictions. And that everything that he decides for these suspects, together with the aforementioned administrators, be executed without appeal, aggravation or any recourse, that is not to My Royal Person immediately.[43]

---

41 *Alvará* and *regimento* of 2 August 1771, in Silva, *Collecção da legislação portuguesa* (1763–1774), 561.

42 Since its foundation in 1759, the Pombaline "Aula de Comércio" also imposed "double entries" and rational accounting on the country's commercial elite. This method was also adopted in the *Erário Régio* (Royal Treasury) in 1761. See, for instance, Cunha, "Administrative Centralisation, Police Regulations and Mining Sciences".

43 "[s]*endo certo, o Intendente Geral, e os administradores, que presenceão occularmente os factos, que constituem as causas dos despejos, são os que delas podem julgar mais competentemente: Determino, que a jurisdição do mesmo Intendente seja nestes casos de despejos, privativa, e exclusiva de toda, e qualquer outra jurisdição. E que tudo o que Elle a estes suspeitos decidir em Junta com os sobreditos Administradores, se execute sem appellação, aggravo, ou recurso algum, que não seja para a Minha Real Pessoa imediatamente*". All sources quoted in the body of the text have been translated by the author.

Thus, according to the *Alvará* of 1771, the Royal Extraction was to be overseen by one Intendant, acting as its main figure and, serving directly under him, one *fiscal* and three *caixas*. Meanwhile, this institution was subordinated to a parallel directive institutional board (*Junta*) with a seat in Lisbon, headed by the president of the Royal Treasury.

It is also relevant to note that, a couple of months after the enactment of the Regiment of 1771, the Crown, "considering the information that it would be useful", applied a minor modification to the Royal Extraction that was also quite revealing of its whole intention.[44] In February 1772, the King established that the *fiscal* of the Royal Extraction should not be a "layman, of private appointment by the Governors of the mines", but a "Minister of letters appointed by me" ("Ministro de Letras por Mim nomeado"). This change would tighten the grip of the royal authority in the region, by controlling the nomination of the Royal Extraction officials in command. It would also create the possibility of adding a couple of steps to the career of royal officials who went through the Royal Extraction: some *fiscals* became intendants later on, proving that this could be a position to acquire experience with less risks of being coopted by the local authorities.

4 Local Problems and the Regiment of 1771 Against the Grain

In his study about fiscality and administration in the Diamond Demarcation, Angelo Carrara has characterised the years between 1729 and 1734 as a period of "hesitancy" from the Crown's side. The inexperience of the royal administration in diamond mining motivated a succession of different *diplomas* with the goal of controlling the exploration, which gradually replaced the overall standard applied throughout the rest of the captaincy of Minas Gerais.[45]

The dense network of norms intended to regulate the administration of the region might be observed as impregnated with inexperience, but one of another kind: inexperience in the face of the complexity, particularity and plurality of the region of Minas Gerais and its population. These new local problems had a normative dimension that cannot be ignored: they drove certain reactions and normative repercussions of their own. They also demanded the flexibility of different tools, whose use paved the way for new meanings of law.

44 *Decreto* of 17 February 1772, in Silva, *Collecção da legislação* (1763–1790), 301.
45 Carrara, "Desvendando a riqueza na terra dos diamantes".

As legally mediated communication, the *leis, decretos, ordens regias, bandos, portarias, editais* and *regimentos* had a procedural role in shifting or translating local complexity into normative information that could be processed by the Crown. By focusing on the problems that these rules tried to solve and contrasting these documents with others, such as letters, reports, etc., legal historians can reconstruct – even if only partially – the normative expectations that were involved in their creation.

It is no coincidence that the Crown attempted three distinct systems of administration in the region between 1730 and 1845. The administration of the diamond lands represented a constant challenge for the metropolitan power. Although the Portuguese Empire had experience with the diamond trade and extraction in some places, such as the East of Golconda, the exploration of this resource with their "own hands" was a complete novelty.[46] This was one of the first problems that the Crown had to handle: to create a system capable of having sufficient control over production, and one that respected the acquired rights of the miners at the same time.

Indeed, D. Lourenço de Almeida had sufficient knowledge about how the activity was carried out in the *Estado da India*; after all, it was precisely there where he made his fortune with the diamond trade, while serving as an official of the Crown for 17 years.[47] Nonetheless, in this case, instead of imitating the system of the *Estado da India*, the Governor of Minas Gerais decided to replicate a system that was already in practice in the region: that of gold extraction.

After advice from people he "trusted", who had "the knowledge of the form in which the diamonds were taken", D. Lourenço de Almeida decided upon the provisions of the Regiment of 1730, destined to regulate diamond extraction, in agreement with the "Ouvidores Gerais of this county and a few other people who could tell the whole truth in this matter".[48] Here, we may already start to notice how the first regulations on diamond mining were produced through negotiations and dialogues between the Governor and the local authorities. Given this arrangement, it may not come as a surprise that, in the end, the power of decision on the matter was placed in the hands of the usual, deeply rooted, local authorities. The "Regimento da Mineração dos Diamantes" determined, as already mentioned, that the Royal Magistrate (*ouvidor*) of Vila do Príncipe would simultaneously be the Superintendent of the Diamond lands of

---

46 McPherson, "Anglo-Portuguese Commercial Relations".

47 Romeiro, "O governo dos povos e o amor ao dinheiro".

48 ANTT, cod. Manuscritos do Brasil, fol. 8r.

the county. In addition, for the exploration, a "head tax" (capitação) should be collected; and the "slaves" should be registered in the book of the Intendency.[49]

Despite some scholars pointing out, correctly so, that this decision by the Governor was motivated by personal interests and was beneficial to the interests of the local elites as well, it is also true that this measure was agreed on according to a political imaginary well diffused in corporative monarchies during early modernity.[50] In the context of an empire whose extension presented difficulties in facing a highly multifaceted social reality, the Portuguese deployed strategies of governance that were often passive and decentralised. On many occasions, due to the limitation of material conditions, the best strategy was to take advantage of the existing structures in the local places; in some cases, this included adopting native institutions and rules for resolving conflicts or regulating social life.[51]

By replicating the regulation of gold mining, D. Lourenço de Almeida could use an administrative apparatus already established in the region, with officials and a tax system that was familiar to both the royal officials and the local population as well. From this perspective, the problem was being resolved (at least so far) by considering the "miner's equity" and considering the various normative expectations at stake.[52]

In addition to being very diverse, the population of the district had various expectations connected with the mining, mainly, of gold. Despite some economic diversity in the region,[53] the mining of gold was the main activity in the region and gave birth to a *modus vivendi* of its own.[54]

Initially populated by *bandeirantes*, who were chasing gold deposits,[55] the society of what would later be the Diamond District was also made up of

49 At that time, the administration was that of "gold and diamonds". The Intendency solely dedicated to the diamond extraction administration was only created in 1734.

50 Cardim, "Religião e ordem social"; Hespanha, "A senda amorosa do Direito".

51 Hespanha, *Filhos da Terra*.

52 ANTT, cod. Manuscritos do Brasil, fol. 8r.

53 Quintão, "Para a felicidade pública dos mineiros"; and Quintão, "A Real Extração e o abastecimento do Distrito Diamantino".

54 In this sense, the mineralogist José de Vieira Couto defined the spirit of the population as "miners above all". Couto, *Memória sobre a Capitania das Minas Gerais*.

55 The *bandeirantes paulistas* were the ones who trailblazed their way to the region and discovered the first gold mines, driven by promises of reward from the Crown (many of which remained unfulfilled). These *paulistas* have already been described as an "ethnic group", who had their fair share of past encounters with the Crown for their services in Palmares and the Guerra do Açú. After the discovery of the mines, many Portuguese and other men from the north migrated to the mining region to try their luck with the possibilities of enrichment. The struggles and quarrels quickly began between these two

the Portuguese, who had migrated from the Minho in search of wealth, and enslaved people who were used as labour in mining.[56] Many of the *bandeirantes* carried with them specific practices and knowledge about mining, which they had acquired in other places or through contact with "slaves" who had experience with the activity on the African coast.[57]

It is not a far-fetched consideration that many of them had a pretty good notion of how the relationship with the Portuguese Crown could be beneficial to them, and how to work to get what they wanted. Many of these individuals wished to ascend socially and economically, be it by winning *ofícios*, privileges, land-tenure or favours from the Crown.

In this sense, the very demographic characteristics of the region triggered a multiplicity of normative expectations that were entangled within the activity, which the Crown had to harmonise *amorosamente* with its own expectations.[58] The conflict and overlap between the expectations of the gold miners and the Crown's economic interest in the diamonds were causes of continued tensions throughout the period of Portuguese rule in the region.[59] This mishmash of different representations about what was fair or unfair, and the normative notions that shaped it, was relevant when the Crown had to decide or legislate on matters of the region.[60]

---

groups. The *paulistas* claimed their privilege in owning land, holding titles and in receiving permission for the extraction of gold in the region through the argument of their right of conquest. The rival group, dubbed mockingly as *emboabas*, used the bad reputation of the *paulistas* to make a case for why they should be preferred in the graces of the King. In the end, the *emboabas* were granted with the governorship of the region, but the semantics of resistance, insurgent tradition and negotiation by the *paulistas* survived as a trademark of the *mineiros* later. The Guerra dos Emboabas that ecloded later was a repercussion of this tension. Romeiro, *Paulistas e emboabas no coração das Minas*.

56 Beyond the reality of the district, the society of the captaincy of Minas Gerais represented a complex panorama during the 18th century. According to the literature, the mining activity not only generated some structures of exclusion by itself but also allowed, at least symbolically, the dismantling of other hierarchies. Thus, for example, some historians characterise the "gold society" as a social reality where there was a "tendency to live lavishly", in which the possibility of profit permeated a wide variety of relationships and impacted the normative conception of the agents. See Azeredo, *Da Justiça em Nome d'El Rey*; and Souza, *Norma e conflito*. For an overview of the demographic characteristics, see Mancilla-Órdenes, *The Crown as an Apprentice*, and all the revision of the literature there.

57 See Holanda, *A mineração: antecedentes luso-brasileiros*; Holanda, *Metais e pedras preciosas*.

58 Hespanha, "A senda amorosa do Direito"; Cardim, *Religião e ordem social*.

59 ANTT, cod. Manuscritos do Brasil, fol. 7r.

60 BNP, Pba-691, 70–73.

The royal officials were aware of the difficulties that had to be handled in the everyday life of the administration. On 19 December 1731, José Rodrigues de Oliveira, *capitão de dragões* of the county of Serro do Frio, depicted an overview of the activity to the cardinal da Mota (counsellor of D. João V). According to Rodrigues de Oliveira, it was necessary to pay more attention to the abandonment of some economic activities in the region – and, among them, the mining of gold was mentioned: carelessness with this activity could result in scarcity of coins and paralyse the trade of other products.

From the same perspective, the migration of gold miners to diamond mining could entail problems as well, such as a) the size of the stones (small by nature) made them easier to hide and avoid payment of the "fifths"; b) the lack of miners overall, which would end up diminishing the collection of the *quintos do ouro*; and c) private individuals preferred to sell the diamonds to foreigners, even at a lower price, rather than letting them arrive at their destination in Portugal.[61]

The local conditions presented obstacles to the regulatory desires of the metropolis. If we think about law as a field in constant dispute, the diversity of situations and agents could discourage or even obliterate those desires.[62] When we think about the materiality of documents, said conditions could also directly interfere in the time it would take for royal regulations to reach the intended place. More importantly, they forced a permanent adaptation of the legislation to the emerging needs.[63]

As someone acquainted with the complexity of the Brazilian hinterland, Rodrigues de Oliveira had some ideas about how the law ought to be in such circumstances. From his point of view, law should be flexible: "because, as Solórzano wrote, according to the varieties and alterations of businesses and trades, the Monarchies and their decrees will vary". This piece of wisdom was even more applicable to the specific case, since the mining of diamonds was a "matter whose knowledge depends more on experience than on reason".[64] The reference to Solórzano Pereira, taken from his *Politica Indiana*, also attests to

61 AHU, Minas Gerais, box 19, doc. 52.

62 Hespanha, "Uncommon Laws"; Thompson, *Whigs and Hunters*, 258. Furthermore, among the documents related to diamond mining, it is fairly common to find letters and reports detailing the state of the affairs. In them, the most abundant topics are the everyday problems of the activity and what might be the best ways to resolve them. In this regard, the Crown had a constant flow of normative information. For another report example, see, among others, AHU, Minas Gerais, box 63, doc. 77.

63 For a deeper approach to this idea, see the presentation by Fragoso and Monteiro (eds.), *Um reino e suas repúblicas no Atlântico*.

64 AHU, Minas Gerais, box 19, doc. 52.

some degree of self-reflection about the particularities of the colonies on the part of royal officials.[65]

Insofar as that experience revealed new problems, the royal agents in the colony were also trying to adjust their regulation. In this sense, the *bandos* of 7.1.1732 replaced the "head-tax" through a system of renting *lavras* – which was the same system that the Portuguese had in India. It also established the condition that diamonds of over 20 carats would be reserved for the Crown. This *bando* was repeated on 9 January 1732. This attempt of adjustment failed since there was little interest in the purchase of lands from the region.[66] As some sources show, the miners considered land investment a "high risk business" since there was no exact certainty whether the acquired land possessed diamonds or not.[67]

Shortly after, on 2 December 1733, the *bando* of the Governor André de Melo e Castro, *Conde das Galveias*, modified the "head-tax" again. This time around, a tax of 40,000 *reis* per "slave" was established for the owners; and punishment against smugglers and "negas de tabuleiro" was reiterated. Both the increasingly assertive mechanisms to collect taxes and to control smuggling generated permanent problems for the metropolitan power.[68]

Moreover, the biggest obstacle that the diamond administration dealt with between 1729 and 1734 was of an economic nature; the urgency and priority of rationalisation and control of this activity had to do with how the diamonds generated specific problems in the economy. Unlike gold, for example, the quantity of diamonds in the market influenced its price: the higher the amount of this commodity in circulation, the lower its value. Because of this, it was almost impossible for a system that followed the example of gold activities in the region to be successful.[69] The abundance of *lavras*, the illegal *garimpo* and trafficking all provoked an accelerated increase of diamonds available

---

65 It seems that Rodrigues de Oliveira is paraphrasing the libro V, cap. XIII, 451 of *Politica Indiana*, in which Solórzano Pereira is discussing warnings given to the *audiencias*, stressing that "nunca pudo ser loable en varones aventajados en el gobierno de las Repúblicas, estarse siempre firmes en un parecer, porque en uno mismo negocio es lícito mudarle, si se varían los tiempos, y las razones, y aunque no se varíen, reformando en nuestro propio dictamen". Solórzano Pereira, *Politica Indiana*.

66 For more on *bandos*, see Arthur Curvelo's chapter in this volume.

67 RAPM, 251–355.

68 As Angelo Carrara pointed out, this fact also explains the composition of the group of sources that we have of the zone in this period. Carrara, "Desvendando a riqueza na terra dos diamantes".

69 Carrara, "Desvendando a riqueza na terra dos diamantes"; Furtado, "Relações de poder no Tejuco", 301.

for international trade[70] and the price collapsed.[71] Attentive to this issue, in addition to noticing the "rare" payment of the taxes (*quintos*), the Crown suspended the *lavras* of diamonds in the county between 1734 and 1739.

Alongside the suspension of the *lavras*, formalised by the *bando* of 19 July 1734, the Portuguese Crown created the *Intendencia dos Diamantes* that same year. Meanwhile, it also ordered the demarcation of the district, whose centre of operation would become the *Arraial do Tijuco*. This was not only to have greater control over the flow of people who could be involved in diamond trafficking, but also to define an exclusive jurisdiction.[72] Finally, the system of the contractors was implemented, already explained above.

In these contracts, some obligations for "good administration" were established – for example, a specific delimitation of the mining areas, and a limitation imposed on the number of slaves used for the activity (none of which were respected in practice). There was also the obligation to cast out of the demarcation every person without occupation or office or who had been charged with something, especially smuggling. And finally, there was the obligation to send to Portugal a determined amount of diamonds.[73]

According to the instructions given to the first Intendant of Diamonds appointed for the district, Rafael Pires Pardinho,[74] control of the contract's obligations was in his hands (something that would later be reiterated in the contracts themselves).[75] In case of suspicion that someone was a buyer or "extractor" of diamonds, the Intendant had to "take information" from him and, if "found guilty by the testimony", sentence him. The Intendant also became the private judge of matters of extraction. Finally, he oversaw the annual investigation "not only in this region but in the other demarcated lands as well",

70 "Mas a Europa aterrada com Diamantes, pela immencidade, que por todas as partes se espalharão, e raríssimos os que pagarão o tributo, de forma q'era quazi nenhuma consideração o que Rendia, obrigou a Corte a nomear Intendente Geral dos Diamantes ao Dezembargador Rafael Pires Pardinho, e fazendo o passar imediatamente ao Brasil, levou as ordens do Conde das Galveas para que fizesse cerrar inteiramente aquella Mina não permitindo mais a extração daquele perciozo gênero". Noticias das Minas de Diamantes. BNL, seção de reservados, Avulsos, cód. 7167, fol. 10r.

71 Furtado, *O livro da capa verde*, among others.

72 See Mancilla-Órdenes, *The Crown as an Apprentice*.

73 In practice, the contractors proved to be ingenious in finding different strategies to avoid these rules.

74 For an analysis of Pires Pardinho's career in the context of the *Ancien Régime*, and his conflicts with Governor D. Lourenço de Almeida, see Mancilla-Órdenes, *The Crown as an Apprentice*.

75 BNL, seção de reservados, Avulsos, cód. 7167, fol. 11r.

where he still had to approach the inhabitants to inquire about extraction and investigate possible frauds that caused "damage" to the Royal Treasury.

The six contracts signed throughout this period established – with a few changes over time – the following main obligations: i) conclude the extraction, in principle, within four years (in practice, however, some contracts were renewed or granted for a longer period); ii) resume mining with the limited amount of 600 slaves (if any more were found, they had to be confiscated, and if a captured slave ran away or died, the administrators and overseers had to notify the *Intendente* within 48 hours); iii) respect the frontiers of the demarcation where the stones could be extracted; iv) any person who had no trade or position in the land, alongside smugglers, had to leave the district within a period of two months (if they were seen again in the demarcation, they would be compelled to pay 100 octaves of gold, and if they were repeat offenders in this act, they would be assigned to *Nova Colônia*, to *Rio Grande* or to the *Ilha de Santa Catarina*); and v) all the diamonds and gold extracted in the services had to be collected in a company safe, which was in the *Real Fazenda* in the *Intendência dos Diamantes* and, later, to Rio de Janeiro, where they would be delivered in small boxes to the officers and commanders of warships to be delivered to the elected attorneys at the Court of Lisbon.[76]

However, by the end, around 1770, the problems related to this system of contractors were "so many that it is impossible to put in a paper", according to the advisors of the Crown.[77] For example, the administration of the *contratadores* did not stop the trafficking of diamonds: even worse, some contractors were proved to be involved in it. This inobservance of the rules of the contracts was frequent, and it resulted in less profit for the mining activity.[78] In order to put an end to both the "scandalous and excessive embezzlement of diamonds"[79] and the "great disorder of the unlimited quantity of rented negroes", the Decree of 2 July 1771 established the cessation of exploitation by private individuals.[80] From that year, the activity was in the hands of the Royal

76 *Códice Costa Matoso*, vol. 2, 634.

77 AHU, Minas Gerais, box 67, doc. 43, fol. 1r.

78 Wehling, *Administração portuguesa no Brasil*, 111.

79 *Decreto* of 12 July 1771, ANTT, col. Documentos do Brasil.

80 With this, the Crown manifested its discontent with the "harmful and intolerable abuses" introduced in the mining of diamonds. The "disorder" in ploughing the land, which was causing the clogging of rivers and the "exorbitant and superfluous number of slaves [...] employed in the mining services" were outlined as being the "evils" to cope with. For them, the norm attested that the "particulars" lacked within their strengths the remedies to deal with this. Therefore they "indispensably" demanded the actions of the "Royal Arm" (*regimento* of 12 July 1771).

Treasury (*Fazenda Real*). During the same year, the Crown implemented the *Real Extração dos Diamantes*. This institution acted as the direct hand of the Crown overseas, with the *Intendente* as its head in Brazil, while functioning alongside a corresponding institution in Portugal.

In this way, as already mentioned, the *Alvará* of 2 August 1771 established mining as a complete and direct royal monopoly. But, more importantly, it concentrated even more administrative and judicial powers in the *Intendente dos Diamantes*, who now directed a larger institution, the *Real Extração*. Some of these powers had previously been in the hands of the *câmeras* or even the governor of captaincy.[81]

After the Regiment of 1771, the *Intendente* was empowered with exclusive jurisdiction on the demarcation to decide on evictions as well as with the entry control of the general population and registry of slaves. Concerning the evictions, he could judge them "summarily" (an oral procedure, in which he could be both witness and accuser, without the possibility of appeal for the defendant).[82]

The *Real Extração* centralised all control of matters that could directly or indirectly influence the mining activities,[83] such as supplies, weights and measures, control of prices, commerce, etc. It was not unusual that this situation created an overlap in jurisdictions and political conflicts with other local authorities. For example, for the *câmera* of Vila do Príncipe, which lost control of trade over the *Vila*, this meant the loss of one of the main sources of income, which came from the taxes that the establishments had to pay to be able to sell their products.[84]

This institutional and legal change was both ignited by the intellectual shifts around the concept of "police" (also with the emergence of the

81 For a deeper analysis, see Mancilla-Órdenes, *The Crown as an Apprentice*.

82 While historiography on the region always raises questions about the effectiveness of the regiment, and whether the jurisdiction of the *Intendente* really brought about substantial change in the way conflicts were managed in the region, these questions are not the main focus of this chapter. See, for instance, Furtado, *O livro da capa verde;* and Furtado, "Relações de poder no Tejuco". For a relativisation of this point, see Fonseca, *Arraiais e vilas d'el rei*. Indeed, in relation to the social practices, the legislation (and the administration) involved soft enforcement, not unlike what happened in the rest of the captaincy or even in the rest of colonial Brazil. Instead, what is important here is to observe how these changes elicited a reaction from various agents who, beyond trying to protect their individual interests, mobilised different normative concepts (such as custom) to express their dissatisfaction with changes that did not align with what they had previously known as fair, as can be seen in the following section.

83 Wehling, *Administração portuguesa no Brasil*, 111.

84 For a deeper analysis, see Mancilla-Órdenes, *The Crown as an Apprentice*.

Policeywissenschaft and the cameral sciences) and by the necessity of economical control of the prices of the diamonds in the international market. But most of all, it was the aftermath of a series of trials and errors by the Portuguese royal administration in attempting to deal with the complexity of the colonies.

From the point of view of the Crown, one of the main failures in the administration of the contracts was the informational confusion it produced. A more rational administration, therefore, required a systematisation of how the institutions kept their papers and communicated with the centre. In fact, after establishing the new system, one of the first orders was to practice the *escripturação*.[85] To control the information was also to govern; that is why the Crown demanded from this new institution a detailed day-to-day record of the situation in the district, the periodic update of the record books (in a way that was much more sophisticated than in previous periods), the presentation of yearly balances and a continuous correspondence with the *Junta da Real Extração* in Lisbon.[86]

The Crown urged the officers to follow "good commercial faith"[87] while imposing the elaboration and delivery of tables and records and the application of the double entry method.[88] Although often with tardiness,[89] the officials of the Royal Extraction seemed to have fulfilled their duties. The correspondence

85 ANTT, PT-TT-RED-A-001_m0012–13TIF (12 July 1771).

86 "Dentro dos primeiros seis Meses de cada Anno se lhe aprezentara huma Conta final do Anno proximo precedente feita por orçamento: no fim de cada semestre selhedaria hum rezumo do estado, em que estiver o mesmo negocio, para sempre se achar calcullado o estado desta Administração e me ser prezente tudo o que for a ella concernente. As cartas de Ordens, que se expedirem para as Minas, serão todas registradas pela ordem chronologica em hum livro intitulado Copiador. O qual com o jogo dos outros livros Auxiliares, que necessarios forem estarão sempre escripturados em dia com as Cartas e Papeis, que se receberem collegidos em termos tao exatos, que a toda hora se achem promptos para Eu os mandar ver, quando me parecer justo, ou julgar necessario, e as existencias para elle feitas serão sempre pagos, e pagos no Meu Real Erário, como os Contratadores particulares o practicarão até agora: para assim se conhecerem melhor as utilidades rezultantes desta Administração. Os livros della serão guardados na Caixa da mesma Administração até serem por mim aplicados, como entender, que há de mais conveniente. As commas de dinheiro, que necessarias forem para se comprarem no Contrato que acacaba, as Fabricas que deixa: e para satisfação das Letras de Costeamento, serão supridas por emprestimo pelos cabedaes do Meu Real Erário, debaixo dos recibos dos trez Directores assima nomeados: para reporem os mesmos dinheiros nos Cofres donde sahirem pelos productos da sua Administração depois de liquidados." ANTT, PT-TT-RED-A-001_m0012–13TIF (12 July 1771). See also, ANTT, PT-TT-RED-A-001_m0013.TIF, among others.

87 ANTT, PT-TT-RED-A-001_m0012–13TIF.

88 AHU, MG, box 110, doc. 33.

89 TCP, box 4088, fol. 167r.

was filled with tables many times, each time more detailed, about the shipment of diamonds. Although the elaboration of maps with information on the precious stones and the organisation of the extraction were within the tasks of the contractors, they tended to be very broad and general. From 1771 on, the structure of the tables changed, with the addition of specific columns not only about the *oitavas*[90] but also about the provenience of the diamonds – which were then divided into extracted diamonds (*diamantes explorados*) and confiscated diamonds (*diamantes confiscados*). Likewise, the practice of elaborating tables designed to organise the expenses (of the most varied sort) that the administration incurred in order to maintain the continuity of its services was instated.[9192]

In the discourse, the concept of "utility" of the service acquired more relevance than in the earlier period, or at least it was considerably more heavily emphasised in the orders given to the officials. Even some traditional meanings

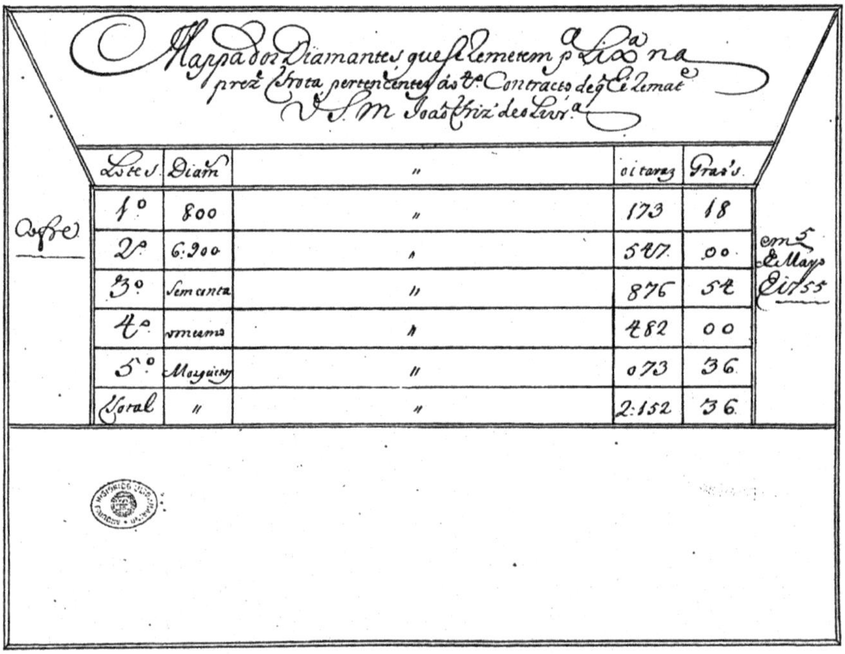

Lotes	Diam.	"	oitavas	Grãos.
1º	800	"	173	18
2º	6:900	"	547	00
3º	[illegible]	"	876	54
4º	[illegible]	"	482	00
5º	[illegible]	"	073	36
Total	"	"	2:152	36

FIGURE 9.1 'Mapa' of the diamonds by the *Intendente* Tomas Roby de Barros Barreto for the Marquis of Pombal on 4 April 1755[92]

90 Type of measure of the weight of diamonds.

91 Quintão, "Cultura material e trabalho nos serviços de mineração do Distrito Diamantino".

92 AHU, Minas Gerais, box 67, doc. 31, fol. 3r.

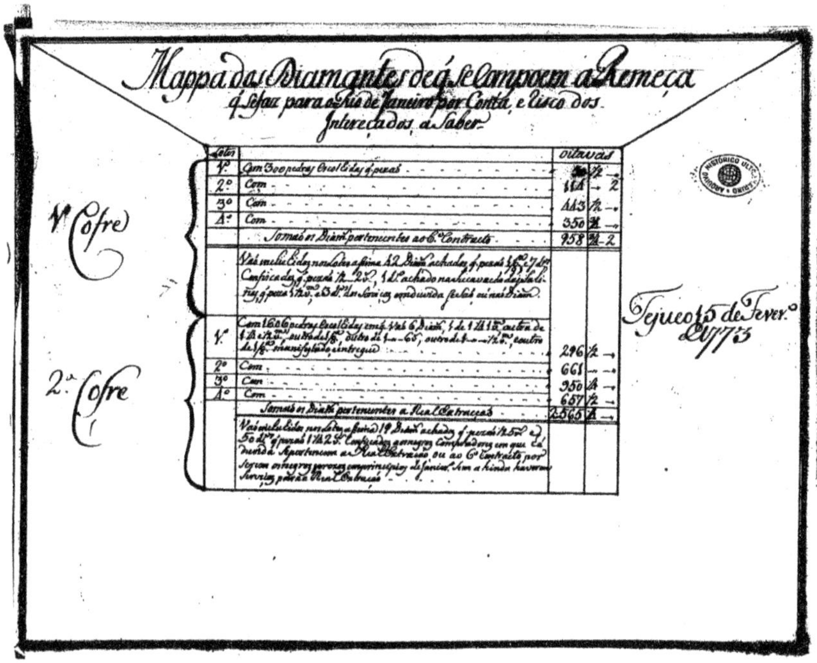

FIGURE 9.2 'Mapa' of the diamonds by the *Intendente* João da Rocha Dantas e Mendonça for Martinho de Melo e Castro on 15 February 1773[93]

were combined with new logics: the good order was presented as necessary for the "best economy possible" ("a maior economía possivel").[94]

Control over the population continued to be one of the most essential topics. The surveillance and inspection of those who circulated in the region, alongside records of their occupations, and the eviction of smugglers and vagrants, which were matters already regulated, were reiterated by the Regiment. In the use of these powers, it is still not possible to describe a radical change from the previous aims and scope. Some documents show us how they were still used to avoid subversion of the "natural order", sanctioning luxury and the extravagant use of ornaments or clothes that tended to blur social distinctions.[95] The case of the *cabra* Francisco Gonçalves may be one of the most illustrative: in 1777, he was arrested for disorder under the argument of wearing unsuitable clothes

93 AHU, Minas Gerais, box 104, doc. 35, fol. 4r.

94 ANTT, PT-TT-RED-A-001_m0014.TIF, *Carta de 22 de Agosto de 1771*.

95 For an extensive review of the *alvarás* on this matter, see Seelaender, *Polizei, Ökonomie und Gesetzgebungslehre*; and Seelaender, "A polícia e o rei-legislador".

when he paraded through the centre of the Tijuco with the uniform of the *destacamento de dragões*.[96]

Moreover, both the concepts of "utility" and "good order" not only implied the disciplining of the population in general, but especially of the officers themselves. Indeed, the problems with the administration of the *contratadores* revealed the need for more control and professionalisation of the officers. After acknowledging the actual state of affairs of the business, the diamond administration in Lisbon decided to divide and specify the functions of the ones in charge of extraction. With the objective of putting an end to quarrels over delimitation of activities, the Crown determined that each service would be under the care of a specific administrator and his troops. It also tried to establish a hierarchical chain in cases where the service covered an extended piece of land and demanded more than one administrator. In said cases, it was also considered that these administrators might be subordinated to a general one.[97]

The attempt to discipline the officials did not end there. As Régis Clemente Quintão clearly shows in his investigation about corruption in the Diamond District, the Regiment of 1771 brought about a change regarding the application of sanctions to officers who deviated from the obligations of their position. This led to the appearance of the crime typification of prevarication and even to the convictions of some officials of the Royal Extraction.[98]

---

96 APM, SC, cód. 240, fol. 62v. From another perspective, remaining with the same source, Junia Furtado analyses this case to exemplify the lack of effectiveness of the Regiment of 1771. Gonçalves' case would supposedly show how the social order in the district was not far different from what prevailed anywhere else in colonial Brazil: the law would be applied, in a marginal way, against the lower layers of society and in practically insignificant cases (like this one), while the local elites would remain unscathed by it. Observing this case through the lenses of how police ordinances operated in early modernity shows exactly the opposite. The logic of the sanctions was precisely the social disciplining of the lower layers of society, directed at not altering the harmony of the presupposed natural order. In this sense, it was not a matter of lack of effectivity or inequality in application, but rather that the rule, from the start, was only aimed at being applied to certain subjects. Among others, see Hespanha, "Justiça e administração".

97 "Em quanto à disciplina da gente empregada nos serviços parece conveniente o metodo que VM aponta de encarregar o governo principal de cada serviço ha um só administrador para por este meio evitar não só as competencias de Jurisdicções que costuma haver entre as diverssas pessoas empregadas com igual authoridade mas também as multiplicadas despezas que se seguem de haver varias tropas em hum mesmo serviço, nomeandose alguns outros administradores que ajudem e servão de conselho ao primeiro mas sempre a elle saber a elle subordinadas naquellas serviços os quais pela sua distancia grandeza e maior numero de escravos não se poderiao bem governar por hum so Administrador". ANTT, PT-TT-RED-A-001_m0014.TIF.

98 Quintão, *Corrompidos pelo interesse*, 59.

Although the problems that occurred in the "bureau" of the administration occupied a considerable part of the concerns of the metropolis, the functioning of the Royal Extraction also showed that the biggest problems occurred in the day-to-day activity, that is, in the mining sites.[99] The centralisation of the administration and extraction of the diamonds in a single institution forced it to handle problems that were previously externalised to contractors. Consequently, even though there were strong bonds between the Royal Extraction and the central power, the former was also an eminently local institution, permeable to local specificities and with a relevant role in localising the law.

Different letters contain advice for the officials of the Royal Extraction about the necessity of considering the local conditions and their differences with Portugal. In March 1772, for example, the *Direção do negócio dos Diamantes* in Lisbon instructed Caetano José de Sousa, one of the administrators in the district, on the prices and supplies of the region. The instruction was twofold. First, the local administrator should regulate the prices and supplies in accordance with the needs of consumption. Second, he should also take advantage of the local circumstances: due to the heat, produce scarcity was an issue in the Tijuco because the groceries could not be conserved for more than one year; without price speculation the Crown could acquire them for smaller amounts of money.[100] The reason for this was to maintain "good order", but also due to the "utility" of the service.[101]

Weather conditions posed problems for the administration, which had to act quickly while also anticipating future situations. The §§ II, III and IV of the Regiment of 1771 established the forms and periods of the year in which ploughing and extraction should be executed. Although mining was previously prioritised during dry periods, the Regiment established that it should occur during rainy periods as well, in an attempt to increase the "utility" of the service. Likewise, there was an order to calculate the amount of diamonds that could be extracted, taking the observations of the administrators who were in the district into consideration.[102] In fact, the planning of the services seems to have been a matter of priority for the administrators, who, in trying to extract diamonds during rainy periods, started using "grupiarias"[103] and "tabuleiros"

99 *Códice Costa Matoso*, fol. 325r.

100 ANTT, PT-TT-RED-A-001_m0015.TIF.

101 ANTT, PT-TT-RED-A-001_m0015.TIF.

102 In the same way, for example, it was discussed how the scarcity of wood could affect the production of stones. *Memorias economicas da Academia Real das Sciencias de Lisboa*, vol. 1, 204.

103 Name that is given to gravel stone on the ground.

that could be employed during the wet season.[104] Through said planning, they also sought to lower the costs of slave rental in times of lower extraction, as well as to optimise the quality of labour.[105] It was in the constant flow of communication between the Royal Extraction and the director board in Lisbon that some of the devices of the Regiment were taking shape.[106]

Even if the institution was established with centralising purposes, this informational circuit allowed it not only to respond to local complexities, but also to deal with and adapt to the diverse expectations of the district's inhabitants. The law was constantly calibrated in the face of such expectations, either by considering them or by setting them aside. In fact, in June 1755, after an exchange of letters with the Intendant João Rocha Dantas e Mendonça, the Marquis of Pombal asked the official to be especially careful not to apply excessive taxes on the population, which only consisted of people who "had their work" ("tem o seu trabalho").[107] This recommendation was also generated by fear that local discontent could turn into revolts. Aware of the dangers that the discontent of the population in the Minas Gerais region could cause,[108] he could not completely disregard the *modus vivendi* of the miners even when trying to foster the "utility" of mining.

If we observe the Regiment of 1771 as a type of police ordinance, then we may be able to improve our understanding of said regulation through the logic of its own time. In this way, it makes it easier for us not to fall into hasty judgements about its "effectiveness". Certainly, this is a widely discussed topic within social history, oscillating between a narrative of despotic rule of the region and another of total ineffectiveness of the Regiment in the face of the impossibility of controlling the diamond traffic. However, I maintain that its relevance should be evaluated in relation to the normative expectations that it was able to mobilise on the part of the various historical agents. In this sense, even

104 TCP, liv. 4099, fol. 148r; TCP, liv. 4089, fol. 41r.
105 AHU, Minas Gerais, box 167, fol. 55r.
106 TCP, liv. 4088, fol. 139r; TCP, liv. 4088, fol. 133r; ANTT, PT-TT-RED-A001.
107 TCP, liv. 4088, fol. 171.
108 The revolt of Vila Rica from 1720, perhaps not a distant memory for the agents of the Crown, surely serves as an example here. There, a group of influential men insufflated the population against the measures of the Governor. The revindications were to lower the taxes, to diminish judicial costs and to abolish the monopolies and the *casas de fundição*. At first, Dom Pedro Miguel de Almeida Portugal e Vasconcelos, the *Conde de Assumar*, yielded to the demands of the mob. But he later executed some involved in the conspiracy and went on to reinstate the measures. The *Conde de Assumar* went on to produce a text reflecting on the events of the revolt. See Monteiro, *O rei no espelho*; and Monteiro, "Catilinária mineira".

though the implementation of the new regime faced a series of obstacles,[109] it is undeniable that it mobilised disputes around a much more instrumental vision of law.

5 From "Justice" to "Utility": New Meanings of Law in the Administration of the Diamond Demarcation

Reflecting on the transformation of law in early modernity also involves considering the changes that society was experiencing. If, in the *Ancien Régime*, law played a central role in articulating and transcending a large part (or all) of social relations,[110] then, the intellectual constructions of the jurists are like "paintings" of the functioning of the societies of the time. They illustrate the logic with which the images of that world were constructed.[111]

The conceptual transformation of the Crown into a pole of normative production during the second half of the 18th century is an example of this. During the first decades of the 18th century, the King was commonly praised for his passive stance, as one who was not a lawmaker.[112] Since the law was conceived as an expression of a natural and harmonic order, its alteration meant the subversion of this order as well. In this sense, the law was 'unavailable' to the King.[113] The role of the ruler was to enforce law by dispensing justice. In fact, in the scholastic tradition, *Iustitia* was the main virtue of the Prince,[114]

109 This even produces doubt about the opinions of the officials themselves concerning the proposed utility of the institution. In 1794, a report (*parecer*) by the Intendant Luis Beltrão de Gouveia de Almeida planned a reform of the Royal Extraction basing itself in that "it is currently onerous to the Royal Treasury", although not due to the smuggling, but because there was too much expenditure with the "payment of labour and supplies to feed the slaves".

110 Thus, for example, it was usual for legal disputes to arouse great interest on the part of the population, rather than being restricted to the "parties" involved in them. Hespanha, *Caleidoscópio do Antigo Regime*, 37.

111 Hespanha, *Como os juristas viam o mundo*, 2.

112 Seelaender, "A polícia e o rei-legislador", 96. When dealing with the author Diogo Guerreiro C. de Aboym (1663–1709), Seelaender notices this tendency in his quotes: for Aboym, the King was essentially a "benign star", who would dispense grace and justice, "dissipating the clouds of pleas". Also, because the "preexistent statutes" ("leis preexistentes") were "santíssimas, puríssimas, justíssimas", and "the purer the more ancient", as stated by the *Desembargador* Joao Pinto Ribeiro (†1649), the King should not innovate but preserve the given order.

113 Among others, see Hespanha, "Justiça e administração".

114 As Hespanha points out, "There was an essential relation between *imperio* and *iurisdictio*", which meant that "the acts of power, even the ones that were comprehended in the

and the most important political power. Through the influence of moral theology and other strains of thought, this conception would be sustained until the end of the *Ancien Régime*.[115]

As the Portuguese Empire expanded its knowledge of the colonial world and its ability to control overseas domains, the law itself acquired new tonalities.[116] During the second half of the 18th century, the colonial administration, the problems it generated and the wealth derived from it all played a fundamental role in the transformation of the monarch's function from a judge-king to a lawgiver-king, one who was gradually more active.[117] Some legal historians highlighted the function that police ordinances had in this transition, and consequently for the transformation of the concept of law itself.[118] In fact, since police ordinances were pragmatic orders with the goal of having a direct and immediate effect, they were a useful tool to (attempt to) transform behaviour patterns and social order. Beyond the effectiveness of these attempts, their failure triggered some shifts in the concept of law as well, at least for colonial administration.[119] Some documents from the *distrito diamantino* show how the need to adapt to the diverse circumstances of the colony led to "creative legal solutions", even more so considering that diamond trade was fundamental for the Crown's economy.

We may encounter examples of this in the patterns and types of legislation. Certain charters (*diplomas*) gained greater relevance over others for solving problems, be it inland or overseas. This was the case for the *alvará*, a type of

sphere of mere *imperio*, were subjected to the minimum requirements of *iustum iudicum*, namely, a previous hearing of the interested parties (*citatio* [*late suptma*]). And that was valid even in the centre of the 'political' matters." Hespanha, "Justiça e administração", 139. On the other hand, according to the same author, during the 17th century in Portugal, even when what was at stake was public utility, the power did not cease to be limited by the jurisdictional nature of its prerogatives, and the King was obliged to exercise them according to the typical manners of the judiciary order. This essential link between *iurisdictio* and *imperium* only became controversial in the 17th century, and their separation became more radical in the context of Portuguese Enlightenment. Hespanha, "Justiça e administração", 139.

115 Hespanha, "Justiça e administração".

116 Cardim and Baltazar, "A difusão da legislação régia".

117 Seelaender, "A 'polícia' e as funções do Estado", 95.

118 Seelaender, *Polizei, Ökonomie und Gesetzgebungslehre*; Kotkas, *Royal Police Ordinances in Early Modern Sweden*.

119 As Marc Raeff reminds us, the role of the "colonial experience" was fundamental to the innovation of the art of politics and, consequently, it had normative implications as well. Although Raeff concentrates on the Jesuit experience of governance, it is still interesting that his intuition has not yet been explored in depth. Raeff, *The Well-Ordered Police State*, 23 and 30–32.

legislation of lower hierarchy than *Cartas* or *Leis Régias*, which normally had a validity of one year.[120] Since in the Portuguese context there were no proper police ordinances until 1749, the so-called police norms appeared commonly as pragmatics (*pragmáticas*).[121] As the legislative action of the king was reaching its climax during the second half of the 18th century, the *alvará* became the tool par excellence of legislative action on the police matters of this period.[122]

For the region of the Diamond District, this shift towards the use of the *alvará* was also essential. In fact, during the first decade of the 18th century, the *bandos* from the governor of the captaincy were the prevailing form of regulation.[123] Starting from 1750, following the Crown's efforts to centralise the control over diamond extraction, local matters began to be increasingly regulated by *alvarás*. In other words, the *bandos*, which were a decentralised method of regulation, started to lose space to the *alvarás*, which were direct instruments of legislation from the Crown. Between 1729 until 1739, five *bandos* were published by the governors of the captaincy of Minas Gerais with the purpose of regulating the exploration of diamonds in the region. In turn, between 1752 and 1808, seven *alvarás* formed part of the body of legislation for said purpose.[124]

Some sources show how as early as during the 17th century, although not in a generalised way, some *alvarás* designed to regulate colonial spaces of great importance for the Portuguese Empire (for example, in the case of Goa) had

---

120 *Ordenações Filipinas*, liv. 2, tit. XL. In formal terms, this type of *diploma* normally began with the expression "Eu el-Rey". Cardim and Baltazar, "A difusão da legislação régia".

121 According to Seelaender, unlike German and French pragmatics, in 17th- and 18th-century Portugal, these *diplomas* mainly dealt with police matters. Seelaender, *Polizei, Ökonomie und Gesetzgebungslehre*, 102.

122 For an extensive analysis on this, see Seelaender, *Polizei, Ökonomie und Gesetzgebungslehre*. As Seelaender reminds us, important innovations were made in matters relevant to the strengthening of the Crown via *alvarás* and *alvará com força de lei*. Examples are changes in colonial policy, reforms of the Portuguese administration, a new urban design for Lisbon, etc., Seelaender, "A polícia e o rei-legislador", 102–105.

123 For an analysis of the role of *bandos* in the governance of colonial Brazil, see Curvelo, "Governar à distância", 19.

124 There were also changes in the formal procedures of the *alvarás*. The *alvarás* had at least two formal requirements of validity that began to be relativised to better suit their ends. One of them was the requirement that the proposal of a charter should go through chancery inspections, and the second was the temporal limitation of validity of just one year. The relativisation of these requirements was an important step to try to guarantee the solution of problems as quickly as possible, at a time when the dissemination of royal legislation depended on innumerable material circumstances. Cardim and Baltazar, "A difusão da legislação régia".

their duration extended beyond one year.[125] Notwithstanding that, it is after 1750 that we notice a multiplication of *alvarás* and the extension of their temporal validity. This is followed by a "growing disregard for formal criteria", like the textual inclusion of a warning that said a charter did not pass through the chancery.[126] Beyond the practical effects of granting the legislator-king the prerogative to decide and intervene directly with law (without the interference of councillors or within a council) this measure also affected how legal order was conceived. In Portuguese institutional architecture, the *Chanceler-mor* was considered to be the "guardian of the coherence of the legal order":[127] by downplaying his function, little by little a trend was set towards redefining the normative chain, in which the sovereign gained pre-eminence.[128]

Both the *Alvará* of 1753 and the *Alvará* (also called Regiment) of 1771 had temporal validity that far exceeded a year. In addition to these changes, the Regiment of 1771 was accompanied by two important innovations: a) it systematised previous norms in one sole *diploma*;[129] and, at the same time, b) after said *Alvará*, apparently, there was no further repetition of the rules regulated in it, but rather they stuck to the guidelines of the interpretation contained in the normative text.

Furthermore, to only analyse the text of these norms while attempting to describe the potential changes that they intended to entail is still an insufficient historical exercise. The reason for that is that legislation of this period was rarely understood as an imperative command to be applied at all times, regardless of the situation or those involved. Even if the aim of the Crown was to increase the collection of diamonds by guaranteeing the observance of orders from the kingdom and the application of penalties, the measures had

---

125 *Alvará* of 26 March 1631; *alvará* of 20 January 1646.

126 Seelaender, "A polícia e o rei-legislador", 103.

127 S. Paio, *Prelecções de direito*, 75 and ss. For a similar reading of this and other sources, see Seelaender, *Polizei, Ökonomie und Gesetzgebungslehre*.

128 Mello Freire's separation of government and justice, linking the former to arbitrary power, serves as an example here. In this sense, he states that "jus actiones subditorum pro arbitrio dirigendi". Mello Freire dos Reis, *Institutiones juris civilis Lusitani*, vol. 1, lib. 1, tit. 1, 2.

129 The disposition XI of the *regimento* states: "Mando que na conformidade do Capitulo II do Regimento do Governador D. Lourenço de Almeida, do Bando do outro Governador Gomes Freire de Andrade, publicado em: 26 de agosto de 1739 e das penas acima estabelecidas, fiquem proibidos em todos os arraiais diamantinos assim as negras de tabuleiro, como no Tijuco, as vendas por casas das negras e dos negros dentros das vendas e lojas ou a comprar ou a vender"; XXXII "Os caixas administradores pagarão pontualmente e sem demora a parte que tocar aos denunciantes ou às pessoas que fizeram as tomadias na forma determinada pela minha Lei de 11 de agosto de 1753 (…)".

to be applied "slowly and with ease" ("com vagar e sossego").[130] In the logic of early modernity, "police" was still invariably intertwined with notions of *prudentia, iustitia* and *aequitas*.[131]

This paradigm of "justice" in the interpretation of law was never completely surpassed in this period. What is remarkable in the transition to the second half of the 18th century, though, is that this paradigm of "justice" started to appear as overlapping with that of "utility" in normative communication. Furthermore, these tensions were felt by the various historical agents involved. Specifically, in the Diamond District, the establishment of the Diamond Intendancy and the separation of the intendant's office from the *ouvidor's* role led to several jurisdictional disputes.[132] Consequently, certain petitions by the district's inhabitants reveal that from their perspective, the conflicts that involved the *lavras* had to be solved with "justiça" and "letras" from the *ouvidor-geral* and the *corregedor* of the *comarca* indistinctly. From the opposition, the actions of the *Intendente* were described as "despotism" and "abuses".[133] In the same petition, some officers from the municipal council of Vila do Príncipe conveyed their discontent about the "little observance" of local customs ("a pouca observancia do costume") by the new royal officers ("os Ministros que por V. Mag. são mandados").[134] The complaint was that the *Intendente* had not presented himself to the municipal council, with the respective *provisões*, and did not inform them of his jurisdiction. Although it is obvious that the locals defended their own particular interests (they had, effectively, lost the right to mine diamonds freely), it is also noticeable that the logic of the "polícia" provoked a frustration in their normative expectations.[135]

130 This "vagar e sossego" was also a way to understand the government and the function of sanctions in the *Ancien Régime*, where the symbolic function of law as a form of social harmonisation took precedence over the effective appliance of a punishment. Hespanha, *As vésperas*, 494. Besides, as already mentioned, passive administration was the standard. Hespanha, *Caleidoscópio do Antigo Regime*, 12. For an example of this, see the famous letter from Alexandre de Gusmão sent in 1745 to Inácio da Costa Quintela, *Desembargador* and *Corregedor do Crime da Corte e Casa*, ANTT, PT/TT/MSLIV/1012/00011.

131 In fact, the regulations, measures and official correspondence of the royal authorities usually exhorted officials to act "according to equity", and to "be just" and "particularly careful". Among others, see "Regimento ou instrução que trouxe Martinho de Mendonça e Pina e de Proença". *Códice Costa Matoso*, vol. 1, 297, and Portaria of 8 November 1734. ANTT, col. Manuscritos do Brasil, Iiv. 32.

132 Carrara, "A Demarcação Diamantina: administração e fiscalidade, 1730–1771".

133 AHU, Minas Gerais, box 33, doc. 64.

134 AHU, Minas Gerais, box 33, doc. 64.

135 AHU, Minas Gerais, box 33, doc. 64, fol. 2r.

The values of justice and equity were not completely abandoned, even from the side of the royal officers, but rather they were either presented in tension or in harmony with those of "utility". But it is clear that the paradigm of "utility" subverts the logic of legal interpretation: the goal-oriented character acquired more relevance than tradition or custom, and legislation started to be increasingly regarded as an imposing command of a rational authority striving for common wellbeing. Compliance with the norm became necessary for the achievement of the imagined goals and a generically conceived "common wellbeing". In this sense, the norm should not merely be applied whenever it maintained equity and justice, avoiding breaks with the preexisting order, but rather it should always be enforced regardless of said order.

This shift is perceivable in the exchange of official letters between the Diamond District and the Portuguese Empire. At first, the focus of these letters was entirely on "justice". Their communication based itself on this concept, while at the same time very vividly maintaining values of honour and of ceremonial structure. But, after 1750 and especially after the establishment of the Royal Extraction in 1771, their communication started to increasingly revolve around the concept of "utility". The agents also started to incorporate notions specialised of "policey" and cameralistic ideas into their discourses.

In this shift, three movements are noticeable. First, there was growth in the number of letters and the influx of communication from both sides, from Crown to local authorities and vice versa. For perspective, the letters doubled in comparison with the previous period.

The second movement is that this increased quantity was followed by a change in the information contained in the letters, a change in the interests in matters or themes of regulation. The main subject of the letters was no longer a detailed description of the daily life in the district, rather they started to focus on the problems that needed to be solved – in this case, "police" was the main tool for solving them. The matters involved orphans, smuggling, the prices in the market, the supply of food to the region, slavery, vagrancy and so on. The localisation of the law is easily perceived by focusing on the local circumstances described by the letters.

The application of the regiment's rules about accountability and food supply was mediated by the exchange of letters. For example, in an epistolary exchange between the Intendant and the President of the *Junta* da *Real Extração* in Lisbon, the local authorities were instructed to consider the influence of the weather on food storage by the merchants. The Crown advised local authorities not to buy food at a higher price, instead waiting for it to depreciate in value due to the impossibility of storing it during hot weather.

The third movement is that these letters increasingly began to discuss how to apply the law and how it should be understood. This last movement could be described as an increase of normative content in the official communication.

At this point, the first period may be illustrated with two documents. The first one is the Regiment or Instruction brought by Martinho de Mendonça de Pina e Proença, dated 30 October 1733 and redacted by Alexandre de Gusmão. It stated that the officer should inform the Governor of "the different judgements and opinions that have taken place regarding the collection of fifths" and "on the means of preserving the reputation of diamonds", so that the best way to use the Royal Treasury to "facilitate the collection" of taxes could be chosen. However, it was emphasised that this decision should be "fair and in accordance with the rules of equity" and one that caused the "least possible vexation".

The second document is the *Portaria* of 8 November 1734. According to it, "being convenient to the service of His Majesty that in the diamond district of the comarca of Serro do Frio all occasions of fraud be avoided" and the entrance "of people and slaves" in the district "after the discovery of diamonds" should be prevented. But, once again, the normative text remarks that the *Desembargador Intendente* Rafael Pires Pardinho should be "particularly careful in proceeding against Blacks from any other district and their lords with the penalties of my *Bando*". Pires Pardinho was also requested to send a report of all the *lavras* to determine which ones could continue according to their old permissions.

In controlling the activity of the contractors, the distinction between fair/unfair was not subject to strict compliance with the clauses established in the contracts. Justice and equity limited the excessive burden (potentially seen as despotism) that could fall upon the subjects stemming from the strict observance of the clauses.

With the letters of 1771 onwards, the situation changed. Labels that came from tradition, such as "justice", were refunctionalised. The official letter issued in April 1787 by the Auditor of Diamonds, Luis Beltran de Gouveia e Almeida, in April 1787, to the Secretary of State for the Navy and Overseas' Dominions, Martinho de Melo e Castro, portrays this:

> When laws lose their force and ordinary remedies lose their strength, there is no other recourse than representation to the supreme legislator who can enforce the transgressed law or save the obligation of the one in charge of promoting its execution; this is the object of this official letter aimed solely at knowing, but by charging the enormous and useless expense that this administration is making

due to the inconsiderate term that it granted with the mining, the royal treasury had been emptied by despotism or fear that those in charge of its management do not dare to confront an armed power.

In my official letter of the 20th of (?), Your Excellency is aware of the disorders practiced in the demarcation of the Serra de S. Antonio de Itacambira Sul either due to the laxity or bad faith of some of the employees in those diamond services; as well as by the hidden intelligence of the Military Troops deployed in that place, as well as of smugglers and traffickers as far as the former are concerned, as the remedy depended on me in the expulsion of some and in the change of others, I cut short the evil as much as possible: by effect of my zeal I have the satisfaction in showing that certificate in which your Excellency will see what having been the yield of the previous three months of 73 octaves of diamonds in the immediate following my reform of the 106 with which it is well proven the damage that the royal treasury suffered for some years in which mining continued in that state: with regard to the military corps that is not hampered by §27 of the regiment of 2 August 1771, it has not changed the system in which it was when I visited those services and that already by the presence of Your Excellency in the aforementioned letter. I thus also will resume any execution of §11, 12, 18 and 23 and a number that cannot be understood because I dismissed the overseers; the peddlers or traffickers or *comboyeiros*, the Black tobacconists and women still find help and reception there.

Of all that I name in the presence of Your Excellency, I will determine what is most useful in accordance with the Royal Service.[136]

---

136 AHU, Minas Gerais, box 126, doc. 36, in the original: "Quando as leis perdem o seu vigor e os remedios ordinarios perdem a sua força, nao ha outro recurso mais do que a representação ao supremo legislador que pode vigorar a ley transgredida ou salvar a obrigação daquela que tem a seu cargo promover a execuçao della: este he o objeto do presente oficio dirigido unicamente a saber mas pela imputação pela enorme e inutil despesa que essa administração esta fazendo pelo inconsiderado termo que concedeo com as lavras a fazenda real hajasse esvaziada pelo dispotismo ou pelo medo os que tem a seo cargo a direção della, nao se atrevem a afrontar hum poder armado.

No meu oficio de 20 de (?) le presente a V Excelencia das desordens praticadas na demarcação na serra de S Antonio de Itacambira Sul tanto pela frouxidão ou ma fé de algum dos hempregados naquelles serviços diamantinos; como pela inteligencia da Tropa Militar destacada naquelle lugar, como dos extraviadores e traficantes pelo que respeita aos primeiros, como o remedio dependia de mim na expulsão da humos e na mudança de outros atalhei o mal quanto me foi possível: o efeito do meu zelo tenho a satisfação de o mostrar na certidão 3 na qual vera V. Excelencia que tendo sido o rendimento dos 3 meze anteriores de 73 oitavas de diamantes logo no seguinte imediatos a minha reforma as 106 com que fica bem provado o prejuízo que a fazenda real padeceu por alguns annos em que as lavras continuarao naquelle estado: pelo que respeita ao corpo militar que se nao

For another example, in a dialogue between José Antonio de Meireles Freire, then serving as Intendant, and D. Pedro José de Noronha Camões de Albuquerque Moniz e Sousa, the then *Marquês de Angeja*, the Intendant enquired about the interpretation of the ninth paragraph of the Regiment. This paragraph concerned how to proceed with "slaves" that were possibly involved in the traffic of diamonds within the demarcation. The Intendant was unsure of how to deal with those that were caught outside the demarcation. The Marquis answered that indeed the rule was only applicable to those who were found inside the demarcation, but that it was possible to punish them if they were caught with diamonds or caught mining:

> With regard to the doubt raised by the said Intendant, as to whether the provision of paragraph 9 of the said Regiment should be applied to those who, outside the demarcation of the said Lands, are found only with mining tools: Since this provision is limited to Slaves who are found with these tools within the said demarcation and outside it there is another *ministério* for which they can serve; only those who are found either with diamonds or in the act of mining them in any place, or even with the said tools in the one in which they will be allowed to do some mining or service, should be punished.[137]

But more than just specific dispositions were discussed. The letters were not only a means to demand enforcement of the Regiment or to question how to apply it specifically; they were also the media through which these interactions shaped a network of normativity, which in turn acted to communicate the self-description of the law and its functions. For example, in the same letter we can observe the shift from a jurisdictional paradigm of law, more centred in equity, to another that aimed to prevent violations of the norm by applying the law in an abstract way: "that the greatest diligence and care must be taken in repressing the smugglers who infest the Diamantina Lands, as determined

---

embaraça com o S (de paragrafo) 27 do regimento de 2 de agosto de 1771 nao tem alterado o sistema em que estava quando visitei aquelles serviços e que ja por via precença de V Excelencia no meo referido oficio assim também excecucao algum os § 11, 12, 18, 23 e numero que no se entiende porque os feitores que despedi; os mascates ou traficantes ou comboyeiros, as pretas de taboleiro e mulheres ainda ali encontrar auxilio e recepção. De tudo o que nombro na presença de V. Excelencia me determinarao a que for mais util e conforme ao Real Serviço". Translated by the author.

137 TCP, box 4088, fol. 171r.

by the Regulation of 2 August 1771, since prompt punishment is the means of curbing crimes".[138]

When it came to a fundamental economic resource for the Portuguese Empire, and when the contingency of local affairs seemed too fast and too much to handle, a departure from the paths of traditional justice was fundamental. Resolving these matters "judicially" only left the interests of the Crown adrift, and potentially lost, among the traditional tricks of rhetoric that jurists practiced when making decisions.[139]

This bypassing of contentious jurisdiction was conceived not only through the creation of a parallel jurisdiction of the Intendency, and its supportive institutional structure, but also through strict prohibitions of the interpretation of the new laws concerning police matters. Dispositions prohibiting legal interpretation were present in the *Alvará* of 1760 that created the *Intendência Geral de Polícia* in Lisbon. But directly of interest to the present research is the presence of the same disposition in the last paragraph of the Regiment of 1771. There, it was demanded that the Regiment should be "executed literally, and in the exact form in which it is written, without interpretation or intelligence of any kind". The reasoning presented for this was that, whenever necessary, the interpretation and understanding of the laws of the King should fall upon himself, and no one else. The disposition also highlights how the prohibition was directed to every person, of any status and "dignity"; and prescribed sanctions for those who disobeyed it – such as losing their office titles, payment for losses and damages following the violation, nullification of all acts caused by said violation or the suspension of magistrates involved.[140]

---

138 TCP, box 4089, fol. 66r.

139 "E como huma Administração tao laborioza e de tão importantes consequencias e implicancias necessariamente hao de occorrer novos acontecimentos cujo remedio não esteja totalmente prevenido, esperamos que VM de acordo com o Administrador Geral fazao toda a necessaria dispozição como entenderem ser mais justo ao Serviço do Rey e do publico, obrando em algum acontecimento como o pedir a razao ate que deca va(?) a approvação ou a reprovação necessaria sendo alias certo que nesta qualidade de governo há muitas occazioens em que he precizo deliberar neste sistema fugindo algumas vezes das ambages judiciais e dos Termos forences, que servem de sucitar questoes e animar o terror panico para não buscar a verdade sabida num deliberar sobre ella como he da mente do rey e do ministerio." ANTT, PT-TT-RED-A-001_m0013.TIF.

140 It would be wrong to think of this provision as a total prohibition on interpretation, not only because total control over this activity would be materially impossible, but also because during early modernity interpretive activity was deeply linked to the legitimisation of the Crown itself, be it, in the first instance, indirectly through the delegation of the power to judge or, in the second instance, as a way of ensuring one's own sovereignty (Stolleis, "Was bedeutet‚Normdurchsetzung' bei Policeyordnungen der Frühen Neuzeit"). Considering the latter, the question that gains relevance is: what type of interpretation is

Following the same direction, an *Alvará* from 1772 quickly adjusted one detail from the institutional structure of the Royal Extraction: it created the requirement for all those appointed to the office in the role of a *fiscal* to possess a degree in law. The intention was clearly to increase control over the choice of personnel in charge of the administration of the district. The students of law could be directly sent to the district after finishing the course and their classes of *direito pátrio*, and stay there in Brazil under the guidance of the intendant. This also created possibilities of a quasi-professional career: some *fiscais* became intendants in the next step of their professional path.

The process that is being observed here is only clearly noticeable when looking at it over a longer duration and it can be described as one of legal change. But this legal innovation did not arise from great leaps or ruptures, rather it was an innovation gradually woven through continuous communication between different agents. In this sense, when the ways of talking about the law change, then law itself and the normative expectations of the various agents change as well.[141]

Even though the implementation of the new form of administration faced a series of obstacles, it is undeniable that it mobilised disputes around the concept of law. Moreover, at the beginning of the 19th century, the jurisdiction of the intendant was extended outside the boundaries of the district and, with it, the instrumentalised vision of law expanded.[142]

6 Conclusions

By examining the case of the Royal Extraction, this chapter has demonstrated the role of colonial institutions in the process of legal change during early

---

the one that seeks to control? In the context of Portuguese Enlightenment, the idea that prevailed was that the traditional structure of the *ius commune* became an impediment to the proper functioning of the State (Bravo Lira, *Constitución y Reconstitución*, 77). Therefore, restricting jurisdictional hermeneutics was essential. In this sense, the application of *direito pátrio* could only be guaranteed by removing the possibility that these matters could be decided by the more traditional offices, because the "vereadores e almottacés regularmente são homens rústicos, sem ideias alguma, nem conhecimento de que é policia e economia da cidade". Mello Freire dos Reis, *O novo código do direito*, 354.

141 On this process in the political context, see Koselleck, *História de Conceitos*, 309.

142 On the other hand, it must be considered that these processes of jurisdictional expansion were not a peaceful matter. An example is the dispute between the governor of Minas Gerais, Rodrigo José de Menezes, and the Intendant João da Rocha Dantas regarding the discovery of diamonds in the Itacambira Sul area in 1780, which at the time was outside the jurisdiction of the diamond district.

modernity. The reconstruction of the implementation of this institution, along with the web of normativity associated with it, has shown how the law during the *Ancien Régime* emerged from a complex communication process. Within this process, various spaces, conditions, historical agents and diverse normative expectations were decisive. In this context, the legislation and, especially, the Royal Extraction was one strategy, among others, that the Portuguese Crown used to deal with the complexity and specificities of the normative context of the Diamond District.

At a conceptual level, the regulations related to Diamond Demarcation could be categorised as *Policey* regulations. They regulated police matters, and their flexibility enabled the Crown to address local conditions and the daily challenges of administering diamond mining, thereby attempting to maintain control over an activity that was crucial for the Kingdom's economy. In this sense, it is possible to conceptualise colonial law as a type of police regulation. When we observe this regulation in this way, and we perceive that these norms were not envisioned to be top-down commands, then it is possible to see which agents were involved in normative production and to see the social impact of said norms.

These norms were the product of an active dialogue between the many *pouvoir intermédiaire* that composed the society of the *Ancien Régime*. And this was not different for the colonies. The royal authorities had intense communication with the colonies, and they enacted statutes in accordance with the information received. Also, it is clear that there was an effort to conform the regulation to the normative expectations of the addressees, especially when it came to "miners". At this point, it is important to highlight the relevance of reports and letters in the normative production of the early modern period. Early modern law was significantly shaped by the continuity and discontinuity of its own communication. Letters were a crucial media through which normative information circulated during this period, encompassing instructions and debates about the interpretation of norms and the meaning of law itself. Therefore, letters provide a valuable lens through which we can observe how this process resulted in a web of normativity.

Moreover, it is relevant to consider that the problems of the colony were propelling normative changes. The complexity of the unfamiliar problems (like the weather, the geography, the *sertão*, etc.) and the diversity of the population, with its array of normative expectations, posed obstacles that the Crown thought were unlikely to be surpassed using traditional legal forms. But the rupture with tradition did not come at once: what happened was the overlapping of old and new, with the latter gradually gaining ground with time.

It was not so much a great increase in their application that made these statutes a matter of posterity, but rather the fact that they modulated law by establishing firmer rules of interpretation and that they carried with them different understandings of law. Their symbolic effect was not to be disregarded, and the fact that the population of the district burned the Regiment book during a revolt is evidence that they perceived it as a profound infringement on the natural order of things. The capability of effectivity of law in this context must not be measured according to enforceability or coercibility of law, but rather according to its capability of mobilising normative expectations and building a web of normativity around it.

Acknowledgements

This chapter is a culmination of efforts resulting from my Ph.D. and postdoctoral research within the CoCoLaw project. I extend my gratitude to Airton Seelaender, Heikki Pihlajamäki, Gustavo Cabral, Gustavo Zatelli, Luisa Stella Coutinho, Manuel Bastias Saavedra and Nuno Camarinhas for their feedback on earlier drafts of this work. Additionally, I am thankful to the peer reviewer, whose careful reading has further refined and strengthened the arguments presented herein.

Bibliography

Manuscripts

Arquivo Histórico do Tribunal de Contas de Portugal, Lisboa (TCP), box 4088.
Arquivo Histórico do Tribunal de Contas de Portugal, Lisboa (TCP) box 4089.
Arquivo Histórico do Tribunal de Contas de Portugal, Lisboa (TCP), box 4099.
Arquivo Histórico Ultramarino, Lisboa (AHU), Minas Gerais, box 33, doc. 64.
Arquivo Histórico Ultramarino, Lisboa (AHU), Minas Gerais, box 63, doc. 77.
Arquivo Histórico Ultramarino, Lisboa (AHU), Minas Gerais, box 67, doc. 31.
Arquivo Histórico Ultramarino, Lisboa (AHU), Minas Gerais, box 67, doc. 43.
Arquivo Histórico Ultramarino, Lisboa (AHU) Minas Gerais, box 104, doc. 35.
Arquivo Histórico Ultramarino, Lisboa (AHU), Minas Gerais, box 126, doc. 36.
Arquivo Histórico Ultramarino, Lisboa (AHU), Minas Gerais, box 167.
Arquivo Histórico Ultramarino, Lisboa (AHU), Minas Gerais, box 19, doc. 52
Arquivo Histórico Ultramarino, Lisboa (AHU), Minas Gerais, box 110, doc. 33.

Arquivo Nacional Torre do Tombo, Lisboa (ANTT), cod. Manuscritos do Brasil.
Arquivo Nacional Torre do Tombo, Lisboa (ANTT), col. Manuscritos do Brasil, Iiv. 32.
Arquivo Nacional Torre do Tombo, Lisboa (ANTT), col. Documentos do Brasil.
Arquivo Nacional Torre do Tombo, Lisboa (ANTT), ordinance of 2 December 1729.
Arquivo Nacional Torre do Tombo, Lisboa (ANTT), PT/TT/MSLIV/1012/00011.
Arquivo Nacional Torre do Tombo, Lisboa (ANTT), PT-TT-RED-A001.
Arquivo Nacional Torre do Tombo, Lisboa (ANTT), PT-TT-RED-A-001_m0012–13TIF.
Arquivo Nacional Torre do Tombo, Lisboa (ANTT), PT-TT-RED-A-001_m0013.TIF.
Arquivo Nacional Torre do Tombo, Lisboa (ANTT), PT-TT-RED-A-001_m0014.TIF.
Arquivo Nacional Torre do Tombo, Lisboa (ANTT), PT-TT-RED-A-001_m0015.TIF.
Arquivo Público Mineiro, Belo Horizonte (APM), SC, cód. 240, fol. 62v.
Biblioteca Nacional de Lisboa, Lisboa (BNL), seção de reservados, Avulsos, cód. 7167.
Biblioteca Nacional de Portugal, Lisboa (BNP), cód. 1612, fols. 113v–114.
Biblioteca Nacional de Portugal, Lisboa (BNP), Pba-691, 70–73.
Códice Costa Matoso, 2 vols., Belo Horizonte 1999: Fundação João Pinheiro, Centro de Estudios Históricos e Culturais.
Revista do Arquivo Público Mineiro (RAPM) 7 (1902), 251–355.

Printed Sources

Couto, José Vieira, *Memória sobre a Capitania das Minas Gerais: seu território, clima e produções metálicas*, Belo Horizonte 1994 [1799]: Sistema Estadual de Planejamento, Fundação João Pinheiro, Centro de Estudos Históricos e Culturais.
Freitas, Joaquim Ignacio de, *Colleção da legislação antiga e moderna de Portugal*, vol. 2: Da legislação Moderna, Coimbra 1819: Na Real Imprensa da Universidade (for *alvarás* before 1749).
Mello Freire dos Reis, Paschoal José de, *Institutiones juris civilis Lusitani*, vol. 1: De jure publico, Conimbricae 1827: Typographia Academio-Regia.
Mello Freire dos Reis, Paschoal José de, *O novo código do direito publico de Portugal*, Coimbra 1844: Imprensa da Universidade.
Memorias economicas da Academia Real das Sciencias de Lisboa, vol. 1, Lisboa 1789: Na Officina da Academia Real das Sciencias.
Ordenações Filipinas, ed. Almeida, Candido Mendes de, Rio de Janeiro 1870: Typographia do Instituto Philomathico.
Silva, Antônio Delgado da, *Collecção da legislação portuguesa*, Lisboa 1830 (1750–1762), 1829 (1763–1774), 1844 (1763–1790), 1828 (1775–1790), 1828 (1790–1801), 1826 (1802–1810): Na Typografia Maigrense (for *alvarás* after 1760).
Solórzano Pereira, Juan de, *Politica Indiana. Dividida en seis libros*, Amberes 1703: Henrico y Cornelio Verdussen (https://libros.uchile.cl/665).

S. Paio, Francisco Coelho de Souza e, *Prelecções de direito pátrio público e particular*, Coimbra 1793: Real Imprensa da Universidade.

Literature

Agüero, Alejandro, "Las categorías básicas de la cultura jurisdiccional", in *Cuadernos de derecho judicial*, no. 6 (2006), 19–58.

Azeredo, Claudia Atalah, *Da Justiça em Nome d'El Rey*, Rio de Janeiro 2016.

Benton, Lauren, "Colonial Law and Cultural Difference: Jurisdictional Politics and the Formation of the Colonial State", in *Comparative Studies in Society and History* 41:3 (1999), 563–588.

Biedermann, Zoltán, *(Dis)connected Empires. Imperial Portugal, Sri Lankan Diplomacy, and the Making of a Habsburg Conquest in Asia*, New York (NY) 2018.

Bravo Lira, Bernardino, *Constitución y Reconstitución. Historia del Estado en Iberoamérica 1511–2009*, Santiago de Chile 2010.

Brendecke, Arndt, *Imperio e información. Funciones del saber en el dominio colonial español*, Madrid 2012.

Cabral, Gustavo César Machado, "Case Law in Portuguese decisiones in the Early Modern Age: Antonio da Gama's Decisiones Supremi Senatus Lusitaniae", in *forum historiae iuris* (2015) (https://forhistiur.net/2015-06-machado-cabral/?l=en).

Cabral, Gustavo César Machado, *Uma teoria do direito para a América Portuguesa (Séculos XVI–XVIII)*, Porto Alegre 2021.

Camarinhas, Nuno, "O aparelho judicial ultramarino português: O caso do Brasil (1620–1800)", in *Almanack Braziliense*, no. 9 (2009), 84–102.

Cardim, Pedro, "Religião e ordem social. Em torno dos fundamentos católicos do sistema político do Antigo Regime", in *Revista de História da Ideias* 22 (2001), 133–175.

Cardim, Pedro, "'Nem tudo se pode escrever': Correspondencia diplomática e información «política» en Portugal durante el siglo XVII", in *Cuadernos de História Moderna* (2005), 95–128.

Cardim, Pedro and Miguel Baltazar, "A difusão da legislação régia (1621–1808)", in Fragoso, João and Nuno Gonçalo Monteiro (orgs.), *Um reino e suas repúblicas no Atlântico. Comunicações políticas entre Portugal, Brasil e Angola nos séculos XVII e XVIII*, Rio de Janeiro 2017.

Cardim, Pedro, Tamar Herzog, Jose Javier Ruiz Ibanez and Gaetano Sabatini (eds.), *Polycentric Monarchies. How Did Early Modern Spain and Portugal Achieve and Maintain a Global Hegemony?*, Brighton 2012.

Carrara, Angelo, "Desvendando a riqueza na terra dos diamantes", in *Revista do Arquivo Público Mineiro* 41 (2005), 40–59.

Carrara, Angelo, "A Demarcação Diamantina: administração e fiscalidade, 1730–1771", in *Tempo* 28:2 (2022), 22–42.

Cunha, Alexandre Mendes, "Administrative Centralisation, Police Regulations and Mining Sciences as Channels for the Dissemination of Cameralist Ideas in the Iberian World", in Marten Seppel and Keith Tribe (eds.), *Cameralism in Practice: State Administration and Economy in Early Modern Europe*, Suffolk 2017, 155–178.

Curvelo, Arthur, "Governar à distância nas capitanias da América portuguesa: comunicações políticas entre governadores e autoridades locais (Pernambuco, séculos XVII e XVIII)", in Gaudin, Guillaume and Roberta Stumpf (eds.), *Las distancias en el gobierno de los imperios ibéricos. Concepciones, experiencias y vínculos*, Madrid 2022, 235–254.

Duve, Thomas, "Rechtsgeschichte als Geschichte von Normativitätswissen?", in *Rechtsgeschichte – Legal History* 29 (2021), 41–68.

Duve, Thomas, "The School of Salamanca: A Case of Global Knowledge Production", in Duve, Thomas, José Luis Egío and Christiane Birr (eds.), *The School of Salamanca: A Case of Global Knowledge Production*, Leiden 2021, 1–42.

Fonseca, Cláudia Damasceno, *Arraiais e vilas d'el rei: espaço e poder nas Minas setecentistas*, trans. Maria Juliana Gambogi Teixeira and Cláudia Damasceno Fonseca, Belo Horizonte 2011.

Fragoso, João and Nuno Gonçalo Monteiro (eds.), *Um reino e suas repúblicas no Atlântico. Comunicações políticas entre Portugal, Brasil e Angola nos séculos XVII e XVIII*, Rio de Janeiro 2017.

Furtado, Junia, "Distrito Diamantino: o avesso da memória", in *Varia Historia* 9:12 (1993) 80–94.

Furtado, Junia, *O livro da capa verde: o regimento diamantino de 1771 e a vida no distrito diamantino no período da Real Extração*, São Paulo 1996.

Furtado, Junia, "Relações de poder no Tejuco; ou um teatro em três atos", in *Tempo* 4:7 (1999), 129–142.

Grossi, Paolo, *A ordem jurídica medieval*, São Paulo 2014.

Hannula, Henri, Nathaly Mancilla-Órdenes, Heikki Pihlajamäki, Airton Ribeiro, Gustavo Zatelli, "Unpacking Early Modern Colonial Law: A Brief Overview of the Literature of the Last Twenty Years", in *Zeitschrift für Neuere Rechtsgeschichte* 46:1-2 (2024), 138–157.

Härter, Karl, "Gesetzgebungsprozess und Gute Policey. Entstehungskontexte, Publikation und Geltungskraft frühneuzeitlicher Policeygesetze", in *PoliceyWorking Papers*, no. 3 (2002) (https://akpolicey.univie.ac.at/wp-content/uploads/pwp_03.pdf), 1–32.

Herzog, Tamar, "How to Approach Colonial Law?", in Duve, Thomas and Tamar Herzog (eds.), *The Cambridge History of Latin American Law in Global Perspective*, Cambridge 2024, 141–249.

Hespanha, António Manuel, *As vésperas do Leviathan. Instituições e poder político. Portugal – séc. XVII*, Lisboa 1984.

Hespanha, António Manuel, "Justiça e administração entre o Antigo Regime e a Revolução", in Clavero Salvador, Bartolomé, Paolo Grossi and Francisco Tomás y Valiente (eds.), *Hispania entre derechos propios y derechos nacionales: atti dell'incontro di studio Firenze-Lucca 25, 26, 27 maggio 1989*, vol. 1, Milano 1990, 135–204.

Hespanha, António Manuel, "Porque é que existe e em que é que consiste um direito colonial brasileiro", in *Quaderni fiorentini per la storia del pensiero giuridico moderno* 35:1 (2006), 59–81.

Hespanha, António Manuel, "A senda amorosa do Direito: Amor e Iustitia no discurso jurídico moderno", in Petit, Carlos (ed.), *Paixões do jurista: amor, memória, melancolia, imaginação*, Curitiba 2011.

Hespanha, António Manuel, *Caleidoscópio do Antigo Regime*, São Paulo 2012.

Hespanha, António Manuel. "Uncommon Laws. Law in the Extreme Peripheries of an Early Modern Empire", in *Zeitschrift der Savigny-Stiftung für Rechtsgeschichte: Germanistische Abteilung* 130:1 (2013), 180–204.

Hespanha, António Manuel, "The Legal Patchwork of Empires", in *Rechtsgeschichte – Legal History* 22 (2014), 303–314.

Hespanha, António Manuel, *Como os juristas viam o mundo. 1550–1750: Direitos, estados, coisas, contratos, ações e crimes*, Leipzig 2015.

Hespanha, António Manuel, "Prefácio", in Fragoso, João and Nuno Gonçalo Monteiro (orgs.), *Um reino e suas repúblicas no Atlântico. Comunicações políticas entre Portugal, Brasil e Angola nos séculos XVII e XVIII*, Rio de Janeiro 2017, 9–11.

Hespanha, António Manuel, *Filhos da Terra. Identidades Mestiças nos confins da expansão Portuguesa*, Lisboa 2019.

Hespanha, António Manuel, "Southern Europe (Italy, Iberian Peninsula, France)", in Heikki Pihlajamäki, Markus D. Dubber and Mark Godfrey (eds.), *The Oxford Handbook of European Legal History*, Oxford 2018, 333–358.

Holanda, Sérgio Buarque de, *A mineração: antecedentes luso-brasileiros. História Geral da Civilização Brasileira: a época colonial*, tomo 1, vol. 2, São Paulo 1985.

Holanda, Sérgio Buarque de, *Metais e pedras preciosas. História Geral da Civilização Brasileira: a época colonial*, tomo 1, vol. 2, São Paulo 1985.

Iseli, Andrea, *»Bonne Police«. Frühneuzeitliches Verständnis von der guten Ordnung eines Staates in Frankreich*, Epfendorf 2003.

Knemeyer, Franz-Ludwig, "Polizei", in *Economy and Society* 9:2 (1980), 172–196.

Koselleck, Reinhart, *História de Conceitos*, Rio de Janeiro 2020.

Kotkas, Toomas, *Royal Police Ordinances in Early Modern Sweden: The Emergence of Voluntaristic Understanding of Law*, Leiden 2014.

Langfur, Hal, *Adrift on an Inland Sea. Misinformation and the Limits of Empire in the Brazilian Backlands*, Stanford, CA 2023.

McPherson, Kenneth, "Anglo-Portuguese Commercial Relations in the Eastern Indian Ocean from the Seventeenth to the Eighteenth Centuries", in *South Asia: Journal of South Asian Studies* 19:sup001 (1996), 41–57.

Mancilla-Órdenes, Nathaly, *The Crown as an Apprentice: Policey, Colonial Administration and New Meanings of Law in the Diamond District* (*1771–1808*) (Ph.D. Thesis), Brasília 2023.

Monteiro, Rodrigo Bentes, *O rei no espelho: a Monarquia Portuguesa e a Colonização da América. 1640–1720*, São Paulo 2002.

Monteiro, Rodrigo Bentes, "Catilinária mineira: o discurso da revolta de 1720 em Vila Rica", in Monteiro, Rodrigo Bentes and Sandra Bagno (org.), *Maquiavel no Brasil: dos descobrimentos ao século XXI*, Rio de Janeiro 2015.

Moreira, Joelmir Cabral, *Legislação régia em terras minerais: uma análise do processo de exploração de diamantes na comarca do Serro Frio, 1720–1771* (Ph.D. Thesis), Seropédica 2020.

Nitschke, Peter, "Von der Politeia zur Polizei: Ein Beitrag zur Entwicklungsgeschichte des Polizei-Begriffs und seiner herrschaftspolitischen Dimensionen von der Antike bis ins 19. Jahrhundert", in *Zeitschrift Für Historische Forschung* 19:1 (1992), 1–27.

Pihlajamäki, Heikki, "The Westernization of Police Regulation: Spanish and British Colonial Laws Compared", in Duve, Thomas and Heikki Pihlajamäki (eds.), *New Horizons in Spanish Colonial Law: Contributions to Transnational Early Modern Legal History, Global Perspectives on Legal History*, Frankfurt am Main 2015, 97–124.

Pihlajamäki, Heikki, "Law in Spanish and Portuguese America: The Early Colonial Period", in Mirow, M. C. and Víctor M. Uribe-Uran (eds.), *A Companion to Latin American Legal History*, Leiden 2023, 73–98.

Pihlajamäki, Heikki, Zatelli Gustavo, Ribeiro Jr. Airton and Henri Hannula, "Comparing Early Modern Colonial Laws: Police Regulation Overseas", in *Journal for Digital Legal History* 2:1 (2024), 1–16.

Quintão, Régis Clemente, "A Real Extração e o abastecimento do Distrito Diamantino", in *e-hum* 8:2 (2016), 10–17.

Quintão, Régis Clemente, "Para a felicidade pública dos mineiros ou para a boa administração e aumento das rendas reais: as instruções do Erário Régio de 1775", in *Temporalidades* 8:3 (2016), 492–513.

Quintão, Régis Clemente, "Cultura material e trabalho nos serviços de mineração do Distrito Diamantino (Minas Gerais, século XVIII)", in *Anais do Museu Paulista: História e Cultura Material* 26 (2018).

Quintão, Régis Clemente, *Corrompidos pelo interesse: os diamantes do Brasil e o controle da corrupção* (*Distrito Diamantino, 1729–1821*) (Ph.D. Thesis), Minas Gerais 2022.

Raeff, Marc, *The Well-Ordered Police State: Social and Institutional Change through Law in the Germanies and Russia, 1600–1800*, New Haven, CT 1983.

Ribeiro, Mônica da Silva, "'Razão de Estado' e pombalismo: Os modos de governar na administração de Gomes Freire de Andrada", in Falcon, Francisco and Claudia Rodrigues (eds.), *A "Época Pombalina" no mundo luso-brasileiro*, Rio de Janeiro 2015.

Romeiro, Adriana, *Paulistas e emboabas no coração das Minas: idéias, práticas e imaginário político no século XVIII*, Belo Horizonte 2008.

Romeiro, Adriana, "O governo dos povos e o amor ao dinheiro", in *Revista do Arquivo Público Mineiro* 51:1 (2015), 107–120.

Seelaender, Airton, *Polizei, Ökonomie und Gesetzgebungslehre. Ein Beitrag zur Analyse der portugiesischen Rechtswissenschaft am Ende des 18. Jahrhunderts*, Frankfurt am Main 2003.

Seelaender, Airton, "A 'polícia' e as funções do Estado – notas sobre a 'polícia' do antigo regime", in *Revista da Faculdade de Direito da UFPR* 49 (2009), 73–87.

Seelaender, Airton, "A polícia e o rei-legislador: notas sobre algumas tendências da legislação portuguesa no Antigo Regime", in Bittar, Eduardo Carlos Bianca (org.), *História do Direito Brasileiro: leituras da ordem jurídica nacional*, São Paulo 2012, 91–108.

Silva, Ana Cristina Nogueira da, *Constitucionalismo e Império. A cidadania no Ultramar português*, Lisboa 2009.

Simon, Thomas, *»Gute Policey«: Ordnungsleitbilder und Zielvorstellungen politischen Handelns in der Frühen Neuzeit*, Frankfurt am Main 2004.

Souza, Laura de Mello e, *Norma e conflito. Aspectos da história de Minas no século XVIII*, Belo Horizonte 1999.

Souza, Laura de Mello e, *O sol e a sombra: política e administração na América portuguesa do século XVIII*, São Paulo 2006.

Stolleis, Michael, *Storia del diritto pubblico in Germania*, vol. 1: *Publicistica dell'Impero e scienza di Polizia 1600–1800*, Milano 2008.

Stolleis, Michael, "Was bedeutet ‚Normdurchsetzung' bei Policeyordnungen der Frühen Neuzeit?", in Vec, Miloš and Stefan Ruppert (eds.), *Ausgewählte Aufsätze und Beiträge*, Frankfurt am Main 2011.

Tau Anzoátegui, Vítor, *El jurista en el nuevo mundo. Pensamiento. Doctrina. Mentalidad*, Frankfurt am Main 2016.

Thompson, Edward Palmer, *Whigs and Hunters. The Origin of the Black Act*, London 1975.

Wehling, Arno, *Administração portuguesa no Brasil, de Pombal a D. João (1777–1808)*, Brasília 1986.

Wehling, Arno and Maria José Wehling, "'Sem embargo da ordenação em contrário': a adaptação da norma portuguesa à circunstância colonial", in Venâncio, Renato Pinto, Andréa Lisly Gonçalves and Cláudia Maria das Graças Chaves (eds.), *Administrando impérios. Portugal e Brasil nos séculos XVIII e XIX*, Belo Horizonte 2012, 45–60.

Index

www.ingramcontent.com/pod-product-compliance
Ingram Content Group UK Ltd.
Pitfield, Milton Keynes, MK11 3LW, UK
UKHW022218051026
15624UKWH00001B/230

9 789004 764415